A J. M. Synge
Literary
Companion

A J. M. Synge Literary Companion

Edited by Edward A. Kopper, Jr.

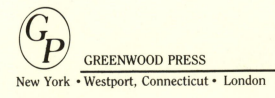

GREENWOOD PRESS

New York • Westport, Connecticut • London

Library of Congress Cataloging-in-Publication Data

A J. M. Synge literary companion / edited by Edward A. Kopper, Jr.
    p.   cm.
  Bibliography: p.
  Includes index.
  ISBN 0–313–25173–8 (lib. bdg. : alk. paper)
  1. Synge, J. M. (John Millington), 1871–1909—Criticism and
interpretation. I. Kopper, Edward A.
PR5534.J24 1988
822′.912—dc 19   87–32295

British Library Cataloguing in Publication Data is available.

Library of Congress Catalog Card Number: 87–32295
ISBN: 0–313–25173–8

First published in 1988

Greenwood Press, Inc.
88 Post Road West, Westport, Connecticut 06881

Printed in the United States of America

∞™

The paper used in this book complies with the
Permanent Paper Standard issued by the National
Information Standards Organization (Z39.48–1984).

10 9 8 7 6 5 4 3 2 1

For Peggy, Eddie, Kevin

Contents

Preface

This volume provides a "companion" for those interested in elucidating Synge's work. It covers all important issues dealt with in Synge criticism from around 1900 to the present; its sources, both the references at the ends of chapters and the Select Bibliography at the end of the book, are of great importance. Throughout the *Companion,* an attempt was made to provide insight into commonly recognized complexities in Synge's works and to permit authors of individual chapters to develop their own specific premises. The contributors are established Irish Renaissance scholars, and all of the chapters are original. Special features of the volume include a glossary of characters, locales, and motifs and representative stage histories that describe productions of Synge's plays in Ireland, the United States, and several other countries. The volume's combining of the fundamental with the specialized will, it is hoped, appeal to a varied audience of intelligent readers and playgoers while providing a lot of material for Synge authorities.

In Chapter 1, Daniel J. Casey synthesizes the major influences on Synge: for example, the Synge Ascendancy background, Synge's studies in Dublin and abroad, his visits to Aran, and his relationships with principals of the Irish Renaissance. Casey maintains tht Synge "lived a life apart, and he did so by choice . . . In a period of political and cultural extremism, he courageously stood the middle ground and called himself 'a temperate nationalist' to rail against extremism on both flanks." Thus Casey believes that "Synge is interestingly complex and in some ways enigmatic, but he is approachable."

In Chapter 2, Thomas J. Morrissey points to a good deal of merit in Synge's often neglected prose, maintaining that "most of the prose canon is vital and original." Although Morrissey regards most of the early writing as weak, he believes that *Etude Morbide* is a good transition to the major prose work *The Aran Islands*. The latter Morrissey examines at length: its concept of time; its structure, including a possible cyclic pattern; its genre; and its "balance of dispassionate description and emotional response." In discussing the later prose, Morrissey sees Synge as an "investigative reporter." Morrissey also includes an appreciative comment about Synge's abilities as a critic.

In Chapter 3, Edward A. Kopper, Jr., analyzes *The Shadow of the Glen* by synthesizing several contemporary accounts that detail the hostile reception of the play in Dublin, especially in the pages of the *United Irishman*, edited by Arthur Griffith. Then, after glancing at two by-products of the debate over the play, the lightly parodic "In a Real Wicklow Glen" and Synge's own bitter unpublished "National Drama: A Farce," Kopper maintains that the best source for an understanding of *Shadow* lies in Synge's essays, which "reveal the Irish rustic with all of his or her warts and wrinkles." These peasants "demonstrate the Rabelaisian streak that infuses Synge's plays with the toughness of the grotesque." Also, Kopper argues for the relevance of Nora's plight to the problems of women in present Western society, and he finds that her characterization is consistent from beginning to end, including her plausible decision to leave with the Tramp.

In Chapter 4, Kopper's discussion of *Riders to the Sea* traces the interaction among Synge and his contemporaries, such as Joyce; stresses Synge's insistence upon verisimilitude in the staging of *Riders*, for example, the need to procure authentic pampooties, a valid keening melody, and a convincing spinning wheel; and emphasizes that the belief that the play was received without controversy, still held by many, is erroneous—many critics in 1904 censured the work's supposed morbidity. Kopper then discusses dimensions beyond the literal that Synge added to *Riders* through his biblical allusions and, especially, through his subtle incorporation into the play of many Irish folk customs. The chapter also summarizes criticism concerning two key issues regarding *Riders*: its genre, that is, whether it be truly tragic, and the symbolism surrounding Maurya's characterization. Treatment of the last two points in the chapter is admittedly cursory (although, it is hoped, seminal), and the reader is urged to address the sources at the end of the chapter.

In Chapter 5, interweaving critical opinions that range from Yeats's pronouncements to modern newspaper accounts of the play's performances, Leslie D. Foster describes *The Well of the Saints* as ironic comedy and focuses on Yeats's insistence on the dream element in the work. Thus the "glory of Synge's characters" is revealed in the "aspirations they are moved by." The Douls' rejection of renewed sight does cause Foster to demur, however, since he believes that their choice of blindness is not a "desirable solution."

In Chapter 6, Rosemarie A. Battaglia suggests that part of the appeal of *The Tinker's Wedding* lies in its characterization and in its theme, the latter expressing the "dialectical" opposition between the Establishment and the tinkers, who are disestablished, or between ritual and anti-ritual. Battaglia finds, though, that the "tinkers, like the Aran Islanders, are able to live with the contradictory claims of marginality and orthodoxy."

In Chapter 7, Zack R. Bowen reveals that *The Playboy of the Western World* is as puzzling and complex today as it was in Synge's time, when the work "became itself a metaphor for art, tried and martyred by a mob of philistines." Bowen cites reasons for the hostility directed against *Playboy,* emphasizing the satiric treatment of the three "fathers" in the work; discusses *Playboy's* comic differences from the somber original *Oedipus;* explains the causes of the audience's ambiguous attitude of identification with the play; examines language as "subject matter," wherein, in *Playboy,* the language "becomes signified instead of signifier"; analyzes Synge's use of hyperbole in regard to Old Mahon, as well as Christy; fits the term *shifts* into the play's clothing imagery; and ends by citing *Playboy's* "magnificent ambiguity."

In Chapter 8, Michael H. Begnal avers that in *Deirdre of the Sorrows* Synge's focus is on the human side of his protagonists; the play embodies the dramatist's wish to "encompass the full spectrum of passion and emotion." Rather than *Deirdre* being a play about fate, Begnal insists that "it is the concept of *choice* which is the prime factor in the unfolding of the plot." Thus Deirdre and Naisi are certainly not victims; they forge their own destiny, and they do so "in concert." Also, Begnal shows that the scene in which Deirdre sends her lover off with a seeming ruthlessness that appears to repudiate seven years of love, a gesture that many critics have cited to prove that Deirdre is a predator, actually reveals Deirdre's putting Naisi's "needs before her own."

In Chapter 9, Leonard Orr avers that an accurate assessment of the worth of Synge's poetry has been hampered by the overshadowing presence of Yeats and by the prefaces of the poems written by Yeats and by Synge. He then points out that some critics have praised the brutality of Synge's verse, challenges the claim that Synge's poetry was a great influence on Yeats's work, shows the eclectic nature of Synge's selection of sources for his verse, cites Synge's techniques and themes in the poetry, and analyzes some of the more representative poems.

In Chapter 10, Anthony Roche's detailed examination of Christianity and paganism in *Riders, Wedding, Well,* and *Playboy* is derived in part from a scrutiny of primary Synge materials housed at Trinity College, Dublin. Roche emphasizes the continuing role that religion played in Synge's life and work, albeit a religion sans hell, the concept of eternal damnation having terrified Synge in his youth. This religion assumed a form of pantheism as Synge and his cousin Florence Ross explored nature; the sense of an "Edenic interaction with the natural world," obliterated by puberty, is revived in some of Synge's writings that attempt to recapture this "paradise lost." Also, Roche stresses that Synge was much influenced by the ancient St. Patrick-Oisin debate and by the idea of the Celtic otherworld. Thus *Riders* suggests an ocean governed by the Irish sea deity

Manannan Mac Lir, and Christian metaphor in *Playboy* is undercut by pagan allusions to Cuchulain and by human love, the "lovers' otherworld."

In Chapter 11, in his discussion of Synge's use of Irish mythology, Reed Way Dasenbrock asks why Synge, who had always opposed the "Cuchulainoid" or "spring-dayish" renderings of the sagas by his contemporaries, turned to the Deirdre legend at the end of his life. Dasenbrock maintains that Synge, who read the saga material in the original, did not object to the subject matter of the myths but rather to the treatment accorded them by others such as AE (pseudonym of George Russell) and Yeats. Ironically, it was the public ire over *Playboy* that urged him toward the Deirdre legend and "the conscious demythologizing of Irish mythology": "If a Pearse could denounce Synge, yet celebrate a Cuchulain whose exploits make Christy Mahon look like the parish priest, the time had come to show the Irish some of the truth about their own mythology."

In Chapter 12, Richard Fallis, in his comprehensive study of literary influences on Synge, situates Synge solidly in the modernist tradition. Synge, who maintained that all art is a collaboration, was indeed a "literary sophisticate" after his studies in Paris. Paraphrasing Julia Kristeva, Fallis locates in Synge's texts "clear examples of intertextuality with their mosaics of citations in which every text absorbs and transforms others." Fallis cites Synge's discriminating assessment of French Decadent writers; holds that with de Jubainville's version of Irish literature, Synge was helped to regard civilizations comparatively; finds that Arthur Griffith was probably correct in sensing that *Shadow*, despite its Aran Islands source, also had European origins; and sees in *Deirdre,* besides its obvious sources in Gaelic mythology, traces of Villiers de l'Isle-Adam, Wagner, Maeterlinck, and Villon. Synge then was in a nonpejorative sense a "profoundly *influenced* artist" who "understood himself most thoroughly when he was constructing texts responsive to other texts, overtly responsive."

In Chapter 13, Patrick A. McCarthy cites the divergent opinions of Synge and Joyce toward the Irish Revival and posits the important influences on Synge of the dialect of Hyde and Lady Gregory and of Synge's own study of Irish literature and language. McCarthy emphasizes differences between Yeats and Synge in regard to their attitudes toward Irish mythology, the Irish past, and the concept of the individual's place within a "coherent community"—with Synge from the start preferring "outcasts and dissenters." To McCarthy, the "conflict between individual and community that is central to Synge seems at times almost a paradigm of the tension between the literary movement and its public."

In Chapter 14, Bonnie Kime Scott details relationships among Synge and several women, including his mother, Cherrie Matheson, some intelligent Europeans, and Molly Allgood, in whom he "may have found a combination of natural sexual attraction and the type of the artist-women who had helped him recover from the Matheson affair." Scott's focus is on the capacity of Synge's women chartacters "for speech. This relates to the feminist issue of silence imposed upon women as authors, members of society, and in literary representation." She maintains that Synge, "unlike many male authors, delights in women's talk, and makes powerful speakers, storytellers, advisers, and even prophetesses of his female heroes." Scott traces examples of female communication in *Riders, Deirdre,* and *The Aran Islands* and discusses at length Synge's association of women (and courting males) with external nature. Also, Synge's early work has affinities with contemporary French feminist theory, which "concerns itself with a return to a pre-Oedipal ancient mother as a source of language and even literary form."

In Chapter 15, Mary C. King avoids the distracting and overworked issue of "vernacular authenticity" and instead concentrates on Synge's preoccupation with the nature of language itself. King finds aspects of Synge's modernism in "the metaformal and metalinguistic features of his work." She feels that Synge's early discovery of Darwin was important: "If language . . . evolved, the Word was not a divinely underwritten literal expression of Ultimate Truth." King finds that the book-lined setting of *When the Moon Has Set* "predicates [in its two-act version] the self-conscious textuality of the work," which contains many "metatextual devices," such as letters and manuscripts. In *Well,* the "word itself can be considered a kind of act." In *Playboy,* Christy's past, "like his dream of future freedom and integrity, is mediated by language." In summary, King maintains that Synge, like Joyce, "refuses, while celebrating the creative power of language, to grant any ultimate privilege to the aesthetic word."

In Chapter 16, Kopper tries to avoid a listing of Synge's assets and debits; rather, the reflections are meant to provoke future thinking as well as to tie matters together. Kopper's open-ended suggestions might be considered "workpoints" for further Synge scholarship. Also, the postscript to this chapter deals briefly with matters such as the sources that are available for tracing the critical reception accorded Synge's works, primary bibliography for Synge, Synge in translation, Synge's language, and Synge's letters as a means of understanding his work.

Throughout this book, all references to Synge's works are to *J. M. Synge: Collected Works* (4 vols, ed. Robin Skelton. London: Oxford University Press, 1962–1968; reprint, Washington, D.C.: The Catholic University of America Press, 1982). The references in the text are indicated in parentheses by volume number in roman numerals followed by a comma and page numbers in arabic.

Robin Skelton's edition of *Poems* (vol. I, 1962) includes fifty-eight entries under "Poems," thirty-four published for the first time; prefaces by Yeats and Synge; three fragments of poetic dramas; twenty-four translations, including seventeen from Petrarch; worksheets for two poems, "Is It a Month?" and "In Kerry"; a reprinting of the story of the Lady O'Conor from *The Aran Islands*; and a variant reading of "Danny."

Prose (vol. II, 1966), edited by Alan Price, consists of four parts. The first part, "The Man Himself," contains the "Autobiography," "Vita Vecchia," "Etude Morbide," "On a Train to Paris," and "Under Ether"; the second part has *The Aran Islands*; the third part has *In Wicklow, West Kerry, and Connemara*; and the fourth part provides several short pieces, ranging from Synge's comments on Geoffrey Keating and Anatole Le Braz to an unpublished letter to the Gaelic League. Previously unpublished material makes up less than 25 percent of the volume.

Ann Saddlemyer's edition of the *Plays* (vols. III and IV, 1968) consists of Synge's six produced plays, the one-act version of *When the Moon Has Set,* several fragments of plays, and scenarios for other contemplated works. The two volumes contain full variant readings, detailed descriptions of other editions, appendices of first-draft versions of the works, and excerpts from relevant non-dramatic prose that clarify passsages in the plays.

Acknowledgment

The editor wishes to thank Slippery Rock University for granting him the university's First International Development Award, which defrayed the cost of research into Synge's work that he conducted on the Aran Islands, in Dublin, and in other parts of Ireland during the summer of 1986.

A Brief Chronology

1871, April 16.	Edmund John Millington Synge born into an Ascendancy family, with churchmen dating from seventeenth-century Ireland. Youngest child of John Hatch and Kathleen (Traill) Synge, at 2 Newtown Villas, Rathfarnham, Dublin.
1872, April 13.	Father dies.
1881 forward.	Sporadic schooling, with Synge's education gained to a great extent through home tutoring.
c. 1885.	When "about fourteen" (II, 10), read Darwin and went through a (temporary) religious crisis of doubt; beginning interest in systematic study of nature.

Note: A full chronology may be found in both volumes of Ann Saddlemyer's edition of the *Collected Letters*, and many of the above dates are cited in the Greene-Stephens biography, *J. M. Synge, 1871–1909*.

1889, February-December 15, 1892.

Attendance at Trinity College, where Synge shows interest in Irish antiquities and language, including Hebrew, but in little else. (Graduates from Trinity with a gentleman's or pass degree.) Pursues separate studies almost concurrently at Royal Irish Academy of Music.

1893, July 29-June 1, 1894.

Studies music in Germany, mainly with the von Eickens.

1895, April.

Enrolls at the Sorbonne and studies medieval literature under Petit de Julleville (and other aspects of French culture with other professors).

1896, fall and early winter.

More study at the Sorbonne.

February 18, 1898.

Starts study of comparisons between Irish and ancient Greek cultures under d'Arbois de Jubainville.

February 14, 1902.

Begins study of Old Irish with de Jubainville, with Synge often being the only student in attendance at his lectures.

1896, June.

Proposal of marriage rejected by Cherrie Matheson, presumably because of differences in religion.

1896, December 21.

In Paris, first meeting with Yeats, with Yeats giving Synge the famous admonition to leave France and go to the Aran Islands (but with Synge not following up on the lead until a year and a half later).

1898, May 10-June 25.

First visit to Aran; four others follow, the last in fall 1902.

1901, September

Visit with Lady Gregory and Yeats at Coole Park, which, possibly, was the occasion for their rejecting the two-act version of his *When the Moon Has Set*.

1903, March.

Spends about a week in Paris with Joyce debating the merits of *Riders* and other literary matters.

1903, October 8–10.

The Shadow of the Glen produced by the Irish National Theatre Society at Molesworth Hall (Dublin).

1904, February 25–27.

Riders to the Sea produced at Molesworth Hall.

1905, February 4–11.

The Well of the Saints produced at the Abbey Theatre.

1905, June 3-July 3.	With Jack Yeats, the poet's brother, Synge tours the Congested Districts of western Ireland to secure material for articles commissioned by the *Manchester Guardian*.
1906, January 12.	Max Meyerfeld's translation of *Well* produced as *Der heilige Brunnen* in Berlin.
1906, February 7.	Karl Mušek's translation of *Shadow* performed in Prague.
1906, late February.	Synge's affection for Molly Allgood, who now plays the role of Nora Burke, becomes public knowledge.
1907, January 26.	First night of *The Playboy of the Western World* at the Abbey, the start of a week of disturbances and riots.
1907, spring.	*The Aran Islands* published by Maunsel and Elkin Mathews.
1907, early summer.	Synge spends about three happy weeks with Molly at Glencree in County Wicklow, a pastoral setting that is reflected in *Deirdre of the Sorrows*.
1907, December.	*The Tinker's Wedding* published by Maunsel.
1908, October 26.	Synge's mother dies.
1909, March 24.	Synge dies.
1910, January 13.	*Deirdre,* with Molly in the lead, performed at the abbey.
1910, November 22.	Maunsel publishes the four-volume *Works*.

John Millington Synge: A Life Apart

And so when all my little work is done
They'll say I came in Eighteen-seventy-one,
And died in Dublin... What year will they write
For my poor passage to the stall of Night?

                                        "On an Anniversary"—J. M. Synge

Because Synge's drama so often mirrors the experiences reported in the fragmented *Autobiography*, the manuscripts and the letters, serious critics have scrutinized volumes of such documents in an effort to interpret more accurately the writer and his works. In fact, to the diligent scholar, Synge himself offers insights and commentary otherwise not found that provide a ready entrée to the playwright's canon. Because his personal life was his material, a study of the *Life* cannot help but pay generous dividends to the reader.

John Millington Synge repudiated his Anglo-Protestant birthright and sought a life uncomplicated by a tradition that he believed stifled the artistic imagination and demanded a too-rigorous adherence to concerns of class. The Synges had, after all, come to Ireland in the seventeenth century and had produced, in addition to five bishops, a long line of clerics and missionaries. They had, through intermarriage with the Hatches, who were land barons of standing, acquired substantial holdings throughout Leinster and had established a family seat at Glanmore Castle, an ostentatious Ascendancy showplace. Apart from a brief time when their properties fell under the jurisdiction of the Encumbered Estates

Courts, they were well provided for, even through the leaner years of the late nineteenth century, a period of dwindling Ascendancy fortunes.

Synge's father, John Hatch Synge, was a barrister with a practice in land conveyances. Synge's eldest brother, Robert, immigrated to South America and managed an uncle's vast estates in Argentina; a second brother, Edward, oversaw holdings as an agent in Wicklow and the West. Samuel, a third, served the church as a medical missionary in China. His sister Annie married well. Apart from the playwright himself, then, the Synges were Establishment to the core.

Kathleen Synge, the playwright's mother, was a devoted daughter of the Reverend Robert Traill, an evangelical zealot from Antrim who had been "exiled" as rector to Schull in County Cork, a remote backwater district on the edge of the Atlantic, for intemperate diatribes against popery. So vehement was the reverend that, on more than one occasion, he was forced to enlist constabulary protection against the Catholic agrarian societies in the district. After Traill's death in 1847—ironically, he died of famine fever—his wife relocated the family first to Blackrock, a coming residential suburb, and thence to Monkstown, the neighboring suburb. In 1856, after summer holidays in Wicklow, Kathleen Traill married John Hatch Synge, fourteen years her senior.

The Synges reared five children in relative comfort. (Three others had died in infancy.) Edmund John Millington Synge—that was, in fact, the playwright's christened name—was born on April 16, 1871, in Rathfarnham, another suburb. But when his father contracted smallpox and died the year after John's birth, Kathleen Synge shifted the family to 4 Orwell Park in Rathgar, to a house next to her widowed mother. Mrs. Synge had sufficient income from land rents— about £400 a year from some Galway holdings—to live a rung or two above genteel poverty and provide her children an education befitting their station. Although finances were at times strained, the Synges had the wherewithal to carry on in true Ascendancy style. There were servants and nurses and tutors, and there were holiday outings and summers by the sea. The moral tenor at 4 Orwell Park, however, was dictated by religious fundamentalism presided over by a mother and grandmother of extremely narrow views. The Reverend Traill would have smiled his approbation.

John Millington Synge, the youngest, was a sickly child, plagued by frequent bouts of asthma and colds, and his formal schooling was intermittent. At age ten he attended Mr. Herrick's Classical and English School on Leeson Street in Dublin, about a half hour's walk from home. At thirteen, he went to the Aravon House-Bray School in Wicklow. For the rest, he received thrice-weekly tutorials at home and religious education at the Zion Church Bible School in nearby Rathgar. His childhood was spent in comparative isolation, a situation that apparently did not overly concern his mother.

What he recalls fondly in the notebooks, however, is his informal education: the wanderings in Rousseauesque abandon through the woods of Rathfarnham and Wicklow with his brother Sam and his cousin Florence Ross; collecting specimens of moths and butterflies and charting their progress on small notepads;

caring for a menagerie of rabbits, pigeons, guinea pigs, canaries, and rabbits; and scanning the heavens with a ten-shilling telescope (II, 6). For young Synge, these summer activities in Greystones, an insignificant fishing village, with excursions into the hills beyond, prompted the metaphysical inquiries that inevitably led him to a study of Darwinism. In effect, they prompted a questioning that would soon dismiss revealed religion as inadequate. His mother was heart-scalded at his apparent abandonment of God. In a letter to Robert, she lamented, "Oh how I pray for him, the lost child, far from God" (Greene and Stephens 19).

Synge wrote in 1896:

When I was about fourteen, I obtained a book of Darwin's. It opened in my hands at a passage where he asks how can we explain the similarity between a man's hand and a bird's or bat's wings except by evolution. I flung the book aside and rushed out into the open air—it was summer and we were in the country—the sky seemed to have lost its blue and the grass its green. I lay down and writhed in an agony of doubt. (II, 10)

He was distressed and terrified by the awesome discovery that the faith of his fathers had come up short. By age sixteen, however, he had stopped his brooding about eternal hellfire and damnation and sought sympathetic company in the membership of the Dublin Naturalists' Field Club:

Natural history did [much] for me . . . To wander as I did for years through the dawn of night with every nerve stiff and strained with expectation gives one a singular acquaintance with the essences of the world. The obscure noises of the owls and rabbits, the heavy scent of the hemlock and the flowers of the elder, the silent flight of the moths I was in search of gave me a passionate and receptive mood like that of early [man] . . . The forces which rid me of theological mysticism reinforced my innate feeling for the profound mysteries of life. (II, 9–10)

Fortunately, Synge had a romantic rather than a scientific bent and, in the next eight years, found his solace in music and in poetry. He had traded the morbidity and melancholy of early adolescence for the wild ecstasy of "the finest art." He tells us: "I threw aside all reasonable counsel and declared myself a professional musician" (II, 15). Wordsworthian poetry offered a credo and music a mystical language. "Every life is a symphony, and the translation of this life into music, and from music back to literature or sculpture or painting is the real effort of the artist," he reflected (II, 3). He studied violin under Patrick Griffith in Dublin and, with the Academy Orchestra, played two memorable concerts in the Antient Concert Rooms and in Molesworth Hall, both of which would later figure prominently in Irish Literary Revival history. He also won prizes for counterpoint and harmony.

In 1888 Synge put aside the violin to prepare for the entrance examination at Trinity College. His mother wrote that he only "squeaked by," although, given her humorless personality, the pun must have been unintended. For four years, guided by his tutor and his kinsman Anthony Traill, he applied himself to the study of modern languages, excelled in both Irish (Gaelic) and Hebrew, and developed a particular fascination for antiquities. He also had an awareness of politics, although it was not fine honed. He put it this way:

Soon after I had relinquished the Kingdom of God I began to take a real interest in the kingdom of Ireland. My politics went round from a vigorous and unreasoning loyalty to a temperate Nationalism. Everything Irish became sacred . . . and had a charm that was neither quite human nor divine, rather perhaps as if I had fallen in love with a goddess. (II, 13)

Although he later spoke with almost derision of his college years and the Trinity "Divines," that experience was essential for what was to come; it established, after all, the foundation for his Irish dramas.

In those days if an odd undergraduate of Trinity felt a vague longing to know more of Ireland and her past than he could learn from his teachers or companions, he had to wander on Aston's Quay and Bachelor's Walk, picking up ugly pamphlets with Grattan's Speeches in them, or Davis's Poems on the true History of Ireland from before the Flood. If he wished to learn a little of the Irish language and went to the professor appointed to teach it in Trinity College, he found an amiable old clergyman who made him read a crabbed version of the New Testament, and seemed to know nothing . . . about the old literature of Ireland, or the fine folk-tales and folk-poetry of Munster and Connaught. (II, 384)

He was protesting the silent neglect of the indigenous culture by those of the Garrison mentality. In his study of antiquities—tramping Petrie-like through the glens of Wicklow, rough-sketching rural ruins, capturing the poetic cadences of the local dialect—he was discovering the "fascinating newness of the old," to use Patrick Kavanagh's apt phrase. Here was a heroic literature, pristine and pure, that was ignored by the hyphenate inheritors of the Celtic past. No wonder he slipped further from the myopia of Ascendancy Ireland and fell under the spell of the Wicklow *seanchaí,* no wonder he spoke so disparagingly of those Trinity years.

In spite of his disappointment with Trinity, where he received a "gentleman's pass," Synge published "Glencullen," a nature sonnet inspired by Wordsworth in *Kottabos* (the college magazine), and continued to read voraciously in Irish texts and to study violin at the Royal Irish Academy of Music, although it was becoming clear that his temperament was too fragile for the concert hall.

By his graduation from Trinity in December 1892, he had renounced the Anglo-Protestant tradition. He had, to his family's great consternation, totally rejected Evangelicalism and Ascendancy values. To him, scriptural evidence and divine revelation were only convenient deceptions, and rank and privilege came at too high a price. He reasoned that a religion that frightened little children into submission had "probably caused more misery than many customs that the same people send missionaries to eradicate'' (II, 4–5). His favorite brother Sam, confounded by his refusals to repent, finally settled for John's admission that ''Christianity is good for depraved humanity such as cannibals and the heathen in general'' (Greene and Stephens 43). Sam finally embarked for the China missions on the best of terms with his errant brother.

John remained as unshaken in his agnosticism as he was in his ''temperate nationalism.'' He was, moreover, embarrassed by the notoriety of the Synges and the Traills in recent Irish history. Uncle Alec (the Reverend Alexander Synge), a missionary to Aran, had earlier received bad press when he ran a fishing vessel in unfair competition with the local islandmen, and more recently, Synge's brother Edward rivaled Captain Boycott as an ''undertaker'' and land agent. In 1887 a particularly ruthless eviction on the Glanmore Estate made the *Freeman's Journal*. Mrs. Synge's justification for all of this was simple: they (the Protestant gentry) were God's chosen, whereas the Catholic majority were ignorant and inferior. ''What would become of us if our tenants in Galway stopped paying the rents?'' she once asked (quoted in Skelton 12). There could be no reconciliation on matters of faith, morality, or politics.

Synge's intellectual convictions, although not yet fully defined, had by age twenty-three already cost him dearly. A ''loner,'' he found himself alienated from family and friends: ''I laid a chasm between my present and my past and between myself and my kindred and friends. Till I was twenty-three I never met or at least knew a man or woman who shared my opinions'' (II, 11). His romance with Cherry Matheson was surely dashed by that ''unorthodoxy.'' A member of the puritanical Plymouth Brethren, Matheson was ''quite shocked'' at his candor, and she rejected his several proposals (Greene and Stephens 55). Although Synge's unorthodoxy may have defied prescribed Victorian behavior and beliefs, he was hardly a radical free thinker. He was no more a committed atheist than he was a committed nationalist. He had simply opted for independence, and he needed to distance himself from Ascendancy Ireland to try himself. An English cousin of his father's who was a concert pianist, Mary Synge, provided him the opportunity.

Mary Synge persuaded the family that John should accompany her to Germany and seriously pursue his career in music, and in July 1893 he met her in London and the two traveled to Coblenz together. The visit to Germany was another turning point in his life. Music was no longer a useless preoccupation. The von Eiken boardinghouse, where he lodged, became his novitiate and his refuge, and Valeska von Eiken became his confidante. From Coblenz he traveled to Oberwerth and Würzburg to perfect techniques in violin and piano, but to his dismay, he discovered what he had already suspected, that he had neither the inclination nor the confidence to continue his music. Perhaps more importantly, he had begun writing poetry in earnest and sketching outlines for plays. The poetry was forced and the plays were melodramatic, but they were, nevertheless, apprentice pieces that set his imagination whirring.

He confessed, ''I wished to be at once Shakespeare, Beethoven and Darwin;

my ambition was boundless and amounted to a real torture in my life'' (II, 12). Shakespeare was winning out. When he returned to Ireland in the summer of 1894, he was a changed man, a man with a sense of mission. In October, when he left again for Paris after a brief stopover in Oberwerth, he was determined to channel his energies toward language and literary criticism. In Paris he met Stephen MacKenna, the journalist, and formed a lifelong friendship with him. He found a room with a French family and supported himself by teaching English privately. One of his students, Thérèse Beydon, a Protestant art teacher and a feminist, had a profound influence on him (more, perhaps, than more critics have imagined), and he broadened his horizons and became immersed in a modern world of ideas. He continued drafting his poetry and dramas, and when he returned to Ireland the following summer, he confessed to Cherry Matheson, ''It is very amusing to me coming back to Ireland to find myself looked upon as a Pariah, because I don't go to church and am not orthodox, while in Paris amongst the students I am looked upon as a saint, simply because I don't do the things they do'' (Greene and Stephens 51–52).

As a graduate student at the Sorbonne in 1895, he read philosophy and politics; attended lectures by Sebastien Fauré, the noted anarchist; and joined the university debating club. He was also surveying Petrie and the Irish language and pursuing a keen interest in Italian language and culture. In February 1896 he traveled to Rome for four months to realize a life's ambition. At the *pension* where he boarded he met three young women—Miss Capps, Marie Zdanowska, and Hope Rea—and discussed art, religion, and Cherry Matheson. On his return to Ireland that summer and apparently acting on their counsel, he again proposed marriage to Matheson, who again rejected him. It was a hard blow that sent him wandering back into the Wicklow hills to assuage his wounded pride.

From Italian exercises translating Dantean poetry and Petrarchan love sonnets, Synge turned now to writing poems of agony and despair and autobiographical notes that would become, in time, the grist for *Vita Vecchia* (1895–1897), a collection of fourteen philosophical pieces with connected prose narrative. *Étude Morbide* (1899), a prose diary, would follow suit. There are also indications that, during the period, he drafted *When the Moon Has Set* (1901), a heavy drama that rehearsed a familiar theme of unrequited love between believer and unbeliever, a dark autobiographical drama drawn from the Synge-Matheson relationship.

On December 21, 1896, came the historic meeting with W. B. Yeats outside the Hotel Corneille in Paris. It probably was not as dramatic a meeting as Yeats recollected, although, in truth, Synge would never measure up to Arthur Symons as a critic of French letters and he would (some seventeen months later) hie off to Aran ''to express a life that has never found expression'' (III, 63).[1] What was significant was the catalyst introduced by Yeats and Maud Gonne and other Irish emigrées that would draw Synge further into a literary and political movement from which there was no escape. He had, after all, been well primed by Fauré, by his readings of Marx and Morris, by his university debates, and by his Irish studies to involve himself in Yeats's renaissance and Maud Gonne's Irish League. But Maud's gospel was too extreme, and Synge's politics smacked of "temperate nationalism." He was no revolutionary. He resigned from the league, stating, "I wish to work in my own way for the cause of Ireland, and I shall never be able to do so if I get mixed up with a revolutionary or semi-revolutionary movement" (Saddlemyer, *Collected Letters* I, 47).[2]

During the summer of 1897 Synge returned to Ireland. His mother, sensing what she regarded as dangerous socialist leanings, refused to lend further financial support to his associations with the Parisian Decadents and the Irish movement abroad. Writing to Robert in Argentina, she complained, "But then men like Yeats and the rest, get round him and make him think Irish literature and the Celtic language and all those things that they are trying to revive are very important and, I am sorry to say, Johnnie seems to believe all they tell him" (Greene and Stephens 130). On holiday in Wicklow he explored desolate glens and wild places—Aughavanna, Glenmalure, and the like—and soon discovered the mystical and occult in the poetry and the plays of Yeats and Russell. The Celtic twilight offered him glimmerings of an aesthetic scheme in which a mythology could suddenly come alive against his Irish haunts.

Synge showed the early signs of Hodgkin's disease—a malignancy that would eventually kill him—in the summer and autumn of 1897, when his hair began to fall out in clumps and a glandular swelling formed on his neck. On December 11 he entered Dublin's Mount Street Nursing Home for surgical removal of the offending gland. "Under Ether," a personal essay, recalls his psychic experiences under the anaesthetic—vivid sensations of death, consciousness, and elation. Undaunted by the operation and topped by a black wig and a black felt hat (his trademark), he recuperated well and reentered the land of the living. En route to Paris in January, he stopped off to see Yeats in London and enlist in the "Company."

At the Sorbonne his studies in medieval and modern French literature gave way to Irish literature and Celtic languages. He now attended twice-weekly lectures by the eminent Celticist H. d'Arbois de Jubainville, who developed a theory comparing the primary literatures and put Irish heroic literature on a par with the Homeric epics. It was perhaps that revelation, more than Yeats's dictum outside the hotel, that convinced Synge to embrace Aran and the Irish-speaking West. His five visits to the islands, between 1898 and 1902, were unquestionably the making of him as a dramatist.

In the Aran notebooks, later published as *The Aran Islands* (1907), Synge recognized the stark cultural disparity that stood between the islanders and himself: on his second trip, he entered:

In some ways these men and women seem strangely far away from me. They have the same emotions that I have, and the animals have, yet I cannot talk to them when there is much to say, more than to the dog that whines beside me in a mountain fog. (II, 113)

But with each succeeding visit to Aran the distance was narrowing, while the allurement for the people and their ways increased.

By October of 1902, when the text of his *Riders to the Sea* was complete, Synge's imagination was teeming with folktales and myth, epic, and fairy tales, for he had in that time continued his Celtic studies at the Sorbonne, reviewed for *The Speaker* four Irish titles—*Danta Amhrain Is Caointe Sheathruin Ceitinn, Cuchulain of Muirthemne, Donegal Fairy Stories,* and *Foras Feasa Ar Éirinn*—written the essay "La Vielle Littérature Irlandaise," participated in the Breton folk revival, and compiled and edited nearly a score of notebooks in *The Aran Islands*.

The Aran sketches furnished plots for his dramas, and his reflections added the aesthetic perspective. Pat Dirane, the *sqéalaí* of Inishmaan, provided "He That's Dead Can Do No Hurt," and the oldest man on the island gave him the details of the infamous Lynchehaun murder mystery. The playwright shifted Dirane's tale to the Harney cottage, a familiar place in the Wicklow hills, and made *The Shadow of the Glen* of it. He removed the ancient's tale of the patricide from Achill Island and the Arans to a shebeen in Mayo and there created *The Playboy of the Western World*. Although he adapted the plot of *The Well of the Saints* from a medieval French farce, he also remembered his Irish teacher's miraculous well at *Teampall an Ceattrair Alainn* (*The Church of the Four Comely Persons*), where blindness and epilepsy were cured. *Riders to the Sea* had the urgency of place, however; it was set on Aran, and it was worked directly from the materials at hand.

Although he translated the Deirdre story from the Irish on Inishmaan, his final play owed only some nuances of language to Aran itself. *The Tinker's Wedding*, a Wicklow tale, had no Aran ties. Four of Synge's six published plays owed their origins to the Arans because the islands provided plot and character and setting and because their mood harkened to antiquity and drew a strength from the pagan fatalism that pervaded the place.

Synge also perfected a marvelous cadence and style that emanated from those Aran experiences, although he was the first to admit that he had only reproduced the Gaelic idiom of Aran. The Tramp's memorable supplications at the end of *Shadow*, Maurya's monologue at the conclusion of *Riders*, and Deirdre's final defiance of old age and death were taken from the spoken Irish and from letters he had read. The language was occasionally heightened by literary context, but in spite of the purists' protests to the contrary, the dialogue was literal transcription of that Irish-English he heard on Inishmaan from 1898 to 1902. In a letter, in 1907, he explained:

I look upon *The Aran Islands* as my first serious piece of work—it was written before any of my plays. In writing out the talk of the people and their stories in this book, and in a certain number of articles on the Wicklow peasantry which I have not yet collected, I learned to write the peasant dialogue which I use in my plays. (Saddlemyer, *Collected Letters* II, 103)[3]

He had transformed and translated Celtic imagery and the poetic vernacular into exquisite phrasing and, for the first time, realized the grand vision of his art. He had finally fallen in love with the goddess, and Jubainville's theories on the kinship of Irish and Grecian myths were now borne out by Synge's own readings and observations.

In 1898, before returning to Wicklow from Aran, Synge accepted Lady Gregory's invitation to Coole, and, with Yeats, he visited Edward Martyn at Tullira. They discussed ideas for plays, and Synge learned that Gregory, Martyn, and Yeats, with George Moore, had already laid the groundwork for an Irish literary theater they hoped to launch the following spring. Synge marveled at his fortune—a privileged access to the inner sanctum—but secretly, he questioned the extent of his own contribution to such a scheme.

Back in Wicklow he edited the Aran notebooks and sent a trial essay to the *New Ireland Review*. "A Story from Inishmaan," Synge's first published prose piece, was accepted and appeared in the November issue of that journal. He was especially delighted since in those notebooks were contained all of his observations and dreams and aspirations.

That autumn, when he renewed old friendships in Paris, he realized that he had again fallen in love—this time with Margaret Hardon, a young American art student. Hardon's rejection of him (in fact, she twice rejected him) was traumatic enough to drive him back to the melancholy of *Étude Morbide*. In time, though, he found respite in Breton language lessons and in a fortnight's excursion to Brittany. He was also beginning to discover Le Braz, Loti, and Renan, the prime movers in the Breton Renaissance. But in May he was back in Dublin for the premiere performances of plays by Yeats and Martyn for the new Literary Theatre.

Martyn's *Heather Field* was well received by audiences, but Yeats's *Countess Cathleen* was not. Cardinal Logue, the Catholic primate, condemned the play as heretical, and protesters continuously disrupted the performances with hisses and jeers. Yeats ordered in the police to quell the disturbances to see the drama to the final curtain—not an auspicious start but an unfortunate preview of riotous things to come in Irish theater.

Synge finished the text of *Riders to the Sea,* his tragic masterpiece, and *The Shadow of the Glen,* his adaptation of Pat Dirane's stark folktale, in 1902 and went to work on *The Tinker's Wedding,* a dangerous bit of an anticlerical farce for an Ascendancy castoff. On his farewell visit to Paris, in March 1903, "the mad fiddler" met James Joyce. Neither writer was particularly impressed with the other: Synge saw Joyce as "an ego with a mind like Spinoza's"; Joyce saw him as "a dark tramper of a man" (Gorman 101, 254). Synge, at last satisfied that he had a contribution to make, left Paris and went home to Dublin to stay; he was now even more resolved to cast his lot with Yeats.

The Irish National Theatre Society, which would, in 1904, become the Abbey, performed *The Shadow of the Glen* on October 8, 1903, and *Riders to the Sea* on February 25, 1904. The first was denounced by rabid nationalists as "a libel on Irish womanhood,'' for Synge's sending the Irish wife off to tramp the roads with a blathering vagabond. (''And what else might one expect of a Big House wastrel whose brother had put impoverished tenants on the road?'' they whispered.) The performance of ''Riders'' was met with guarded praise from the Dublin critics and rave reviews from London and elsewhere. John Masefield, Arthur Symons, and G. K. Chesterton at once recognized Synge's genius.

Yeats and Lady Gregory had not only welcomed their prodigal back to Ireland but they took enormous pride in touting his accomplishments. Synge responded by fierce dedication ''to theatre business and the management of men'' and set to shaping Abbey drama in the likeness of his own. Unlike Wilde and Shaw, he remained in Dublin, determined to produce Irish plays on Irish themes for Irish audiences. From 1904 until his death five years later, he sat on the Reading Committee, selected the fare, edited and revised promising manuscripts, toured with the company, and directed and rehearsed his own plays and those of others. In 1905 he was vested a director of the Irish National Theatre Society with Yeats and Lady Gregory and, in a few short years, set the course of modern Irish drama.

In spite of all of his theater activity, Synge found time to write prose and verse. He was an accomplished journalist with a keen eye for detail, even if, at times, he was ''selective.'' *The Aran Islands,* published in 1907, remains central to an understanding of his plays, although it is important to realize that it was not his only reportorial work. He published a series of reflections on the Wicklow peasants that he had known since childhood. He visited Dingle, Iveragh, and the Blaskets each summer from 1903 to 1907 and, at Philly Harris's cottage in Mountain Stage, touched the soul of rural Ireland and captured there a dialect less archaic and more vibrant than that heard on Aran. These were the utterances of the bards of Munster that gave voice to *The Playboy of the Western World.* In 1905 Synge and Jack Yeats accepted a commission to travel four weeks in Connemara and produce a dozen illustrated articles on the Congested Districts for *The Manchester Guardian.* They wandered the most depressed sections of western Galway and Mayo and discovered ignorance and poverty and hunger beyond belief. But what struck Synge even more than the deprivation of the peasants and the landscape were the base instincts of the groggy-patriot-publican-general shopmen, the druid-priests, and the petty swindlers who terrified them, fleeced them, and preyed on their ignorance. The essays were acclaimed for substance and style and illustration, but more importantly, they set the stage for *Playboy.*

Taken together, these prose works complement *The Aran Islands* and offer yet other insights on the playwright and his plays. They show moods as varied as his subjects—in Wicklow, Synge is the pensive romantic; in Kerry, the exuberant fiddler; in Connemara, the restrained reformer. Like the *Autobiography,* they offer dimensions denied the common reader of plays and establish a common ground for the anthropologist, folklorist, historian, linguist, sociologist, and literary critic to meet Synge on his own terms.

Although *The Tinker's Wedding* was completed before *The Well of the Saints*, it was withheld from production because it was thought by Yeats and Lady Gregory to be too inflamatory. In fact, it took nearly fifty years to get it to the Abbey stage. Based on a story told him in Wicklow and later written as "At a Wicklow Fair," the play, given the period and the mood, was offensive, even if faithful to its source. Nonetheless, Synge accepted defeat and filed the script for a later publication. *The Well of the Saints* was first performed at the Abbey on February 4, 1905, and *The Playboy of the Western World* on January 26, 1907.

The Well of the Saints opened at the Abbey to small houses because Synge was, in 1905, still embroiled in a controversy with the nationalist crowd over *Shadow*. The play did, however, bring Molly Allgood (later "Maire O'Neill") to the stage. Although Molly was fifteen years his junior, the playwright was smitten by the passionate, beautiful young woman, and she with him. There followed a relationship that has been described as "tempestuous." His paternalizing and jealousy were answered by her impatience and resentment. During their frequent separations, he wrote to her daily, often long, querulous letters complaining of her inattentions. He moved house twice, to Rathgar and Rathmines, ostensibly to be nearer the theater but in truth to be nearer Molly and escape his disapproving family. The ecstasy and torments of the romance with Molly carried over to his final days. In 1906 they were secretly engaged. *The Playboy of the Western World,* which he had begun with notes in 1903, suddenly became a vehicle for Molly, and *Deirdre of the Sorrows* became *her* play.

When *Playboy* opened, it was not to small houses but to hostile audiences outraged by what they saw as peasant caricature, foul language, and a slur on Irish womanhood. Pearse denounced the Abbey as "a sort of evil spirit in the shape of Mr. J. M. Synge," and others welcomed the play as the beginning of the end of "Anglo-Irish" drama. But Yeats and Lady Gregory stood by Synge, and Yeats summoned the police and castigated its detractors as pseudopatriots who had again brought disgrace to Ireland.

Synge's response to the riots was typically laconic, and although he told an interviewer he didn't care a rap, he actually did. To make matters worse, his health was steadily deteriorating—the symptoms of Hodgkin's disease were now recurring with alarming regularity. He postponed his marriage to Molly to undergo surgery three times, and he found it increasingly difficult to concentrate on *Deirdre* and on his poetry. Deirdre's lament over Naisi came straight from the heart's core, and, remembering Molly's sad refusal to attend his funeral, he wrote:

> I asked if I got sick and died, would you
> With my black funeral go walking too,
> If you'd stand close to hear them talk or pray
> While I'm let down in the steep bank of clay.

And, No, you said, for if you saw a crew
Of living idiots, pressing round that new
Oak coffin—they alive, I dead beneath
That board,—you'd rave and rend them with your teeth. (I, 64)[4]

He made excursions to Kerry and Coblenz now to restore memories of happier days, but while he was in Germany, his mother died leaving him mournful and depressed. No escape! No escape!

On March 24, 1909, Synge died in the Elpis Nursing Home in Dublin, and the Abbey suffered a hard blow. *Poems and Translations* was published post-humously and *Deirdre of the Sorrows,* edited by Yeats, Lady Gregory, and Molly Allgood, opened under Molly's direction at the Abbey Theatre on January 13, 1910, with Molly as Deirdre. Synge's work was done.

David H. Greene, Synge's biographer, has suggested that we are not likely to come by any startling revelations about the writer because all evidence appears to be in.[5] Yet for all of the evidence—Synge's *Autobiography*, letters, com-mentaries, and journals—the playwright's personality remains an enigma, and the distortions still abound.

Biographers have made much of Synge's childhood infatuations, adolescent agonies of self-doubt, and the melancholy of his later years. Synge was, in fact, a reticent individual accustomed to, and comfortable with, his solitude. He lived a life apart, and he did so by choice. He was afflicted with chronic asthma and suffered the symptoms of Hodgkin's disease, but he was, for most of his life, physically robust, an outdoorsman, and not a hypochondrical invalid. He was also a product of his hyphenate Ascendancy culture, in spite of all of the pro-testations and repudiations and the anarchistic and socialist leanings. He never switched horses and rode for the nationalist camp. As he said himself, "I wish to work in my own way for the cause of Ireland." In a period of political and cultural extremism, he courageously stood the middle ground and called himself "a temperate nationalist" to rail against extremism on both flanks.

Synge's "atheism" was never an atheism at all but a rejection of Christianity, especially the evangelical strain hammered home by a family of devotees. He was, at heart, an inquiring, meditative, deeply religious man, but his sense of religion was pantheistic—encompassing a divine scheme promoting uniformity and cosmic harmony in nature. He dabbled in occultism, read the mystics, even turned to Thomas à Kempis occasionally for direction.

Synge is interestingly complex and in some ways enigmatic, but he is ap-proachable. Since this sketch is meant as an introduction to the man, rather than a critical response to his works, it deliberately skirts the texts and leaves that task to the critics who follow. It is, however, important in summing up to put him in perspective. As the master playwright in a theater movement that reached beyond Ireland—to all of modern drama—Synge is especially significant and central. He has offered a unique comic-tragic blend and a vision of rural Ireland that somehow melds the romantic and realistic without ever jarring. His plays give voice to heightened poetic dialogue that suggests a Shakespearean dignity.

Always the consummate artist, Synge was true to an aesthetic that promotes the language of drama as an extension of the spiritual, but since it also projected life on stage—all of human life—the outrages to the spirit could not, in his mind, be suppressed. Accordingly, despotic husbands, tyrannical priests, and greedy shopkeeps were made flesh and offered to audiences that recoiled in horror at their mirror likenesses.

The nationalist gallery was especially wounded because Synge's Irishman was a contradiction of their own; home-grown critics, like George Moore, Daniel Corkery, and Frank O'Connor, who objected that the "lack of veritism," "synthetic language," and "slight plots" were inherent weaknesses of Synge's style, were out of sync with the major critics in "the Big World."

Synge's reputation is secure, and on the basis of *Riders to the Sea* and *The Playboy of the Western World,* his genius has been universally recognized. It is essential, though, that that genius also be understood. So this sketch, summing up his life and his comments, is offered to the reader as a starting point for further Synge studies.

Notes

1. Other than correcting the date of the Paris meeting, Yeats did nothing to dispel the erroneous impression that he was solely responsible for Synge's Aran journeys. See Gerstenberger.

2. April 6, 1897.

3. To Leon Brodzky, a writer and publisher, December 12, 1907.

4. The poem is titled "A Question."

5. Greene, "J. M. Synge." Greene, as Synge's biographer and most intimate critic, wrote with authority on this point.

References

Gerstenberger, Donna. "Yeats and Synge: 'A Young Man's Ghost.' " *W. B. Yeats, 1865–1965: Centenary Essays on the Art of W. B. Yeats.* Edited by D. S. Maxwell and S. B. Bushrui. Ibadan, Nigeria: Ibadan University Press, 1965. Pp. 79–84.

Gorman, Herbert. *James Joyce.* London: Bodley Head, 1949.

Greene, David H. "J. M. Synge: A Centenary Appraisal." *Éire-Ireland* 6, no. 4 (1971):71–86.

Greene, David H., and Edward M. Stephens. *J. M. Synge, 1871–1909.* New York: Macmillan, 1959.

Saddlemyer, Ann, ed. *The Collected Letters of John Millington Synge, I: 1871–1907.* Oxford: Clarendon, 1983.

———. *The Collected Letters of John Millington Synge, II: 1907–1909.* Oxford: Clarendon, 1984.

Skelton, Robin. *J. M. Synge and His World.* New York: Viking; London: Thames and Hudson, 1971.

Prose

Synge's prose works are overshadowed by the plays and are often seen principally as sources of autobiographical or critical evidence. The pre-Aran writings merit no higher status, but most of the prose canon is vital and original, the work of an attentive stylist destined to make his name in another genre. Synge's prose is in itself multigeneric, ranging from three distinct modes of autobiography through several modes of reportage to literary criticism. Sometimes even these distinctions are blurred, for *The Aran Islands* is a unique blend of reportage and spiritual autobiography. Although the prose has engendered considerable critical controversy, virtually every critic since Daniel Corkery (1931) agrees that most of the work displays lasting literary value independent of the plays.

Pre-Aran Writings

None of the prose pieces in the *Collected Works* grouped under the rubric "The Man Himself" had reached a final form or had been published before Synge's death, although editorial changes were made as late as 1907. Each is autobiographical to some extent, and each has been augmented by Alan Price with material from Synge's notebooks. The dozen or so page *Autobiography* (1896–1898) is a spare, seemingly understated account of the author's youth up to his early twenties. The work is generally a straightforward progression of details and commentaries—the early fear of hell and love of nature, a close friendship with a girl cousin, the discovery of Darwin and subsequent abandonment of Christianity, the unsettling onset of puberty, the initiation into music and literature. The *Autobiography* is universally regarded as a useful but tantalizingly brief source of information, although one commentator, Lanto Synge, asserted without proof that it is also a work of art and social history (121).

Synge continued his autobiography in veiled form in *Vita Vecchia* (1895–1897) and *Étude Morbide* (c. 1899), neither of which is held in high regard by most critics. Nicholas Grene's description of the pieces as "lamentable" (23) is, however, harsher than most in print. *Vita Vecchia,* a collection of verse with prose links, recounts an unhappy love affair and concludes with some melancholic observations on the meaning of life and art. Robin Skelton found the poems overly melodramatic and called the prose narrative a "perfunctorily disguised version of his affair with Cherrie Matheson" (11). T. R. Henn's commentary on one section seems to sum up his opinion of the work as a whole: the poetry is Synge's morbidity transformed into lyricism, but the prose is highly derivative (113). Declan Kiberd constructed an elaborate argument to show that the mixing of prose and poetry and heavy use of alliteration in the poems represent a conscious adoption of conventions common to Irish romances such as *The Three Sorrows*. The operatic structure of the romance gives Synge the opportunity to blend his love of music with his interest in native literary forms. Unfortunately, said Kiberd, the native form is an inferior one that invites redundant prose narrative and stilted poetry; thus Synge's good intentions are thwarted by reliance on a weak model, and the result is a literary failure (84–85).

In a letter to Yeats, Synge himself called *Étude Morbide* "a morbid thing about a mad fiddler in Paris, which I hate" (II, x), so it is no wonder that it has not earned much critical praise other than as a source of Synge's thinking on personal and aesthetic issues. *Étude Morbide* is the diary of a feverishly intense violinist who fails in his concert debut, contemplates suicide, is saved by reading *The Imitation of Christ,* travels to Brittany, and then renounces art. One of his potential lovers dies insane and the other turns down marriage for the life of an ascetic. Although the work has autobiographical overtones, Price wisely warns that *Étude Morbide* and *Vita Vecchia* together comprise an "expression of dreams and ideas, longings and discoveries, rather than a record of actual lives or material events" (II, 16n). Thus trying to establish a precise correlation between the female characters and women in Synge's life is a risky undertaking. Robin Skelton was still on safe ground, however, when he wrote that the work is concerned with major issues in Synge's life, such as "his doubts about his own musical abilities, his meditations upon religious truth, his appreciation of peasant life, as well as his difficulties with his girlfriends" (14).

Étude Morbide is an artistic dead end, but several critics see it as a fitting prelude for the great *Aran Islands,* notes for which Synge was drafting while working on *Étude*. Jeanne Flood argued that *Étude* is the turning point in Synge's early autobiographical writing, for it was there that he modified his view of art as rarefied creation independent of and superior to objective reality. Through self-discovery, the narrator realized that the artist's emotional life is inexorably tied to the material world and that because he cannot yet live with this realization, he must give up art. Although Robin Skelton thought the diarist's withdrawal was a surrender to a decadent dream world, he found in many passages of *Étude* sentiments very similar to those expressed in *The Aran Islands* (15). To Nicholas Grene, Synge was, in 1898, poised uncomfortably between two poles, the first French decadence, the other the primitive and folk studies of Pierre Loti and Anatole Le Braz (21); *Étude Morbide* is at the first pole, but *The Aran Islands* is at least midway to the second. Thus the principal issue in dealing with Synge's earliest prose is not deciding whether it is any good but judging how great an attitudinal gap separates these trivial explorations from the extraordinarily rich *Aran Islands*.

Price included two other selections in this section, the fragment "On a Train to Paris" and the essay "Under Ether." The first recounts a train ride in which Synge is seated with a troupe of French ballet dancers. Although the essay was never finally edited, it displays an emotional irony befitting a pre-Aran piece. At first Synge is condescending and pitying, but he ends up envying "their high spirits and good humour" (II, 38). "Under Ether" is a description of Synge's experience with anesthesia during his first Hodgkin's disease operation in 1897. Anyone old enough to have had ether can appreciate his comments, which T. R. Henn said are worthy of Thomas de Quincey (111). His struggle with self-control and fear of surrender looks forward to the "Dream on Inishmaan" episode of *The Aran Islands*.

The Aran Islands

The Aran Islands is the most complex and pivotal of Synge's prose works. Critics generally agree with David H. Greene that the five annual trips to the islands beginning in 1898 and the book that resulted from them mark Synge's transition from failure to artist (Greene and Stephens 74). Although the book contains the rudimentary plots of several of the plays as well as abundant samples of the Gaelicized English spoken by the characters of the drama, what concerns us here are two principal questions: first, what is the nature of Synge's artistic achievement in the book, and second, what does this say about the process that led to his sudden emergence as a major literary figure?

The Aran Islands is a multidimensional travel book in which the author moves in time as well as space. To live among the islanders is to live in the past. Furthermore, to read *The Aran Islands* is to glimpse the author's personal and artistic growth over a five-year period. Divided into four parts corresponding to Synge's first four western journeys, the book is arranged as a kind of undated diary. The sometimes jarring juxtaposition of realistic description, commentary, and supposedly verbatim transcriptions of the islanders' conversations or stories creates the image of a narrator who is at once an objective journalist or ethnographer and a subjective artist and pilgrim. The narrator's relationship to his subject matter changes slightly from part to part. The author maintains overall mastery of the book through careful sequencing of episodes and expert control of prose styles.

Time is a thematically, stylistically, and structurally important element in *The Aran Islands*. Synge regarded Aran culture as premodern: "the life is perhaps the most primitive that is left in Europe" (II, 53). Robin Skelton reminded us that the repetition of terms such as *pagan* and *primitive* is anything but perjorative, for the people's primitivism enhances their sensibility (33). Weldon Thornton went the farthest when he asserted that the culture is literally prehistoric, a Celtic and, therefore, Indo-European survival owing little to Greco-Romanized European culture (*J. M. Synge and the Western Mind* 51ff.). Because they live in a premodern culture, the islanders exhibit unusual attitudes toward time. They have no conception of clock time, something that intrigues Synge. They eat when they are hungry, and they further accommodate themselves to natural rhythms by building their houses with doors in front and back so that they can realize the greatest warmth and light from the sun. Faced with hardships and threats to life, the people live largely for the present, making the most out of ordinary experiences. Donna Gerstenberger accurately observed that Synge admired the people for their existential persistence (29).

The style and structure of the book reflect Synge's concern for time. The book begins "I am in Aranmoor" (II, 49); the ensuing narration has a present-time immediacy that heightens the credibility of Synge's reportage and lends to the descriptive passages an almost photographic quality that many critics have noticed. In his excellent essay "The Prose of John Millington Synge," T. R. Henn provided examples of both the monosyllabic, laconic style and "contrasting brushwork" (112) that vivify the prose. In fact, the disarming simplicity of the descriptions and the authentic sound of the transcriptions of native speakers make the occasional highly personal meditative passages seem all the more acceptable in spite of their obvious subjectivity. In any case, the prose style makes the reader know that Synge was really present on the islands and that he developed a keen awareness of the old culture he found there.

Although the book's structure owes much to the issue of time, critics are not in agreement over how tight the overall structure is. Both the structure of each of the four parts and the relationship among the parts are at issue. Corkery, Henn, and others have noted how Synge characteristically inserted a phrase or sentence that sums up or interprets one or more descriptive passages. These occasional pithy bombshells remind us that we and the narrator are undergoing a progressive learning experience. Embedded within the thirty-three-line, eight-paragraph description of a curagh ride is this brief commentary: "It gave me a moment of exquisite satisfaction to find myself moving away from civilisation in this rude canvas canoe of a model that has served primitive races since men first went on the sea" (II, 57). In this example, the shift from reportage to interpretation is unmarked by a change in prose style; sometimes, however, the change is dramatic, as in the famous dream passage first published in *The Green Sheaf*, "A Dream on Inishmaan" (II, 99–100). Gerstenberger defended her existential interpretation by noting that the structure of each part mirrors life: each begins with an arrival and ends with a departure, and what lies between is difficult (23–24). Ann Saddlemyer made the boldest assertion concerning the internal structure of the four separate parts. She claimed that the structure is not chronological but cyclical and that each cycle peaks with a cathartic experience that renders the narrator less reserved and more empathic. She maintained that circles and cycles are the basis of the book's structure (107–8). Thornton, who certainly appreciated the book's cathartic elements, charged in his bibliographical essay "J. M. Synge" in Richard Finneran's *Anglo-Irish Literature: A Review of Research* that Saddlemyer did not demonstrate that the cyclical pattern continues throughout the book (358).

Critics have long noted a change in mood from one part to another. Corkery observed that the narrator moves from delight to distress from Part I to Part II (119). Emphasizing that the book is a record of a learning process, Skelton claimed that the recording consciousness becomes more selective in the later parts (30). Keith Hull posited that Synge changed his attitude toward the relationship between the people and nature. Thornton demonstrated how, throughout the work, the narrator learns to appreciate and respond to the islanders' strange worldview (*J. M. Synge and the Western Mind* 75–76).

It took Synge five years to write *The Aran Islands,* and as Grene showed, he gradually edited the manuscript material as he developed a firmer perspective on his experiences. The extent to which he recreated that learning process in the final product tells us a good deal about how alien the Aran experience was for him. The question of how and if he managed to tell the objective story of Aran and the subjective story of his own growth brings us head to head with the issue of the book's genre: just how journalistic or how autobiographical is *The Aran Islands*? What is Synge's relationship to the subject? The extent to which he is objective or subjective has been hotly debated by critics. Is the book a personal myth or a documentary? The spectrum of critical thought is broad.

Daniel Corkery, the first commentator to consider the book in detail, presupposed that Synge's Protestant Ascendancy background limited his perspective on the Aran culture. He noted that the objective descriptions of the islands are as real as paintings by Jack Yeats or Paul Henry (114). He praised Synge's appreciation of the islanders' spontaneity and enthusiasm and his ability to learn and accept that as an outsider he can never be one of them (121). At the same time, however, he saw Synge as a "colourist . . . even a sensationalist" (115) capable of exaggeration and blindness. Thus is the author eager to hear and comment upon the people's quaint paganism but willfully ignorant of the primacy of their Catholic orthodoxy (116). He also contended that Synge spent most of his time on the islands either by himself or in the company of the least authoritative men; the essential reality he was seeking transcends the facts he could have learned from more respectable sources (112).

Nicholas Grene thought the book was Synge's unique and not always objectively accurate impression of the islands. For him, Synge was an artist above all: "he saw Aran as it was significant to himself, and the normal selectivity of any individual's impressions is heightened to the level of artistic vision" (29). Tracing the development of the book through Synge's notes and early drafts, Grene showed how the author revised transcriptions of the islanders' speech. Often it makes what they say sound more idiomatically Irish, but occasionally, Synge toned down the Irishness to suit his needs (24–29). Furthermore, he evidently exaggerated the danger to the fishermen of drowning and underplayed the degree to which native workers specialize in particular crafts (30). What is important about the island culture is that it is a microcosmic world, that its essence is accessible because of the absence of modern social structures (34). Ultimately, Grene concluded, the emendations and small inaccuracies are artistic devices for conveying the essential truth about the islands, a truth in which Synge believed and one that he made believable to readers (40).

In *The Writings of J. M. Synge* Robin Skelton devoted considerable attention to the question of the author's relationship to his subject. Skelton claimed that the book is not a "self-portrait of the narrator" but the exposition of how the narrator responds to "a system of values alien to his previous experience, and perspective" (30). This is an important observation because it accentuates Synge's culture shock; he must process what he sees in order to understand it. Pointing to the narrator's frequent use of the verb *seem* and the expression "in a certain sense," Skelton observed that the book is very subjective and that the narrator "may be simply establishing himself a personal myth which makes sense of his disturbed feelings on facing this environment" (37). Skelton's use of the auxiliary *may* makes his conclusion look a bit tentative, however.

Gerstenberger, Saddlemyer, and Thornton thought that *The Aran Islands* was definitive and relatively objective. As T. R. Henn pointed out, most of the text is direct reporting (124). Gerstenberger thought Synge was being essentially objective. For her, the book was "analogous to the documentary" with Synge serving as a cameralike observer (22). Ann Saddlemyer asserted that Synge's search for a suitable persona, what she called the "prepared personality," was a consuming problem for him as he struggled to assimilate and express the Aran experience. What he accomplished is the reconciliation of objectivity with individual personality. Her description of the narrative perspective of *The Aran Islands* is the most concise and accurate in print:

The Aran Islands poises delicately and surely between objective, amoral, deliberate description of the hardships of the islander's daily life and the luxurious evocation of Synge's own mystical reaction to the inner life as he sensed its reflection in the primitive world about him. (107–8)

The balance of dispassionate description and emotional response gives us a work that is at once an account of the life of the islands and the personal development of the author. Saddlemyer's judgment is accurate, for we believe the reporting because it looks so objective, and we accept the commentary because it appears to come from an artist who knows himself honestly and thoroughly and who is, therefore, in control of his material. Saddlemyer believed that Synge saw art as a collaboration between the artist and reality, but that it works only when the artist is "in tune with life and nature" (118).

Weldon Thornton went further still in *J. M. Synge and the Western Mind* when he asserted, in spite of Corkery and Grene, that *The Aran Islands* is an accurate account of a Celtic society that by 1900 existed only in the Gaeltacht, most notably Aran. For him, Synge's artistic consciousness was awakened by encountering the islanders' archaic attitudes and thought processes. The visits to Aran showed Synge a competing worldvision that allowed him to break free of the intellectual and emotional strictures inherited from thousands of years of rationalism. Thornton made a convincing case in support of his claim that Synge regarded the islanders as untamed Celts; to prove that they really were such would require a more exhaustive anthropological study than we are given.

The Aran Islands is in some ways the culmination of Synge's autobiographical efforts, but it is much more than that. This unique prose piece conveys with power and sensitivity the lives of turn-of-the-century Aran islanders, the freshness of Synge's youthful discovery, and the maturity of his successful introspection.

In Wicklow, West Kerry, and Connemara

In the prose volume of the *Collected Works*, Alan Price gave us the contents of the 1911 library edition with additions to five essays and two other essays, only one of which had been previously published (II, 187n). Like *The Aran Islands*, all of the essays are written in the first person, and the Wicklow essays are in many ways the most personal because they are set in Synge's home county. *In West Kerry*, published in three installments in *The Shanachie*, contains less personal reports of life in the Munster Gaeltacht. The pieces in the Connemara section were commissioned by *The Manchester Guardian* as reports of economic and social conditions in the Congested Districts of Connaught.

The essays set in Wicklow are excellent companion pieces to the plays, especially *The Shadow of the Glen*, because they paint such a vivid picture of the gloomy beauty and lingering vitality of this wild, hilly county. As in the later essays, here Synge underscored the material poverty of the people. The deprivation that they endure is different from that in Aran, where the people were relatively undisturbed natives; in Wicklow they were the dispossessed: tramps wandering the roads ("The Vagrants of Wicklow") or the young apple thief in "A Landlord's Garden in Wicklow." "An Autumn Night in the Hills" and "The Oppression of the Hills" evoked the spiritual problems of life in the foggy glens. Synge wrote that "this peculiar climate, acting on a population that is already lonely and dwindling, has caused or increased a tendency to nervous depression among the people" (II, 209). The notebook fragment "People and Places" celebrates the richness of the peasant life that modern Europeans miss (II, 199). But the freest of all are the tramps, who, though homeless, have "a world for habitation'' (II, 236). Although Harold Orel contested this portrait of the vagrants in ''Synge's Concept of the Tramp,'' there can be no doubt that Synge was inspired by those fallen peasants and impractical artistic nomads (II, 202–8). Synge seemed to know his Catholic neighbors well, which was unsettling to Corkery. He suggested that these essays are probably the best crafted that Synge ever wrote but missed in them Synge's sense of mild despair at never really being able to be one with the native people that he found in *Aran, West Kerry,* and *Connemara* (121). In contrast to this opinion, Price contended that all of the essays from *Wicklow* to *Connemara* display an emotional distancing that distinguishes them from the more emotive *Aran Islands* (96).

What Gerstenberger said of all later essays is especially true of the West Kerry and Connaught pieces, which is that the people suffer from a ''fatal separation from life'' that results in ''a povery of mind and spirit'' (32). *In West Kerry* opens with a westward train trip. But neither the train nor the sidecar ride bring Synge to the primitive world; only the curagh ride to the Blaskets can do that. Even there, life is not what it is in Aran. Synge enjoyed the music, dance, and talk, but he never wrote of his host with the warmth he lavished on Pat Dirane or Old Mourteen, the Aran storytellers. In fact, although he did not comment directly upon the episode, the imperious behavior of his host, ''The King,'' who awakens a daughter at six in the morning to bring him a glass of whiskey, is unlike anything in *The Aran Islands*. Price observed that Synge derived little joy from attending either the shoddy circus or the Puck Fair, the ancient annual event that is the talk of Kerry (99). Synge's sense of isolation is apparent throughout; even his Irish does not break down as many barriers as it did in Aran because he has trouble with the Munster dialect.

What is most startling about the *Connemara* essays is their raw objectivity. Paraphrasing Sir Philip Sidney, Price noted that unlike anything else Synge wrote, these essays strive to instruct rather than delight (102). The opening phrase, ''Some of the worst portions of the Irish congested districts'' (II, 283), sets the tone. We then learn about the poverty, hunger, cruelty, ignorance, and despair, an almost unremitting tale of human suffering. Describing the toil of the kelp-burners, he boldly defended the people against charges that they are lazy (II, 309). At every turn, what little there is of local tradition is in danger. Emigration deprives people of their children and their future. Despite the Gaelic League, Irish is dying. Synge did not much like the dwellings built by the Congested Districts Board because they seemed out of place with their slate roofs and cement floors, but he allowed that with a turf fire, they seemed a little more authentic (II, 324). But Synge was not a sentimentalist in these essays. The final piece, ''Possible Remedies,'' proposes that the ultimate sense of futility comes from the lack of any semblance of political control. Despite what Yeats might have said about Synge's unfitness for political thought, the final essay takes a firm stand in favor of Home Rule, stating that it would do more to improve life in Connaught than ''half a million creameries'' (II, 343).

It is hard to believe that the author of *Vita Vecchia* and *Étude Morbide,* two melodramatic and self-absorbed practice exercises, could have developed into the chronicler and spiritual autobiographer of *The Aran Islands* or the investigative reporter of the later essays. Yet the progress is there for us to see.

Literary Criticism

From time to time during this amazing transformation, Synge also tried his hand at criticism. He was a good, if not a prolific, literary critic. Aside from the prefaces to the plays, his critical production consists of notebook fragments and articles, mostly reviews, published in various periodicals, all of which occupy a scant fifty pages in the *Collected Works*. Taken together, several articles, including two written in French, illuminate his attitudes toward the literary revival in Ireland. In "La Vielle littérature irlandaise," he asserted with firmness the primordial importance of Irish writing: "Dans nos légendes et dans les cycles dont je viens de parler, on trouve une mythologie qui forme avec la mythologie greque de la première époque, un noyau de croyances les plus primitives que nous ayons des races indo-européennes" (II, 354). In "Le Mouvement intellectuel irlandais," he indicated that the first decade of the twentieth century was momentous for Ireland, highlighted by the rediscovery of the Irish language, agricultural reform, "une nouvelle activité intellectuelle qui est en train de nous créer une littérature" (II, 387), and a lessening of sectarian hostility. His reviews of works of Irish, French, and Breton arts and letters give us a picture of his broad interests and suggest probable influences on his own art. More specifically, the essays reveal a critic devoted to language and style. His review of Fiona Macleod's *The Winged Destiny* demonstrates his intolerance of bad writing. With mock politeness, he echoed the author's vacuous prose when he described one of her sentences as "Words which may have profound meaning, but which, it is to be feared, will appear to many as a terrible reality of wind and vastness" (II, 388). Overall, then, Synge's criticism mirrored his principal literary concerns, although it remains an interesting, well-crafted sidelight to his major efforts in prose and drama.

From the time of *The Aran Islands*, Synge's prose demonstrates that he could have made a career as an essayist or journalist had his first love not been the theater.

References

Corkery, Daniel. *Synge and Anglo-Irish Literature: A Study.* Dublin and Cork: Cork University Press; London: Longmans, Green, 1931. Reprint. New York: Russell & Russell, 1965.

Flood, Jeanne. "The Pre-Aran Writing of J. M. Synge." *Éire-Ireland* 5, no. 3 (1970):63–80.

Gerstenberger, Donna. *John Millington Synge.* Twayne's English Authors Series 12. New York: Twayne, 1964.

Greene, David H., and Edward M. Stephens. *J. M. Synge, 1871–1909*. New York: Macmillan, 1959.

Grene, Nicholas. *Synge: A Critical Study of the Plays*. Totowa, N.J.: Rowman and Littlefield, 1975.

Henn, T. R. "The Prose of John Millington Synge." *J. M. Synge: Centenary Papers, 1971*. Edited by Maurice Harmon. Dublin: Dolmen, 1972. pp. 108–26.

Hull, Keith N. "Nature's Storms and Stormy Natures in Synge's *Aran Islands*." *Éire-Ireland* 7, no. 3 (1972):63–71.

Kiberd, Declan. "Synge's *Prós* and Verse in *Vita Vecchia*." *Éire-Ireland* 15, no. 3 (1980):75–85.

Orel, Harold. "Synge's Concept of the Tramp." *Éire-Ireland* 7, no. 2 (1972):55–61.

Price, Alan. *Synge and Anglo-Irish Drama*. London: Methuen, 1961.

Saddlemyer, Ann. "Art, Nature, and 'The Prepared Personality': A Reading of *The Aran Islands* and Related Writings." *A Centenary Tribute to John Millington Synge, 1871–1909: Sunshine and the Moon's Delight*. Edited by S. B. Bushrui. New York: Barnes & Noble, 1972. pp. 107–20.

Skelton, Robin. *The Writings of J. M. Synge*. Indianapolis and New York: Bobbs-Merrrill, 1971.

Synge, Lanto M. "The Autobiography of J. M. Synge." *A Centenary Tribute to John Millington Synge, 1871–1909: Sunshine and the Moon's Delight*. Edited by S. B. Bushrui. New York: Barnes & Noble, 1972. pp. 121–40.

Thornton, Weldon. "J. M. Synge." *Anglo-Irish Literature: A Review of Research*. Edited by Richard J. Finneran. New York: The Modern Language Association of America, 1976. pp. 315–65.

———. *J. M. Synge and the Western Mind*. Irish Literary Studies 4. New York: Barnes & Noble, 1979.

The Shadow of the Glen

In the Shadow of the Glen (the *In* was dropped after the first season of performances) was Synge's third play to be completed, following *When the Moon Has Set* (in its two-act version) and *Riders to the Sea*, and his first to be performed. In the fall of 1902, Synge brought *The Shadow* (and *Riders*) with him on a visit to Coole Park and showed both plays to Yeats and Lady Gregory. After the first of the year, the plays were read "with much approval" (III, xvii), according to Synge, by Lady Gregory in her rooms at Queen Anne's Mansions in London on January 20, 1903, and by Yeats who read the plays on February 2 in one of his regular Monday gatherings in Woburn Buildings. Unlike *Riders*, *The Shadow* was accepted immediately by the Irish actors, and in a letter to Synge on March 29, 1903, Lady Gregory wrote of the Fay company, "They were much taken by it & I shd. think will be sure to act it, but their hands are pretty full just now" (Saddlemyer, *Theatre Business* 42). *The Shadow* was produced along with Yeats's *The King's Threshold* by W. G. Fay's Irish National Theatre Society at Molesworth Hall on October 8, 1903. It was published by Yeats in *Samhain* in December 1904.

Maire Nic Shiubhlaigh, who was cast in the part of Nora Burke upon the defection of Maire Quinn, expressed amazement at the hostility that was directed against *The Shadow* by Dublin newspapers: "Indeed, the attacks were launched so suddenly that few of us were even able to gather what they were all about" (43). Yet even before the first performance there were signs of trouble. Joseph Holloway, who was not yet the anti-Synge zealot that he was soon to become, wondered in a diary entry of September 4, 1903, how an audience would greet

The Shadow because "the tone of it is not quite Irish" (25). An editorial in the *Irish Independent,* printed hours before the first evening performance, took up this theme of foreign influence, describing the two plays of Synge and Yeats as "unwholesome productions" (Greene and Stephens 145). Also, Dudley Digges, who had acted in Willie Fay's troupe from the start, refused to perform in *The Shadow* but instead staged a public walkout on opening night, along with Maire Quinn, his future wife, and Maud Gonne, who had been Synge's acquaintance since 1896 and who had been present at Yeats's reading of the play the previous February 2.

Still, the opening-night crowd took the production in stride. There was some hissing during the play that continued when Synge acknowledged his authorship at the conclusion, but the cheers overcame the demurs. Joseph Holloway said that the play received a "mixed reception" (27). He added that "most present applauded the . . . literary and dramatic merits of the play [areas in which the opaque Holloway unfortunately rarely speaks with authority]" (27). However, they had "little to say in favour of the matter of the story contained therein" (27). Perhaps the temperate atmosphere of the audience was typified by their amused response to George Roberts (Dan Burke) as he was seen creeping into bed to feign death (to test his wife's fidelity) before the play began (Hogan and Kilroy 72), this response coming despite the fact that many of the patrons had heard the warning that in attending the performance of *The Shadow* they would be witnessing the spectacle of a wife who runs away from her husband.

Although the *Freeman's Journal* of October 9 called the performance of the previous evening "quaint" and "true to nature" (Kopper 1), and although the *Daily Express* of the same date termed the play a "gem" (Kopper 1), other newspapers were emphatic in their denunciations of Synge's work. The *Irish Times,* confounding artistic integrity with national self-image, found *The Shadow* to be "an extraordinary choice of subject for a society that claims to have a higher and purer standard than ordinarily accepted in things dramatic" (Hogan and Kilroy 74). The *Dublin Evening Mail* situated *The Shadow,* with its stress on the loveless marriage and marital infidelity, in the school of the "problem play," espoused by Henry Arthur Jones and Sir Arthur Wing Pinero (Kopper 2–3).

By far the most cogent and enduring opposition to *The Shadow* was that led by Arthur Griffith, the feisty, intelligent, lucid, ultranationalist who edited the *United Irishman.* This publication, although of small influence outside of nationalist circles, was read and believed by the same type of partisans who were to forbid a hearing of *The Playboy of the Western World* in 1907.

Griffith admitted in the *United Irishman* of October 10 that he had not yet seen or read Synge's play, but then, on October 17, he launched a full-scale attack on *The Shadow.* Griffith implied that Yeats and Synge were merely West Britons—English sympathizers living in Ireland who welcomed the praise of the British press. He found *The Shadow* to be simply a new version of *The Decameron* inspired by a corrupt and decadent European society. In a charge that was to resurface in a renewed attack on *The Shadow* in February 1905, provoked then by Griffith's opposition to *The Well of the Saints,* he maintained that Synge was "influenced by the ancient story of the Widow of Ephesus" (Kopper 2).

Also, in this October editorial, Griffith chided Yeats for abandoning his patriotic ideals, calling *The Shadow* "an inferior substitue for *Cathleen ni Houlihan*" (Kopper 2). In addition, Griffith wondered how a theater that has cut itself off from its country's soil can call itself national. He maintained that when the Irish National Theatre Society "ceases to be national, it will also cease to be artistic, for nationality is the breath of art" (Hogan and Kilroy 79). Finally, Griffith charged Synge with falsifying not only the morals and mores of his peasants but their speech. He thought that a tramp would never address a rustic wife as "lady of the house" and that an Irishwoman from a cottage who has treated a traveler with hospitality (and, by the way, who is about to go away with him) would not call him "stranger" (Hogan and Kilroy 78). Griffith's adjurations continued in the October 24 issue of the *United Irishman,* where he shrilly proclaimed the "fact which all of us know—that Irishwomen are the most virtuous women in the world" (Kopper 2)—and on October 31, when he castigated Synge for spending most of his time away from Ireland, in contrast to Padraic Colum, who was more acceptable to nationalists.

A typically intelligent rebuttal to Griffith was offered in the *United Irishman* by Yeats and his father J. B. Yeats and later by Lady Gregory in *Our Irish Theatre.* The elder Yeats pointed out on October 10 and on October 31 that Synge's play *is* really an attack on the loveless marriage. W. B. Yeats wrote on October 24 that Irish traditions, such as popular songs, do include the cases of the occasional women who will take lovers when they are victims of such a union. On October 10 he had argued in anticipation of the controversy that the theme of the faithless wife is universal and, at any rate, urged his readers to accept Synge's satiric viewpoint: "Aristophanes held up the people of Athens to ridicule, and . . . they invited the foreign ambassadors to the spectacle" (Kopper 3). Lady Gregory, in her trip to America with the Irish actors in 1911–1912, learned from an old Irish-born nursemaid that *The Shadow* was a common "hearth tale" or "fireside story" (66).

One effect of the contentiousness over *The Shadow* was that when the Irish National Theatre Society applied for a patent for the Abbey Theatre in 1904 one of the charges brought against the group was that it had produced "a play which was an attack on marriage" (Lady Gregory 35).

The renewed attack on Synge early in 1905, occasioned by Griffith's objections to *The Well of the Saints,* was sporadic, short lived, and inconclusive. Griffith charged once again that Synge had found his source for *The Shadow* in the old-world libel on women, the tale of the Widow of Ephesus; Yeats demanded a specific reference from Griffith to support his allegation; Synge sent the *United Irishman* both a letter and a separate summary of his source of this play, the tale that he had heard from Pat Dirane on Inishmaan; and Griffith, while printing the letters of Yeats and Synge in the February 4 and February 11, 1905, issues (respectively) of his paper, refused to publish Synge's account of his source, averring that it did not merit space in his columns.

Reasons for the opposition to *The Shadow* by Griffith and his followers are as varied as the personalities and aims of the Irish Renaissance period. In terms of the politics of the age, the controversy was seen by Lady Gregory and Yeats as an attack by the nationalists on the Irish theater movement generally and on Yeats in particular, with Synge being merely a secondary target. Apparently, Griffith was irritated by Yeats's rapidly evolving resistance to the Irish theater's being used for political purposes; Yeats was growing more and more adamant in insisting that art must be free from national purpose. This conflict between politics and art was exacerbated in the stir caused by the political gaffe that was committed during the staging of *The Shadow*, although the incident seems trivial today. Through courtesy, the chief secretary of Ireland and his party of six were seated in the front row at Molesworth Hall, and to make matters worse, the chief secretary was seated in a chair upholstered in the hated British color of red (Fay and Carswell 141–42).

More important in causing the disturbances was the realism of *The Shadow*. As Ann Saddlemyer pointed out, "the production emphasized the reality of the life he [Synge] depicted. Dan Burke's cottage was scrupulously copied from life . . . Harney's cottage in Glenmalure, County Wicklow" (III, xviii). Also, the play presented the dissolution of a marriage, an outcome rarely seen in a play that purported to be "comedy," and the "sexual ebullience" (Greene and Stephens 153) of Maire Nic Shiubhlaigh in portraying Nora did not help assuage puritanical attitudes. In addition, as Francis Bickley stated, "Satires on Irish town life, such as Mr. George Moore's *Bending of the Bough*, could be tolerated, but satire on the Irish peasantry . . . was in no wise to be borne" (15–16).

The final result of this realism, both physical and psychological, was to leave the audience in a state of shock. As Weldon Thornton pointed out, the audience brought to the theater a "perceptual set" (100). They were inclined to "read into the play a pattern very common in Western literature . . . they see in the play what they expect to see" (100). The *Irish Times'* reviewer's description of Nora's leaving with a "young suitor" stemmed from the " 'lovers' triangle' stereotype" that had been implanted in his mind (Thornton 101). As Thornton averred, "The dramatist's proximate goal is to elicit expectations and then confuse them, to throw us into perceptual—specifically, aesthetic—shock" (107).

One antedote to the bitterness occasioned by the 1903 protests over *The Shadow* is seen in the mildly satiric skit "In a Real Wicklow Glen," which was signed by "Conn" and appeared in the *United Irishman* of October 24, 1903 (Hogan and Kilroy 148–52). The heroine, Norah, has been married for ten years, for security, to an elderly "hard" man, and although it is difficult to marry without love, says the old lady Mrs. Shaughnessy, the playlet's wizened prophetess, Norah is a good wife and mother. Norah's old love arrives on the scene ragged and with "that dreadful look of drink" (150). Mrs. Shaughnessy advises John to stop drinking in case Norah should one day be in a position to remarry.

Fortified by this slender hope, John promises, "So help me, God, I will be a man worthy of her love" (152). The implication to the piece is perhaps that Synge's Nora should have waited for Dan's real death; today's audience might ask: and for a change of character in the grasping Michael Dara?

Another bit of writing to stem from the controversy over *The Shadow* is one not so humorous in intent and one that affords a side glance at Synge's attitudes toward the Irish middle-class Catholic nationalists. Synge's fragment "National Drama: A Farce" (III, 220–26), unpublished in his lifetime, was probably written in response to the attacks on *The Shadow,* although Yeats mistakenly thought in later years that the riots over *The Playboy of the Western World* had inspired it. The setting of this "farce" is "a national club room," where a debate is scheduled on the topic of what constitutes national drama. The start of the play sees the entrance of Mr. Fogarty, a florid gentleman who enjoys telling dirty jokes and fantasizing about high-kicking music-hall dancers. Fogarty scans the contents of the book shelf lining the room where the debate is to be held. The books include direct tie-ins with Griffith: "How to be a Genius, by a Gaelic Leaguer. The Pedigree of the Widow of Ephesus. The complete works of Petronius and Boccaccio, unabridged. The Plays for an Irish Theatre, abridged and expurgated by a Catholic critic" (III, 221).

In the ensuing debate, the national drama is one "in short which contains the manifold and fine qualities of the Irish race" (III, 222). The debaters discuss foreign authors that they might model their own dramas upon (a practice that Synge abhorred). Molière, Shakespeare, and Ibsen are all ruled out. Molière was "always making fun of his own country, till the holy bishop wouldn't take his corpse when he was dead" (III, 222). Shakespeare is "infected with the plague-spot of 'sex' " (III, 223), and Ibsen deals with "livid realities" (III, 223).

The best "answer" to Griffith and the nationalists and the best means of understanding *The Shadow* is an examination of Synge's prose: *The Aran Islands,* which was not published until 1907 although completed about five years earlier, and his short essays written around the time of *The Shadlow*. These prose writings reveal the Irish rustic with all of his or her warts and wrinkles and, in their portrayal of the hidden passions, sexual and otherwise, of the Irish peasants, demonstrate a side of Ireland that Griffith did not want publicized abroad. Synge's men and women are far different from the pathetic stage Irishman and from the mystic Gael who was never far from a smile or a tear. They demonstrate the Rabelaisian streak that infuses Synge's plays with the toughness of the grotesque that was a part of Synge's characters.

The complexity of Synge's portrait of Irish rustics is seen first in two old men, Old Mourteen (Martin Coneely), Synge's tutor on Inishmore, and Pat Dirane, his *shanachie* on Inishmaan. On one occasion, Old Mourteen showed Synge one of the well-preserved beehive dwellings and with "earthy humour" began to tell him "what he would have done if he could have come in there when he was a young man and a young girl along with him" (II, 56). Again, as part of his tour, Old Mourteen stopped to describe the occupant of a slated house, a "kind of schoolmistress." Synge related that then "his old face puckered with a gleam of pagan malace," and he asked, "wouldn't it be fine to be in there, and to be kissing her?" (II, 56).

Pat Dirane also exhibited at times the slight leer of the sensualist. Once he saw a "grotesque twopenny" doll lying on the floor of the McDonough cottage (where Synge stayed during his visits to Inishmaan) and asked the old woman in the cottage if she had brought "that thing into the world" (II, 70). But Pat can be helpful from time to time; once he confided to Synge a secret that he had never told to another soul, that the way to ward off the faeries was to keep a sharp needle under the collar of his coat. This instrument takes on symbolic meaning as the Tramp of *The Shadow* sews (seemingly) to while away the time and as he sings the *De Profundis*, another sure method of discouraging evil creatures.

Pat tells the story of the unfaithful wife (the source for *The Shadow*) using the first-person approach for authenticity. Once as he was walking from Galway to Dublin, he stopped outside of a rustic cottage, and although he saw a dead man inside, he decided to enter. The young woman of the house asked him to stay with the corpse so that she could summon help. Then, having returned with her lover, she entered the bedroom with him. The dead man and old Pat approached the couple with two sticks that the old husband had used to keep "down his wife" (II, 72). The dead man "hit him [the lover] a blow with the stick so that the blood out of him leapt up and hit the gallery [critics of Synge, ignoring the Spanish influence on the western part of Ireland and the structure of many Irish churches in the West, wondered how a "gallery" came to be part of an Irish cottage and falsely scented a European origin in the term]."

Another element of Synge's complexity in *The Aran Islands* is seen in the effects of the repression of women, which is so pronounced on Aran that it is not difficult to find in the book the sources of passionate but frustrated heroines such as Pegeen Mike and Nora Burke or to understand why the woman rebel is at the heart of Synge's drama. According to Synge, the finest quality the men of Inishmaan see in a woman is that "she should be fruitful and bring them many children" (II, 144). Thus although the sex instincts "are not weak" on Inishmaan, Synge found, they rarely lead to marital infidelity. Indeed, the life on Aran is still "at an almost patriarchal stage, and the people are nearly as far from the romantic moods of love as they are from the impulsive life of the savage" (II, 144). The Aran women typify many female rustics, and it is not surprising that the emotionally starved Pegeen Mike can be led by Christy's poetry almost to escape from her sterile environment or that Nora Burke, with trepidation, decides to follow the Tramp after his poetically intense description of the possibilities of external nature outside of her repressive cottage.

Sometimes in *The Aran Islands* the women compensate for their lack of emotional freedom by displacing their feelings, by going underground in a sense. Of such are the frenzied women who, after an emotional scene in which pet pigs are shipped to England for marketing, start to ridicule Synge on the deserted boat slip, to begin "jeering and shrieking" at him because he is not married: "they were taking advantage of the absence of their husbands to give me the full volume of their contempt" (II, 138). In contrast to these women is the "wonderfully humorous girl" (II, 143) whom Synge came to know well in Book Three of *The Aran Islands,* who finds another way to compensate for her romantic frustrations. She spent her time spinning in the kitchen of the McDonough cottage, and on the night before Synge's departure, she told him that after he left he was "to marry a rich wife with plenty of money, and if she dies on me I am to come back here and marry herself for my second wife" (II, 144). With her deft grasp of human practicalities, this girl resembles the Aran women who approached a peddlar just arrived on the boat slip at Inishmaan: Synge was surprised when he noticed that "several women who professed to know no English could make themselves understood without difficulty when it pleased them" (II, 138).

Of more direct relevance to an understanding of *The Shadow* is Synge's essay "The Oppression of the Hills," which was written between 1898 and 1902 and first published in the *Manchester Guardian* on February 15, 1905. One passage encapsulates Nora Burke's depressing existence in Glenmalure and, by implication, that of her husband, although this fact is not stressed by critics:

Among the cottages that are scattered through the hills of county Wicklow I have met with many people who show in a singular way the influence of a particular locality. These people live for the most part beside old roads and pathways where hardly one man passes in the day, and look out all the year on unbroken barriers of heath. At every season heavy rains fall for often a week at a time, till the thatch drips with water stained to a dull chestnut and the floor in the cottages seems to be going back to the condition of the bogs near it. (II, 209)

As Synge averred, these conditions cause various kinds of neurasthenia and sometimes lead to madness; "every degree of sadness . . . is common among these hills" (II, 209). One such person to be ruined by this desolation provides the source for the characterization of Patch Darcy. This "poor fellow" drank two glasses of whiskey and, overcome by "some excitement,"ran naked into the hills where he died amidst darkness and rain, and his body was nearly devoured by crows (II, 210). Another half-demented cottage dweller is a woman that Synge met who had "lived by herself for fifteen years in a tiny hovel near a cross roads much frequented by tinkers and ordinary tramps" (II, 210). She confided her fears to Synge, and her timorous approach to itinerants, suggesting her fear of rape, differs markedly from Nora's dealings with the Tramp: "what would I do at all if one of them lads was to come near me?" (II, 210).

Two other essays of Synge are helpful in a discussion of *The Shadow.* In "An Autumn Night in the Hills," published in *The Gael* (New York) in April 1903, Synge related his trip to a cottage to retrieve a dog for a friend. None of the men is at home because all have gone to bring back the body of Mary Kinsella, a young woman with two children who went mad, was sent to Richmond Asylum, and died two days before under peculiar circumstances: "maybe they thought the sooner they were shut of her the better" (II, 188). Also, in this essay Synge admitted that he had often heard "strange noises in the cliff" (II, 189) when fishing at night; in his description of the sound of sheep after he has left the cottage, the reader finds an analogue for his sensitive depiction of nature in *The Shadow*: "On the other side of the road flocks of sheep I could not see coughed and choked with sad guttural noises" (II, 192).

Finally, it is "The Vagrants of Wicklow," probably written in 1901 or 1902, with its description of the savagery hidden just below the surface of the Irish rustic's veneer of control, that serves to clarify the febrile emotions portrayed in *The Shadow*. One such emotional peasant is a drunken flower-woman who fights so ferociously with policemen who are trying to evict her from a village that her clothes begin to come off, and the police leave her alone to prevent a scandal. Another peasant detailed in this essay, who is different from the stereotype promulgated by Griffith, is the man who claims with some likelihood, according to Synge, that he is 102 years old. Synge wrote: "When he was over ninety he married an old woman of eighty-five. Before many days, however, they quarrelled so fiercely that he beat her with his stick" (II, 203). On her complaint, he was remanded for a month to Kilmainham Jail.

Assessing such background material as nationalistic opposition to Synge, Synge's response to his critics, and the clarifying prose documents written around the time of the play's composition, literary critics have viewed *The Shadow* in terms of both the Irish Renaissance and, in recent years, the more universal aspects of literature. Some of the resultant critical controversy focuses upon the character of Nora. Daniel Corkery, writing from an ardently nationalistic viewpoint, pictured her as a "piece of naturalistic flesh and blood, wearing her lusts upon her sleeve, a being all appetite and no faculty" (II, 125). Corkery remarked that Dubliners may just as well have looked to a foreign playwright for guidance as to an Irishman who pictures a woman leaving her husband without the "least trouble of conscience" (II, 132). Also, Corkery, although posing the important question of Nora's vacillating motivations, becomes sidetracked on the pedestrian issue of whether the play is a comedy or a tragedy. Una Ellis-Fermor thought that Nora has used the Burke cottage as "a garrison against the mountain's power" (II, 168). Alan Price admitted that Nora has indeed indulged in a dream, marriage with Dan and a farm, but that this dream has become a "nightmare" (II, 125). Eugene Benson averred that although some commentators argue that "The life of the Tramp offers hope to Nora . . . it is difficult to accept this interpretation" (II, 77). He added: "There is no evidence in the play that the Tramp has a wisdom superior to that of Patch Darcy or Peggy Cavanagh, or that he will not go the way of Patch Darcy" (II, 77). In a more moderate vein, Ann Saddlemyer viewed Nora as a victim of "horizon-fever" ("Synge and the Nature of Woman" 62), and Weldon Thornton viewed Nora as "the mountain

ewe [that] will prove too much for timorous Michael to handle" (105). Denis
Johnston, though, pictured Nora as someone whom Dan is probably better off
without. In describing the end of *The Shadow,* Johnston wrote, "And the old
man—who, after all, cannot help being old—settles down with a bottle by the
fire, and with a sense of peace that suggests that he may be well able to look
after himself in spite of his wife's prophecies to the contrary" (14–15).

Other critics have evaluated the play's faults from a broader perspective. Donna
Gerstenberger, for example, thought that Synge had not "dramatically realized"
in *The Shadow* the conflict between the world of Dan and Darcy (39). Frank
O'Connor thought that the ending of the play is literary in a middle-class sense,
not true to life.

The majority of commentators on Synge, however, have accepted the play's
prominent status and have cited reasons for its permanence. Robin Skelton
thought *The Shadow* was a transitional play but one in which Synge's themes
and characters are fully realized, and he considered the work to be a precursor
of dark comedy. Gérard Leblanc examined patterns of reversal in the work, and
Nicholas Grene also approached *The Shadow* through recurrent patterns, the
chief of which is the "shadow of the glen itself" (101). Declan Kiberd demonstrated that the play owes much of its richness to the conventions of the Irish
wake that Synge incorporated into the work. Thomas J. Morrissey believed that
in Dan Synge's depiction of a "distorted type of Christ" (159) the sheep and
shepherd symbolism is "biblically inspired" (161). Toni O'Brien Johnson discussed the Tramp in the context of the "fool-figure" (118), averring that he has
"many salient characteristics of the literary fool" (120). She related the play's
feigned death motif to French and Italian medieval literature, "and the motif of
the faithless wife . . . appears with remarkable frequency in French medieval
literature" (163). Jean Alexander and Mary C. King focused on Synge's language
in *The Shadow*. Alexander pointed out that "on the most basic level, the physical
act of beating with a stick until blood spurted [in the original tale of Pat Dirane]
becomes a verbal attack with images of death" (22). She thought *The Shadow*
was the beginning of Synge's theme of the "verbal transformation of reality"
(24). Finally, King, in a contemporary approach to the play, stated, "Daniel
Burke, hater of the creative word and guardian of the authoritarian *fiat*, is an
incarnation of those defenders of dying truth" (67).

Much criticism of *The Shadow* views Nora as more symbol than person, a
type of Synge's trapped heroines doomed to grow old in an unfulfilling environment while they conjure up images of almost preternatural creatures, such
as Jaunting Jim, Patch Darcy, and a literally patricidal Christy Mahon. This
same criticism, unfortunately, often fails to address the fact that Nora is a
character drawn with utmost realism and with complete consistency. A close
analysis of Nora's characterization from beginning to end of the play reveals
that whatever "confusion" there might be about her motivation is not on Synge's
part; *The Shadow* presents a compelling portrait of a woman with no real answers,
a far different matter. Nora knows that she is unhappy, and she dreads growing

old. In dealing with her depression, augmented by the lonely, mist enshrouded environment in which she lives, she acts in a practical manner, one that seems to envision no long-term goals or to possess the idealism demanded by some playgoers. But in doing so, Nora is in good company; her characterization looks back to Hardy's Sue Bridehead and forward to many contemporary women who, when forced to choose between two unpleasant alternatives—in Nora's case, life alone on the backroads and life with the Tramp—choose the less destructive of the two. One must recall that Nora was driven from her home by Dan in spite of her effort to rekindle what must have been at least a bit of warmth in their married relationship.

The stage directions at the start of the play suggest a number of motifs in *The Shadow*. The two cups might be set for Michael and Nora in the unlikely event that the old man is really dead, an actuality that Nora doubts from the start. The homemade cake becomes an emblem of her entrapment as she later laments that cake baking formed one part of her sterile existence. The money that she is careful to hide in her pocket becomes less important as Nora realizes that marriage to Michael will be not much different from marriage to Dan.

Nora's bantering with the Tramp is an outlet for her emotions and probably resembles her conversations with the "power of men" that assuaged her loneliness through talk, not as Dan and many critics insist (without evidence) through sexual encounters; in fact, this "talk" may well be the link between the Tramp and the hypersensitive Darcy. Nora tells the visitor of Dan's coldness, which continues after his death in his injunction that she must not touch his body. This aridity marked his nights as well as his days, Nora relates, as she covers Dan's face again, perhaps signaling her displeasure to this dead man who might well be "queer" enough to stage a trick such as the simulacrum of his own demise.

Nora's continued conversation with the Tramp reveals Synge's use of artistic control and demonstrates further Nora's tough-minded realism. Although she repeats that she lives "with no house near me" (III, 37), Nora does not fear "beggar of bishop" (III, 37), neatly vaulting the social spectrum. She speaks of Darcy with interest, then with sorrow, and states the nature of their relationship: "he'd always look in here and he passing up or passing down, and it's very lonesome I was after him a long while" (III, 39). In contrast, Nora queries after the mincing Michael, an early Shawn Keogh, with a "*half-smile*" (III, 39). An added touch of realism, a Rabelaisian note, is added to Nora's characterization by her ability to whistle, and ironically it is Dan who boasts: "Did ever you hear another woman could whistle the like of that with two fingers in her mouth?" (III, 41–43)

After the Tramp has fallen asleep, Nora tries to express her deepest emotions to Michael: her mistake in marrying for security; her fear of aging and becoming like the desiccated Peggy Cavanagh; her perception of the fog and mist, to which she imputes an almost malevolent nature; and her dignity in the midst of loneliness. Michael is as unreceptive to this desperate recital as was Ibsen's Torvald Helmer: he sees her relationships with male friends in crass sexual terms; he believes that, with her imaginative and sensitive view of external nature, she is invading the male domain; his obsession with money contrasts sharply with Nora's questioning of the processes of growth and decay; and his gross simplification that all Nora needs is a "young" man is a shallow answer to Nora's fearful surmise: "God forgive me, Michael Dara, we'll all be getting old, but it's a queer thing surely" (III, 53).

Nora's decision to leave with the Tramp is the result of a careful weighing of options and is not inconsistent with what has gone before in the play. Immediately after his resurrection, Dan, with Synge reversing the ending of Ibsen's *Doll's House,* tells Nora that she must leave: "You'll walk out now from that door, Nora Burke, and it's not . . . any day of your life, that you'll put in your foot through it again" (III, 53). Michael suggests the union. Then Nora, with a moment of wifely solicitude, advises Dan: "let you be getting up into your bed, and not be taking your death with the wind blowing on you" (III, 55). Her concern is met only with Dan's reiteration that she must leave, and Nora's answer to the Tramp's optimistic statement that although it is raining now, a fine morning may eventuate, is a realistic evaluation of her situation: "What good is a grand morning when I'm destroyed surely, and I going out to get my death walking the roads?" (III, 55)

Nora, then, does not decide to leave Dan; that decision is made for her. Her decision to go with the Tramp is based upon the realistic attitude that life will not be all that happy for her. What the Tramp and nature offer is *distraction* from the processes of aging, not a halt to them. Involved in nature, Nora will not be hastening her old age (as she would have done by brooding in her cottage); nor do the larks and thrushes talk of Peggy Cavanagh's decay. Nora knows that the Tramp's answer is not a panacea, for in some ways he is as obtuse as Michael and Dan. Even though she pictures herself "wheezing" and "lying down under the Heavens when the night is cold" (III, 57), she detects that the Tramp does have a "fine bit of talk," though he is no Christy Mahon, and Nora decides to go with him on the road.

It is no wonder that *The Shadow* was disquieting for Synge's audiences. It depicts an Irish rustic set completely opposed to the image that nationalistic Ireland was promoting: a cold and brutal husband; a cowardly and mean-spirited would-be lover; a tramp, who, while exhibiting some kindness toward Nora at the end, is filled with blather and blarney; and a thoroughly discontented woman. But the work is enduring literature, as well as a commentary upon the loveless, mercantilistic Irish marriage of Synge's time, and the issues that Synge raises are as relevant today as they were to playgoers of 1903.

References

Alexander, Jean, "Synge's Play of Choice: The Shadow of the Glen." *A Centenary Tribute to John Millington Synge, 1871–1909: Sunshine and the Moon's Delight.* Edited by S. B. Bushrui. New York: Barnes & Noble, 1972. pp. 41–51.

Benson, Eugene. *J. M. Synge*. Grove Press Modern Dramatists. New York: Grove, 1983.

Bickley, Francis. *J. M. Synge and the Irish Dramatic Movement*. London: Constable; Boston and New York: Houghton Mifflin, 1912.

Corkery, Daniel. *Synge and Anglo-Irish Literature: A Study*. Dublin and Cork: Cork University Press; London: Longmans, Green, 1931.

Ellis-Fermor, Una. *The Irish Dramatic Movement*. London: Metheun, 1954.

Fay, William G., and Catherine Carswell. *The Fays of the Abbey Theatre: An Autobiographical Record*. New York: Harcourt, Brace; London: Rich and Cowan, 1935.

Gerstenberger, Donna. *John Millington Synge*. Twayne's English Authors Series 12. New York: Twayne, 1964.

Greene, David H., and Edward M. Stephens. *J. M. Synge, 1871–1909*. New York: Macmillan, 1959.

Gregory, Lady. *Our Irish Theatre: A Chapter of Autobiography by Lady Gregory*. Gerrards Cross, Bucks: Colin Smythe, 1972.

Grene, Nicholas. *Synge: A Critical Study of the Plays*. Totowa, N.J.: Rowman and Littlefield, 1975.

Hogan, Robert, and James Kilroy. *Laying the Foundations, 1902–1904*. The Modern Irish Drama: A Documentary History 2. Dublin: Dolmen; Atlantic Highlands, N.J.: Humanities Press, 1976.

Holloway, Joseph. *Joseph Holloway's Abbey Theatre: A Selection from His Unpublished Journal "Impressions of a Dublin Playgoer."* Edited by Robert Hogan and Michael J. O'Neill. Carbondale and Edwardsville: Southern Illinois University Press; London: Feffer & Simons, 1967.

Johnson, Toni O'Brien. *Synge: The Medieval and the Grotesque*. Irish Literary Studies 11. Gerrards Cross, Bucks: Colin Smythe; Totowa, N.J.: Barnes & Noble, 1982.

Johnston, Denis. *John Millington Synge*. Columbia Essays on Modern Writers 12. New York and London: Columbia University Press, 1965.

Kiberd, Declan. *Synge and the Irish Language*. Totowa, N.J.: Rowman and Littlefield, 1979.

King, Mary C. *The Drama of J. M. Synge*. Irish Studies. Syracuse: Syrcuse University Press, 1985.

Kopper, Edward A., Jr. *John Millington Synge: A Reference Guide*. A Reference Publication in Literature. Boston: G. K. Hall, 1979.

Leblanc, Gérard. "Ironic Reversal as Theme and Technique in Synge's Shorter Comedies." *Aspects of the Irish Theatre*. Cahiers Irlandis I. Edited by Patrick Rafroidi, Raymon de Papot, and William Parker. Paris: University of Lille, 1972. pp. 51–63.

Morrissey, Thomas J. "The Good Shepherd and the Anti-Christ in Synge's *The Shadow of the Glen*." *Irish Renaissance Annual* 1 (1980):157–60.

Nic Shuibhlaigh, Maire (Mary Walker). *The Splendid Years: Recollections of Maire Nic Shuibhlaigh as Told to Edward Kenny*. Dublin: James Duffy, 1955.

O'Connor, Frank. "Synge." *The Irish Theatre*. Edited by Lennox Robinson. London: Macmillan, 1939. pp. 29–52.

Price, Alan. *Synge and Anglo-Irish Drama*. London: Metheun, 1961.

Saddlemyer, Ann. "Synge and the Nature of Woman." *Women in Irish Legend, Life, and Literature*. Edited by S. F. Gallagher. Gerrards Cross, Bucks: Colin Smythe; Totowa, N.J.: Barnes & Noble, 1983. pp. 58–73.

Saddlemyer, Ann, ed. *Theatre Business: The Correspondence of the First Abbey Theatre*

Directors: William Butler Yeats, Lady Gregory, and J. M. Synge. Gerrards Cross, Bucks: Colin Smythe; University Park: Pennsylvania State University Press, 1982.

Skelton, Robin. *The Writings of J. M. Synge*. Indianapolis and New York: Bobbs-Merrill, 1971.

Thornton, Weldon. *J. M. Synge and the Western Mind*. Irish Literary Studies 4. New York: Barnes & Noble, 1979.

Riders to the Sea

Riders to the Sea was written, along with *The Shadow of the Glen*, during the summer of 1902 in a villa in County Wicklow called Tomrilands House. This rented farmhouse was the usual summer vacation resort of the Synge family, and Synge divided the days from July 21 to September 6, 1902, between a limited social schedule at Tomrilands House with his mother and wandering through the glens of Wicklow, finding further inspiration for *The Shadow of the Glen*. We know that Synge composed *Riders* first through a letter of December 12, 1907, to Leon Brodzky, the founder, in 1904, of the Australian Theatre Society. Synge stated, "By the way 'Riders' was written *before* the Shadow of the Glen, though Shadow of the G. was the first played" (Saddlemyer, *Collected Letters* II, 103).

Before leaving for the Aran Islands on October 14 for what was to prove his fifth and final visit, Synge spent from October 8 to October 13 at Coole Park discussing *Riders* and *The Shadow of the Glen* with Lady Gregory and Yeats and submitting his two plays to their scrutiny. Changes, apparently minor, were needed in Synge's plays, and after they were made, the works were received enthusiastically in January 1903 by several early members of the Irish theater movement. As Ann Saddlemyer explained, "Both plays were read aloud by Lady Gregory in her rooms at Queen Anne's Mansions in London on 20 January 1903 . . . A repeat performance occurred at Yeats's regular Monday gathering in Woburn Buildings on 2 February" (III, xvii). In a diary entry of January 20, 1903, Synge noted that Lady Gregory read *Riders* "with much approval" (Saddlemyer, *Theatre Business* 39).

This enthusiasm of several prominent Irish Renaissance figures for *Riders* was shared by the literary critic Arthur Symons, who suggested to Lady Gregory that Synge might wish to publish the play in the *Fortnightly Review* before having it appear in book form, thereby receiving double profit on the work. Lady Gregory repeated Symons's advice to Synge in a letter of February 12, 1903, adding, "See what a run there is on your play!" (Saddlemyer, *Theatre Business* 39) Matters did not work out, however, and in a letter to Lady Gregory written on March 26, 1903, Synge stated that his play was rejected as not suitable for the purposes of the *Fortnightly* (Saddlemyer, *Theatre Business* 41). Subsequently, *Riders* was published by Yeats in the October issue of *Samhain*. It was first produced by the Irish National Theatre Society at Molesworth Hall on February 25, 1904.

Synge's relationship with James Joyce during this period of nascent playwrighting is intriguing and not merely because of Joyce's questioning of whether *Riders* was true classic tragedy, an issue that is still debated by critics. Synge arrived in Paris on March 6, 1903, and spent about a week there debating several issues over lunch with Joyce, including the merits of *Riders*. The twenty-one-year-old Joyce had been reading Aristotle seriously and applied his theories stringently to Synge's play. Joyce also might have been jealous of Synge because in the preceding January Yeats had expressed to Joyce his view that *Riders* was truly Greek. At any rate, Synge brought the play in typescript form to Joyce's hotel room in Paris, where Joyce was studying medicine, and as Richard Ellmann averred, "No manuscript was ever read with less sympathy" (129).

Joyce objected first to the brevity of *Riders*: a one-act play, a "dwarf-drama," he told Synge, cannot be a "knockdown argument" (quoted in Ellmann 129). Also, in a letter to his brother Stanislaus of March 9, 1903, he announced that he had so picked apart Synge's plot that there was not a "sound spot" left, adding, "but thanks be to God, Synge isn't an Aristotelian" (quoted in Ellmann 129). Joyce's attitude persisted, and in his program notes to the production of *Riders* in Zurich in 1918, he again cited Aristotle's doubts about a brief play qualifying as tragedy.

These disclaimers aside, however, it is obvious that Joyce did not dislike Synge's play so much as it would seem on the surface. Even while Joyce was denouncing *Riders* to Synge's face in Paris, he was attracted by the music of Synge's lines and had already memorized Maurya's last speech. In the year of Synge's death, 1909, he translated *Riders* into Italian; then in July of that year, he tried to have the play produced in Italy, only to be frustrated by the Synge Estate. On June 17, 1918, Joyce and the English actor Claud Sykes, cofounders of the English Players, produced *Riders* at the Pfauen Theatre in Zurich. Joyce's wife, Nora, played a part in the production because Joyce thought that, coming from Galway, she could teach the others the proper brogue.

Miraculously, Synge managed to hold his own among the diverse personalities of the Irish Renaissance, and nowhere is his determined individuality better seen than in his insistence upon authentic stage properties for the opening of *Riders,* on February 25, 1904. Far from being, as Hugh Kenner suggested, a "fuss about . . . pampooties" (265), the cowskin footwear worn by the Aran islanders, Synge's need for verisimilitude argues that the symbolism imputed to his play is anchored in a meticulous reproduction of the commonplace. Also, the quest for the right properties reveals a great deal about the interaction of the principals in the early years of the Irish theater, as they collaborated, they maintained, to add dignity to Ireland.

Synge's demand for realism centered, first, on the chanting of the *caoine,* the funeral lament at the end of *Riders.* Lady Gregory finally located an old peasant woman originally from Galway and then living in a tenement near Dublin who promised to teach the actresses how to keen. Unfortunately, she could not practice her art without a corpse, and George Roberts, who had played the part of the "dead" Dan Burke in *The Shadow of the Glen,* filled the role perfectly. Synge insisted, too, that Sara Allgood, who played Cathleen in *Riders,* be taught to spin in order to add realism to the opening of the play, and he did the instructing himself.

Also, the spinning wheel had to be authentic. Lady Gregory was told by the nuns at Gort, the market town nearest Coole, of the whereabouts of a spinning wheel that had been in the family for one hundred years. This prop arrived the day before the first performance, as Lady Gregory noted in an entry in her *Seventy Years* (414). Synge's interest in the implement was continuing: he insisted on its being carried to London for the opening performance of *Riders* on March 26, 1904, although in 1906 he finally admitted to Lady Gregory that a new spinning wheel might be in order now that the first one was giving out. In the same letter, Synge stated that Molly Allgood must learn to spin "so that there may be no fake about the show" (Saddlemyer, *Theatre Business* 122).

The same care was expended on the actors' clothing. Synge was unsuccessful in securing pampooties from his friends on the Aran Islands, but Lady Gregory was glad that they had to be made in Dublin. She saw no need to bring "local smells into the theatre" (415).

Despite the zeal for cooperation, the insistence upon realistic portrayal, and the excitement engendered by Synge's play among the leaders of the Irish Renaissance, Dublin critics greeted the work with such vehement denunciation that it is difficult to see how the author of Lady Gregory's recent biography (1985) could state, "John Synge's second [*sic*] small masterpiece *Riders to the Sea* . . . was the only one of his plays produced during his life to give no offense to anyone" (Kohfeldt 167). Indeed, the attacks upon *Riders* would probably have been even more severe were it not for the catharsis brought about by the vituperation directed against *The Shadow of the Glen* by the nationalists after its first performance on October 8, 1903. Then the opposition to this work, which was denounced as a libel against Irish women, was led by Arthur Griffith, editor of the *United Irishman,* a weekly newspaper. *Riders,* the patriots felt, might be morbid, influenced by the decadence of Europe, and based upon an ignorance of Irish Catholicism; but it was not, to their minds, so great a slander against Ireland as the previous production.

Among these attacks on *Riders* was one led by the *Freeman's Journal,* which charged that Maurya's expression of relief that she need no longer spend her nights praying for the safety of her sons ignores the true beliefs of the Irish peasant, who, upon the death of her last son, would have begun, not ended, her supplications (Hogan and Kilroy 19). Another complaint was directed against the introduction upon the stage of an actor portraying a corpse. The display was seen as the "cheap trick of the Transpontine dramatists" (Fay 73). The *Irish Times* found the length of time the corpse lay exposed to be "repulsive," arguing that realism should not be equated with art (Fay 73). Finally, it is the judgment of the drama critic of the *Leader,* Arthur Clery, known as "Chanel," that encapsulates much of the adverse response to *Riders.* Chanel called the play the "most ghastly" stage production that he had ever seen (Saddlemyer, *Collected Letters* I, 79). He found some hope for Synge, however, if he would abandon his morose view of life and stress the healthy side of existence.

These negative views are only partially mitigated by the praise of a critic such as Max Beerbohm, who after the first performance of *Riders* in London recognized the play as a masterpiece (455–57) and by the appreciative London theatergoers who chanted a keen as they left the production. The majority opinion seems to have been represented by those Dublin patrons who left Molesworth Hall depressed before the play was over.

It seems, too, that Synge's close associates, who should have known better, did not truly understand *Riders.* The actor Frank Fay was relieved to learn that Synge's next two plays would not contain any corpses. He may have been concerned that first-time patrons would think that Synge's somber play typified the Irish theater offerings and would be driven away from the movement. Frank's brother Willie, who played Bartley in the premiere, wanted desperately to play the part in a manner that would shock the audience by his stretching his neck over the edge of the table (Saddlemyer, *Theatre Business* 43). Also, Karel Mušek, who translated *Riders* and *The Shadow of the Glen* into Bohemian, wrote to Synge in May 1906 to inform him that the manager of the National Theatre in Prague judged *Riders* to be a "little too sad" (Saddlemyer, *Collected Letters* I, 169). Moreover, Synge did not assist in the chore of fathoming the play's meaning when he told Padraic Colum that the impetus for its composition was his foreboding of death and his depression over the process of his own aging (Mikhail 66).

Part of the reason for the unenthusiastic reception accorded *Riders* was the inability of critics and audience to comprehend that the play has several levels of meaning beyond its literal statement. For example, Synge added depth to the work by his Hebraic-Christian symbolism and by his many subtle references to Irish folklore. The biblical allusions may be briefly parsed, but Synge's use of folklore provides a major key to an understanding of the play.

Several events in *Riders* suggest the Crucifixion and its aftermath. To Errol Durbach, Maurya's keen over Bartley implies the *Pietà,* the suffering Mary lamenting the loss of her son (364). The procession of mourners toward the cottage, Mary C. King concluded, might be an "antitype of Easter morning, when the women came and found the tomb empty" (62). The missing nails, King thought, could represent Maurya's freedom from a crucifying living condition (64). In addition to this Crucifixion imagery, David R. Clark recognized in Michael the St. Michael who is the patron of mariners in Normandy in Mont-Saint Michel (44). Alan Price viewed Maurya as a priest conducting a requiem service (188). All of this religious symbolism is highly evocative, and it is unfortunate that the usually perceptive Nicholas Grene viewed the imagery in reductionistic terms, averring that the "physical difference" between the cake of bread and the Euchristic wafer nullifies a view of the bread as sacramental (52).

The horses in Synge's play also have a biblical source; once again, the imagery adds richness while avoiding an exact allegorical correspondence. As several Synge critics have maintained, the term *Riders* in the title suggests the four horsemen of the Book of Revelation (6:1–8). The horses in Revelation are white, red, black, and pale, and the most relevant verse seems to be Revelation 6:8: "And I looked, and behold a pale horse: and his name that sat on him was Death." The crown that is given to the rider of the white horse and the white robes that are given to all the slain parallel the new clothes of Michael as he rides the gray pony, while the name Michael, seen in connection with the other religious symbolism in *Riders,* implies the warrior who drove the dragons (or devils) into Hell, in Revelation (12:7). Finally, one is reminded of Exodus 15:1: "the horse and his rider hath he thrown into the sea."

More important are the folkloric ingredients of *Riders,* which might be examined under the following categories: first, the nature and mission of dead spirits or fairies, who are not the amiable, although slightly mischievous, creatures depicted by non-Irish commentators; second, Maurya's twice failing to complete the prayer that may have warded off the specter of Michael, which she beholds *after* her parting benison for Bartley, for the second time, chokes in her throat; and third, the lapses in ritual of Maurya and her remaining family as they violate the prescribed rites of the Feast of St. Martin, November 11, which is combined in the play with the pagan November festival of *Samhain.*

The Irish fairies, sometimes seen as spirits of the dead, are scarcely benign, and it would seem that Michael has joined their host. Denis Johnston argued that "the ghostly Michael . . . is the killer of his younger brother" (22) and found that this central movement of *Riders* springs from the Irish peasant's deep-rooted fear that the dead, at times through loneliness, will return to take one of the living. Irish fairies are often "malevolent," Johnston held (22), and they frequently spirit away the living with false promises. In this regard, the gray pony, according to Declan Kiberd, is a type of púca that "appears in the form of a horse to lure people to death" (164). Nor do the dead countenance the use of their property by survivors. Michael must have been offended by Bartley's taking his shirt and by Maurya's using his walking stick. In the folkloric context, then, the boat destined for Galway becomes a Death Ship, with the choice of Bartley as victim being an example of the Aran Islanders' belief that the returning spirit will often single out a former partner (often over even a relative) as his companion in the world of the dead.

The evil influence of Michael could have been mollified had Maurya been able to bless Bartley either before he left the house or when she saw him at the spring well. As John Messenger pointed out in his study of the Aran Islands, "the magical incantation, 'God bless you' . . . automatically opposes the power of God to that of the witch" (106). In fact, "God bless you" was the ordinary greeting on the Aran Islands of Synge's time, and the salutation had to be answered by the ejaculation "God and Mary bless you." In addition, half a prayer was far worse than none on the Aran Islands, and great danger could result from failure to reply to the opening religious phrase. Moreover, the islanders knew that, from the time of St. Patrick, fishermen embarking on a journey always said the "Prayer to Guide You Safely" and that, if "two mistakes are made in its recitation," the trip was delayed or postponed (Messenger 46).

The Feast of St. Martin on the Aran Islands blends Christian and pagan elements in ostensibly commemorating St. Martin of Tours but actually honoring a holy miller who was crushed to death by a millstone and whose martyrdom initiated the practice of refraining from spinning and baking bread around the time of the feast, a practice abrogated by Cathleen. It is no coincidence that Bartley never receives the soda bread and that Michael is identified by his clothing, through the dropped stiches. Also, the Sunday before St. Martin's Day was known as Bloody Sunday, and at that time an animal was sacrificed. Maurya's family allows the pig with the black feet to run about nibbling at the rope that is to be used to lower the coffin. The family should have sacrificed the pig to Manannan Mac Lir, the Irish Poseidon, who often can be prevailed upon to prevent drownings.

The remaining folklore elements, examined as above by Messenger and by Kiberd, may be briefly summarized. They include the injunction never to mention a priest when discussing fishing; the rule that when once embarked on a journey, one must not return for a forgotten article, as Bartley does for the rope; and the ironic symbolism surrounding the spring well, in *Riders,* a representation of false hope for rebirth and, in Celtic lore, often a symbol of death.

Allusions to religous tradition and to Irish folklore notwithstanding, however, the main source for *Riders* is *The Aran Islands,* which Synge wrote before any of the produced plays, although it was not published until 1907. This prose description of life among the islanders is based on four (of five) summer visits that Synge made to the Aran Islands from 1898 through 1902. *The Aran Islands* is a storehouse of information crucial to an understanding of *Riders,* and any serious attempt to interpret the play must take the book into account. Because many commentators on *Riders* have discussed the volume as the principal source of the play, only a cursory glance at the work is presented here.

Even a brief glimpse at *The Aran Islands* supports Synge's contention that the book sheds a "good deal of light on my plays" (II, 47). One finds detailed descriptions of pampooties, curaghs maneuvering through a dangerous sea, red petticoats, spinning, the scarcity of vegetation on an island where a bush is almost synonymous with a tree, and funeral rites complete with keen. The reader learns of a mother whose prayer choked in her throat and the need for a rope to be used as a halter on a wild pony because there is only one bit and saddle on Aranmore, the largest of the three islands. The pages also define the emotions of motherhood on the islands and help to clarify Synge's portraiture of Maurya: "The maternal feeling is so powerful on these islands that it gives a life of torment to the women" (II, 108).

Two sections of *The Aran Islands,* both involving drownings, are of direct relevance to *Riders*. The first concerns the dead "Mike," who was washed ashore in Donegal. His mother, after several days, still visits the beach hoping to find his body; then his sister is able to identify her brother from a description that she has been given of the few remaining effects of the drowned man: "one pampooty . . . a striped shirt with a purse in one of the pockets, and a box of tobacco" (II, 136). In the second instance, a headless corpse is recovered, but it cannot be buried until boards are borrowed from a neighbor and until a decayed corpse is removed from a shallow grave to make room for the next occupant.

With its complex blending of realism and symbolism, it is no wonder that *Riders* has generated a good deal of critical controversy. One of these problem areas is the issue of whether the play is tragic, even though from the beginnings of the Irish theater movement several critics have assumed parallels with specific Greek counterparts. Yeats's exclamation "Aeschylus!" as he read the play aloud before its first production (Gogarty 300) was echoed by Ernest Boyd in 1916 when he stated: "Maurya takes on the profound significance of an Aeschylean figure, in her vain protest against Fate, and her ultimate resignation" (322). A. C. Partridge, writing in 1984, cited the play's brevity; yet he found an "undoubted likeness to the *Hippolytus* of Euripides" (218). Robin Skelton, writing twelve years earlier, in 1972, located elements of both Hippolytus and Freudian incest archetypes in *Riders* when he compared the drownings of Bartley and Hippolytus (32). Johnston discerned an Orestean parallel in the play (20), and T. R. Henn detected a similarity between Hecuba's lament over the body of Astyanax and Maurya's keen over the dead Bartley (108–9). D. S. Neff traced at length parallels between *Riders* and *Hecuba* of Euripides, at one point seeing Michael as a Polydorus figure (81). Several critics have limned the presence of the Three Fates—Clotho, Lachesis, and Atropos—behind the three central females in *Riders*.

One difficulty commentators have found with classifying *Riders* as tragedy in the Aristotelian sense is its brevity. Joyce thought that the play was "dwarf-drama," and nine years later, in 1912, P. P. Howe implied that *Riders* violates classical unity of time because so much happens in the half hour required for the stage presentation (59). Robert Heilman called the play "slight," more elegy than tragedy; two genres, he maintained, that critics tend to confuse (38–39). Henn wondered how so short a play, a "miniature" tragedy as he called it, can achieve the momentum necessary for a classic tragedy (209). Henn thought that *Riders* goes part of the way to solving this difficulty of momentum by "simplifying the conflict of *Man* vs. *Necessity* into *Man* vs. *The Sea*" (202).

On the other hand, Clark believed that *Riders* succeeds as classic tragedy because it does provide a catharsis (50). Grene thought that the play contains the illumination common to Greek tragedy, which, in *Riders,* is one presented in a single moment of revelation (57). Northrop Frye, while exploring his theory that comedy, as opposed to tragedy, frequently consists of repetition that is purposeless or overdone, maintained about *Riders* that "if it had been a full-length tragedy plodding glumly through the seven drownings one after another, the audience would have been helpless with unsympathetic laughter long before it was over" (168). Finally, Weldon Thornton insisted that Synge did not write *Riders* with any particular genre or philosophical system in mind. If Synge's play does not inculcate Aristotle's perception of existence, said Thornton, it was not intended to do so. The world view in *Riders* is "pagan and archaic, pre-Western and pre-tragic . . . Greek tragedy, Christian theology, scientific empiricism, however different in other respects, all present nature as ordered . . . We do not find that in *Riders to the Sea*" (111).

Crucial to an understanding of the tragic nature of *Riders* is a defined viewpoint concerning Maurya and her vision. Many critics have perceived Maurya as being a universal picture of suffering motherhood. Price viewed Maurya as representing "all humanity" (191). Daniel Corkery considered her the "universal mother" (141), and Seamus Deane thought that Maurya is the "voice of humanity uttering its resignation to an incurable human plight" (60). Robin Skelton compared Maurya's loss of her sons to the losses of mothers whose sons died in Vietnam: in Maurya, Synge "portrayed a figure of wracked and grieving motherhood so absolutely convincing and so universal in its application" (38). Ryder Hector Currie and Martin Bryan believed that Maurya combines elements of the Great Mother and of Mara, the "nightmare figure," to form the "fused duality that is woman" (146). King wrote about Maurya's vision of the dead Michael: "Maurya is narrating at this point not a literal encounter, but a *visionary tale,* and like the folk tales in *The Aran Islands,* the vision is a translation into story of what is happening to Bartley as he takes the horses to the fair" (56). Conversely, Malcolm Pittock, in a brief but often cited article, held that the vision is implausible because it depends upon the acceptance by a "modern audience" (448) of the superstitions of peasants; Eugene Benson contrasted Maurya with the "queenly" Cathleen Ni Houlihan, comparing her instead to the depleted Mrs. Moore of *A Passage to India* (66). Finally Leslie D. Foster provided a full analysis of opinions about Maurya and the "extravagant terms" (98) used to describe her character.

The differing critical opinions about Maurya and about the tragic nature of *Riders* resemble the beginning misinterpretations of Synge's purposes by his Dublin audiences and by his friends; they indicate that the play is an even more complex work than has been previously supposed. Both founded in reality and deviating from it for purposes of symbolism, *Riders* is a hymn of praise to the Aran Islanders, who welcomed Synge. Yet it is founded in the hardness of life that Synge, from the beginning of his playwriting career, believed was an essential ingredient in the portrayal of his people. As did Joseph Conrad in *The Nigger of the Narcissus,* whose earlier, proposed title was *Children of the Sea,* Synge saw both the godlike and the human in his subjects. Maurya is a priestess; she is also a tired old woman who bickers with her daughters and son. However, despite Synge's often perplexing dual vision, critics have recognized the consummate worth of *Riders* and have assured that it or *The Playboy of the Western World* finds a place in virtually every anthology of modern drama. In other words, *Riders,* like all classic literary works, gives much more than is paid for it.

References

Beerbohm, Max. "Some Irish Plays and Players." *Saturday Review* (London), April 9, 1904, pp. 455–57.

Benson, Eugene. *J. M. Synge.* Grove Press Modern Dramatists. 1982. Reprint. New York: Grove, 1983.

Boyd, Ernest. *Ireland's Literary Renaissance.* Dublin: Maunsel; London and New York: Knopf, 1916.

Clark, David R. "Synge's 'Perpetual Last Day': Remarks on *Riders to the Sea.*" *A Centenary Tribute to John Millington Synge, 1871–1909: Sunshine and the Moon's Delight.* Edited by S. B. Bushrui. New York: Barnes & Noble, 1972, pp. 41–51.

Corkery, Daniel. *Synge and Anglo-Irish Literature: A Study.* Dublin and Cork: Cork University Press; London: Longmans, Green, 1931. Reprint. New York: Russell & Russell, 1965.

Currie, Ryder Hector, and Martin Bryan. "Riders to the Sea: Reappraised." *Texas Quarterly* 11, no. 4 (1968):139–46.

Deane, Seamus. *Celtic Revivals: Essays in Modern Irish Literature, 1880–1980.* London and Boston: Faber and Faber, 1985.

Durbach, Errol. "Synge's Tragic Vision of the Old Mother and the Sea." *Modern Drama* 14, no. 4 (1972):363–72.

Ellmann, Richard. *James Joyce.* New York and London: Oxford University Press, 1959.

Fay, Gerard. *The Abbey Theatre: Cradle of Genius.* New York: Macmillan, 1958.

Foster, Leslie D. "Maurya: Tragic Error and Limited Transcendence in *Riders to the Sea.*" *Éire-Ireland* 16, no. 3 (1981):98–117.

Frye, Northrop. *Anatomy of Criticism: Four Essays*. Princeton, N.J.: Princeton University Press, 1957.

Gogarty, Oliver St. J. *As I Was Going Down Sackville Street: A Phantasy in Fact*. London: Rich and Cowan; New York: Reynal and Hitchcock, 1937.

Gregory, Lady. *Seventy Years: Being the Autobiography of Lady Gregory*. Edited and foreword by Colin Smythe. New York: Macmillan, 1974.

Grene, Nicholas. *Synge: A Critical Study of the Plays*. Totowa, N.J.: Rowman and Littlefield, 1975.

Heilman, Robert Bechtold. *Tragedy and Melodrama: Versions of Experience*. Seattle and London: University of Washington Press, 1968.

Henn, T. R. *The Harvest of Tragedy*. New York: Barnes & Noble, 1966.

Hogan, Robert, and James Kilroy. *The Abbey Theatre: The Years of Synge, 1905–1909*. The Modern Irish Drama: A Documentary History 3. Dublin: Dolmen; Atlantic Highlands, N.J.: Humanities Press, 1978.

Howe, P. P. *J. M. Synge: A Critical Study*. London: Martin Secker, 1912.

Johnston, Denis. *John Millington Synge*. Columbia Essays on Modern Writers 12. New York and London: Columbia University Press, 1965.

Kenner, Hugh. *A Colder Eye: The Modern Irish Writers*. New York: Knopf, 1983.

Kiberd, Declan. *Synge and the Irish Language*. Totowa, N.J.: Rowman and Littlefield; London: Macmillan, 1979.

King, Mary C. *The Drama of J. M. Synge*. Irish Studies. Syracuse: Syracuse University Press, 1985.

Kohfeldt, Mary Lou. *Lady Gregory: The Woman behind the Irish Renaissance*. New York: Atheneum, 1985.

Messenger, John C. *Inis Beag: Isle of Ireland*. Case Studies in Cutural Anthropology. 1969. Reprint. Prospect Heights, Ill.: Waveland, 1983.

Mikhail, E. H., ed. *J. M. Synge: Interviews and Recollections*. Foreword by Robin Skelton. New York: Barnes & Noble; London: Macmillan, 1977.

Neff, D. S. "Synge's Hecuba." *Éire-Ireland* 19, no. 1 (1984):74–86.

Partridge, A. C. *Language and Society in Anglo-Irish Literature*. Totowa, N.J.: Barnes & Noble; Dublin: Gill and Macmillan, 1984.

Pittock, Malcolm. "*Riders to the Sea*." *English Studies* 49, no. 5 (1968):445–49.

Price, Alan. *Synge and Anglo-Irish Drama*. London: Methuen, 1961.

Saddlemyer, Ann, ed. *The Collected Letters of John Millington Synge, I: 1871–1907*. Oxford: Clarendon, 1983.

———. *The Collected Letters of John Millington Synge, II: 1907–1909*. Oxford: Clarendon, 1984.

———. *Theatre Business: The Correspondence of the First Abbey Theatre Directors: William Butler Yeats, Lady Gregory, and J. M. Synge*. Gerrards Cross, Bucks: Colin Smythe; University Park: Pennsylvania State University Press, 1982.

Skelton, Robin. *J. M. Synge*. The Irish Writers Series. Lewisburg, Pa.: Bucknell University Press, 1972.

Thornton, Weldon. *J. M. Synge and the Western Mind*. Irish Literary Studies 4. New York: Barnes & Noble, 1979.

Additional Sources

Bauman, Richard. "John Millington Synge and Irish Folklore." *Southern Folklore Quarterly* 27, no. 4 (1963):267–79.

Casey, Daniel J. "'An Aran Requiem: Setting in 'Riders to the Sea.' " *Antigonish Review* 9 (1972):89–100.

Collins, R. L. "The Distinction of *Riders to the Sea*." *The University of Kansas City Review* 13 (1947):278–84.

Combs, William W. "J. M. Synge's *Riders to the Sea*: A Reading and Some Generalizations." *Papers of the Michigan Academy of Science, Arts, and Letters* 50 (1965): 599–607.

Donoghue, Denis. "Synge: *Riders to the Sea*: A Study." *University Review* 1 (1955):52–58.

Figgis, Darrell. "The Art of J. M. Synge." *Fortnightly Review*, ns. 110 (1911):1056–68.

Free, William J. "Structural Dynamics in *Riders to the Sea*." *Colby Library Quarterly* 11, no. 3 (1975):162–68.

Holloway, Joseph. *Joseph Holloway's Abbey Theatre: A Selection from His Unpublished Journal "Impressions of a Dublin Playgoer."* Edited by Robert Hogan and Michael J. O'Neill. Carbondale and Edwardsville: Southern Illinois University Press; London and Amsterdam: Feffer & Simons, 1967.

Levitt, Paul M. "The Structural Craftsmanship of J. M. Synge's *Riders to the Sea*." *Éire-Ireland* 4, no. 1 (1969):53–61.

Rollins, Ronald G. "Portraits of Four Irishmen as Artists: Verisimilitude and Vision." *Irish University Review* 1, no. 2 (1971):189–97.

Van Laan, Thomas F. "Form as Agent in Synge's *Riders to the Sea*." *Drama Survey* 3 (1964):352–66.

The Well of the Saints

The poet William Butler Yeats, who encouraged Synge in his work, is surely one of the greatest interpreters of Synge's *The Well of the Saints,* the first full-length play by Synge, although his fourth play. But Yeats wrote by indirection. His criticism that I am thinking of is in his "Preface to the First Edition of the Play," which bears the subtitle "Mr. Synge and His Plays" (1905). What would be the *experience*—not the idea, the concept, that is too inconsequential—of being created in the image of God? Something of this innocent experience (innocent of theory and doctrine) is what Yeats saw in all of Synge's plays to that date (and Yeats let his observation stand when he edited his prose works many years later).

Of Synge's language, Yeats wrote while the play was in rehearsal:

Above all, he made word and phrase dance to a very strange rhythm, which will always, till his plays have created their own tradition, be difficult to actors who have not learned it from his lips. It is essential, for it perfectly fits the drifting emotion, the dreaminess, the vague yet measureless desire, for which he would create a dramatic form. It blurs definition, clears edges, everything that comes from the will, it turns imagination from all that is of the present, like a gold background in a religious picture, and it strengthens in every emotion whatever comes to it from far off, from brooding memory and dangerous hope. (III, 64)

Yeats said Synge had no desire to change or reform things but wanted his people to "pass by as before an open window, murmuring strange, exciting words" (III, 65).

To relate Synge's diction and thought to his themes and preoccupations, Yeats continued:

> Mr. Synge has in common with the great theatre of the world . . . a delight in language, a preoccupation with individual life. He resembles them [the great dramatists] also by a preoccupation with what is lasting and noble, that came to him, not, as I think, from books, but while he listened to old stories in the cottages, and contrasted what they remembered with reality. (III, 66–67)

He said that every writer who has belonged to "the great tradition" "has had his dream of an impossibly noble life, and the greater he is, the more does it seem to plunge him into some beautiful or bitter reverie" (III, 67). The "earliest poets of the world" gave that dream "direct expression"; others "mingle it . . . subtly with . . . reality" (III, 67).

The glory of Synge's characters is in the aspirations by which they are moved:

> Mr. Synge, indeed, sets before us ugly, deformed or sinful people, but his people, moved by no practical ambition, are driven by a dream of the impossible life . . . and those two blind people of *The Well of the Saints* are so transformed by the dream that they choose blindness rather than reality. (III, 67)

Returning to fuse his comments on Synge's language with these concerns, Yeats summed up: "It is the preoccupation of his characters with their dream that gives his plays their drifting movement, their emotional subtlety" (III, 67). Indeed, it may be that being "created in the image of God" is secondary (if that) to the "brooding memory and dangerous hope" (III, 64).

In *The Well of the Saints,* it is only the Saint who is a theologian, and he appears twice, in the first and third acts. Martin had dreamed that with sightedness he would see "all the fine things is walking the world" (III, 85). In the Saint's first appearance, he has a grim view of what the dream of life might be, as he tries to still Martin's and Mary's disillusionment with one another's appearance:

> May the Lord who has given you sight send a little sense into your heads, the way it won't be on your two selves you'll be looking—on two pitiful sinners of the earth—but on the splendour of the Spirit of God, you'll see an odd time shining out through the big hills, and steep streams falling to the sea. For if it's on that you do be thinking, you'll not be minding the faces of men, but you'll be saying prayers and great praises, till you'll be living the way the great saints do be living, with little but old sacks, and skin covering their bones. (III, 101)

This is indeed sad: *teaching the blind to see* the miracle and "wonder" (III, 79) and *healing the blind,* and we will see that Martin Doul, the blind beggar, will remember it. Anticipating this miracle giving them sight, Martin had said: "And we'll be seeing ourselves this day."

Synge is neither a naturalist nor a realist to have a miracle at all, but the symbolism is clear: The church shows man to himself as ugly and calls it a miracle. Nicholas Grene said that Synge gives the Saint Synge's own pantheist views here by making the Spirit of God in nature. But the irony makes it too clearly the Saint's own pantheism. Mary Doul calls the Saint "a simple fellow" when she first hears about him (III, 83). The people have a dream.

But at the end of the play, before the Saint curses Martin and calls down God's wrath and that of the townspeople on him, he tries to reason with Martin to let his sight be restored a second, permanent, time. How can Martin not want to see the wonders of the world, the Saint asks. Martin says he has seen a lifetime of "wonders" and doesn't care to see any more. Says the Saint: "I never heard tell of any person wouldn't have great joy to be looking on the earth, and the image of the Lord is thrown upon men" (III, 139). Here we have the theology of man created in the image of God. Martin responds, tying together the two appearances of the Saint and what the Saint represents of the dream:

That's great sights, holy father. . . . What was it I seen my first day, but your own bleeding feet and they cut with the stones, and my last day, but the villainy of herself that you're wedding, God forgive you, with Timmy the smith. That was great sights maybe. . . . And wasn't it great sights seeing the roads when the north winds would be driving and the skies would be harsh, and you'd see the horses and the asses and the dogs itself maybe with their heads hanging and they closing their eyes—. (III, 141)

The view I try to present is my understanding of what W. B. Yeats wrote about the play when it was being readied for its first production in 1905. I think of two brief formulations. *The Well* is the story of the sightedness created by the Saint, the Hell it leads to, and its rejection by Martin and Mary Doul. Or it is the story of the search for the dream of man, not an idea or a theory, but the experience.

Critics have not been sure what this play is, and so they have differed about its achievement. It is fair to ask, what is its *myth (mythos,* plot) and what is its presiding spirit? With my view of the myth frankly given, I will try in what follows to examine some of the important criticism other than that which I have dealt with already. The presiding spirit is ironic comedy, where the chattering, blocking society is undefeated and the hero and heroine are driven out, giving the play overtones of tragedy.

Synge evidently had trouble with the cast in the rehearsals for the first performance (1905). Willie Fay, who played Martin Doul as "a very repulsive old man overwhelmed in sensuality" (quoted in Grene 127), said the cast "realized" all the characters were bad tempered and would make the audience bad tempered too. He suggested to Synge (not changing his own characterization) making the Saint or Molly (the shallow, cruel epitome of the opposition to Martin) more good-natured or lovable, but Synge wouldn't allow it, saying he was doing a monochromatic canvas. The emphasis the players wanted would have been to make the chattering society the norm, heroic in driving off the would-be usurpers

Martin and Mary Doul, blind again. Both Grene (1975) and Eugene Benson (1983) tried to walk this line. But if the Saint and Molly are the "dreamers," then Yeats is a fool and Synge the defender of the status quo. Joseph Holloway saw both the 1905 performance, where Yeats and Synge had talked together, and the revival in 1908, when Synge was ill and away. Of the earlier performance, Holloway wrote that the play was a "harsh, irreverent, sensual representation of Irish peasantry with its strange mixture of lyric and dirt," and he was happy to see the Dublin curtains close. Of the 1908 revival, Holloway wrote:

The wild beast nature of 'Martin Doul' was artistically kept in check, and it made him a far more agreeable personage . . . Arthur Sinclair [the lead in the second version] made him more of a dreamer with a longing for the beautiful. . . . In fact, the play was lifted out of reality into the realm of fancy where it should have been from the first. (quoted in Grene 127)

Grene, however, thought Holloway dependably always has things reversed in his commentary (Grene 127). Benson follows Grene in that (Benson 103, *passim*).

The controversy reminds one of one of the first critical disagreements in the history of literature, in Aristotle's *Poetics*. Aristotle had just said that a figure in serious literature must have a certain stature and dignity. Then, responding to prejudice of the times, Aristotle said that even a slave and a woman may be figures in serious literature—that is, may have dignity and stature—but this is not often presented because audiences do not want to believe it. Martin and Mary must have dignity and stature for Synge's play to work, however much they also may have shared in the unpleasantness of the villagers and the Saint, and that is the heart of the interpretive problem of the play.

One of the earliest commentators on *The Well of the Saints* was P. P. Howe, in his *J. M. Synge: A Critical Study* (1912). Howe is not always accurate in details but he quotes accurately (III, 113) when he sums up his view of Synge's characters who need not be ugly and depressing:

In all Synge's people there is something of the little children of whom Martin Doul speaks, who "do be listening to the stories of an old woman, and do be dreaming after in the dark night that it's in grand houses of gold they are, with speckled horses to ride, and do be waking again, in a short while, and they destroyed with the cold, and the thatch dripping maybe, and the starved ass braying in the yard." (Howe 43)

Is this where "the dangerous hope" begins?

Maurice Bourgeois (1913) gave us the full early account of what Synge's sources might have been. He is of special interest, however, in what he said Synge did with the fable he began with. The fable was "among the simplest and most moving ones" ever chosen for a modern drama, and it offers "all the searching beauty of an ancient parable" (183). But the play was a disappointment to Bourgeois: "it is perhaps of all Synge's dramatic works the one in which we find embodied the truest expression of his pessimistic view, if not philosophy, of life. Nothing can be more pathetic and also more depressing than the two blind people's disillusionment'' (192). Bourgeois himself preferred the view of Maeterlinck in *Sister Beatrice,* which is the opposite of Synge's view: "Life is worth living; let us therefore risk to live." In the end, Bourgeois took the play as chiefly autobiographical: "in this gloomy pathos, *in this ascetic pity,* we seem to find the dramatic externalization of Synge's inmost consciousness" (192–93, my emphasis). That is a clear enough standard: Bourgeois preferred the affirmation of life, and he did not find it in the "gloomy pathos" and "ascetic pity" of the brooding author. That may not be grounds enough to reject a work of art, but even if we take the standard as our own, we still have to deal with the "dangerous hope" that Bourgeois apparently did not find here, although he apparently did find the "ascetic pity" of the Saint as a kind of norm: "two pitiful sinners of the earth" (III, 101). Nonetheless, the dream is not easy to sustain, certainly less so than in Maeterlinck.

In 1932 Brooks Atkinson reviewed a hotel production of *The Well of the Saints* for the *New York Times,* finding the ensemble unsatisfactory but the work "a strangely exalting play." He concluded: " 'The Well of the Saints' has compassion, love of humanity and a faith in the poetic ideal that only a trained company could engender" ("The Play" 15). The play came back to Atkinson twenty-seven years later (1959), when he found the key to a fine performance in the actor taking the part of Martin Doul: "Although the character is a wretch and a mendicant, Mr. Germain does not forget that he has a keen mind and a capacity for bold decisions." Atkinson also counted off the qualities of the play: iconoclastic, with characters who are rugged individualists; the figures have high opinions of themselves and low opinions of others—they are vigorous, hard headed, sharp tongued, alert, and irascible under the flowing imagery of the dialogue (*"The Well of the Saints"* 15). Here the compassion and love of humanity serve for the dreaming dignity of another day.

In 1943 *The Times* of London printed a review that said it would pass over the trifling plot for the poetry it brings along with it, and the reviewer thanked the revival. Chief is the character who presents Martin:

Mr. W. G. Fay plays the blind man with the exquisite humour which makes for tears rather than laughter. His frantic courtship of the pretty young Molly perhaps lacks a little the air of likelihood which Mr. Arthur Sinclair was used to give it long ago, but Mr. Fay beautifully carries off the realistic conclusion that darkness with hope is infinitely better than clear sight with despair. (6)

We have the dream of a greater world.

The Times in 1954 took note of a new revival of *The Well* by an Irish company stating that it was acted so well as to raise the question of whether *The Playboy of the Western World* is Synge's best play. It took the play to be a work of "cruel realism" where a wrong marriage and brutal disillusionment lead even the confident minor characters to begin to be self-conscious. The critic seemed to have Bourgeois's perception of gloomy pathos unhampered by Bourgeois's distaste for it. *The Times* came back to the play once more, in 1970, with Michael Billington writing on the Old Vic production. He called the play part of the "best work" of Synge and concluded that "this is Synge done proud." The theme is of "the need for the human imagination to create a new world once one's original illusions have been shattered." The play comes close to naturalism: "There is . . . no attempt to invest with a spurious sentimentality, and the furious intolerance both of the blind couple themselves and of the village community that stones them for their ingratitude is heavily underlined." Hardest for a modern audience to believe is the miracles, so the part of the saint is praised for doing so well: "endowing this Christ-like figure with a serene authority that conceals a vein of angry impatience" (7). The Douls, not the Saint, are still the inheritors.

I have difficulty understanding Martin and Mary Doul's rejection of renewed sight as a desirable solution, just as I find it sad that Christy Mahon, in *The Playboy of the Western World,* leaves Pegeen to wander the world telling tales of the fools there are in Mayo. That, too, is ironic comedy, in which Christy leaves because he has been just too much tormented by Pegeen, when, indeed, she is at last ready to marry him if he will just ask her. In *The Well of the Saints,* Martin tells Mary when he returns to her that he has begun to appreciate her, although she does not have physical beauty. If he can learn that, he can learn what he needs, to be sighted. Illusion is not the opposite of brutal reality; blindness may be better than dark, tormenting reality, but human vision is not unreality. The problem continues to be with which are the blocking figures in the play and with where the truer society lies more surely. The more valuable world lies with Martin and Mary, rather than with the people they live among, but it is more valuable not because they are blind. The new world is too weak to establish itself in the East, we are led to believe. This is Synge's story of the Eastern world, just as *Playboy* is of the Western world. Both are ironic comedy, and we cannot berate Martin and Mary Doul for not establishing a redeemed society in the Eastern world. (They head for the Southern world, where, some critics believe, they will die.)

There was little scholarly criticism of *The Well of the Saints* in the beginning of the last half decade of this century, in the years before the flurry of work on Synge brought about by his centenary in 1971. I mention some of the former. David H. Greene and Edward M. Stephens published their biography of Synge in 1959 and told us a little about the play. Alan Price studied Synge's plays in a 1961 book. There was Donna Gerstenberger's book on Synge in the Twayne English Authors Series (1964), in which she described the play as a disappointment and a failure in eight closely argued pages. Finally, there was Pat Barnett's helpful study of the use of poetry to characterize the figures in the plays, a topic studied fruitfully by him and others as well, notably T. R. Henn and Vincent Nash, whose works were inspired by the centenary.

Greene and Stephens showed us that in late August 1904, with Synge in Kerry, W. B. Yeats wrote a letter, dictated to Lady Gregory, to Synge about the rehearsals of *The Well of the Saints*. Yeats thought, from the first act, that William Fay would be "as fine as possible" as Martin Doul, and Frank Fay would be good as the saint, but the women were less satisfactory—something objectionable in a voice, or not having "a right ideal," whatever he meant by that. With the text of the play, there was a problem of a suggestion of *King Lear* and Cordelia, with whose gentleness surely he wouldn't want any of the women compared, and there were too many "Almighty Gods," which irritate the ear (Greene and Stephens 165–66).

Despite his asthma problems, Synge returned to Dublin, presumably for the rehearsals, on September 1. But he changed his mind about staying and left again on September 17. Arguments that Synge was leading the cast into a definitive performance (Grene 127: "There can be little doubt that Fay's Martin Doul was as Synge intended the part to be played; and Benson 103) are not clearly supported by the historical data. It is clearly untrue to suggest that Synge "saw the play through its rehearsals." Beyond this information, including the information Synge was being troubled by asthma, Greene and Stephens fell silent.

An important early analysis, including in its purview *The Well of the Saints*, that needed to be done is Pat Barnett's essay "The Nature of Synge's Dialogue," which appeared in *English Literature in Transition (1880–1920)* in 1967. Barnett argued that the figures in the plays are characterized by the poetry in their speech. He took it as given that criticism has finally settled that the speech of the plays is authentic Irish, or Gaelic, and he focused on the "function and variation" in the speech among the different characters. The two levels of speech he identified are "the common everyday speech of peasant conversation, and the passages and phrases of poetic lyricism and rhythm" (119). It is the latter of these two types that needs discussion, he believed. He said that in the plays "passion and poetry are always akin," and the gift of language in *The Well of the Saints* belongs only to the Douls, chiefly Martin, with the villagers entirely lacking it (123).

Barnett noted that the entire play lacks Synge's usual good humor, and "much of the language is both bitter and bad-tempered. . . . Most of [the characters] deliberately rise to their greatest poetic hights in the passion of invective" (123). Ultimately, for Barnett, it is a matter of the life of the characters that the passion and poetry create: "Not only does lyricism create atmosphere and build character throughout Synge's plays, but theme and character at the same time support and suggest the language; people come alive through speaking in the rhythmic lyric phrases Synge can use" (126). The Douls are endowed with an element of life and vitality that the villagers lack. There should be no question about where the nucleus of the authentic society lies and what is being driven out by the society at the end, by saint and villager.

Donna Gerstenberger's important criticism of the play was reported three years earlier, in 1964, and Barnett referred to her work in general. She took Synge as the author of "at least two plays which have become a part of the canon of modern drama," meaning *Riders* and *Playboy,* and her intention in her book, as she said in her Preface in the Twayne Series is to help in the sifting out of what is and is not enduring in Synge's works, explaining at the same time why his work continues to be of interest. Her view is that *The Well of the Saints* and *The Tinker's Wedding*—that is, Synge's first three-act play and the play that he tried to revise into longer form—are best considered as transitional plays because they have "structural and other weaknesses" not found in his later work. In *Well,* she took the central concern to be with "the power of the imagination to create and to destroy, and the compromises men make with reality." But the play makes "one of the few partial compromises to be found anywhere in his work, for the play ends with a preference for the lie, an insistence upon illusion in place of reality" (55). It is the ending of the play that most troubled Gerstenberger.

She referred to Alan Price's book *Synge and the Anglo-Irish Drama* (1961) and quoted him as stating that the play is "perhaps Synge's most profound and somber work." She believed that Price was misled by his own interest in studying a theme he came to the plays with and so thus read them in terms of his own preoccupations: "that work of art is best which most embodies the critic's concern" (57–58). On the contrary, she viewed the pessimism of the "lie" that the play ends with as contrary to Synge's nature and notebooks, and she wrote of the dramatic failures of the play in lengthy dialogues and failure to achieve dramatic compression. She believed Synge was working with uncongenial material and so was not wholly engaged by his work (56–58). The argument is a species allied to the one she accused Alan Price of: he didn't believe it, he couldn't have meant it.

Gerstenberger presented a generally excellent summary of the plot and the theme of blindness, passages among the finest that have been written on *The Well of the Saints,* but she tied this work to the thesis that it does not necessarily support: at the end, the choice of the Douls "is one that denies the wholeness of the world, the totality of experience; it also denies what Synge himself had learned about reality" (58–61). This is reminiscent of Bourgeois, who wanted life-affirming art and so could not (he thought) like this play. The paradox of Gerstenberger's view is that she can quote some of the characteristically lovely "seeing" that the blind beggars have and at the same time state that when they choose this view they are choosing "illusion" (III, 131, 133):

MARY DOUL: There's the sound of one of them twittering yellow birds do be coming in the spring-time from beyond the sea, and there'll be a fine warmth now in the sun, and a sweetness in the air, the way it'll be a grand thing to be sitting here quiet and easy, smelling the things growing up, and budding from the earth.

MARTIN DOUL: I'm smelling the furze a while back sprouting on the hill, and if you'd hold your tongue you'd hear the lambs of Grianan, though it's near drowned their crying is with the full river making noises in the glen. (Gerstenberger 60–61)

Missing also is the theme the Saint casually brings in, of looking for the beauty of "man created in the image of God," a business about which only the Douls appear to have any concern. Gerstenberger is surely right in stating that it is sad that the Douls choose blindness, when there was a wiser choice that we know could have been made—by someone; still, the theme of ironic comedy is insistent—the redeeming society fails to establish itself and is driven away by the chattering imposters. Is ironic comedy in itself unacceptable? Here is Yeats again: "Mr. Synge, indeed, sets before us ugly, deformed or sinful people, but his people, moved by no practical ambition, are driven by a dream of that impossible life" (III, 67).

But let me give pride of place to Gerstenberger's conclusion about the play, since she evidently struggled greatly to come to terms with it:

Frank O'Connor is correct in his suggestion that " . . . in *The Well of the Saints* [Synge] invokes drastic dramatic machinery and then fails to exploit it." Yet Synge's problems with the play probably have a deeper source, for it is never clear exactly when the machinery of the play was constructed in the first place. It is almost as if, having become involved with the dramatic possibilities of the situation, Synge can find no conclusion that might justify the existence of his machinery. *The Well of the Saints* stands as a reminder of the totality of Synge's dramatic achievement in his best plays, for neither the power of Synge's invention nor the considerable energies of his language can conceal or give meaning to the machinery of *The Well of the Saints*. (62)

References

"Arts Theatre: *The Well of the Saints* by J. M. Synge." *The Times* [London], 18 March 1943, p. 6.

Atkinson, Brooks. "The Play: *The Well of the Saints*." *New York Times*, 22 January 1932, p. 15.

———. "*The Well of the Saints*." *New York Times*, 11 April 1959, p. 15.

Barnett, Pat. "The Nature of Synge's Dialogue." *English Literature in Transition (1880–1920)* 10, no. 3 (1967):119–29.

Benson, Eugene. *J. M. Synge*. Grove Press Modern Dramatists. 1982. Reprint. New York: Grove, 1983.

Billington, Michael. "Simplicity of Synge. Old Vic: *The Well of the Saints*." *The Times* [London], 5 August 1970, p. 7.

Bourgeois, Maurice. *John Millington Synge and the Irish Theatre*. London: Constable, 1913.

Gerstenberger, Donna. *John Millington Synge*. Twayne's English Authors Series 12. New York: Twayne, 1964.

Greene, David H. "J. M. Synge: A Centenary Appraisal." *Éire-Ireland* 6, no. 4 (1971):71–86.

Greene, David H., and Edward M. Stephens. *J. M. Synge, 1871–1909*. New York: Macmillan, 1959. Reprint. New York: Colliers, 1961.

Grene, Nicholas. *Synge: A Critical Study of the Plays*. Totowa, N.J.: Rowman and Littlefield, 1975.

Henn, T. R. "John Millington Synge: A Reconsideration." *Hermathena* 112 (1971):5–21.

Howe, P. P. *J. M. Synge: A Critical Study*. London: Martin Secker, 1912.

Nash, Vincent. *"The Well of the Saints*: Language in a Landscape." *Literatur in Wissenschaft und Unterricht* 5, no. 4 (1972):267–76.

"New Lindsey Theatre: *The Well of the Saints* by J. M. Synge." *The Times* [London] 28 April 1954:6.

Price, Alan. *Synge and Anglo-Irish Drama*. London: Methuen, 1961.

Additional Sources

Eckley, Grace. "Truth at the Bottom of a Well: Synge's *The Well of the Saints*." *Modern Drama* 16, no. 2 (1973):193–98.

Leblanc, Gérard. *"The Well of the Saints,* une parabole ambigue." *Cahiers Victoriens et Edouardiens* 9–10 (1979):241–52.

Roche, Anthony. "The Two Worlds of Synge's *The Well of the Saints*." *Genre* 12 (1979):439–50.

Sidnell, M. J. *"The Well of the Saints* and the Light of This World." *A Centenary Tribute to John Millington Synge, 1871–1909: Sunshine and the Moon's Delight*. Edited by S. B. Bushrui. New York: Barnes & Noble, 1972. pp. 53–59.

Skelton, Robin. *J. M. Synge*. The Irish Writers Series. Lewisburg, Pa.: Bucknell University Press, 1972.

———. *The Writings of J. M. Synge*. Indianapolis and New York: Bobbs-Merrill, 1971.

The Tinker's Wedding

The Tinker's Wedding was begun by Synge in the summer of 1902, while he was at work on *Riders to the Sea* and *The Shadow of the Glen*. It was not published until December 1907. Ann Saddlemyer, the editor of Synge's *Plays* in the *Collected Works*, wrote in the Introduction to Volume IV that *The Tinker's Wedding*, more than any of Synge's published plays, suffered from "the author's keen awareness of its limitations" (IV, xi). Saddlemyer explained that the play was to be rejected twice as "too dangerous" to be played in Ireland (IV, xi). Synge's experience in County Wicklow gave rise to *The Tinker's Wedding*; its first reference occurs in his diary for October 3, 1903, but by the end of 1903 the final draft was completed. Nicholas Grene, in *Synge: A Critical Study of the Plays*, noted that Synge's "The Vagrants of Wicklow" is like a "notebook of themes and incidents" for the Wicklow plays, *The Shadow of the Glen* and *The Tinker's Wedding*. In *The Tinker's Wedding*, Synge used the description of a tinker gathering he heard from a man in Aughavanna, who also told him a story of the tinkers' power of clairvoyance (Grene 87). In Wicklow, which Synge used to visit often, the community was divided into three groups: sheep farmers, who lived in the mountain areas; agricultural laborers, who lived in the villages in the valleys; and the vagrants, tramps, tinkers, and traveling people (Grene 84). Grene stated that the tinkers belong to large clans or tribes, and their social structure is a hierarchy ranging from what we can call the respectable to the disreputable (88). They were always genuine outcasts, and they were resented by farmers.

The Abbey Theatre risked producing *The Tinker's Wedding* sixty-four years after its publication, and it played very well, disproving the discredit it received from its critics (Grene 103). After much controversy, the play was finally first produced on November 11, 1909, despite the decision by Yeats that its performance would be too dangerous at the time. It was first produced in London, by an English Company, The Afternoon Theatre Company at His Majesty's Theatre. Although Yeats and Lady Gregory had championed the play, Yeats was so indignant that he walked out after the first act. A reviewer for the London *Times* commented that it pictured squalid aspects of Irish life and stated that the climax, where the priest is gagged and placed in a sack, was "far-fetched to English audiences." Nevertheless, the reviewer described the play as a whole as a "vivid and effective little work" (IV, xvi). The play was first published by Maunsel in Dublin, 1907, and this publication remained the only edition of the play during Synge's lifetime.

The play consists of two acts. The setting is in Ballinaclash in Wicklow, where the tale is still told of the great tinker fight in which the tinkers took over the village, only to be driven out (Grene 89). The characters are Michael Byrne, a tinker; Mary Byrne, his mother, an old woman; Sarah Casey, a young tinker woman; and a priest. Both acts take place at a roadside near the village. It is the month of May.

Briefly stated, the play consists of a confrontation between the tinkers and the priest, both of whom represent a separate world. Sarah, who has been the longtime companion of Michael and who has borne him children, now wants to be married by a priest to be legitimized as the wife of Michael Byrne. Sarah expresses a longing for the world the priest represents to her, a world she does not know but which Mary describes mockingly in Act Two as a world where "grand ladies do be married in silk dresses, with rings of gold" (IV, 37). A bargain is struck between the tinkers and the priest, who agrees to marry Sarah to Michael, provided he receive payment of a gallon tin can, the product of the tinkers' work, and ten shillings. The bargain is abrogated because Mary has traded the gallon can for a bit of drink and places three empty bottles and straw in its place. When the priest returns the next day to perform the ceremony, his anger is provoked when the empty bottles fall from the bundle supposedly keeping the can. The priest refuses to marry the couple, throwing the ten shillings to the ground. The contract has been ruptured, and the tinkers gag and tie the priest in sacking (IV, 45). The tinkers fear discovery by peelers to whom the priest begins to shout, and the priest is then unbound and ungagged by them. At his freedom he promises not to inform on them. Sarah places her intended wedding ring on the priest's finger and the tinkers gather up their things. The priest, now free, utters a Latin malediction and the tinkers scatter.

Although the plot is relatively simple, it is the theme and characterization that give the play its appeal. Aside from the simple abrogation of a contract, the thematic meaning of the play is to be found in the existence of social boundaries between the two cultures or worlds in the play and the reestablishment of these boundaries after an effort is made to bring these different worlds together.

Although they represent a social polarity in terms of class, the tinkers and the priest share some characteristics. It is Sarah who has "queer thoughts" at the opening and who says "the spring-time is a queer time" (IV, 7), revealing a springtime desire to be wed. Sarah then shows her longing to belong to a finer world, the world of the "rich tinkers" and "young Jaunting Jim," a world where "there wouldn't be any big hills to break the back of you, with walking up and walking down" (IV, 9). Associated with the legitimation of her marriage is her yearning for respectability; she belongs to a class of poor tinkers, and her "queer thoughts" involve not only marriage but also the legitimation of class, which marriage might bestow. In this way, Sarah creates the impetus of the plot's unfolding. Although Michael thinks she is foolish, it is agreed that the priest who enters the scene will marry them. The priest is shown to be worldly, and this depiction reverses our expectations. Michael speaks of him as "playing cards, or drinking a sup, or singing songs, until the dawn of day" (IV, 13). The bargain is struck, and he joins the tinkers' world by drinking porter with Mary. His own longing for the kind of life he sees represented by the tinkers is evident when he states, after Mary comments on his sharing drink with them:

it's well for the like of you that do be drinking when there's drouth on you, and lying down to sleep when your legs are stiff. [*He sighs gloomily.*] What would you do if it was the like of myself you were, saying Mass with your mouth dry, and running east and west for a sick call maybe, and hearing the rural people again and they saying their sins? (IV, 19)

The priest then comments that his life is hard. Overlooking the hardships of vagrant poverty, the priest envies the freedom from constraints of the tinkers' way of life just as Sarah desires release from the hardships of a way of life to one where "big hills" will not "break the back of you." The impetus of the play derives from Sarah's desires, and the priest's willingness to perform the marriage, despite the fear of his bishop's knowledge, derives from the qualities in him that he shares with the tinkers—love of gold and drink. It is after the offer of the gold and the gallon can and the drink of porter with Mary that he agrees to perform the ceremony. Thus although the play presents a dualistic world, the world of the tinkers and the cultivated world of the priest, the boundaries of those worlds momentarily dissolve in the agreement that will join Sarah and Michael in the sacrament that the priest bestows.

Synge's characterization of the priest is anticlerical; he is depicted as worldly, playing cards, drinking, and singing. He will perform the ceremony against the obligation to his bishop. The contradictions he embodies in his role as priest are balanced by the contradictions abiding within the tinkers. Although the tinkers ordinarily despise the world the priest represents, both Sarah and Mary manifest desires to partake of that world. It is not only Sarah who wistfully yearns for the power religious ritual bestows; Mary asks the priest to say a prayer in Latin: "And I'm thinking it should be great game to hear a scholar, the like of you, speaking Latin to the saints above" (IV, 21). There is a seeming incompatibility between the tinkers' need for a priest for the marriage and their rejection of him at the end of the play. The audience must accept the incompatibilities and contradictions in both the tinkers and the priest, and it is the tension engendered by these oppositions that makes for the attraction of the play. It can be speculated here that Synge attempted to solve his own dilemmas, arising from the conflict between his orthodox Protestant upbringing and the intellectual freedom he found in Darwin, for example, in what can be seen as the subtle vindication by the tinkers at the end of the play. For although the stage directions at the end of the play read *"They rush out, leaving the Priest master of the situation"* (IV, 49), there may be a thought in the audience's mind that the priest does not win out and that the tinkers triumph. It is almost as though Synge admired the irreverant freedom of the tinkers by presenting their strong emotions in an almost romantic, poetic way; it is well known that Synge greatly admired the strongly emotional nature of the Aran islanders, among whom he found a solution to his own conflicts between beliefs and reality.

Mary C. King, in *The Drama of J. M. Synge*, discussed the roots of *The Tinker's Wedding*, whose spirit she described as a "playful challenge to conventional judgements and behavior" (88). King described the scene of "a wedding and an anti-wedding," as a version of the traditional *nopces à mitaines*, and she stated that the violence has roots in the carnivalesque folk ritual. She quoted from Mikhail Bakhtin's *Rabelais and His World* that in the carnival idiom we find:

a characteristic logic, the peculiar logic of the "inside out" (*à l'envers*), of the "turnabout," of a continual shifting from top to bottom, from front to rear, of numerous parodies and travesties, humiliations, profanations, comic crownings and uncrownings. (88)

The play presents a dialectical relation between the tinkers and the priest and, thus, in King's words "encourages us to look for the interdependent forces of coherence and incoherence beneath the social surface" (89). The effect of the play is subversive, according to King. The final version has a "pervasive comic irony, in which words, gestures, tropic patterns, and properties all act in collusion to create an effect which is essentially subversive of any attempt to divorce them from each other" (93).

The dialectical nature of the play is revealed in the polarities between flesh and spirit; between the pagan, unorthodox, folk-ritual world the tinkers represent and the orthodox, ritualized world of the Catholic priest; between the underprivileged, marginal itinerant way of the tinkers and the established social position of the priest. The antithesis between flesh and spirit is evident not only in the illegitimate relationship between Sarah and Michael as opposed to the legitimizing marriage the priest is to perform but also in the internalization of this opposition within both tinkers and priest. Sarah longs for the sacrament of marriage, which will establish in her world a place for the spirit, and the priest gives evidence of his own conflict between flesh and spirit when he yearns for the freedom of the tinkers, who can drink when they are thirsty and sleep when tired. The priest cannot do this; he must say Mass even though he is thirsty, go for sick calls even when tired. The tinkers' world is a world of antiritual, despite the roots of the play in the folk ritual of *nopces à mitaines*. A ritual is normally understood as an established, regular mode of performing duties or the religious celebration of important events in human existence, such as birth, coming of age, marriage, and death. According to Grene, Synge invented the tradition of free love implied in the play (107). Nevertheless, it is a *given* in the play that the tinkers do not celebrate marriage with ritual; the life of the tinkers in the play is represented by Synge as free of ties to obligations such as rites and to class restraints, as opposed to the life of the priest, who would under normal circumstances have to obtain the permission of his bishop to perform the ceremony demanded by the tinkers in the play. The priest is tied to ritual and to an established social position; the play shows this opposition between a given antiritualistic world and a ritualistic one, even though the attempts to join the two worlds occur when Sarah requests the sacrament of marriage and when Mary mockingly offers the porter to the priest as a burlesque of the Lord's Supper, "the last sup from the jug" (IV, 21). The marginal, itinerant, disestablished way of life the tinkers represent is opposite to the priest's well-defined and well-established social position. The tinkers' way of life is an undercutting comment on the priest's way, which is based on Western categorical and metaphysical modes of thought, evident in the Catholic theology and philosophy that the priest has espoused as a member of the Catholic clergy. The tinkers' disestablished, uncategorized way shows difference and offers a critique to the mode of existence of the priest, which shows identity, sameness. "Difference" as opposed to "sameness" refers to divergence from established norms and codes, be they social, economic, religious, or philosophical. Difference is a concept that distinguishes between the rigid classification of an easily identified, socially hierarchized, codified group with well-defined rules for thought, feeling, and behavior—a group such as that the priest represents—and the uncodified, nonprescriptive, nonhierarchized, and unstructured opposite, which the tinkers represent. Difference can be applied here philosophically as well, in the refusal of the tinkers to embrace the conceptual underpinnings of the priest's metaphysical ground, which rests upon a tradition of centuries of Western metaphysical thinking. Characteristic of metaphysics is the issue of the "concept" or "category" before the reality, and its social derivations arise in Western patriarchal and authoritarian societies, such as the one the priest represents. Since all of Western philosophy traditionally has been identified as a "footnote to Plato," the traditional Western historical and social derivations of this thought are embedded in structures and institutions that support conceptual, categorical thinking.

It is clear whose side Synge is on. The marginal, "fringe" nature of the tinkers represents a freedom from the constraints and way of thinking the priest must accept as a member of a hierarchized class. The tinkers see and feel reality in a way other than the priest does, who is haunted by the ghosts of Western metaphysics. He tries to exorcise those ghosts when he drinks the porter with Mary, after she sings her "bad, wicked song" in the gesture mocking the Catholic Communion ritual.

The opposition within the play can also be described as a game between conceptual thinking and reality that reflects an opposition Synge had to deal with personally. His reading of Darwin is well known as the source for his questioning the orthodox Protestant beliefs of his childhood, and this conflict had to be solved in some way; his stay among the Aran Islanders helped reconcile this conflict. The stay on the Aran Islands and his great admiration for the strong emotions of the inhabitants and their ability to live with the contradictions of pagan superstition and Catholic orthodoxy enabled him to create a new sense of integration that is represented in the play in the tinkers' way of life. The tinkers, like the Aran islanders, are able to live with the contradictory claims of marginality and orthodoxy. Sarah's request for the sacrament of marriage, although at first scorned by Michael, appropriates orthodoxy for her own needs and purposes. The desire for the sacrament does not disrupt the entire way of life of the tinkers and the sacrament can be incorporated into their world without changing them. It is a very different matter for the priest.

The attempt to join the two worlds in the play is, after all, an impossibility. The renegade nature of the tinkers cannot be accepted within the orthodox world, and the priest's world cannot be reconciled with the tinkers. In a sense, both sides win in the end; the tinkers render the priest powerless by binding and gagging him, and he reestablishes his power by uttering the Latin malediction as the tinkers scatter. The reversal of expectations at the end indicates that there is no closure in the normal sense, and the dualism in the play remains. The "solution" at the end remains problematic, and questions of Synge's intentions remain. Is the priest comic, pathetic, or powerful at the end? After the comic reversals, the play's impossibility produces a comic effect. Although King stated that "Synge does not, however, concede total victory to either side" (101), the tension produced by this ambiguity provides the dramatic power of the play.

According to Weldon Thornton in *J. M. Synge and the Western Mind*, Synge's aim in *The Tinker's Wedding* was "to put his audience through an experience of shock, of cognitive dissonance, similar to what he suffered upon reading Darwin, or to what he enjoyed on the Aran Islands" (98). Thornton further stated that Synge wished to avoid the conventional genres of tragedy or comedy, "representing as they do received Western categories of response" (98). The entire aim of Synge, in form and in meaning, then, in *The Tinker's Wedding*, is to destroy abstract Western categorical modes of thought, feeling, and behavior in a dramatic enactment that creates a solution to his own inner drama.

References

Grene, Nicholas. *Synge: A Critical Study of the Plays*. Totowa, N.J.: Rowman and
    Littlefield, 1975.

King, Mary C. *The Drama of J. M. Synge*. Irish Studies. Syracuse: Syracuse University Press, 1985.

Thornton, Weldon. *J. M. Synge and the Western Mind*. Irish Literary Studies 4. New York: Barnes & Noble, 1979.

Synge: *The Playboy of the Western World*

Even before January 26, 1907, the day of the Abbey's first performance of *The Playboy of the Western World*, the play was the subject of controversy and fears of potentially harsh criticism from an Irish audience for whom this strange and elaborate mixture of exotic language, metaphor, comedy, tragedy, and melo-drama was to become such a cause célèbre that unprecedented audience response would be generated during its initial performances in Ireland and in subsequent productions in the United States. It was destined eventually to become one of the most profoundly controversial dramas in the Western world. Critics today, though distanced by history, are as deeply enmeshed in the perplexities of mean-ing and interpretation as were the rioters who disrupted Abbey performances during the opening week in 1907. In fact the response of the audience has generated as much scholarly interest during the past eighty-one years as the play itself.

This attention is entirely appropriate, since the audience's response to the play was so intimately bound up with the meaning, language, and nature of the dramatic action portrayed. At least one entire book (Kilroy, *The 'Playboy' Riots*) and several major articles (e.g., Kain and Suss) document the history of the *Playboy* riots. Synge himself added fuel to the fire, declaring in a newspaper interview shortly after the production that the play was simply an "extravaganza" and that he "did not care a rap" about the public's response. His statement on January 29 in *The Evening Telegraph*—that "the play was suggested to him by the fact that a few years ago a man who committed murder was kept hidden by the people on one of the Aran Islands until he could get off to America and also by the case of Lynchehaun'' (quoted in Hirsch 101)—tended to undercut Synge's argument that his intent was not to depict Irish life realistically so much as to glorify the joy and extravagance of its language and propensity to develop its own fiction.

Whether or not the *Playboy* was an accurate representation of the Hibernian mentality, it was not what the audience wanted. In a perceptive essay, Edward Hirsch discussed the psyche of an audience who wanted and needed to see their own hopes, dreams, illusions, and beliefs embodied in a drama in order to identify with them. When the characters did not conform to these expectations, the audience felt subverted and undermined. In a way, they had a right to feel cheated. A preliminary announcement published in the *Freeman's Journal* the day the play opened emphasized Synge's truthful portrayal of the peasants of Western Ireland, his expertise in having lived with them, his thorough knowledge of "their speech, their humours, their vices, and virtues," and the claim that the *Playboy* was founded on an actual incident (Hirsch 90; Kain 177). In the parlance of the Irish nationalistic movement, this equaled humble and long suffering, if occasionally quaint Irish bravery.

The origin of the Abbey Theatre at the turn of the century is tied closely with the revival of Irish language and traditions. Its playgoers expected to see not the buffoonery of the English-stage Irishman, which they universally deplored, nor, for that matter, Irishmen with any serious vices at all but rather a west-of-Ireland peasant embodiment of Irish virtue and purity. But the Mayo citizens of Synge's *Playboy*, besides being either drunkards or priest-panicked wimps, were a short-sighted, meanspirited lot, characterized by a speech that despite Synge's ad-monitions of verisimilitude, seemed more caricature than reality. Although Synge had caught the rhythms of the West as well as its hyperbolic language, its present participles, and other idiosyncratic constructions, at the same time he had created a speech more metaphoric than literal, a language heightened by the artistry of the dramatist into an action that imitated not reality as we normally conceive of it but a metaphoric, perhaps tragic, perhaps comical, burlesque truth that went far beyond the boundaries of Mayo or turn-of-the-century Ireland.

The audience was right about one thing, however. The *Playboy* was not merely a story of young innocence and love but of the mentality and actions of an entire community. It was the judgment of the collective Mayo citizenry that both surprised and upset that opening-night audience. At the end of the first act, Lady Gregory reported to Yeats that they seemed to be receiving the play well, but by the end of the second act they grew more restive and, finally, incensed by the word *shift* in what is now one of the most famous speeches in Western drama, the audience erupted into open hostility. Critics have later pointed out that *shift* and *shifts* had previously been used in the works of Douglas Hyde and Lord Tennyson, without critical notice or comment, and it is difficult for a contem-porary reader, even with allowances for the delicate sensibilities of a 1907 Irish audience, to conceive that they might have responded so violently to such an apparently innocuous word. But the offending speech was only the catalyst for a deeper discontent. Newspaper accounts the next day, although noting the point at which the rioting began, also commented that the play was a degrading representation of Irish sensibilities. After all, the play was about patricide and how in Mayo the idea of such an act, instead of inspiring horror, inspired praise, even awe, for its daring and lawless nature. Literary historians have explained the townsfolk's sympathy with the deed as being the empathy of an oppressed people with anyone who rebelled against authority. The crowd that came to hear Synge's play and to see themselves glorified as fellow members of a race oppressed but pure resented the implication that they, too, glorified lawlessness and shameful acts. Christy Mahon, the would-be patricide, was simply an unacceptable hero.

The play gained so much notoriety that after the first night many besotted viewers attended more to participate in the jeering spectacle than to see a drama, and they can hardly be regarded as an unbiased audience. What amounted to minor disruptions on opening night blossomed into riotous behavior in subsequent performances, although box office receipts indicate that the unruly audiences were comparatively small.[1] The play, running the rest of the week under the auspices of police protection, become itself a metaphor of art, tried and martyred by a mob of philistines, until W. B. Yeats called for a public debate on the issue the following Monday. During the rancorous and voluble exchange, Yeats was virtually alone against the crowd.

The *Playboy*'s glorification of Ireland through its love of poetry, its rich relationship to Elizabethan rhetoric, its treatment of deep and traditional tragic themes, its vitality of dialogue and extravagant poetry, its romantic love affair, and its theme of liberation and freedom were all overlooked. As Hirsch pointed out, what the audience wanted was a play with a cast of characters who would celebrate Irish objects and the disembodied and essentially apocryphal Irish way of life, not a play that celebrated its own rhetoric and the joy of its own exuberance. Lively, joyful, hyperbolic peasants were not the cliché essentials the audience was looking for. In degrading the motives of the Mayo citizenry, which the audience saw as an extension of itself, the play degraded the viewers. The irony is that art means so much in Ireland that its citizens identify themselves with fictive characters, see their own lives and struggles embodied in the images of art, and connect the imaginative metaphors and language of drama so strongly with reality itself. There are few countries in the modern world in which an artistic work assumes such importance. The audience was saying in effect that they would never act the way the characters were, and neither would any other Irishman. Synge's language and images had such a dramatic and telling effect upon its audience that they saw the play as a representation of reality, rather than as a work of art. It is, then, the very power of Synge's language of metaphor to promote, shape, define, and become reality that this play is all about. Becoming the playboy of the Western world, it seems, lies merely in believing that it is so. Just as Christy's rise to playboydom lies in his being convinced that he is a playboy, so ironically does the conviction that the play misrepresents Ireland

become for its audience the overwhelming resulting reality. Thus the audience
mob coalesced with the chorus of townspeople in the play, vilifying the author
when they saw their nationalistic illusions become a dirty deed before their eyes,
and unable themselves to distinguish between metaphoric language and reality.

There were other, more subversive, sources of annoyance to Synge's audience.
Additional themes and parodies degrading to traditional Irish morality lurked
just under the surface. Although the audience may not consciously have been
aware of it, certain shibboleths were under playful attack. The three fathers in
the play provide cases in point. Christy's father, old Mahon, is an individual
with scant regard for the citizens with whom he is surrounded, both in Mayo
and at home. He feels superior to them, a sort of Godlike figure, with a son
appropriately named Christy. Christy's perception of his own superior playboy
status in life comes first after he receives gifts from three local Mayo maids, an
echo of the gifts of the venerating Magi. Christy's enticing words, like Christ's
sermons, enhance his stature in the eyes of his disciples, and he is nurtured by
a degraded, almost demonic Holy Mother, the Widow Quin, who is able to
divine his flawed humanity but still loves him. Christy's passion, which follows
his winning donkey ride, consists of the mob's judgment and vilification after
the second "murder." Like Christ, he is wounded in the process and abandoned
before achieving final playboyhood and romping off through life in the Western
world. Physical resurrections from the dead occur not once but twice in the play,
in addition to Christy's spiritual resurrection, inspiring the degraded and the
comic Godlike figure old Mahon to follow his newly reborn son to mocking and
vilifying the mob from the Olympian heights of their superiority. The degradation
of Irish Roman Catholicism in this biblical father-son parody may not have been
consciously perceived by the distraught audience that first night, but surely some
subliminal hackles must have been raised.

The second father, Michael James Flaherty, Pegeen Mike's father, was precisely the sort of bibulous if lovable drunken Irishman that had been so often
caricatured on the British stage. He is off at Kate Cassidy's wake all during Act
Two and returns in Act Three singing a drunken song about being thrown in
jail. He spies Christy and shakes him "drunkenly by the hand," conferring the
following blessing:

The blessing of God and the holy angels on your head, young fellow. I hear tell you're
after winning all in the sports below; and wasn't it a shame I didn't bear you along with
me to Kate Cassidy's wake, a fine, stout lad, the like of you, for you'd never see the
match of it for the flows of drink, the way when we sunk her bones at noonday in her
narrow grave, there were five men, aye, and six men, stretched out retching speechless
on the holy stones. (IV, 151)

It is this father who bestows high honors on the act of patricide during the first
act and spends the second act in drunken comic verbosity and the third act leading
the townsfolk in their chastisement and vilification of Christy. In short, old

Flaherty is the epitome of the Irish father stereotype the Dublin audience was so eager to rid themselves of.

The third father is an ecclesiastic. Although Father Reilly is never seen on stage, his ever-present specter haunts the every action of Shawn Keogh. From marital dispensation through guilt to fears of torment beyond the grave, the sanctions of Father Reilly and the image of his clerical being render Christy's Mayo rival, Shawn, a simpering, cowardly, child. Reilly truly is the father of repression, the heavy hand of the church in making impossible any sort of free existence for the Irish peasant in his sniveling obsequiousness and fear. Father Reilly's specter is part of the yoke of authority that makes these Mayo citizens initially so sympathetic to patricide and to the destruction of the old order of forces that govern them. Certainly, the opening-night audience could not have failed to get that message. In his representation of the effects of the Irish priesthood on its citizenry, Synge was presenting in a comic but degrading form the institution that shapes the lives of most Irishmen. The picture could not have been other than an additional irritant to many. Under the circumstances, it would have been a wonder if they hadn't rioted.

A number of critics have dealt with Synge's sources for the themes and situations of *The Playboy*. M. J. Sidnell and Diane E. Bessai, for instance, viewed the old Ulster sagas, notably "The Championship of Ulster," with its ritual beheading ceremony, as a source Synge drew upon in having Christy murder his Da with a loy, while another critic, Diderik Roll-Hansen, thought *The Playboy* was a possible Irish *Peer Gynt*. These speculations as to Synge's sources are not developed at any length here, because I am doubtful that they can add much to our understanding of the play. On the other hand, Synge is obviously drawing on traditional tragedy and mythology in making patricide the operative center of his plot. The mythic dimension of patricide is indigenous to all of Western civilization. The establishment of one's own place in the continuity of life involves, in psychological as well as evolutionary terms, the search for freedom from one's heritage in one's own life. Sophocles's play *Oedipus Rex* dealt squarely with the theme. Killing one's father without knowing it, although it may be a necessary evil in evolutionary terms, represents a paramount sin in psychological terms, because it involves in essence the destruction of one's origins. Synge adapted the Oedipal theme into a vastly different vision of history and heroism.

Synge was ostensibly writing a comedy rather than a tragedy, that is, a play with a happy rather than a tragic ending. Throughout the history of drama, however, we have associated serious action with tragic implications, and Synge, perhaps beginning a new genre in Irish drama, blended the farcical, the comic, and the lighthearted with actions we normally associate with tragic, even disastrous results. Synge's mixture of traditional opposites paved the way for his two great Irish successors, Sean O'Casey and Brendan Behan, both of whom posed tragic dilemmas in an atmosphere of ribald, often zany, comic language, characters, and situations. The confusion of tragedy, with its serious moral and ethical Aristotelian implications of the recognition of some truth in our Jungian shadow side and of the underlying onerous fatalism of human life, was also part of the response of the early audiences of the play. Synge's early statement that he was writing a comic extravaganza encouraged expectations of a vastly different sort of play. Although tragedy touches the inmost soul, comedy has a more realistic bent. Comic characters are more like ourselves. We do not need, as Aristotle suggested, a protagonist who is better or of more noble import than the audience, nor do we have to aspire to identify with comic characters, who are often less noble than the audience. They have foibles that the audience, even if it condescends, recognizes in itself, and comedy seeks to set right our vaunted ideas of our own tragic nature. In fact, comedy aims to arrive at truth through a debunking process, through displaying to its audiences their own lower natures, eventually culminating in Sancho Panza truths when the audience entered thinking themselves Quixotes. The original Irish audience, seeking an encomium to the essential Irishman as a noble sufferer, was shocked to find Synge's portrait mixed with ignoble, often ludicrous, if lovable, motives and activities. Thus what began as an Oedipal theme from Sophocles, patricide, ended in the protagonist's vision of romping through life a likely gaffer after all. Mary Rose Sullivan has delineated the Sophoclean elements in *Playboy*:

Both plays deal with a man who enters a society as a stranger to everyone—even to himself—to be hailed as a savior by that society because of some distant epic deed that has renewed the barren land; however, in the course of attempting to learn the facts about his own identity and the mysterious deed, the hero uncovers a truth which proves too harsh for the society to accept—with the result that he is forced to leave it as he came, a stranger and alone. (243)

The mysterious stranger destined to be the restorer of a barren land was, even in Sophocles's time, a traditional archetypal character. That Christian mythology derives from the archetypal lineage is, as we have seen, a major factor in Synge's dramatic scheme. The Sophoclean parallels are even closer, as Sullivan pointed out, in Christy's version of the original slaying: " 'I hit a blow on the ridge of his skull, laid him stretched out'—echo Oedipus' version: 'By one swift blow from the staff in this hand he was rolled right out of the carriage, on his back' " (242). Sullivan also noted that Synge pushed the similarities a little further in hinting at an incest theme in *Playboy*. Old Mahon had intended Christy to marry the woman who had suckled him, and Christy's involvement with the Widow Quin also has overtones of a matriarchally incestuous relationship. It is, however, what Synge does with these initial parallels that turns his play into something far lighter and different from the earlier tragedy. The townsfolk, through their adoration, are themselves responsible for raising Christy's self-esteem to the point of his independence from society and his father. Although the fatalism of Sophocles's play would doom any possibility of reversing the tragic outcome, old Mahon is twice resurrected. Furthermore, Christy's eventual knowledge does not concern either the irreversible nature of his crime or his self-destructive hubris but is in fact the very cause of his hubris, his vaulted ideas of himself, enabling him through deed and more importantly through his speech to bring about his own independence and manhood. In fact the hubris and pride that were the bane of tragic heroes are Christy's salvation.

Blind self-preservation and a list of vague provocations in the form of humiliations cause the first murder. The second is more purposeful, and the third, a metaphoric murder in which Christy simply subjugates his father by assuming the superior role, is the most purposeful of all. Hence guilt, pride, and the laws of fate are reversed in the *Playboy*. Whereas Oedipus wanders off blind to a life of humble solitary chagrin, Christy begins his journey through life in triumph and with scorn for the society of weaker beings. Like Oedipus, Christy has achieved manhood through knowledge, but the knowledge that Synge imparts to Christy is triumphal self-assurance, whereas Oedipus's lot is the certainty of his own unworthiness. The tragic loss, according to Sullivan, is society's. Christy is free, independent of the villagers, but Pegeen's last lament "acknowledges society's belated recognition of all that it has lost in clinging to the myth and evading the truth" (Sullivan 253). Man, Sullivan thinks, needs myth to discover his heroic potential, but at the same time he must unmake myth to realize that potential. It is this blend of the serious, the comic, and the tragic that enables him to do so.

The audience, like the townspeople in the play, had choices to make in either identifying with Christy and affecting the liberation through their imaginations, or by siding with the townspeople's condemnation of Christy's second act of attempted murder. Synge put the audience in a bind. If they chose the latter course, they identified with the deservedly oppressed Mayo men and lost their right to become themselves playboys, with all of the heroism that such an alliance entails. In a sense, Synge made the play a didactic reflexive drama, just as the audience expected it would be. But the audience, instead of siding either with the townfolk or, more likely, with Christy, revolted, stating in effect that no such parallels could be drawn because the situation portrayed in Mayo simply could never exist, except in the demented, totally biased and mischief-making mind of the playwright. Their anger in a sense mirrored the anger of the townsfolk in condemning Christy, so that Synge himself became the martyred playboy in the reflexive real-life drama caused by the play.

The ironies are patently apparent. It is, as Pegeen Mike says, the difference between a gallous story and a dirty deed. Bruce M. Bigley discussed the ambiguity that Synge has caused in the mind of an audience who, like the chorus of Mayo pub crawlers, once the violent act is reperformed in their presence and they are called upon to affirm their complicity in a defiant metaphor that suddenly becomes apparently a real act, bow to the authority of the English law and rejoin Shawn's church-dominated, patriarchal society. The audience in the theater, since they have distanced themselves from the beginning from Christy's Mayo men on the stage, are left with the implicit responsibility to join Pegeen in choosing between Christy Mahon and Shawn Keogh, with the uncomfortable implications of that choice. These implications include the approval of patricide in Act One and a rejection of the "reality" of everyday Mayo life in Act Three. On the other hand, should the audience like Pegeen and the townsfolk choose the Shawn Keogh role model, they submit themselves to the oppression of a colorless, humdrum servitude to church and foreign rule: "The act of the imagination which frees Christy from the tyranny of the actual is revolutionary; and although the political currents in this play are less clearly relevant to the Irish Question than some have assumed, this revolution has social and political as well as psychological and epistemological implications" (Bigley 160).

The *Playboy* contains major ambiguities. It begins with the confusion of the tragic and the comic modes, and its end, baffling to some, ambiguous to all, caused a natural response of fear and revulsion in an audience whose social and political expectations led them to believe they were a part of the play itself, both historically and literally. The riots in Boston and later the arrests in Philadelphia were brought about by people who had neither seen nor read the *Playboy* and for whom the play was merely a symbolic threat to their own patriotic ideals. So their response, although interesting, is of less consequence than that of the first-night crowd who had experienced the identification with the play directly.

Other factors, however, make audience identification more difficult. The setting in the wild, wind-blown country of violence in nature and society and the notorious lawlessness of Kerry and Mayo remove its activities slightly from the urban eastern center in which it was played. In the original Aran Islands story, despite the temptation of a substantial reward, no one betrayed the patricide who eventually escaped to America. In more recent productions Pegeen's betrayal has been played down. Successful modern revivals of the *Playboy* tend to emphasize comedy and lack the brutality that was so apparent in its first engagement. Christy is a more harmless lover in the new versions, even a *miles gloriosus* figure. This braggart-parody of the epic hero found its way into formula Irish literature through the *Lomarbhaigh*—the tradition of the boastful dispute or contest such as the one in which Christy and the townsfolk engage. George Moore early complained that the *Playboy* continually switched genres and that the result was a confusion of audience expectations (Benson 135–36). The other side of the argument is that Synge blends traditional figures and patterns in unsettling new combinations, resulting in an ambiguous hybrid form which involves the audience in the dilemma without traditional clues as to how it should respond.

Following the Greek lead, even attempted homicide does not occur on the stage. However, the branding, the violence done by Pegeen to the captive Christy, takes place in full view of the audience, and this melodramatic action removes the play from the realm of metaphors to graphic reality. Although villainous violence has been traditional theatrical fare since the Renaissance, in *Playboy* the violent act is circumscribed by mean and petty intent, which when cloaked in the sanctity of righteous judgment assumes comic overtones, which in turn diminish villainy to commonplace nastiness. The low act is meant to contrast with the highly charged, highly imaginative, implausibly metaphoric speeches and language that have by Act Three become so pervasive a presence that they have assumed a significance almost greater than the literal actions of the play.

From Christy's tentative opening speeches to the resounding triumphal conclusion of the play, the language itself became increasingly important as the prime shaper of events and action. Its centrality was intentionally prompted by Synge, who never intended the fantastic action of the play to be represented as anything more than metaphoric, the process and product of language itself.

Scholars have eagerly cooperated in their search for metaphoric correspondences. The process has led James Kilroy to view Christy as a parallel to Stephen Dedalus and to interpret the *Playboy* as principally being about the growth of the artist-poet as a young man. Kilroy viewed Christy's development as a poet from his first simple account of his early life and the murder. Although initially in his father's eyes Christy was a sort of dreaming idler, the protagonist's growing awareness of his own poetic abilities prompts a conclusion in which he makes, like Stephen, a declaration of his own independence and freedom (Kilroy, "The Playboy as Poet").

On the other hand, Hirsh thought Christy's symbolic role and self-aggrandizement were the glorification of the peasant gone awry. In Hirsh's view it was not the reality of the play that so infuriated its audience but its depiction of their own vain attempts at glorification so inflated that they became the further subject and butt of English ridicule. Indeed, Synge's inviting comparisons of Christy with illustrious predecessors such as Christ and Oedipus was part of the comic hyperbole that informed the language of the play.

Thus language is not only the vehicle of structure, plot, and character, it is the subject matter of the *Playboy*. Critics such as Patricia Spacks and Donna Gerstenberger have treated language as the central consideration. The *Playboy* is about the ability of language to create a reality far greater than empirical fact. Language makes a playboy of Christy, language sustains him through his trial, and language affirms his triumphal position in the end. When the glory of the language contradicts the apparent horror of an event that takes place before the eyes of the townsfolk, the choice to believe that the act is a dirty deed is ironically more ignoble than the belief in the magic of language itself. Weldon Thornton perhaps put it best:

In *Playboy*, language acts as a mediator between actuality and potentiality, between reality and abstraction, for it is largely through language—through his successive accounts of the murder and his self-surprising eloquence in wooing Pegeen—that Christy projects and brings into being one of his potential selves that had until now lain dormant. (140)

Donna Gerstenberger said that *Playboy* was Synge's homage to joy, stemming from an instinctive blow and evolving into an image of self, fostered principally by Christy's own language and the language of others. She thought Synge's linguistic extravagance was the play's source of energy, joy, and salvation. To restate the case in contemporary critical terms, language is so important that it becomes signified instead of signifier, the subject as well as the means of describing other subjects. Its major importance in *Playboy* is transformative. It becomes the means of transforming the comic-tragic genres, the aims of the play, the nationalism, and the expectations of the audience. Extravagant language transforms mundane ideas into great ones or debases them by calling into question the relationship betwen language and reality itself. Synge's Preface to the *Playboy* confines itself to the subject of language, criticizing Ibsen and Zola as "dealing with the reality of life in joyless and pallid words" (IV, 53). For Synge a play must have both reality and joy. He thought the *Playboy* was a celebration of the language of the Irish and hence a tribute to the people:

In a good play every speech should be as fully flavoured as a nut or apple, and such speeches cannot be written by anyone who works among people who have shut their lips on poetry. In Ireland, for a few years more, we have a popular imagination that is fiery and magnificent, and tender; so that those of us who wish to write start with a chance that is not given to writers in places where the springtime of the local life has been forgotten, and the harvest is a memory only, and the straw has been turned into bricks. (IV, 54)

Perhaps surveying a few of the characteristics of Synge's peasant speech will serve as an introduction to its imaginative qualities. The imagery, for example, is couched in a combination Gaelic and Anglo-Irish common to the west coast of Ireland. The idiom has certain identifiable syntactic as well as metaphoric features. Alan J. Bliss has compiled a brief but substantially comprehensive list:

The syntactic features in questions [*sic*] are the following:
1. emphasis by means of introductory *it's*, etc.;
2. the use of "progressive" tenses formed with present participle;
3. the form *do be*, etc.;
4. the construction *I am after doing*, etc.;
5. the subordinate clause introduced by *and* and lacking a finite verb;
6. the imperative formed with *let*. (41)

These are but a sampling of the most common idiomatic expressions that lend the speech a lilting, almost metric pattern. The rhythm proved unusual enough to cause considerable difficulty for the players. Even Yeats admitted that Synge's words and phrases danced "to a very strange rhythm, which will always, till his plays have created their own tradition, be difficult to actors who have not learned it from his own lips" (quoted in Bliss 44). Even an accomplished actress such as Maire Nic Shiubhlaigh had to admit:

At first I found Synge's lines almost impossible to learn and deliver. . . . It was neither verse nor prose. The speeches had a musical lilt, absolutely different to anything I had heard before. Every passage brought some new difficulty and we would all stumble through the speeches until the tempo in which they were written was finally discovered. (quoted in Bliss 44)[2]

All of the characters use the same idiosyncratic patterns, but the most important aspect of the language, the exaggeration, varies with each character. Exaggeration and hyperbole are the joyous celebration of the imagination of speakers who deliver wild, sometimes incongruous metaphors and similes, people who in fact have raised exaggeration to a fine art. Christy's exaggerated imagery is complemented by the same quality in the language of most of the Mayo townspeople. To command their respect Christy's language must be so exaggerated as to draw attention even in that crowd of hyperbolizers. Ironically, Christy's honestly stated belief that he killed his father will do for a start. They see the admission as an exaggerated metaphor rather than a simply stated fact. Even so mundane a character as Shawn Keogh knows how to color his threats and fears with hyperbole. "Leave me go, Michael James, leave me go, you old Pagan, leave me go or I'll get the curse of the priests on you, and of the scarlet-coated bishops of the courts of Rome" (IV, 65).

The timid pre-playboy Christy gives an early indication of his imaginative powers in his description of his father's position in life: "And I the son of a strong farmer [*with a sudden qualm*], God rest his soul, could have bought up the whole of your old house a while since from the butt of his tail-pocket and not have missed the weight of it gone" (IV, 69). The Mayo men are swayed by the metaphoric power of Christy's crime, and they imbue him with such honor that his exaggerated speech begins to rise to heroic proportion. It is good to remember that the title, "Playboy of the Western World," remains to this day a cliché that bears connotations of comic exaggeration. Christy's rise to playboyhood during the drama is hardly a Horatio Alger story, nor is becoming Playboy of the Western World much like becoming a lawyer, doctor, engineer, accountant, computer programmer, or dentist, occupations long on serious purpose and short on imagination or comedy. Christy aspires to be and presumably does become a metaphor with little precise denotation. His title, like those of Chaucer's pilgrims, suggests his occupation, but there is a comic vagueness about it, more image than a means of getting a livelihood.

When Christy begins his short journey to playboyhood, his speech becomes increasingly exaggerated. His second account of the murder of his father is far more elaborate than the first, embellished by a hyperbolic description of the widow his father had chosen for him to marry: "she a hag this day with a tongue on her has the crows and seabirds scattered, the way they wouldn't cast a shadow on her garden with the dread of her curse" (IV, 103). Christy also adds a few graphic images to his description of his father's corpse, "stretched out, and he split to the knob of his gullet" (IV, 103).

The pubcrawlers note that his telling of the tale becomes grander, as his language rises to their expectation of the glories inherent in patricide. Christy tells the tale again and again to repersuade people of his significance, but his continual retelling of the story as Pegeen informs us, serves to lower him in the estimation of the long-suffering listeners. He clearly has to say something new. The second murder, in Act Three, causes the townspeople to turn on Christy in part because the idea of the patricide is redundant, robbed of both originality and of metaphoric imagination. This time they see the stark reality of a gallous act, deprived of imaginative linguistic significance. Although Christy has performed seemingly heroic acts in winning the athletic events and races, we must remember they too are merely metaphors for life's activities, an unimaginative recreation of more realistic tests of manhood, events that draw their power not from language but from mundane physical aptitudes such as donkey jockeying. Christy also extends his victories to the social realm: "and he after bringing bankrupt ruin on the roulette man, and the trick-o'-the-loop-man, and breaking the nose of the cockshot-man" as well as "winning all in the sports" (IV, 133).

But all of these activities are a prelude to the linguistic battlefield on which he must vie with Pegeen. Even though Christy is well on the road to becoming "a likely gaffer," he is easily routed by Pegeen when he rouses her ire by telling her that girls have come four miles to listen to his by now oft-told tale. When she questions the distance, Christy answers by saying that only bona fides lived in the area (people who were privileged to drink on Sunday and after hours because they lived more than four miles from the pub and were thus bona fide travelers). Pegeen counters with the observation that they are bona fide only in that if they come by the road the distance to their houses is four miles, but their journey is short if they leave the road and come by the river. Not satisfied with disparaging that bit of hyperbole, Pegeen continues with her observation of what it would be like to hang for murder: "Ah, that should be a fearful end, young fellow, and it worst of all for a man destroyed his da, for the like of him would get small mercies, and when it's dead he is, they'd put him in a narrow grave, with cheap sacking wrapping him round, and pour down quicklime on his head, the way you'd see a woman pouring any frish-frash from a cup" (IV, 107). The reference to frish-frash, an Indian meal ("raw cabbage, boiled down as thin as gruel"), adds a bit of domestic hyperbole to a standard horror story to give it a specially intense flavor. Pegeen's nastiness inspires Christy's self-pitying image of a lonely Byronic hero:

It's well you know it's a lonesome thing to be passing small towns with the lights shining sideways when the night is down, or going in strange places with a dog nosing before you and a dog nosing behind, or drawn to the cities where you'd hear a voice kissing and talking deep love in every shadow of the ditch, and you passing on with an empty hungry stomach failing from your heart. (IV, 109)

Like Pegeen's speech, there is enough realism (the dogs nosing around) to add a certain sense of the immediate to this otherwise hyperbolic account.

Even though the stage directions call for the speech to be grimly delivered, there is a perpetual element of comedy in his exaggerations. It has led Northrop Frye and others to consider Christy a traditional braggart hero, the *miles gloriosus* whose essentially ludicrous and comic figure exempts him from being a subject of serious action. For Christy to be regarded as a serious hero, he has to be seriously challenged. Such a challenge comes collectively from the Mayo men and also from the woman he loves. There is also a dark side to Christy. It is recognized immediately by the Widow Quin, who constantly calls attention to the similarities between herself and Christy. She is half Madonna, half demonic, gifted with Teresian divination and engaged in life's serious actvities, for she "has buried her children and destroyed her man" (IV, 131). Christy's plea to her takes the form of Christian exaggeration suggesting a comically exalted parallel between himself and Christ: "Aid me for to win her, and I'll be asking God to stretch a hand to you in the hour of death, and lead you short cuts through the Meadows of Ease, and up the floor of Heaven to the Footstool of the Virgin's Son" (IV, 127–31). It sounds like Christ pardoning the penitent thief on Calvary. At any rate, Christy's supplication impresses the widow, and she replies, "There's praying!" But voices are heard calling out. "Christy! Christy Mahon!" and Christy turns back again and says to the widow, "They're coming. Will you swear to aid and save me for the love of Christ?"(IV, 131) This identification of Christy with Christ, although hyperbolic and more than a little blasphemous, keeps the exaggerations of the speech from becoming wholly comic, as Synge walks the linguistic line between comedy-farce and drama-tragedy.

One of the problems in all of these exaggerations is exactly how much of old Mahon's account of his worthless, beaten, scapegoat son to believe. Mahon's version of the younger Christy is a little hard to reconcile with even the frightened fugitive of the first act. "Didn't you hear me say he was the fool of men, the way from this out he'll know the orphan's lot with old and young making game of him and they swearing, raging, kicking at him like a mangy cur" (IV, 139). But Mahon's exaggeration becomes fact, and his version of the past a fore-shadowing of the future, when the mob eventually turns on Christy. Although old Mahon possesses some linguistic prowess, he does not have his son's imag-ination. Old Mahon is, like Pegeen's father, a heavy drinker. He believes only in what he sees, not in the power of language to transform. His life is guided by realities not metaphors. If those realities seem illogical, they must therefore be hallucinations. That is why he is so easily persuaded by the Widow Quin that the vision of his son winning a race and being cheered by the crowd must, like the other products of his drunken hallucinations, be merely a failing of his mind: "There was one time I seen ten scarlet devils letting on they'd cork my spirit in a gallon can; and one time I seen rats as big as badgers sucking the life blood from the butt of my lug; but I never till this day confused that dribbling idiot with a likely man. I'm destroyed surely" (IV, 143). It is the Sancho Panza investment of the mundane with eternal truth that makes old Mahon such a comic figure. Exaggerations for him are the product of hallucinations.

On the other hand, when reality overtakes the townspeople and they learn that Christy is not a patricide, they become like the derisive mob who have ridiculed Christy all his life, and their taunts help drive him to the second attempted murder. "CROWD: [*jerringly*] There's the playboy! There's the lad thought he'd rule the roost in Mayo. Slate him now, Mister" (IV, 161). "Keep it up, the two of you. I'll back the old one. Now the playboy" (IV, 163). Their attitude inspires Christy's most powerful speech, strong because truth finally overtakes exaggeration: "Shut your yelling, for if you're after making a mighty man of me this day by the power of a lie, you're setting me now to think if it's a poor thing to be lonesome, it's worse maybe go mixing with the fools of earth" (IV, 165).

As the action in Act Three becomes more serious, there is an increased incidence of Christian imagery. Christy answers his increasingly abusive and insistent father's demands for retribution by protesting that he never hurt anyone except for that one "single blow":

MAHON: [*loudly*] If you didn't, you're a poor good-for-nothing, and isn't it by the like of you the sins of the whole world are committed?

CHRISTY: [*raising his hands*] In the name of the Almighty God. . . .

MAHON: Leave troubling the Lord God. Would you have him sending down droughts, and fevers, and the old hen and the cholera morbus? (IV, 161–63)

The coincidence of Christian imagery with the rise in dramatic intensity is typical of most Christians in whom stress automatically invokes references to deities, salvation, and the like. That old Mahon takes Christy's epithet so literally even in this troubled scene adds a comic dimension that undercuts the seriousness of the action.

Another minor and more obvious metaphor that bears mention in this comic-literal pattern is the identification of Christy with his clothes. He wears several costumes in the play: the dirty clothes in which he appears in Act One, Shawn's suit in which he begins the games, the jockey's clothes in which he wins the race, and the petticoats of the women, Sara and Widow Quin, who try to save him in Act Three. Their attempt to fit him into Sara's petticoat is ironically linked with the cataclysmic line about shifts that so drew the ire of the Irish audiences. CHRISTY: "It's Pegeen I'm seeking only, and what'd I care if you brought me a dirft of chosen females, standing in their shifts itself maybe, from this place to the Eastern World" (IV, 167).

Although the image outraged Irishmen by referring to undergarments, it was not outrageous in terms of the action, in which the women were frantically trying to fasten Sara's petticoat around Christy to disguise his appearance. Whereas his former changes of clothing increased his stature, this disguise degrades him. The reference to shifts combined with the Freudian irony of the wielder of the phallic loy clad in petticoats must have at some subliminal level played a part in the violence of the audience's action at the moment. Yet his very degradation is the source of his inherent nobility. The crowning irony is that the phrase made the play and its author famous. With all apparently lost, Christy, like his creator, finally turns on the crowd and asserts his independence.

The growth of Christy's new and more convincing freedom is increasingly apparent throughout the last act, first, in Christy's beating his father once more, which, though it seems degraded to the townspeople, becomes an ennobling act of liberty. Then in defying the short-sighted morality of the townspeople and Pegeen, Christy achieves a final manhood. Metaphor, or language, has finally become one with reality. In escaping from the acceptance of others' images of himself, Christy performs an act of genuine heroism by defying the mob and even his love for Pegeen Mike. She is, after all, not just a member of the mob, but its leader.

Critics and audiences have for years debated the need for the graphic violence of torturing Christy on stage. The answer lies at the heart of this extended discussion of metaphor. Synge drew this celebration of imaginative language to a violent climax in which the reality of Christy's pain is unadorned by description or linguistic distortion. When Pegeen aligns herself with the morality of the town, the church, and an English law supreme over all the rest, she surrenders her individual sense of decency and freedom. Her imagination, her willingness to submit herself to the idea, image, metaphor, of a playboy of the Western world is superseded by her subservient involvement with reality. In a sense, if there is a tragedy, it is Pegeen Mike's in her final recognition that she will never be able to share life with her playboy image. On the other hand, at the end of the play we have only Christy's assurance that he'll "go romancing through a romping lifetime from this hour to the dawning of the judgment day" (IV, 173). The last bit of exaggeration is no more than Christy's final version of himself, and while both Pegeen and the audience tend to believe in the image, in our soberer moments we may indeed be grateful that we don't have to join Christy's romp. If the audience believes this final hyperbole, Synge has been successful in coalescing language and reality.

Despite Christy's heroic defiance of the mob, Pegeen's concluding recognition affirming that the metaphor of the title has become the truth of the play would not have been possible without the two love scenes that inspired her anguish. This is especially true of the second scene, which reaches new rhetorical heights in Act Three. Both Christy and Pegeen are new to the rhetoric of romance. Christy, amazed that this language has the power to generate tenderness, respect, and perhaps even love, pushes his metaphors to greater and greater heights of exaggeration. Pegeen, who is unused to saying anything pleasant about anybody, let alone speaking the language of romance, is surprised at herself: "And to think it's me is talking sweetly, Christy Mahon, and I the fright of seven townlands for my biting tongue" (IV, 151). Her remarks, which counterpoint Christy's exaggeration, offer a quiet assurance of his poetic artistry and his dark romantic nature.

Pegeen begins by teasing that his proposal of marriage is mere rhetoric and that he will leave for some other girl, "when your father's rotten in four months, or five" (IV, 147). The thought that he might be regarded as insincere prompts one of Christy's greatest exaggerations of the play: "It's little you'll think if my love's a poacher's or an earl's itself when you'll feel my two hands stretched around you, and I squeezing kisses on your puckered lips till I'd feel a kind of pity for the Lord God is all ages sitting lonesome in his golden chair" (IV, 147). The hyperbole of Pegeen's kisses inspiring pity for the solitary Almighty himself is comic exaggeration carried to sublimity. It prompts Pegeen's unabashed admiration: "any girl would walk her heart out before she'd meet a young man was your like for eloquence or talk at all" (IV, 147). Encouraged, he conjures up a romantic picture that is just this side of the burlesque in its intensity. "Let you wait to hear me talking till we're astray in Erris when Good Friday's by, drinking a sup from a well, and making mighty kisses with our wetted mouths, or gaming in a gap of sunshine with yourself stretched back unto your necklace in the flowers of the earth" (IV, 149). Her response, "I'd be nice so, is it?" inspires him to blend a dash of ecclesiastical hyperbole with his mixed biblical and epic metaphor: "If the mitred bishops seen you that time, they'd be the like of the holy prophets, I'm thinking, do be straining the bars of Paradise to lay eyes on the Lady Helen of Troy, and she abroad pacing back and forward with a nosegay in her golden shawl" (IV, 149). Christy's worship of the woman with "the light of seven heavens in . . . [her] heart alone" inspires the most abject humility of both Christian and Pagan worship: "If I wasn't a good Christian, it's on my naked knees I'd be saying my prayers and paters to every jack-straw you have roofing your head, and every stony pebble is paving the laneway to your door" (IV, 149). The scene is so overblown in its exuberance as to be intentionally funny. But lest we miss its comic intent, it is juxtaposed against Michael's drunken exaggerations as he interrupts the love scene and compares Christy's sporting prowess with the drinking bout at Kate Cassidy's wake: "you'd never see the match of it for flows of drink, the way when we sunk her bones at noonday in her narrow grave, there were five men, aye, and six men, stretched out retching speechless on the holy stones" (IV, 151).

In his piety Michael proceeds with another biblical metaphor to admonish Christy for not bringing his father's body westward thrown over the back of a Kerry mule, "like holy Joseph in the days gone by, the way we could have given him a decent burial and not have him rotting beyond and not a Christian drinking a smart drop to the glory of his soul" (IV, 153).

The comic element is never far from the linguistic heart of the *Playboy*. It provides vitality to the imagination, and imaginative language is the cause of Christy's romance with Pegeen. The old high way of love, language, is the foreplay of blissful dreams. But its effect is undercut by the earth-bound Pegeen, who has enough imagination to consent to wed Christy but has her roots in the floor of a licensed premises. She is just as quick to condemn and punish a dirty deed as she is to experience romantic ecstasy.

The *Playboy* weaves the primitive reality of comedy into the linguistic wings of imagination. The Mayo townsmen-characters and the audience, who are, after all, their surrogates, may either fly on these wings of language to some higher appreciation of Irish vitality or be revolted by those earthbound realistic aspects of the play that degrade its meaning. They chose the latter when they rioted eighty-one years ago. Those of us in the contemporary audience who are entranced by the play's idioms and identify its fanciful language with reality have missed still another point: that Synge's metaphors and hyperbolic exaggerations have their comic, low side, rooted in a reality as formidable as the loy Christy uses on his father. We are left then, with the magnificent ambiguity of a drama that became the model for those tragic comedies of O'Casey and Behan to follow, with an artistically accurate portrait of a major side of the Irish psyche and with a classic of Western theater.

NOTES

1. The most detailed account of the riots and subsequent trials drawn from newspaper accounts if offered in *The Abbey Theatre: The Years of Synge, 1905–1909*, by Robert Hogan and James Kilroy, pp. 123–62.

There is one significant point that has never been made about the *Playboy* riots and that is that they were caused by a small number of people. When the theater was full (a rare occurrence), it held 562 people, and a full house represented about £ 32 in box office receipts. Here is a list of the receipts for each performance during *Playboy* week:

January 26 (Saturday)	32.14.10£
January 28 (Monday)	5.2.6
Janaury 29 (Tuesday)	12.10.1
January 30 (Wednesday)	24.13.2
January 31 (Thursday)	19.8.1
February 1 (Friday)	22.18.9
February 2 (Saturday matinee)	13.7.3
February 2 (Saturday evening)	29.15.0

From these figures it can be seen that on Monday night there were only about 80 people in the theater, on Tuesday night only about 210 people, and on Wednesday night, a fairly good house, about 420 people. However, a certain, fairly significant proportion of the audience did not engage in the disturbances. From these figures one might conclude that relatively few people can make a loud noise. (144)

2. For a detailed analysis of Synge's language see Kilberd, *Synge and the Irish Language*.

References

Benson, Eugene. *J. M. Synge*. Grove Press Modern Dramatists. 1982. Reprint. New York: Grove, 1983.

Bessai, Diane E. "Little Hound in Mayo: Synge's Playboy and the Comic Tradition in Irish Literature." *Dalhousie Review* 48, no. 3 (1968):372–83.

Bigley, Bruce M. *"The Playboy of the Western World* as Antidrama." *Modern Drama* 20, no. 2 (1977):157–67.

Bliss, Alan J. "The Language of Synge." *J. M. Synge: Centenary Papers, 1971*. Edited by Maurice Harmon. Dublin: Dolmen 1972, pp. 35–62.

Gerstenberger, Donna. *John Millington Synge*. Twayne's English Authors Series 12. New York: Twayne, 1964.

Hirsch, Edward. "The Gallous Story and the Dirty Dead: The Two *Playboys.*" *Modern Drama* 26, no. 1 (1983):85–102.

Hogan, Robert, and James Kilory. *The Abbey Theatre: The Years of Synge, 1905–1909*. The Modern Irish Drama: A Documentary History 3. Dublin: Dolmen; Atlantic Highlands, N.J.: Humanities Press, 1978.

Kain, Richard M. "The *Playboy* Riots." *A Centenary Tribute to John Millington Synge, 1871–1909: Sunshine and the Moon's Delight*. Edited by S. B. Bushrui. New York: Barnes & Noble, 1972, pp. 173–88.

Kiberd, Declan. *Synge and the Irish Language*. Totowa, N.J.: Rowman and Littlefield; London: Macmillan, 1979.

Kilroy, James. "The Playboy as Poet." *Publications of the Modern Language Association of America* 83, no. 2 (1968):439–42.

———. *The 'Playboy' Riots*. The Irish Theatre Series 4. Dublin: Dolman, 1971.

Roll-Hansen, Diderik. *"The Playboy of the Western World—An Irish Peer Gynt?"* *Studies in Anglo-Irish Literature*. Edited by Heinz Kosok. Wuppertaler Schriftenreihe Literatur 19. Bonn: Bouvier, 1982. pp. 155–60.

Sidnell, M. J. "Synge's Playboy and the Champion of Ulster." *Dalhousie Review* 45 (1965):51–59.

Spacks, Patricia Meyer. "The Making of the Playboy." *Modern Drama*, 4, no. 3 (1961):314–23.

Sullivan, Mary Rose. "Synge, Sophocles, and the Un-making of Myth." *Modern Drama* 12, no. 3 (1969): 242–53.

Suss, Irving D. "The 'Playboy' Riots." *Irish Writing* 18 (1952):29–42.

Thornton, Weldon. *J. M. Synge and the Western Mind*. Irish Literary Studies 4. New York: Barnes & Noble, 1979.

Deirdre of the Sorrows

The first problem that faces a reader of *Deirdre of the Sorrows* is the text. When John Millington Synge died in 1909, he was still at work on the manuscript, so what was finally performed at the Abbey Theatre and published by the Cuala Press in 1910 is a version culled from more than a thousand manuscript pages by William Butler Yeats, Lady Gregory, and Molly Allgood. Despite this confusion, Ann Saddlemyer thought that the text we have is almost certainly what Synge himself had arrived at in his ongoing process of revision (IV, xxx), and it must stand as the final version. In his preface to the play, Yeats stated that he and Lady Gregory "thought it better to have the play performed, as it is printed here, with no word of ours" (IV, 179). Whatever the case, it is clear that Synge intended to add more, to enlarge the part of Owen and to strengthen the speeches of Deirdre, but obviously we must deal with what now remains.

It seems that Synge had been fascinated by the Deirdre story for many years, and he could have read original versions of the tale in the *Book of Leinster* and the *Yellow Book of Lecan*, which were both available to him in the library of Trinity College, Dublin. He had published his own translation in 1898. He was enthusiastic about Lady Gregory's adaptation in *Cuchulain of Muirthemne*, published in 1902, but it was not until late 1907 that he began writing in earnest on the new theme. In some ways, he envisioned the play as a vehicle for Molly Allgood, to whom he would become engaged, and he wrote to her in November of that year: "You mustn't mind my letters being a little dry these times, because I am pouring out my heart to you in Deirdre the whole day long" (Saddlemyer, *Letters to Molly* 214).

Synge decided that the new play was to be written in prose, but just what kind of prose was the initial problem. He was determined to turn away from peasant drama, with the lyrical and poetic flights of language he had created in a play like *The Playboy of the Western World*, since the heroic world of Deirdre and the sons of Usna demanded something different. Above all, he wanted to be realistic, to avoid the artificial rhetoric that was associated in the public mind with the giants of the sagas, and to get to the heart of real motives in real language. "Is the drama—as a beautiful thing a lost art?" he asked. "The drama of swords is" (IV, 394). If it were impossible to know what individuals in the far distant past could conceivably be like, it would be necessary to bring these individuals into the present.

Paradoxically, although *Deirdre* is certainly not another peasant drama, the characters in the play often do sound more like Irish peasants than fabled kings and queens. When Lavarcham complains about the unruly behavior of her charge, the young Deirdre, Conchubor cautions: "Let you not be talking too far and you old itself," and the serving woman replies: "I'm after telling her one time and another but I'd do as well speaking to a lamb of ten weeks and it racing the hills" (IV, 189). For Synge, this is modern language. He saw the play as an experiment, and since what he called "the drama of swords" had no place in the modern world, he transformed his royal characters into beings who speak and who are motivated in ways that would be familiar to a contemporary audience. None of the characters was meant to appear as a refugee from an idyllic and aristocratic past.

Consequently, along with an idiom that was deemed more acceptable, Synge was quick to insert into the play what he had earlier identified as a Rabelaisian note. In Act One, for instance, after Conchubor has departed and Deirdre offstage has begun to dress in the garments befitting a queen, the Old Woman peeps into the room and immediately whispers to Lavarcham: "She's thrown off the rags she had about her, and there she is in her skin putting her hair in shiny twists" (IV, 201). She is earlier described as "running out and in with mud and grasses on her feet" (IV, 187). Perhaps the Dublin audience was growing accustomed to the directness of the modern stage (whereas Irish girls in their shifts in *The Playboy of the Western World* caused a riot in the Abbey, Deirdre in her skin did not), but Synge is not sparing in his fairly graphic depiction of human behavior. Indeed, when Naisi and his brothers burst out of the storm into Lavarcham's cottage, they almost seem initially to be a band of brigands intent upon pillage and rape: "there are nights when a king like Conchubor would spit upon his arm ring and queens will stick their tongues out at the rising moon. We're that way this night, and it's not wine we're asking only. . . . Where is the young girl told us we might shelter here?" (IV, 205).

Synge had no intention of shocking the viewer, but he wanted to encompass the full spectrum of passion and emotion. He had to bring the reality of the characters home to his audience, to establish an immediacy that would be vital. Deirdre's recollection of lovemaking, poetic though it is, is somewhat blunt in much the same way: "It's a long time we've had, pressing the lips together, going up and down, resting in our arms, Naisi, waking with the smell of June in the tops of the grasses, and listening to the birds in the branches that are highest" (IV, 231). Consciously or not, Synge is returning to the early realism that informed the relationship of Queen Maeve and Aillil in the *Tain*, a directness that most of the Celtic Revivalists like Lady Gregory did their best to ignore or transcend.

Critical controversy continues over the basic question of whether or not the play can finally be seen as successful. John Rees Moore said that the characters give "full resonance to the mingled sweetness and sorrow of true ecstasy" (94), and Donna Gerstenberger commented that what we have is a triumph: "Synge has created a moving drama out of heroic stuff, without dishonor to his own beliefs" (99). Robin Skelton took a much dimmer view, concluding that "unfortunately the play remains narrative rather than drama for much of its length" (139), and more recently, Nicholas Grene found that *Deirdre of the Sorrows* is an out and out failure (182). Countering, yet another critic went so far as to call this the best of Synge's dramas: "The result is his achieving here a classic simplicity and tranquility of effect that the other plays lack" (Thornton 144).

Synge was well aware of the problems that he faced with the Deirdre story, that the tale had already appeared in many other versions such as those by AE (George Russell) and William Butler Yeats and that the ultimate fate of Deirdre and Naisi was well known and even preordained by the prophecy. Yet Synge wanted to approach the narrative from a different perspective, to investigate basic human motivation that could provide a new dimension to a story that had been too much bathed in the glow of a Celtic twilight. To accomplish this, even with the prophecy of doom hanging over the ill-fated lovers, it is the concept of *choice* that is the prime factor in the unfolding of the plot. As Synge wrote to Lady Gregory two months before he died: "I have done a great deal to Deirdre since I saw you—chiefly in the way of strengthening motives . . . and recasting the general scenario" (IV, xxix). What will happen will happen not because of an ancient curse but because Deirdre and Naisi, together, will decide what their lives' outcomes must be. In each of the three acts, they will come to a crossroads, and at each of these moments they will chart their courses for themselves.

Thus in Act One, the lovers' flight to Alban is not an impetuous rush into the arms of passion solely, but rather it is something they discuss, albeit briefly, and something they believe is the only action possible. Deirdre contemplates the consequences of escape with Naisi from the impending marriage with Conchubor: "It should be a sweet thing to have what is best and richest if it's for a short space only" (IV, 209) before finally arriving at a thought-out position: "wouldn't we do well paying, Naisi, with silence, and a near death? . . . I'm in little dread of death. . . . Isn't it a small thing is foretold about the ruin of ourselves, Naisi, when all men have age coming and great ruin in the end?" (IV, 211) Yet she is not thinking only of herself, and she throws the question back to her lover: "Won't I be in great dread to bring you destruction, Naisi, and you so happy and young?'' (IV, 211) It is the man in love with her who agrees knowingly, as if there were nothing left to discuss: ''Are you thinking I'd go on living after this night, Deirdre, and you with Conchubor in Emain?'' (IV, 211)

What is significant here is the conversation that takes place between the lovers and the conclusion that they are able to reach in concert. Neither overpowers the other. When Lavarcham asks if they are aware of just what it is they are doing—''Are you choosing this night to destroy the world?'' (IV, 213)—the answer is obvious. The prophecy has no force in the face of a natural and inevitable desire to love, as Lavarcham herself realizes: ''isn't [it] a hard thing you're doing, but who can help it? Birds go mating in the spring of the year, and ewes at the leaves falling, but a young girl must have her lover in all the courses of the sun and moon'' (IV, 213). The natural way of the world must take precedence over curse, prophecy, or law.

Act Two once again presents a decision that is arrived at in communion. Publicly, Deirdre responds to Conchubor's supposedly friendly overtures to return to Emain as a dutiful wife should. When Owen tempts her with the prospect of Naisi's growing old and unattractive she answers: ''I will go where Naisi chooses'' (IV, 223); when Fergus implies that the lovers may grow tired of each other, living in squalor without the honors and comfort of a noble life, she replies again: ''I leave the choice to Naisi'' (IV, 227). Yet the problem of how to respond to the invitation is to be decided together by the lovers. At first, Naisi refuses to return, but he is swayed by Deirdre's realization that they cannot remain in a blissful Eden forever, since time will inevitably change the love they have had. To return, whatever the consequences, is not in actuality a submission or a defeat, but it is rather a triumph. Deirdre recognizes and accepts reality:

There are as many ways to wither love as there are stars in a night of Samhain, but there is no way to keep life or love with it a short space only. . . . We're seven years without roughness or growing weary, seven years so sweet and shining, the gods would be hard set to give us seven days the like of them. (IV, 233)

To state that ''it is Deirdre who decides to return and for reasons which are too psychological and interiorized . . . to give dramatic momentum and life to the act'' (Benson, 141) is to pay little heed to what she actually says. Her feelings are clear: ''isn't it a better thing to be following on to a near death, than to be bending the head down, and dragging with the feet, and seeing one day, a blight showing upon love where it is sweet and tender?'' (IV, 231–32). As Robin Skelton noted: ''Deirdre, unlike her sisters in drama, is not possessed by rage against mortality; she accepts that the price to be paid for youth's splendor is its passing, and she triumphs in evading the miseries of age'' (139). There are several factors involved in the situation, and she tells Ardan that perhaps she does not wish to grow old, perhaps she would prefer a quick and a glorious death to a mundane life, and perhaps she also is simply sick to the heart with loneliness for Ireland.

The psychological complexity of their decision to return cannot be, and should not be, easily glossed over. To her, all three are equally valid reasons, and they are completely convincing to Naisi: "We'll go surely, in place of keeping a watch on a love had no match and it wasting away" (IV, 233). His pronouncement to his brothers again places the emphasis on a clear and rational decision, a *choice*: "I and Deirdre have chosen, we will go back with Fergus" (IV, 235) (Nicholas Grene would not agree: "The essence of the situation is that Deirdre and Naisi leave Alban because their heroic destiny demands it, not primarily for any internal emotional reasons" [180].)

There has been further discussion concerning the decision of the couple to leave that concerns the nature of the relationship Deirdre and Naisi have had together. Since Synge tells us virtually nothing about what the lovers have been doing for seven years, several critics have assumed recently that the supposed idyllic quality of their exile has in fact been an unrealistic attempt at playing house. Mary C. King thought that "Alban threatens, for Synge, to become a utopian dream turned dramatist's nightmare. In the woods Naisi and Deirdre do nothing because few, if any, opportunities are open to them for meaningful human activity" (186). Nicholas Grene concluded that "the result of this lack of event in the life in Alban is to make the love of Deirdre and Naisi to some extent unreal. After seven years it is still the lyrical romantic feeling which is appropriately expressed in images of natural beauty. It cannot be seen to have developed into a mature sexual relationship" (177). But it is exactly in these "images of natural beauty" that Synge describes a life in Alban that is as realistic as it is mature and fulfilling.

Certainly, Deirdre and Naisi have not been involved in commerce or in the building of roads and sanitary systems, and they have not made visits to a marriage counsellor. Their exile has provided them with time to grow with each other, to become one with the natural order, as their marriage vow declared: "May the air bless you, and water and the wind, the sea, and all the hours of the sun and moon" (IV, 215). For Synge, nothing could be more realistic than Deirdre's recollection of their days together:

fine nights, watching the heifers walking to the haggard with long shadows on the grass [*with a thickening in her voice*], or the time I've been stretched in the sunshine when I've heard Ainnle and Ardan stepping lightly, and they saying, "Was there ever the like of Deirdre for a happy and a sleepy queen?" (IV, 219)

It is the "*thickening in her voice*" in the stage direction that gives significance to the emotion she feels and that underlines what the time in Alban has meant to her.

There is nothing trivial or unrealistic about such a declaration for a dramatist who could write to Molly Allgood: "Little Heart you dont know how much feeling I have for you. You are like my child, and my little wife, and my good angel, and my greatest friend, all in one! I dont believe there has been a woman in Ireland loved the way I love for you a thousand years" (Saddlemyer, *Letters to Molly* 225). Both Deirdre and Naisi know full well what it is they are leaving and what they will face in the days to come: "Woods of Cuan, woods of Cuan. . . . It's seven years we've had a life was joy only and this day we're going west" (IV, 239). The poignancy, the tragedy, of what is to come is made all the stronger by the validity of their relationship in Alban. Ann Saddlemyer stressed the importance of such natural existence for Synge: "The individual, he believed, could not achieve wholeness in himself until he was in harmony with nature and had attempted a wholeness within the entire cycle of experience" ("Deirdre," 91). She added: "Long before he had begun to write, Deirdre's lament at leaving Alban was part of his own experience" ("Deirdre," 93).

Despite the fact that in the third act it seems inevitable that Deirdre and Naisi must die, there is still one more choice left to make, and that decision concerns the manner of their deaths. Synge provided an ironic moment of hope, when it seems possible that the lovers may be reconciled with Conchubor, but that fleeting chance is dashed when battle is joined outside the tent between Naisi's brothers and Conchubor's mercenaries. Their end is clear. Moments earlier, confronted with the open grave that has been dug for them, Deirdre had behaved humanly and considered flight: "Take me away. . . . Take me to hide in the rocks, for the night is coming quickly" (IV, 249). But Naisi cannot desert Ainnle and Ardan, as Deirdre soon realizes and accepts, and she seems to acknowledge the rightness of Naisi's words: "It's a hard thing surely we've lost those days forever, and yet it's a good thing maybe that all goes quick" (IV, 249). It is the quickness of the resolution of their fates that is paramount to them both. Once again, Synge makes sure that his drama will be played out on a human level, rather than in an airy world of noble kings and queens—Deirdre and Naisi suddenly become jealous of each other, wondering if one of them will take a new lover if either should survive. Naisi comments wryly: "There's nothing surely the like of a new grave of open earth for putting a great space between two friends that love" (IV 251), but we should note that "love" remains in the present tense. They may quarrel, but they are not sundered, and Deirdre, at least momentarily, heals the breach: "If there isn't maybe it's that grave when it's closed will make us one forever, and we two lovers have had a great space without weariness or growing old or any sadness of the mind" (IV, 251).

Perhaps the most controversial moment of the play occurs when the battle has begun, and Deirdre, in a moment of panic, once again beseeches Naisi to escape with her. Torn between love and honor, love for Deirdre and his duty to his brothers, Naisi's heartfelt cry is the only one he could possibly make: "Do not hold me from my brothers. . . . I cannot leave my brothers when it is I who have defied the king" (IV, 255). She cannot come with him into the fray, and certainly, they could not continue to live as dishonored fugitives. Faced with what must be, Deirdre sends him off with a seeming coldness: "Go to your brothers. . . . For seven years you have been kindly, but the hardness of death has come between us" (IV, 255). "I'm well pleased there's no one this place to make a story that Naisi was a laughing-stock the night he died'' (IV, 257). Dumbfounded, Naisi does not understand her intent, and he can only bitterly reply: ''[*looking at her aghast*] And you'll have me meet death with a hard word from your lips in my ear?'' (IV, 255)

Deirdre's words have called down a storm of critical condemnation upon her head, mainly because her intentions have been misunderstood. ''Deirdre, in brutal language, goes on to denounce their seven years in Alban as 'a dream' and demands his death'' (Benson 144). Insensitive, she now cares for no one but herself: ''Synge's presentation focuses not so much on Deirdre's fate or on any all-compelling love for Naisi that she feels, but on her self-centered wish to be free of the old king'' (Thornton 148). She will make a myth of her own misfortune: ''It makes her a prisoner of her own ego. It leads her to be both ruthless and self-centered. It turns her into a heroine who sees her life's only justification to be its tragic pattern, and the poetry of lamentation that can be made from it'' (Skelton 150). Again: ''This act of Deirdre's is the epitome of her hypertrophied romanticism, for in her toying with Naisi, there is a perverse wish to bring to the most poignant pitch possible the end of their lives together'' (Thornton 152). To conclude: ''She may be a heroic and magnificent creature, but she is finally a predator, a monster'' (Skelton 146). The virulence of these diatribes is only matched by their wrongheadedness.

In actuality, however, it seems possible that it is Deirdre's love for Naisi that causes her to act in this way. Realizing that Naisi is torn between two courses of action, in essence she forces him to do what he knows is right, allowing him to retain his dignity and nobility in the face of death. Rather than acting irrationally or egotistically, she knows exactly what she is doing: ''It was my words without pity gave Naisi a death will have no match until the ends of life and time'' (IV 257). She is thinking of him, and not of herself, when she sends him out into the battle, and in this way she puts his needs before her own. She retains her own sense of heroic dignity, but this does not mean that she is concerned solely with herself. Instead of celebrating her status as a tragic figure, she is conscious mainly of their loss: ''Little moon, little moon of Alban, it's lonesome you'll be this night, and long nights after, and you pacing the woods beyond Glen Laid, looking every place for Deirdre and Naisi, the two lovers who slept so sweetly with each other'' (IV, 267).

Synge was careful that the ending of *Deirdre* would maintain his emphasis on the emotional realism of his characters, and thus, although aware of her own stature, Deirdre is not intent upon making of herself a myth. History would do that for her. The center of the play remains the fact that, despite the prophecy, the love and the lives of Deirdre and Naisi cannot be preserved on this earth. The spectre of old age stares them in the face, but it is not simply the fear of growing old that is the cause of the tragedy. They have played out the string. Lavarcham had laid this temporal pitfall of pride to reset in the second act: ''I tell you there's little hurt getting old, though young girls and poets do be storming at the shapes of age'' (IV, 219). By Act Three Deirdre is no longer a young girl, and she cannot be tempted by Lavarcham's well-meant intention to turn her mistress into some sort of romantic icon: "If it's keening you'd be come till I find you a sunny place where you'll be a great wonder they'll call the queen of sorrows, and you'll begin taking a pride to be sitting up pausing and dreaming when the summer comes" (IV 261). Deirdre will have none of it.

What raises the status of Deirdre and Naisi in the end is that they were not victims. They did what they had to do: "It was the choice of lives we had in the clear woods, and in the grave we're safe surely" (IV, 267, 269), and again Synge underlines the mutuality of their *choice*. They did the choosing together, and their story remains as Synge's tribute to the world well lost for love. In many ways, Deirdre's suicide is a celebration, rather than a way out. As she says: "It was sorrows were foretold, but great joys were my share always" IV, 269). As she proclaims in her last words, disaster has fallen upon the lovers, upon Emain and upon Ireland; yet what has happened is: "a thing will be a joy and triumph to [the] ends of life and time" (IV, 269), recalling her earlier words to Naisi. The tale of Deirdre and Naisi, in Synge's rendering, is thus a celebration of an indomitable human spirit that will preserve itself in the face of any obstacles conceivable. Synge noted that "it is impossible to use our own language or feeling with perfect sincerity for personages we know to have been different from ourselves" (IV, 393), but he breached the gap with Deirdre and Naisi and made them our own. He saw with regret that there was little beauty in the contemporary world, and no doubt he realized that his marriage to Molly Allgood would never come to pass, but he was not daunted. *Deirdre of the Sorrows* is Synge's final stay against imminent confusion, and it is a substantiation of his belief that beauty and truth can still be encompassed in art: "there is always the poet's dream which makes itself a sort of world" (IV, 394).

References

Benson, Eugene. *J. M. Synge*. Grove Press Modern Dramatists. 1982. Reprint. New York: Grove, 1983.

Gerstenberger, Donna. *John Millington Synge*. Twayne's English Authors Series 12. New York: Twayne, 1964.

Grene, Nicholas. *Synge: A Critical Study of the Plays*. London: Macmillan 1975.

King, Mary C. *The Drama of J. M. Synge*. Irish Studies. Syracuse: Syracuse University Press, 1985.

Moore, John Rees. "Synge's *Deirdre* and the Sorrows of Mortality." *A Centenary Tribute to John Millington Synge, 1871–1909: Sunshine and the Moon's Delight*. Edited by S. B. Bushrui. New York: Barnes & Noble, 1972. pp. 91–105.

Saddlemyer, Ann. "Deirdre of the Sorrows: Literature First. . . . Drama Afterwards." *J. M. Synge: Centenary Papers 1971*. Edited by Maurice Harmon. Dublin: Dolmen, 1972. pp. 88–107.

———, ed. *Letters to Molly: John Millington Synge to Maire O'Neill, 1906–1909*. Cambridge: Belknap of Harvard University Press, 1971.

Skelton, Robin. *The Writings of J. M. Synge.* Indianapolis and New York: Bobbs-Merrill, 1971.

Thornton, Weldon. *J. M. Synge and the Western Mind.* Irish Literary Studies 4. New York: Barnes & Noble, 1979.

Additional Sources

Fackler, Herbert V. *That Tragic Queen: The Deirdre Legend in Anglo-Irish Literature.* Salzburg Studies in English Literature. Salzburg: University of Salzburg, 1978.

Johnson, Toni O'Brien. *Synge: The Medieval and the Grotesque.* Gerrards Cross: Colin Smythe; Totowa, N.J.: Barnes & Noble, 1982.

Price, Alan. *Synge and Anglo-Irish Drama.* London: Methuen, 1961.

Synge's Poems

Synge's poems, which were few and, with the exception of "Glencullen" (published in an undergraduate magazine), were unpublished at the time of his death, will not attract much critical attention, nor will they ever become central to the study of the Irish Renaissance, modernism, or even Synge's plays. They occupy the place in the Synge canon held by *Chamber Music* or even *Giacomo Joyce* in the Joyce canon. In the Oxford edition of the *Collected Works* they occupy sixty-three pages, two-thirds of which were not chosen by Synge for publication in the Cuala Press edition in the year of his death.

Assessments of Synge's poetry are generally negative (Alan Price and Robin Skelton are the two major exceptions). In 1952 Donald Davie, speaking of Synge's poems and translations, noted that no one "makes any claims of great importance of this part of Synge's work. It is of great historical importance, as a sort of challenge and manifesto" (32). T. R. Henn's "J. M. Synge: A Reconsideration" sets forth in brief the moderate reading of Synge's poems:

Synge was at best a very minor poet. Much of his work is influenced by Wordsworth, both in technique, subject, spirit; and it is suffused with a Wordsworthian melancholy that often becomes morbid. Out of the mass of the poems we might pause on three or four ballad-like pieces, notable for a fierce energy, written in conformity with his theory set out in the *Preface*. It is a challenge to Victorian sentimentality, a plea for a return to realism, even brutality. (*Last Essays* 192–93)

The Synge biographers, David H. Greene and Edward M. Stephens, called Synge's poetry "derivative" and "sentimental" (50) and the technique unimpressive (59); Synge filled notebooks with "fragments of verse, but passages of criticism indicate that he was a much better critic than creator" (100). The poetry Synge was writing in 1902 was "quite as undistinguished as his previous verse" (102). Finally, at the end of their biography, they worked up a qualified point of praise that has since been echoed by Robin Skelton:

With their "unpoetic" language, their naiveté of form, Synge's poems resemble the work of an uneducated man and thus reveal their origin in his observations of Irish peasant life rather than in literary sources. They make an unusual contrast to the delicate lyrics of Joyce's *Chamber Music*, James Stephen's *Insurrections* and Yeats' *The Green Helmet*, all written in the same period. One is inclined to feel that they are at least uniquely different from the work of his contemporaries. (290)

Similarly, Henn, in his edition of *The Plays and Poems of J. M. Synge*, concluded that the poems generally break down "by sheer failure of technique." Henn seemed to find that sometimes the "rhythms are authentic and the words come alive" and that Synge can be "genuine" but clumsy. "The achievement of the Poems, then, is slight. . . . They are valuable for the light they throw on Synge's personality, and on the plays; as well as for some rough vigorous balladry" (278). Price thought that although it "cannot be maintained that Synge's poems and translations are of high merit, yet they, together with his observations on poetry, have a certain historical importance, and some of his poems remain intrinsically valuable. Synge's verse is also interesting as a supplement to his other work, and to our impression of the man" (107). Skelton noted that the poems lack "the thematic richness and profundity of his mature drama. Nevertheless they take up themes and attitudes which are present in his other work and tackle them from a different point of view, and his thoughts about poetry are as interesting and seminal as his thoughts on other matters" (153). Francis Warner found that "Synge was a fine dramatist who was not a good poet. . . . The verses were not vehicles for deep thought so much as occasional fancy. We read them as an act of homage to the man, but turn to the plays to appreciate his genius" (151).

There is equivocation and disappointment in these assessments. In part, this is because of the continuous presence of Yeats in connection with Synge's poetry: Yeats as literary executor, editor, writer of prefaces and reassessments, mythologizer of Synge, and, most devastatingly for Synge's poetic reputation, a contemporaneous poet of far greater achievement. An additional problem is found in the two prefaces to the poems, one by Yeats and one by Synge. Yeats noted that the misfortune of Synge's death is for the living "and not for the dead that having cast off the ailing body is now as I believe, all passionate and fiery, an heroical thing" (I, xxx). Yeats quoted Synge's letter in which Synge explained how unsure he was of the quality of the poems ("yet enough of myself has gone into them to make me sorry to destroy them" (I, xxxi) and that the translations from Petrarch might be put in the book "to make it a little less thin" (I, xxxi).

Yeats ended his Preface by portraying Synge as "all folded up in brooding intellect, knowing nothing of new books and newspapers, reading the great masters alone" (I, xxxv), a peculiar remark considering Synge's reviewing and Abbey Theatre activities.

Synge's Preface, only one page long and following Yeats's remarks, is similarly problematic: "In these days poetry is usually a flower of evil or good, but it is the timber of poetry that wears most surely, and there is no timber that has not strong roots among the clay and the worms. . . . It may almost be said that before verse can be human again it must learn to be brutal" (I, xxxvi). Synge remarked that most of the poems were written "before the views just stated, with which they have little to do, had come into my head." The phrase "flower of evil" has perhaps been responsible for some commentators' searching for the Baudelairean Synge; others found a naturalistic Synge and sought out clay, worm, brutality, as positive virtues in themselves. Thus in Robert Farren's popular introduction to Irish poetry, he admired Synge's roughness, violence, "medieval bite and *danse macabre*," which he thought would have been acceptable to Gaelic poets, even if they were not acceptable to the effete poetic set of Synge's time: "[Synge's] sort of ballad was to those of Allingham and Yeats what an all-in wrestler is to a ballerina. *They* had favoured refined lamentations, allegorical lilts of The Silk of the Kine; but Synge's were more like jute bags stuffed with clayey spuds: murderous action-ballads all about men, and not the one half of a dreamy eye among them" (125). More traditional academic critics have attempted to make the brutal into an aesthetic notion by explaining it epistemologically or psychologically. According to Donald Davie, for example, Synge "proposes this brutality in poetry only as a temporary expedient. He wants to shock the inhumanly exalted poetry of his time by writing poems of all too human degradation; but only in hopes that between the two extremes poetry may come to rest in a central area of human interest and compassion" (38). It was this brutality, Davie concluded, that makes Synge's poetry modern. Alternately, "brutality" may be related to technique and diction. In the only paragraph devoted to Synge in his *A History of Modern Poetry*, David Perkins referred to the Preface by Synge and remarked that "he portrayed the life and imagination of the folk, and in doing so, Synge achieved a powerful coarsening of image, diction, and rhythm, as in 'Danny' " (260–61). Vivian de Sola Pinto, whose overview of poetry from 1880 to 1940 also found space for only one paragraph on Synge, quoted the same lines from the Preface and declared that Synge's poems are "expressions of brutal facts in language of savage simplicity, which is transformed into poetry by the intensity of his passion" (98–99).

Many believe that Synge's importance as a poet is dependent upon his presumed influence on Yeats's poetry, arguing that Synge's brutal and sensual lead was responsible for the changes in Yeats's work after 1910. Skelton read many Synge poems, such as "Patch-Shaneen" and "Danny," as criticisms of early Yeats, such as "Father Gilligan," "The Foxhunter," and "Moll Magee." "It is extraordinary," wrote Skelton, "how much all the poems that Yeats had first printed after September 1908 and that appeared in *The Green Helmet* of 1910 differ from the poems printed before this date'' (165–66). Price found the same profound influence, claiming that Synge had developed his ''new and startling'' aesthetic and poetry that ''is tough, seemingly casual, yet precise; marked by conversational rhythms, colloquial wording, and a feeling for the concrete in word and object'' (116); Price concluded, then, that ''Synge may be no more than a minor poet, but he is one of those minors who have played a part in the major changes of poetry'' (117). Price believed that in 1908–1909, before encountering Synge's poetry, Yeats ''had hardly begun to loosen his allegiance to the Pre-Raphaelites.''

These ''proofs'' do not seem very convincing. I can find no evidence in the letters or elsewhere to indicate that Synge had Yeats's poems in mind when he wrote his own poems, and certainly Yeats, who championed Synge's poetry in essays, the preface, and in his selection for the *Oxford Book of Modern Verse*, did not respond to Synge's poetry as a challenge to his own. It is improbable to find the change in Yeats's poetry, which, after all, was continually changing, in any one cause. Synge's manuscript of poems, sent with his insecure letter asking for Yeats's opinion, followed by Synge's contradictory Preface, probably had much less of influence on Yeats at that time than Ezra Pound's comments, Yeats's bitter experiences with the Abbey Theatre and its ''mobs,'' the marriage of Maud Gonne, and so on. Much more balanced and convincing are Henn's assessments, which emphasize the background, influences, and opinions shared by Yeats and Synge (*Lonely Tower*, ''Yeats and Synge''; *Plays and Poems of J. M. Synge*, Appendix B; see also Gerstenberger 120–21).

Synge read widely in many languages and picked up influences and ideas everywhere, and these things enter into his poetry. In a sense, his small corpus of poetry lacks a unified voice or style because of his eclectic experimenting. Synge claimed as his tradition in poetry Villon, Herrick, and Burns. Skelton added to this: ''He might equally well have looked back to Ben Jonson, John Skelton, or, perhaps most of all, Dunbar'' (169). Everyone agrees on the influence of Wordsworth, his favorite poet, on Synge's earliest poetry (Saddlemyer, ''In Search of'' 185; Gerstenberger 109), but in addition we find echoes of, or claims for, many others: Goethe, Lessing, Schiller, Heine, Ibsen, Maeterlinck, Wilde, Flaubert, Pater, Huysmans, Borrow, Pierre Loti, Lafcadio Hearn, Ronsard, Petrarch, Baudelaire (see Saddlemyer, ''In Search of'' 188–89). This too-long list of possible influences leaves out Gaelic poetry, anonymous ballads and stories, and autobiographical incidents. Greene and Stephens pointed out that Synge's experiences in Kerry were directly behind ''Beg-Innish,'' ''On an Island,'' and ''The Mergency Man,'' among others. '' 'In Kerry' is an interesting example of how [Synge] was able to transform an unsuccessful love lyric by endowing it with a grotesque element he had heard in Kerry'' (144–45). The sequence ''Vita Vecchia'' is based on Synge's affair with Cherry Matheson, and other poems are based on conversations with Molly Allgood (usually about his death and funeral). Given such an array of sources for his poems, it seems most fruitful to consider the poems primarily as private experiments imitating different modes, trying out techniques, taking on various personas, exploring distance and language (this is the only way to read some of the poems and translations with any engagement).

Critical discussion of techniques and devices in Synge's poetry has been fairly limited. Skelton found dichotomies and balance everywhere: "balance of literary with vernacular diction," "counterpointing informal thought with formal manners of speech," "balance of passion and mortality," "balance of explicit and implicit, factual and fanciful, simplicity and sophistication." "Life and death, birth and decay are often in balance here" (155–61). Whereas Skelton found balance, other critics found juxtaposition without purpose. Henn wrote of "improbable Skeltonesque conjunctions" (*The Plays and Poems* 275), and juxtaposition of incongruous subject matter or diction is one of Synge's most obvious structural elements, especially in poems such as "To the Oaks of Glencree" and "Dread" (see Warner 145; Price 110; Gerstenberger 112). Even Skelton momentarily dropped the notion of harmonious balance by noting the "violent juxtaposition of literary with colloquial language" (163). A milder concomitant to this may be seen in the traditional hyperbole and contrast in the love poems (Warner 147; Skelton 160).

Donald Davie noted that Synge wanted to avoid traditional poetic diction "so he uses common or ugly words like 'skinny,' 'ditch,' 'poach,' 'bitch' . . . in doing this, Synge is not, as he seems to think, avoiding poetic diction altogether, but only substituting one sort of diction for another" (35). Synge's use of "vulgar colloquialism" (Skelton 162) is commonly related to his humor, the notion of the "brutal" stated in the Preface, and in the grotesque. Humor in Synge's poetry has been pointed out mainly as coincidental with the humor in his plays. As usual with criticism of modern poets such as Eliot, humor in Synge's poetry does not receive extended analysis and critical vocabulary is very limited. Henn wrote of the "rough humorous incongruity (*The Plays and Poems* 275; see also Greene and Stephens 287; Skelton 160–61; Warner 144).

Synge and the grotesque, until recently, did not receive very much attention; it was usually noted in connection with a juxtaposition of death and the sensuous, images of decay in the love poems, and poems about Synge's own death or illnesses (one of them, quoted in Greene and Stephens 287—"I'll write a masque of liver, kidneys and the spleen"—is inexplicably missing from Skelton's edition of the poems in the *Collected Works*). These pieces, together with the violent poems such as "Danny" and "The Mergency Man," are Synge's most individual and memorable poems. Greene and Stephens wanted to dissociate Synge from Baudelaire and French symbolist or Decadent influences and so claimed that "critics who are tempted to see the influence of Baudelaire in this identification of sex and anatomy of death are wrong. It came to him out of the mouths of Kerry peasants" (145). But being influenced by Decadent authors does not preclude influence by Gaelic grotesque devices; certainly, the reader of "Étude Morbide," "On a Train to Paris," and "Under Ether" in Synge's *Prose* (II) will find the French Decadent and symbolist influence clearly present. The fullest discussions of the grotesque and language devices from the Gaelic that are used by Synge are found in Declan Kiberd's 1979 study *Synge and the Irish Language*; Synge's attraction to the grotesque in medieval literary sources is the subject of Toni O'Brien Johnson's *Synge: The Medieval and the Grotesque* (1982). All of this, however, is poor counter to the argument of Warner and Henn that in much of the poetry the execution of the devices and techniques are clumsy, "slack," forced, and laborious (see Henn, *The Plays and Poems* 274–76).

It is not surprising, in dealing with such a small group of poems, that there is general agreement about Synge's themes and subjects. All of the critics noted the dominance of the theme of death and time passing. Henn found that most of the poems "are concerned with a sick man's vision of his own death" (*The Plays and Poems* 274), and Gerstenberger recognized again and again "essentially the same theme: the ephemeral nature of man's life, the same presence and triumph of death, and man's inability to mitigate the absolute victory of death" (111–12; see also Price 109–10). Skelton located the major themes in the passing of time, the notion of tradition, the "inheritance of the past by the fleeting present," and brutality (Skelton 156, 163, 164; brutality is also considered a theme by Davie 36; Greene and Stephens 174). Warner's list of themes in Synge's poems includes the contrast between love and death, drinking, dancing and conviviality, "aloneness," and the Wordsworthian pastoral (146). Gerstenberger pointed out the use of the local and the rejection of traditional Irish material "in favor of immediate reality" (114, 117).

Only a handful of poems have attracted any extensive commentary. "To the Oaks of Glencree" (I, 47) is often used to illustrate both juxtaposition and contrast and the grotesque. The first stanza with the speaker addressing the oak tree that he physically embraces (predictable lark singing above) is reminiscent of the early nature poems like "A Mountain Creed" and "The Creed." In the second stanza, the speaker thinks of his death and the time when the wood of the oak will be used for his casket. The banality of the first stanza is meant to be offset by the shock of the second, but the clumsiness of the first and third lines of the second stanza interferes with this effect:

> There'll come a season when you'll stretch
> Black boards to cover me:
> Then in Mount Jerome I will lie, poor wretch,
> With worms eternally. (I, 47)

The "poor wretch" of line 3 sounds either self-pitying or there only for the sake of the rhyme, and the double contraction ("There'll," "you'll") in line 1 seems designed only for the meter. Its faults are shared by the stilted short lines of "In May," one of the later poems, according to Skelton (dated 1907):

> In a nook
> That opened south,

You and I
Lay mouth to mouth. (I, 53)

This is unlikely to have caused Yeats any professional envy. "The Curse: To a sister of an enemy of the author's who disapproved of 'The Playboy,' " on the other hand, is like the Yeats of the angry middle period, with an ending reminiscent of the signature and rhyme of Leopold Bloom's poem in *Ulysses* ("*If you so condescend / Then please place at the end / The name of yours truly, L. Bloom*" 678). The poem begins: "Lord, confound this surly sister, / Blight her brow with blotch and blister, / Cramp her larynx, lung, and liver, / In her guts a galling give her" and ends "And I'm your servant, J. M. Synge." (I, 49). This is humorous, though quickly tiresome, and not innovative; both Yeats and Synge were certainly familiar with flyting poems, which is why, no doubt, Robin Skelton is reminded of Dunbar and Skelton.

There seem to be four poems about which there is a positive critical consensus. "Queens" (I, 34) has the speaker and his companion having spent a week naming all of the queens from mythology (Greek and Gaelic), literature (Ronsard and Villon), queens of the Bible, the murderous, the admired, and the vermin-ridden, and those who are queens only metaphorically; the speaker declares that all of these queens of the past are now dead and rotten, but his companion is alive in the sunsine, "so you're the Queen / Of all are living, or have been." This is well-realized and, at twenty-six lines, one of the longest poems, with a sense of logic such as that of Donne's "The Flea." "The Passing of the Shee" (I, 38) will always attract Synge commentators since it presents such a clear rejection of the Celtic twilight use of language and traditional Irish imagery (even in the spelling of the Celtic twilight *Sidhe* as "Shee"). The disgust for the more ethereal and high-toned is compelling, following the subtitle "After looking at one of A.E.'s pictures":

Adieu, sweet Angus, Maeve and Fand,
Ye plumed yet skinny Shee,
That poets played with hand in hand
To learn their ecstasy.

Instead, "We'll search in Red Dan Sally's ditch." But the two poems that seem to stand highest in Synge's canon are "The Mergency Man" (I, 58) and "Danny" (I, 56), both apparently late poems. They both use colloquial diction, deal with the local, use traditional forms. "Danny" in particular is used as the main example of the "brutal" with which Synge's poems are most identified. It is in ballad form with ten quatrains about a group of men (twenty-nine) who beat a man to death for some minor fighting and sexual immorality. The poem has much more gusto than any of Synge's love poems and the ballad form seems well-adapted to Synge.

> But seven tripped him up behind,
> And seven kicked before,
> And seven squeezed around his throat
> Till Danny kicked no more.
>
> Then some destroyed him with their heels,
> Some tramped him in the mud,
> Some stole his purse and timber pipe,
> And some washed off his blood.

In the end, "Danny" seems like a good imitation of a ballad. But the anonymous nineteenth-century poem "The Night Before Larry Was Stretched," used by Synge as the song in *The Tinker's Wedding*, is much more complex and unusual.

It is not very useful to compare Synge's poetry to Yeats's (any more than it would pay to compare Yeats's fiction to Joyce's), and it is time for the critics to move away from the prefaces. Synge was never very certain about the status of the poems and seemed always very shaky about publishing them even at the very end (he allowed Elizabeth Yeats to remove, without explanation, "The Curse" and "Danny"). They imitate many different forms, moods, and styles but are not innovative or original; they were kept in notebooks and frequently revised and with many variants; we might consider them perennially unfinished, always subject to further reworking, which only Synge's death prevented (here I might record my doubts about Skelton's editorial principles and procedures for the *Poems* in the Oxford edition and the real usefulness of this volume; the manuscripts are kept at Trinity College, Dublin; see *The Synge Manuscripts*). They should be treated along with all of Synge's reviewing and prose writing to work out Synge's aesthetic ideas (see Saddlemyer, "A Share"); so far this has not been systematically attempted (one should note, as Weldon Thornton did in his review-essays both entitled "J. M. Synge," that Price's editing of the *Prose* volume of the *Collected Works* is unreliable). Now with all of the correspondence finally available, and with the various bibliographic guides (Kopper; Thornton; Levitt) Synge can at least be examined fully.

References

Davie, Donald A. "The Poetic Diction of John M. Synge." *The Dublin Magazine* ns. 27, no. 1 (1952): 32–38.

Farren, Robert. *The Course of Irish Verse in English*. London: Sheed and Ward, 1948.

Gerstenberger, Donna. *John Millington Synge*. Twaynes English Authors Series 12. New York: Twayne, 1964.

Greene, David H., and Edward M. Stephens. *J. M. Synge, 1871–1909*. New York: Macmillan 1959; reprint New York: Collier, 1961.

Henn, Thomas Rice. *Last Essays: Mainly on Anglo-Irish Literature*. New York: Barnes & Noble, 1976.

———. *The Lonely Tower: Studies in the Poetry of W. B. Yeats*. London: Methuen, 1950.

————, ed. *The Plays and Poems of J. M. Synge*. London: Methuen, 1963.

Johnson, Toni O'Brien. *Synge: The Medieval and the Grotesque*. Irish Literary Studies 11. Gerrards Cross, Bucks: Colin Smythe; Totowa, N.J.: Barnes & Noble, 1982.

Joyce, James. *Ulysses*. New York: Random House, 1961.

Kiberd, Declan. *Synge and the Irish Language*. Totowa, N.J.: Rowman and Littlefield, 1979.

Kopper, Edward A., Jr. *John Millington Synge: A Reference Guide*. A Reference Publication in Literature. Boston: G. K. Hall, 1979.

Levitt, Paul M. *J. M. Synge: A Bibliography of Published Criticism*. New York: Barnes & Noble, 1974.

Perkins, David. *A History of Modern Poetry: From the 1890s to the High Modernist Mode*. Cambridge, Mass., and London: Belknap of Harvard University Press, 1976.

Pinto, Vivian de Sola. *Crisis in English Poetry: 1880–1940*. Rev. ed. Harper Torchbooks. New York: Harper & Row, 1958.

Price, Alan. *Synge and Anglo-Irish Drama*. London: Methuen, 1961.

Saddlemyer, Ann. "In Search of the Unknown Synge." *Irish Writers and Society at Large*. Edited by Masaru Sekine. Irish Literary Studies 22. Gerrards Cross, Bucks: Colin Smythe; Totowa, N.J.: Barnes & Noble, 1985. pp. 181–98.

————. "A Share in the Dignity of the World': J. M. Synge's Aesthetic Theory." *The World of W.B. Yeats*. Rev. ed. by Robin Skelton and Ann Saddlemyer. Seattle: University of Washington Press, 1967. pp. 207–19.

Skelton, Robin. *The Writings of J. M. Synge*. Indianapolis and New York: Bobbs-Merrill, 1971.

Thornton, Weldon. "J. M. Synge." *Anglo-Irish Literature: A Review of Research*. Edited by Richard J. Finneran. New York: The Modern Language Association of America, 1976. pp. 315–65.

————. "J. M. Synge." *Recent Research on Anglo-Irish Writers: A Supplement to Anglo-Irish Literature: A Review of Research*. Edited by Richard J. Finneran. The Modern Language Association of America Reviews of Research. New York: The Modern Language Association of America, 1983.

Trinity College, Dublin [Nicholas Grene]. *The Synge Manuscripts in the Library of Trinity College Dublin*. Dublin: Dolmen and Trinity College Library, 1971.

Warner, Francis. "A Note on the Poems of J. M. Synge." *A Centenary Tribute to John Millington Synge, 1871–1909: Sunshine and the Moon's Delight*. Edited by S. B. Bushrui. New York: Barnes & Noble, 1972. pp. 141–52.

Additional Sources

Corkery, Daniel. *Synge and Anglo-Irish Literature: A Study*. Dublin and Cork: Cork University Press; London: Longmans, Green, 1931.

Stallworthy, Jon. "The Poetry of Synge and Yeats." *J. M. Synge: Centenary Papers 1971*. Edited by Maruice Harmon. Dublin: Dolmen, 1972. pp. 145–66.

J. M. Synge: Christianity versus Paganism

Of all creative oppositions to be found in John Millington Synge, none more fully unites the man, the Anglo-Irish culture into which he was born, and the native Irish drama he did so much to bring into being than the opposition between Christianity and paganism. Synge's diaries and journals reveal a dual strain initially, his ability to accept his family's Christian beliefs and their inability to appreciate or share his interest in artistic expression. More than a decade's worth of sporadic but persistent reading in a number of European literatures, with a particular emphasis on Irish, showed him cultural equivalents for almost all of the strains in his character and life. The Aran Islands completed his growth in personal perception by introducing Synge to a group of people who could mingle the pagan and Christian beliefs that in him were so divided. What he found in the writing of his plays was not an image of himself but a medium in which those conflicting strains of paganism and Christianity could be worked out to their fullest extent and find a resolution through art impossible in life.

Raised in a strongly evangelical household, Synge's crisis of faith led him to write later about the experience: "By the time I was sixteen or seventeen I had renounced Christianity after a good deal of wobbling" (II, 11). The apparent absoluteness of this renunciation was undercut emotionally when he went on to add that although "this story is easily told, . . . it was a terrible experience. By

I would like to thank Auburn University for a research grant-in-aid which enabled me to travel to Dublin in the summer of 1986 to consult the Trinity College, Dublin, manuscripts.

it I laid a chasm between my present and my past and between myself and my kindred and friends'' (II, 11). For the legacy of evangelical Protestantism was not so easily abandoned and left Synge with recognizable traits of mind that marked all of his subsequent pursuits.

But the crisis did propel him away from the self-enclosed world of the Synge family, an evangelical minority within the Anglo-Irish Church of Ireland minority, toward a larger identification: ''Soon after I had relinquished the Kingdom of God I began to take a real interest in the kingdom of Ireland. . . . Everything Irish became sacred'' (II, 13). The language of conversion here is striking. Synge's interest in Ireland as a whole and his apostasy from his family religion did not entail a conversion to the Catholicism of the majority; that was no more an option for him than the reverse would later be for a disaffected Stephen Dedalus or James Joyce. In the manuscript version of the autobiography, Synge is more explicit about what constituted for him the kingdom of Ireland: ''the Irish country, rains, mists, full insular skies, the old churches, MSS. [manuscripts], jewels—everything in fact that was Irish became sacred in my eyes'' (Synge Manuscripts MS 4382, FF 51–52). The Irish imaginative legacy was made up, on the one hand, of the palpable yet shifting qualities of the Irish countryside he would explore in forays through his native Wicklow, West Kerry, and the Aran Islands. From his earliest days, Synge declared himself to be ''passionately fond of nature'' (Synge Manuscripts MS 4382, FF 51–52) and, through his youth, evolved a pantheistic mysticism that significantly increased as his Christianity waned. But in his Wordsworthian progress, the purely instinctual communion with nature soon craved an intellectual dimension and, after an intermediary progress through music, found it in a sustained scholarly application to learning the Irish language (see Kiberd, *Synge and the Irish Language*), studying the ancient manuscripts, and acquiring a solid cultural foundation for his subsequent writing career.

That foundation, first attempted in his studies in Irish at Trinity College, Dublin, in 1892, was securely laid in 1898 when Synge took a series of courses ''sur la civilization irlandaise comparee avec celle d'homere'' (Synge Manuscripts MS 4378, Notebook 10, F 49) with Professor H. d'Arbois de Jubainville at the Sorbonne. Several months later, the first of his five annual visits to the Aran Islands not only brought the texts he had been studying to embodied life but placed him at the furthest geographic and cultural remove within an Irish context from his Anglo-Irish background on the eastern seaboard. While on Aran, Synge's imagination was stirred not by the Catholicism of the peasant islanders, in which he showed scant interest, but in their retention of many of the pagan beliefs predating the arrival of Christianity in Ireland. These beliefs primarily manifested themselves themselves in talk of the fairies, a real presence in the lives of the islanders; of the appearance and intervention of these supernatural beings at moments of crisis; and of the afterlife to which they summoned the island young. The locus for such beliefs was the storytelling, whose preservation of the Gaelic language and method of oral transmission account for the survival into the twentieth century of such archaic beliefs. This imaginative legacy had a profound impact on Synge, helping to transform him from a mediocre man of letters to a playwright of genius.

Of the six plays associated with his name, four are considered. *The Shadow of the Glen*, while it engages the central Syngean theme of a constricting environment and the dream of a fuller life elsewhere, does not do so primarily in terms of Christianity and paganism. *Deirdre of the Sorrows*, since it is set exclusively in the pagan past, has no opportunity to engage the dialectic. But *Riders to the Sea*, the one play in which Irish directly dramatized his Aran experience, represents the same mingling of Christian and pagan beliefs he encountered among the islanders. *The Tinker's Wedding* directly sets a Roman Catholic priest and a trio of Rabelaisian tinkers in opposition on the stage and was for that reason precluded from ever getting there during Synge's lifetime. *The Well of the Saints* treats a similar conflict in a more subtle and distanced way, bringing a latter-day St. Patrick into dialogue with two unregenerate heathens who in their turn evoke the pre-Christian warrior-poet Oisin. Synge's masterpiece, *The Playboy of the Western World*, although it is concerned with much else, makes mock of Father Reilly and the courts of Rome while hinting a resemblance between Christy Mahon and Christ the Son of Man, a potential redeemer for the people of Mayo whom they first acclaim and then reject. Christy also serves to reincarnate a mock-epic modern version of ancient Irish heroism and brings something of the mystical land of promise to the starved imagination of Pegeen Mike. The plays carry on the debate between Christianity and paganism on their naturalistic surfaces, where the opposition tends to be more clear-cut, and in their deep structures, where biblical and mythical symbolic patterns form a complex weave.

The earliest biography of Synge paid scant attention to his religious background. Maurice Bourgeois described Synge's view of life as "nonreligious" and attributed as cause "the desire to return to the relentless savagery of ancient paganism" (218). As a result, Bourgeois's life downplayed the matrix of evangelical beliefs in which Synge was raised. The David Greene and Edward Stephens biography, however, establishes how strong the Protestant legacy was on both sides of the family: "The Irish branch of the [Synge] family produced five bishops, beginning with the first Synge who came to Ireland in the seventeenth century" (16). Vivian Mercier has drawn attention to the wide role of Victorian evangelicalism in unwittingly fostering the Anglo-Irish literary revival and has noted that "John Synge, the dramatist's grandfather, made Glanmore Castle available for clerical meetings at a time when these were a rallying point for the evangelically inclined" ("Victorian Evangelicalism" 61). But the dominant force in Synge's religious formation came not from his father's but from his mother's side of the family; this might still have been the case had his father not died just a year after his son's birth. His mother, Kathleen Traill, was the daughter of Robert Traill, the Protestant rector of Schull, County Cork, whose staunch evangelical zeal "apparently stood in the way of his ecclesiastical advancement" (Greene and Stephens 16). Synge's religious upbringing lay firmly in the hands of Robert Traill's wife and daughter, whose influence was all the greater since his recurrent bouts of illness meant that the young John had little formal education and received most of his schooling in the atmosphere of the home.

In the biography of his uncle, Edward Stephens encouraged the idea that Synge did not so much reject absolutely the religious ideas he had been taught, as his bold declaration of "renouncing Christianity" might suggest, but rather that he went on to use them in a more independent, less orthodox fashion than his family could accept: "His mother's teaching, like a running commentary on all that happened, emphasized the importance of searching out and utilizing every opportunity that life might afford. John applied her wisdom in a way that she could not understand" (34). Of all Synge's critics, Weldon Thornton in *J. M. Synge and the Western Mind* most followed the direction indicated by Stephens to argue in general for the dramatist's profound religious sensibility and in particular that "while he could not accept his family's dogmas, he was in temperament and attitude quite close to them, and that in his own thinking he transmuted rather than rejected their religion" (34). Above all, he stressed Synge's passionate "concern for the truth and for the integrity of his own mind and thought" (32).

The rock on which Synge's earlier unquestioning faith foundered was the Christian concept of Hell and the terrorizing hold it acquired on his youthful imagination:

I was painfully timid and while still very young the idea of Hell took a fearful hold upon me. One night particularly I thought I was irretrievably damned and cried myself to sleep in vain yet fearful/terrible efforts to form a conception of eternal pain. In the morning I renewed my lamentation and my mother was sent for. She comforted me with the assurance that my fears were caused by the Holy Ghost who was now convicting me of sin and thus preparing me in reality for ultimate salvation. . . . [My mother] was always judicious—except perhaps in her portrayal of Hell. From this time religion remained a difficulty and occasioned terror to me for many years though I do not think the brand I was brought up in was peculiarly Calvinistic. The well-meant but extraordinary cruelty of thrusting/throwing the idea of Hell into the imagination of a nervous child has probably caused more misery [than] many customs that the same people send missionaries to eradicate. (Synge Manuscripts MS 4382, v 59; II, 4–5)

Already implicit here is Synge's sense that any religion that might subsequently win his allegiance would do away with the notion of Hell and promote instead the many pagan customs that other immediate members of his family, his uncle Alec or brother Samuel, took as their missionary goal to eradicate at home or abroad.

Synge returns to this idea years later, in 1898 during his studies on Irish civilization with d'Arbois de Jubainville, when his by-now extensive reading gave him the scholarly authority to make the following observation on the "prog-ress" of Irish literature over the centuries: "Observe that idea of *Hell* absent from most primitive texts. Gradually assumes such prominence that it at last completely overshadows idea of heaven. In Irish and non-Christian texts no hell" (Synge Manuscripts MS 4378, F 50). Here was objective testimony of his earlier experience, a cultural parallel of a personal dilemma that both confirmed it and showed him a way imaginatively to escape its constraints. In his autobiography, he had written of his crisis of faith:

Till I was twenty-three I never met or at least knew a man or woman who shared my opinions. Compared with the people about me, compared with the Fellows of Trinity, I seemed a presumptuous boy yet I felt that the views which I had arrived at after sincere efforts to find what was true represented, in spite of my immediate surroundings, the real opinion of the world. (II, 11)

Synge's "sincere efforts to find what was true" testify to Stephens's and Thorn-ton's view of his enduring debt to Evangelicalism and its urgings to devote one's life to a quest for spiritual truth. But the gulf or chasm that he described separating him from his brethren was opened up by the idea of hell; it separated him emotionally from "kindred and friends" and no longer made the attainment of his family's form of salvation possible. Synge's reading of the ancient Irish texts at the age of twenty-seven cemented the association in his mind between the evangelizing zeal of the Christian missionary, the totalizing promotion of the concept of hell, and the consequent extinction of any heavenly intimations.

Six years later, in 1904, the idea of hell made its appearance in *The Well of the Saints* at the close of Act Two. The blind couple have been cured by the wandering Saint, and as one result, Martin Doul is now forced to labor in Timmy the Smith's forge. He shows the effects of his conversion by a perverse prayer of revenge in which the idea of hell, earlier absent from his imaginings, has now assumed such prominence that it completely overshadows the idea of heaven:

Oh, God, pity a poor blind fellow the way I am this day with no strength in me to do hurt to them at all. . . . Yet if I've no strength in me I've a voice left for my prayers, and may God blight them this day, and my own soul the same hour with them, the way I'll see them after, Molly Byrne and Timmy the smith, the two of them on a high bed, and they screeching in hell. . . . It'll be a grand thing that time to look on the two of them; and they twisting and roaring out, and twisting and roaring again . . . it won't be hell to me I'm thinking, but the like of Heaven itself. (III, 123)

But if the idea of hell made acceptance of evangelical dogma impossible to the youthful Synge, another crisis was precipitated by his reading of Darwin's *Origin of Species*. What it introduced was the question of doubt: "Till then I had never doubted and never conceived that a sane and wise man or boy could doubt. . . . It seemed that I was become in a moment the playfellow of Judas" (II, 10–11). Although the reading of Darwin was destructive in its immediate effects, most critics see the longer-term impact of the experience as crucial in Synge's evolution as a playwright. Weldon Thornton argued that it would be wrong to conclude that the event turned Synge into a rationalist; he was "too aware of the mystery behind all things to regard reason as definitive" (40). Thornton analyzed the experience to show that, given Synge's detailed interest in natural history, what he acquired from reading Darwin was not new facts but a new perspective on facts he already possessed. Henceforth, he was to regard no single perspective, Darwin's or his mother's, as adequate. Mary C. King viewed the effect of reading Darwin as equally liberating on Synge's attitude to language, since it not only "undermined the naive historicism of Mrs. Synge's interpretation of the rest of sacred scripture . . . its undeviating literalism" (6). It also prepared the way for Synge's subsequent discovery of the symbolic nature of words, first as a student of foreign languages in France and Germany and then through his exposure to the Hiberno-English speech of the Aran Islands.

But there is a third crisis in the youthful Synge's life to which scarcely any critical attention has been paid. (The Darwin passage has, if anything, been overemphasized.) In addition to the ideas of the Christian hell and of Darwinian evolution, a third sundering force in the area of belief occurred with the onset of puberty, which had the equivalent negative effect on his earlier beliefs that the other two did on his Christianity. I am here referring to the current of pantheistic nature worship that runs through all of Synge's writings and constitutes arguably his greatest religious belief. His earliest childhood imaginings are of this paradisal or Edenic interaction with the natural world: "Even at this time I was a worshipper of nature. I remember that I would not allow my nurses to sit down on the seats by the [River] Dodder because they were [man-] made. If they wished to sit down they had to find a low branch of a tree or a bit of rock or bank" (II, 5). He shared this heightened otherworld of nature with his cousin Florence Ross: "We were always primitive. We both understood all the facts of life and spoke of them without much hesitation . . . [talking] of sexual matters with an indifferent and sometimes amused frankness that was identical with the attitude of folk-tales" (II, 7). Synge was writing with a later awareness of the cultural equivalents to his own development and the suggestion that, through his avid interest in folktales and the "primitive" life of the Aran Islands, he was seeking at some level to reconstruct and recover this paradise lost. What effected the loss was the onset of puberty, the removal of his cousin from his presence, and the casting of his passionate sensuality into the category of "sin." He wrote of this period of trauma: "Sometimes I was obsessed by the ideas that beset man at this period and thought myself a low miscreant because I had a tendency which was quite natural and healthy. . . . Vulgar sensuality did not attract me but I was haunted by pagan dreams of a time when there was yet no fear of love" (Synge Manuscripts MS 4382, F 53). An alternate version of this passage, which breaks off in Synge and is edited out by Alan Price in the second volume of the *Collected Works*, reads: "I was torn with passions" (Synge Manuscripts MS 4382, v 52).

What remains to be considered is the kind of heaven to which Synge was converted, or rather the concept of heaven that his imaginative beliefs and practices presupposed. His readings in early Irish literature first afforded a glimpse of this by showing the pagan vision and version of the afterlife that the arrival of Christianity displaced (but did not destroy). Weldon Thornton and Declan Kiberd, as late as 1979, were the first critics to take account of Synge's scholarly interest in the Celtic otherworld. In *Synge and the Irish Language*, Kiberd wrote:

In 1898 [Synge] had read an old Irish tale from the Mythological Cycle, *The Voyage of Bran*, edited and translated by Kuno Meyer. . . . Meyer's volume contained an essay by Alfred Nutt entitled 'The Irish Vision of the Happy Otherworld and the Celtic Doctrine of Rebirth.' Synge cited this essay and Meyer's text in an essay written in French in 1902 to support his thesis that Old Irish and Greek literature shared a position of major importance in the Indo-European scheme. (168)

The relevant portion of Synge's article "La Vieille littérature irlandaise" for *L'Européen* of March 15, 1902, reads:

I have spoken above of the European importance of this Irish literature and this claim is not exaggerated. . . . Nothing, for instance, is as primitive as that belief common to Greeks and Irish, a belief in an other world where the dead continue to enjoy a life like that of earthly existence without hope of being rewarded for their virtues or fear of being punished for their misdeeds. (II, 354, translation mine)

As Synge put it six years earlier in his extensive notes on Alfred Nutt's essay, the Celtic otherworld is an "Elysium dissociated from eschatological belief (i.e., framed without reference to man's future life)" (Synge Manuscripts MS, 4378, Notebook 10, F 49). It inclines more to the Christian concept of heaven in its promise of endless delight and its exclusion of strife or rancor and has least to do with the unrelenting physical punishment of hell. But the pagan otherworld differs from the Christian heaven, as Synge noted, in being more "like that of earthly existence" and offering a vision of a world in which natural pleasures were extolled; sensuality heightened into artistic patterns of music, poetry, and dance; and the curse of mortality kept at a distance. If his Continental studies in Celtic literature first introduced these concepts to Synge, it would take his voyages to the Aran Islands to bring him into direct living contact with what remained of these ancient beliefs.

A final irony, and a final connection with his family background is that Synge was not the first of his family to visit the islands. When he landed at Aranmore, he was spotted by an older man who told him that evening: "I was standing under the pier-wall mending nets . . . when you came off the steamer, and I said to myself in that moment, if there is a man of the name of Synge left walking the world, it is that man yonder will be he' " (II, 53). John had been preceded there in 1851 by his uncle, the Reverend Alexander Synge, the first Protestant missionary to the Aran Islands, who wrote: "I get on with the people so far very well, but how will it be when we begin to attack their bad ways, religion, etc., I don't know" (Mercier, "Victorian Evangelicalism" 62). Whereas the Reverend Alexander Synge came to the Aran Islands to convert, his nephew John traveled there fifty years later to be converted.

What Synge's prose work *The Aran Islands* records is his imaginative interaction with the oral folktales of which he had so far read only the literary equivalent. Elsewhere in the French essay already cited, he had specifically located the value of the Irish legends and cycles in their "mythology which forms . . . a kernal of the most primitive beliefs of the Indo-European peoples" (III, 354, my translation) before going on to cite a belief in the pagan otherworld as the most primitive of all. The key terms in this assessment, the *mythology* comprised of *primitive beliefs*, recur in Synge's evaluation of the Aran Islands. Aranmore, Inishmaan, and Inishere are ranked by him according to the "primitive" qualities preserved in their environment: Aranmore "has been so much changed by the fishing industry . . . that it has now very little to distinguish it from any fishing village on the west coast of Ireland. The other islands are more primitive" (II, 47). Synge is correspondingly eager to leave Aranmore and sail to Inishmaan, where "Gaelic is more generally used, and the life is perhaps the most primitive that is left in Europe" (II, 53). These remarks make clear the importance of Gaelic for Synge as a linguistic means of preserving and transmitting this primitive culture. (They also help to explain his hostility to the modernizing techniques of the Gaelic League.) For over and over again in his encounters with the islanders it is the body of imaginative beliefs dating from pre-Christian times, "the wild mythology that is accepted on the islands" (II, 54), that draws his interest.

This discernible bias has led to charges that Synge wilfully ignored the deeply held Catholicism of the islanders, downplaying its central role in their lives in favor of exaggerating the remnants of a few prior superstitions. Daniel Corkery is chief among Catholic Irish critics to make the accusation, contending that Synge "did not frequent the really authoritative people on the islands who could have told him everything about everything" but rather "spent most of his days lying alone in the sun or, equally alone, moping around under the stars!" (111–12) But the criticism of Synge's anti-Catholicism has also been made by his international commentators, first and formidably by Maurice Bourgeois:

Synge's archaic quest of the older Gaelic civilization made him blind to the profounder spirit of modern Ireland. . . . at bottom [the Irish peasant] is an ardently religious being, whose whole life is coloured by faith and belief—especially Catholic faith. This aspect of Irish mind is ignored by Synge; it has no place in his works; and on this score his fellow-countrymen are justified in finding fault with his plays. (218–29)

The incident in *The Aran Islands* on which this controversy focuses is Synge's description in Part I of a funeral he attended on Inishmaan. The account is notable for the passionate grief with which the normally reticent islanders are seized and in particular for the wild cry of the keen (from the Gaelic *caoineadh*, lament) through which it is expressed:

> This grief of the keen is no personal complaint for the death of one woman over eighty years, but seems to contain the whole passionate rage that lurks somewhere in every native of the island. In this cry of pain the inner consciousness of the people seems to lay itself bare for an instant, and to reveal the mood of beings who feel their isolation in the face of a universe that wars on them with winds and seas. . . .
>
> Before they covered the coffin an old man kneeled down by the grave and repeated a simple prayer for the dead.
>
> There was an irony in these words of atonement and Catholic belief spoken by voices that were still hoarse with the cries of pagan desperation. (II, 75)

Many of his plays will dramatize the great gap in that irony, between words of Catholic belief and the passionate rage of the pagan. Synge held that the islanders' Christianity was only the merest veneer or layer covering over the earlier pagan beliefs and that, under the pressure of the lives they led on the westernmost edge of the Atlantic Ocean, the islanders' conventional pieties rapidly gave way before sympathies closer to nature mysticism than Christian orthodoxy. His concern was not with the uppermost layer, the Catholicism to which as a Protestant he was antipathetic, but with the underlying strata of primitive beliefs that he thought constituted the islanders' more profound allegiances and to which he could give his own imaginative assent.

There is objective support for such a view. In *Christianity and Paganism*, J. N. Hillgarth pointed out:

since Ireland was never politically or culturally subject to Rome, Christianity was forced to evolve there in ways distinct from those it had naturally assumed. . . . Ireland—unlike Western Europe—possessed a living culture of its own, expressed in a vernacular literature that had not been obliterated by a Roman overlay. (117)

The distinct development was that Christianity adapted itself to the indigenous (and pagan) culture to a much greater extent than anywhere else, so that "if one turns to the literature produced in Irish—much of it probably in monasteries— one finds that the heroes of the pagan past continued to be revered in a way which would be hard to parallel elsewhere in Western Christendom" (Hillgarth 120). This was particularly the case in the remotest areas of the west of Ireland, where the oral tradition in Gaelic continued unbroken into this century and carried with it, as Synge noted, many archaic features that had vanished from the written literature.

Accordingly, the people he sought out on the Aran Islands were not the priests (though when he met any the exchange was cordial enough) but the storytellers, latter-day descendants of the bardic class. Michael, Pat Dirane, and Old Mourteen are the preeminent storytellers of their respective locales and central to the narrative design in *The Aran Islands*. Synge's first encounter with Mourteen climaxes the account of his arrival on the islands: "one old half-blind man spoke to me in Gaelic. . . . [He] had great confidence in his own powers and talent, and in the superiority of his stories over all other stories in the world" and proceeded to relate how "one of his children had been taken by the fairies" (II, 50–51).

The topic of Mourteen's discourse raises the question of the presence and purpose of the fairy lore in Synge's book. Unlike Yeats and Lady Gregory, Synge never recorded such material purely for its own sake, never detached it from the occasion and context of its telling or from the personality of its narrator: "As we talked he sat huddled together over the fire, shaking and blind, yet his face was indescribably pliant, lighting up with an ecstasy of humour when he told me of anything that had a point of wit or malice, and growing sombre and desolate again when he spoke of religion or the fairies" (II, 50). Synge responded to these old men as inheritors of a number of traditions—of the Irish language, of oral storytelling, of beliefs that originally formed part of a pre-Christian religion. But the people retain the emphasis since, in the words of Walter Benjamin, it is only in the "full corporeality" of the "experience which is passed on from mouth to mouth" (84) that these traditions can be restored to full living currency.

Synge not only situated the stories in the personalities of the tellers; he in turn situated those tellers and their stories in the communal life of the islands. His technique can be best illustrated through a consideration of Part IV. Mary C. King, who has provided the fullest account of Synge's narrative technique in this apparently artless book, noted how in the last part "references to dying and to death . . . accumulate until mortality itself becomes the dominant theme" (24). Juxtaposed with the deaths are "the folktale element," which King did not discuss, and three long poems, "political allegories about Ireland's struggle for freedom, [which] act as a counterpoint to the funereal *cantus firmus* of the prose." But the three poems only account for the second half. What the first half counterpoints with the stark realism of the death by drowning of one of the island's young men is the presence and function of storytelling in the lives of the islanders. Storytelling abounds in Part IV of *The Aran Islands* to such an extent that it displaces the primary account of activities on Aran. But then the primary activity with which IV concerns itself is death, not only of the drowned man but of a young woman stricken with typhus. So Synge gathers with the people in their cottage at night for the rituals of storytelling by which they acknowledge the dead and keep their own terror at bay.

Early in Part IV, a story about the sudden, unexpected killing of two neighbors by each other—having wrought a context in which the most fundamental beliefs surrounding life and death are brought into play—is interrupted by "a gust of wind [that] came and blew up a bundle of dry seaweed that was near us, right over our heads" (II, 156). This inspired another old man to a story that tentatively suggested the hovering, airy presences of the Shee or fairy host behind such an intrusion. By this point, the current of pagan belief tapped by the storytelling is gathering momentum: " 'There was more than that in it,' said another man, 'for the night before a woman had a great sight out to the west in this island, and saw all the people that were dead a while back in this island and the south island, and they all talking with each other' " (II, 157). This particular account of the resurrected dead serves not just as reminiscence but as prophecy, with the next page of Synge's text disgorging "The body of [the] young man who was drowned a few weeks ago" (II, 158). In so doing, it establishes a recurrent juxtaposition of story and incident for the rest of the work, oscillating between a verbal land of the fancy where familiar figures enjoy an extended existence and the realm of the real where their decomposing mortal remains are elaborately laid to rest. The only healing refuge in the pages of *The Aran Islands* is found not in the appeal to an avowedly merciful God but in the consolations of storytelling, the communal act by which the islanders' suffering is confronted and assuaged.

Synge drew directly on his experience of the Aran Islands in writing his one-act tragedy *Riders to the Sea*. As almost every critic has pointed out, *Riders* displays the same mixture of pagan and Christian beliefs as Synge encountered among the islanders. Almost the first words we hear are those of the young priest, offering Maurya and her daughters words of consolation: " 'let you not be afraid. Herself does be saying prayers half through the night, and the Almighty God won't leave her destitute,' says he, 'with no son living' " (III, 5). That the play is going to run directly counter to this confident assertion is suggested by the immediate juxtaposition of the priest's disembodied words with Nora and Cathleen's fearful apprehension of the sea's presence. The two women's reading of the factors that influence their destiny provides a much more accurate prophecy than that of the young priest, one more in tune with the climate and pervasive environment of *Riders to the Sea*:

CATHLEEN: Is the sea bad by the white rocks, Nora?

NORA: Middling bad, God help us. There's a great roaring in the west, and it's worse it'll be getting when the tide's turned to the wind. (III, 5–7)

The sea is rapidly established as the center of power and influence in their lives, an association that will continue to develop throughout the drama. But one could expect little else in any naturalistic representation of those who eke out a precarious existence on a small island, even if Synge *has* concentrated all the potential catastrophes on a single, unfortunate house. What is more subtle is the process by which he invests the physical presence of the Atlantic Ocean with metaphysical overtones. The first step has already been noted in the repeated statements by the priest, whose claims about "the Almighty God" establish the sense of a transcendental power operating invisibly in and through the lives of humans. The priest's invocations are at once countered in the play by the opposing power of the sea. In so doing, Synge implicitly calls into being a countervailing metaphysical realm with its own presiding deities and impact on human affairs.

In an important essay, Denis Donoghue argued that the "relationship between 'Catholic' and 'Pagan' becomes one of the most significant of the dramatic tensions established within the context of 'Riders to the Sea': the tension between orthodox, institutional religion and the implacable power of the Sea" (46). But Donoghue did not consider the pagan values or beliefs associated with the sea, merely continuing to insist on that power as "silent" and "inhuman." Rather it was Robin Skelton who enlarged on how Synge "incorporated into the play many images with supernatural significance. . . . Thus there are references to Samhain (or Hallowe'en) the time when ghosts walk, to holy water, and to the 'black hags' that 'do be flying on the sea.' . . . The sea itself is regarded as a godlike power in the play, and the priest is dismissed as being of very little significance" (*J. M. Synge* 32). Skelton stopped short, however, of identifying the god associated with the sea in Celtic mythology as Manannan Mac Lir. The play's very title invokes the sea god Manannan in its distinctive yoking together of horseriding and the ocean. Its preposition points Bartley and his horses not toward the fair on the mainland that he assumes is his destination or even the boat that will transport them thither but the sea to which (and on which?) he will ride. In the Old Irish *Voyage of Bran*, the hero and his comrades encounter Manannan in the midst of their voyage: "When he had been at sea two days and two nights, [Bran] saw a man in a chariot coming towards him over the sea [who] . . . said that he was Manannan son of Lir," and he presented them with a double vision whereby, although the mariners only see "a clear sea. . . . / There are many steeds on its surface / Though them thou seest not" (Meyer 16, 18–20). Declan Kiberd, in his scholarly amassing of the numerous folk beliefs embedded in *Riders to the Sea*, noted that "pigs were sacrificed to Manannan Mac Lir, the god of the sea, in order to ward off evil, including death by drowning," and argued that "by neglecting this duty, the island family has exposed itself to the danger of drowning" (*Synge and the Irish Language* 165). Manannan's presence is pervasive in Synge's play in the actual form of the sea and in the number of references to gestures, sayings, and rituals designed to propitiate him. What Kiberd demonstrated is how all through the play "members of the family have violated folk prohibitions" and so heightened "our sense of the inevitability of Bartley's death" (167).

That significance associated with the sea begins to develop more explicitly with the entrance of the mother Maurya. As the play opens, she is sleeping but her two daughters know that, once awake, "herself will be down looking by the sea" (III, 5). Maurya is repeatedly drawn there by the fact that her son Michael has been missing for a week, hence the sustained scrutiny she directs at the ocean, urging some kind of response to her eloquent unspoken entreaties. Cathleen speculates that "maybe when the tide turns she'll be going down to see would he be floating from the east" (III, 7). Any aural reception of this second line is bound to be influenced by the first in hovering between "sea/see" as actual locale or as source of vision. What Maurya hopes to see there is not yet made explicit: the body of her son washed ashore at the selfsame spot from which he cast off? Unlikely, at best, but possible to a grief-distracted mother. The return of other islanders with the body of her son? Again, unlikely, since the Aran practice is to bury the body where it is recovered, as we learn elsewhere in the play. There is always the possibility of Michael's actual safe return home, but after this length of time Nora and Cathleen have yielded to the unlikelihood of such an outcome. The final possibility is that Michael, having been "away"— that is, taken to the Celtic otherworld by the fairy forces—might yet put in a reappearance, as many others had been reported doing in island lore.

That possibility is confirmed when Maurya returns from pursuing the remaining son Bartley to give him her blessing. What she says indicates that she has had a vision not of this world:

I'm after seeing [Michael] this day, and he riding and galloping. Bartley came first on the red mare; and I tried to say "God speed you," but something choked the words in my throat. He went by quickly; and "the blessing of God on you," says he, and I could say nothing. I looked up then, and I crying, at the grey pony, and there was Michael upon it—with fine clothes on him, and new shoes on his feet. (III, 19).

The colors of the two horses have been taken by more than one critic as a reference to the Four Horsemen of the Apocalypse in the Book of Revelation (Clark 43; Henn 34; King 55). But Nicholas Grene, who is generally resistant to a symbolic reading of *Riders*, argued that "if we are looking for analogues here, we should not be thinking in terms of the apocalyptic image of the four horsemen, but of the folk concept of the conspiracy of the dead" (*Synge: A Critical Study* 54).

The period of the year in which the dead have greatest freedom to return is Samhain, the Celtic feast referred to by Maurya in her long closing lament: "I'll have no call now to be going down and getting Holy Water in the dark nights after Samhain" (III, 25). Prionsias MacCana wrote:

the Celts have treated the festival of Samhain [November 1] . . . as a time apart which was charged with a peculiar preternatural energy . . . [when] the barriers between the natural and the supernatural are temporarily removed, the *sidh* [fairy fort] lies open and all divine beings and the spirits of the dead move freely among human beings and interfere, sometimes violently, in their affairs. (127–28)

As a result, Maurya's wish to see her son again is answered but in a way that brings little satisfaction. Not only does her vision at the well confirm that Michael is drowned but also that his spirit has returned to interfere violently in their affairs by drawing the living Bartley after him. Maurya's Christianity fails her at this crucial intersection, and the words of blessing are stopped in her throat by the superior strangle hold exerted at that moment by the old religion. Her vision of Michael sustains a double loss, not only confirming in retrospect the drowning of one son but serving as infallible prophecy of the death of the other. Cathleen's rational side attempts to deny the truth of what her mother has seen by equating Michael with the remains retrieved from the sea. But in Maurya's reply—"I'm after seeing him this day, and he riding and galloping"—the oppressive facts of death and loss are simultaneously confirmed and counterbalanced by the alternate prospect of his continued active existence in the otherworld, clad not in a few pitiful rags but in the seamless imaginative splendor of "fine clothes on him, and new shoes on his feet."

The question that most concerns the critics is the extent to which Maurya regains a Christian perspective at the close of the play. Robin Skelton would have none of it and argued that the references to "holy water" do not carry the usual Christian connotations: "It may be that she collects it from a Holy Well, even the Spring Well, mentioned in the play, but it is clear that the only time she does collect it is in the nights after Samhain. . . . Thus the Holy Water is much more the magical water of pre-Christian belief than the water blessed by the priest" (*The Writings of J. M. Synge* 51). Nicholas Grene used the holy water to argue the opposite point of view—that Maurya, after reaching the depths of pagan nihilism in the face of death, now attains a Christian quietude and resignation (*Synge: A Critical Study* 56). But Declan Kiberd pointed out that despite her blessing on Bartley, "Maurya's closing speech holds no orthodox Christian promise of a life to come" and goes on to cite instead the Irish faith in another world "where the dead continue a life similar to their terrestrial existence" (*Synge and the Irish Language* 167–68). What is clear is that Maurya's final attitude, like the line in which she refers simultaneously to "Holy Water" and "Samhain," mixes Christian and pagan beliefs and that the conflict between them which the play has staged now attains at least temporary equilibrium in her soul.

The most direct staging of the confrontation between Christianity and paganism in Synge's drama occurs in *The Tinker's Wedding*. The work is also the most problematic and least esteemed of his six plays. Is there a connection between the two—the possibility that the explicit foregrounding of the Christian-pagan conflict leads to dramatic breakdown and that Synge is best when treating the theme as an adjunct of the dramatic action? This question needs to be considered, but it is also worth remembering that *The Tinker's Wedding* has a complicated structural evolution, first emerging as a one-act play, one of the three of the miraculous summer of 1902. It can be argued that the flaws of the play are as much the result of that most difficult of dramatic moves, away from the self-imposed limitations of the one-act toward a full-length play. The best way to demonstrate this is to compare the treatment of Christianity and paganism in the two-act *Tinker's Wedding* with the three-act *The Well of the Saints*, where the confrontation of man of God and uregenerate pagan is equally central and more successfully resolved.

In terms of Synge's artistic treatment of Christianity, *The Tinker's Wedding* is most notable in presenting the first (and only) onstage appearance of a Catholic priest. That appearance was necessitated from the start by the priest's dramatic centrality to the folktale on which Synge based the play, in which a pair of tinkers attempt to trick the cleric into marrying them for nothing. In the earliest version of this play, the only one-act draft preserved, the financial transaction has already taken place and is represented indirectly through reported speech, as with the words of the young priest throughout *Riders*: " 'You're a thieving lot,' says he 'and I'd do right to make you give a pound surely but maybe if I left the like of that bit of money with you you'ld be drinking it below in the fair'' (IV, 273). The climax, however, at which the tinkers fail to present the agreed sum and are sent packing, requires the direct onstage presence and involvement of the priest. In preparation for this, Synge brought him on not in a private capacity (in black) but in full ceremonial costume from the "chapel door" (IV, 275), which is a requirement of the stage directions throughout.

The stage settings of both *Wedding* and *Well* require the combination and severe juxtaposition of two contrasting visual motifs: a church doorway on the one side, the symbolic portals across whose threshold the tinkers and beggars are impelled but which they finally refuse to cross or enter, and on the other side a roadside, sign of the unfettered imaginative life they lead, as social itinerants outside the bounds of bourgeois society. They are also living a life in greater contact with the physical world. Both settings are outside, more open to the influence of nature and so provide an implicit contrast to the settled world of domestic interiors represented by the bond of marriage.

The priest emerges in his surplice from the chapel doorway to complete the monetary details before bringing the tinkers in to marry them. His questions are direct and terse, allowing for no more characterization than already contained in the reported narrative, that of a man whose mind is as much (if not more) on material rather than spiritual matters. When he discovers their imposture, the priest opens up into a full-throated denunciation that while drawing on his full social and spiritual authority as a Catholic cleric also displays an intimate knowledge of the tinkers and their ways: "If I catch you again in this village you bawdy thief I['ll] tell the peelers who it was stole the grey ass" (IV, 276). Mary Byrne, the oldest of the tinkers and the play's Rabelaisian earth-mother most in touch with the Romany traditions, defends their traditional way of living, both in defiance of the priest and in rebuke of her daughter-in-law's perverse desire to get married in the first place: "You and your marriage! Isn't generations and generations we are walking round under the Heavens and what is it we ever wanted with [your like]?" (IV, 276).

So the original one-act draft concludes—in a much more innocuous way than the notorious revised ending Synge was later to provide. But the addition of an entire act is the much more substantial alteration he made to the play. In so doing, Synge went back to the night before (rather than the more leisurely three weeks of the prose) and dramatized the making of the match between priest and tinker as an uneasy liaison between the traditions of Christianity and paganism in Ireland.

Robin Skelton gave the fullest account of the presence of pre-Christian beliefs and customs in Synge's representation of the tinkers. Many of his examples, however, such as the fertility figure of the "green man" invoked by two children (IV, 281), are from earlier, suppressed fragments rather than the finished version. Skelton did, however, make the best argument for Sarah Casey, building on the play's original title of *The Movements of May*: "Disturbed by the 'change of the moon' at the time of the vernal equinox, she is filled with a rising excitement and sense of her own royal beauty, and expresses this in language that conflates folk-tale and ancient belief with the commonplace" (*The Writings of J. M. Synge* 51).

Sarah's pride in her own physical appearance and confidence in her ability to attract another man strike the keynote not only of her personality but of the essentially pagan beliefs of the tinkers. It is in this context that her decision to insist belatedly on a Christian marriage with Michael is viewed by the other two tinkers (and by the play) as at best a temporary aberration, and at worst a betrayal of the values of her itinerant tribe.

Although the priest when stopped by Sarah the night before is initially as brusque as on the following day, the first act builds sympathy for him and shows some unexpected affiliations between the disparate lives of "his reverence" and the tinkers. Vivian Mercier, in his article on the play, carefully showed how the priest reveals a "basic kindliness" ("*The Tinker's Wedding*" 79) in the face of Sarah's tears and, when pressed to it by Mary Byrne, finally lets down his guard and agrees to share a drink with them. As he does so, he admits: "it's well for the like of you that do be drinking when there's drouth on you. . . . What would you do if it was the like of myself you were, saying Mass with your mouth dry?" (IV, 19) It is presumably this behaviour and admission on the priest's part that led Maurice Bourgeois to his verdict on the play. Having remarked how "it was Synge's object to contrast . . . the two types of Irish civilization, the Heathen and the Christian—Ireland before and after St. Patrick," Bourgeois argued that "this attempt at dramatic synthesis . . . remains on the whole incongruous and unsuccessful; for is not the Priest in the play himself a Pagan?" (182) The answer, surely, is no. The priest's confessing to a degree of dissatisfaction with his lot is no more (or less) than human. When Mary proceeds to make fun of his praying in church, he is scandalized by her blasphemy, prepares to leave, and criticizes her in the following terms: "Stop your talking, Mary Byrne; you're an old, flagrant heathen" (IV, 21). But before he departs, he renews his promise to Sarah Casey, and for the reduced price they have agreed. The first act of *The Tinker's Wedding* would, I believe, have been readily accepted by Irish country people as a convincing account of relations between tinkers and priests. Denis Johnston, an Irishman and a fellow playwright, made this claim— up to a point (that of the ending, which we have yet to consider). He argued that the play depicts, "not unsympathetically, the rapacity and practicality of the clergy, who are . . . quite prepared to allow their parishoners to remain living in mortal sin indefinitely if they fail to produce the necessary cash to pay for a sacrament" (27). But the first act is also a superior dramatic representation, moving adroitly between the two poles of belief. The priest shows an unexpected measure of sympathy and insight into the ways of the tinkers, going beyond the pale of his social role but not of his religious beliefs. The tinkers, in their turn, address him respectfully as "your reverence"; Sarah shows a commendable desire for the sacrament of marriage, and it is only with the verbal and physical mischief making of Mary Byrne that matters get out of hand and the boundaries dividing pagan from Christian again reassert themselves.

The second act is far less satisfactory. Too much of it has not been transformed beyond either its folktale or one-act origins. As a result, the character of the priest reverts to being simply a remote authority figure, alternately condemning the tinkers or trying to take their money. Too much of the act centers on the trick whereby Synge, deciding not to have Michael and Sarah directly attempt to cheat the priest, now has Mary Byrne acquire sole blame in making off with the can and selling it for porter. When this is discovered, the full mutually condemnatory exchange, which is retained in all versions, then takes place. But it goes one crucial step further in the final version when the tinkers lay violent hands upon the priest, tie him up in a bag, and threaten to kill him.

The ending has been almost universally condemned by Synge critics and is certainly the reason the play was never staged during his lifetime. In addition to its direct affront to any (especially a Catholic) audience's sensibilities, there are crucial problems of tone here, veering from the farcical (the incident itself) to the serious (when they consider killing him). The tinkers finally, reluctantly, agree to let the priest out of the bag when he gives "a mighty oath" in the name of his God not to turn them over to the police. He emerges with the following lines in the play's overly hasty denouement:

PRIEST: [*lifting up his hand*] I've sworn not to call the hand of man upon your crimes to-day; but I haven't sworn I wouldn't call the fire of heaven from the hand of the Almighty God. [*He begins saying a Latin malediction in a loud ecclesiastical voice.*]

MARY: There's an old villain.

ALL: [*together*] Run, run. Run for your lives. [*They rush out, leaving the Priest master of the situation.*] (IV, 49)

The crude explicitness here is bad enough. But the ending is affected by a more serious and disabling lack of ambiguity, even a downright contradiction, in terms of our theme. I would focus this by looking at the attitudes in the play toward the two rituals by which its beliefs are formulated, prayers and stories. The former are the exclusive preserve of the priest, from the tinkers' point of view, and Mary urges him to recite one over the fire as his contribution. The oral storytelling by which the Irish pre-Christian legends were preserved and transmitted is associated with the tinkers, their migratory way of life, and their regard for and display of fine speeches. The older Mary Byrne is more conscious of this tradition than the younger couple:

let you sit down there by the big bough, and I'll be telling you the finest story you'd
hear any place from Dundalk to Ballinacree, with great queens in it, making themselves
matches from the start to the end, and they with silks on them the length of the day, and
white shifts for the night. (IV, 23)

But in her soliloquy that closes Act One, Mary Byrne reveals a crucial ambiguity
toward the stories in whose telling she takes such pride: "What good are the
grand stories I have when it's few would listen to an old woman, few but a girl
maybe . . . or a little child wouldn't be sleeping with the hunger on a cold night?"
(IV, 27) Perhaps her stories are no more than illusory compensations for the
undeniable facts of her growing old and her aloneness. The play's attitude toward
the storytelling therefore gravitates between admiration and distrust, affirmation
and doubt.

But in the tinkers' attitude toward Catholic prayer, there is not such ambiguity
but rather downright contradiction. In the first half, they display ignorance of
the "queer noise" (IV, 21) people make in church and ask the priest for an
example of something they claim never to have heard. At the end, there is a
certain justifiable fear at the threat of the peelers. But their awe-struck terror
before the priest's Latin maledictions not only comes out of nowhere but contradicts their earlier insouciance toward the metaphysical potency of Roman
Catholic prayer. The ending makes them seem like ignorant, superstitious heathens, an appalling stereotype that the rest of the play—and of Synge's dramatic
career—has been at pains to counter in its sympathetic, complex, and detailed
representation of the figure of the Irish peasant.

In *The Well of the Saints*, staged in the opening months of the Abbey Theatre
in early 1905, priests were still causing problems. As Nicholas Grene pointed
out in his Introduction to his edition of *The Well of the Saints*, the players balked
at performing the line: "Looking on your face is it? And she after going by with
her head turned the way you'd see a priest going where there'd be a drunken
man in the side ditch talking with a girl" (57). Despite writing indignantly to
Frank Fay that "I most emphatically will not change a syllable of it because A.
or B. or C. may think they know better than I do" (Saddlemyer 91), Synge
altered the offending line in his own copy of the 1905 edition to read: "And
she after going by with her head turned the way you'd see a sainted lady going
where there'd be drunken people in the side ditch singing to themselves" (III,
107). Nicholas Grene pinpointed the change as occurring "at the dress-rehearsal
stage after more complaints" and, in his edition of the play, restored the original
line in place of what he termed a "forced bowdlerization" (28).

The protest over this line apart, *The Well of the Saints* had a relatively tranquil
passage, attracting little criticism (and, hence, attention) when first staged. Although Willie Fay wished "that the Saint anyway might be made into a good-
natured easy-going man" (Fay and Carswell 31), and Synge wrote to Lady
Gregory that Padraic Colum "finds my play unsatisfactory because the Saint is
really a Protestant!" (Saddlemyer 94), the character of the Saint did not arouse

the usual protest. There are several reasons for this. One is the deliberate dist-ancing and stylization made possible by Synge's decision to set the play not in the present but *"one or more centuries ago"* (III, 69). This removed the action from the immediate realm of the real to an intermediate zone of fact and fancy where the central miracle would not strain credibility and to an archetypal level of the drama where he could draw more explicitly on mythic forebears. Another reason for the lack of protest is that *The Well* resolves many of the problems attendant upon *The Tinker's Wedding* in terms of satisfactory dramatic develo-ment and a balance of sympathies.

The play engages much more fully with the theme that Bourgeois saw as central to the earlier play: "the two types of Irish civilization, the Heathen and the Christian—Ireland before and after St. Patrick" (182). Although Synge's Saint is never given a name, any critical tendency to associate him with the archetypal Irish saint is corroborated by Synge's placing in his character's mouth words and sentiments taken directly from Patrick. In a letter to Max Meyerfeld, the play's German translator, Synge commented on "the words of women and smiths" (III, 91) that "this phrase is almost a quotation from an old hymn of St. Patrick" (Saddlemyer 121) known as "St. Patrick's Breastplate." In ex-plicitly evoking St. Patrick, he is removing his Saint from the sectarian divisions of the present to a time when the name of Christian transcended the divisions into Catholic and Protestant. Just as with Padraic Colum's accusation, St. Patrick could be seen as either Catholic or Protestant, since he was claimed by both traditions. Vivian Mercier wrote that there "were two patriotic tendencies pe-culiar to the Irish version of Evangelicalism: its interest, however narrow and utilitarian, in the Irish language, and its determined efforts to link the post-Reformation Church of Ireland with the pre-Norman Celtic Church of St. Patrick and his successors" ("Victorian Evangelicalism" 88). The presentation of the Saint therefore allows for greater identification on Synge's part with the "austere asceticism" (Grene, *The Well of the Saints by J. M. Synge* 13) of this spokesman for a spiritual way of life than with the well-fed Catholic clergy of the present day—like the priest in *The Tinker's Wedding*.

With this linking of his Saint with Patrick and our awareness of Synge's scholarly grounding in early Irish literature, we are in a much better position to understand the extent to which the conflict in the play between the Christian Saint and the blind couple is a dramatic treatment of the debates between St. Patrick, representing the new forces of Christianity making changes in the land, and Oisin, aged survivor of the Fenian warriors. In these traditional dialogues, Oisin is the spokesman for a world of pagan values of which he is the sole survivor but which he vigorously defends.

David Krause developed the Oisin/St. Patrick connection in his important essay " 'The Rageous Ossean': Patron-Hero of Synge and O'Casey," where he established the debate between them as the primary example of the dialectic between Christian and pagan values from the Irish literary past. In these nar-ratives, the Fenian hero has returned after a three hundred-year sojourn in Tir na nOg, the Land of Youth or Celtic otherworld, to an Ireland demythologized and Christianized, with Patrick as its spokesman. He is no longer the fine physical specimen preserved in Tir na nOg; having once more come into contact with the earth, he is old, feeble, and blind. The paradox by which a blind old man like Synge's Martin Doul can be said to inhabit the Land of Youth is resolved through this image of Oisin. Although physically much debilitated, what remains as vital and undiminished as ever is his imaginative apprehension of the natural world, his unabashed celebration of the senses and delight in the peculiarities of existence—a vision like that shared by Martin and Mary Doul in Synge's play. So I argued in an essay, "The Two Worlds of Synge's *The Well of the Saints*," that Synge was not only identifying Martin Doul with the figures of Oisin but further representing, through the ironic cure by which he and Mary are disillusioned, the "fall" from the pagan world of the Fianna and the Celtic otherworld into a Christianized world in which the oppressive vision of Patrick dominates. Vivian Mercier has suggested as a mythic archetype for the action of the play that of the biblical Fall of Man: the blind couple are expelled from a visionary state into a postlapsarian world where they must labor in the sweat of their brow and where they become only too conscious of the burden of mortality ("*The Tinker's Wedding*" 82). I think this theory does justice to the world into which they fall but less so to that from which they are banished, particularly when a Christian Saint is the agent of their expulsion.

A sustained comparison between what they perceive when blind and what they confront when cured will bear this out. When Martin and Mary Doul were blind, they were given gold and silver for their storytelling; when they can see, they must labor. When blind, they appeared to each other as the finest man and the finest woman, Mary in particular with her "yellow hair," her "white beautiful skin . . . on your neck and on your brows" (III, 71); when they can see each other, they behold a pair of tattered scarecrows, "things would make the heavens lonesome above, and they scaring the larks, and the crows" (III, 99). When deprived of physical sight, their mind's eye constructed visions, as their correspondingly heightened other senses brought to them "the sound of one of them twittering yellow birds do be coming in the spring-time from beyond the sea" (III, 131). The gold and silver, a beautiful fair-haired woman, the singing birds, the opened natural store of the earth's fecundity—all of these things are specific elements of the pagan nature-poetry of the Fianna and of the otherworld, a celebration of physical beauty in a natural morality devoid of Christian overtones.

It is to just such a perspective that Martin and Mary are restored in Act Three. The knowledge of each other's physical decrepitude that accompanied their "cure" would appear to present too great an obstacle to imaginative conversion now that their sight has failed once more. But as these "saints" of the eternal imagination gaze into "a well, or a clear pool, maybe" (II, 129), the abundance of luxuriant white hair verbally reflected by those visionary waters is finer than the actual, since unsullied by it.

A dissonant note is introduced when the "*faint sound of a bell is heard*" (III,

133). This sound of the bell signals the reentry of the Saint (Patrick) into the play and threatens the destruction of the pagan vision Martin and Mary have only just succeeded in reestablishing. As Krause pointed out, one of "the countless ways in which the Fenian life is superior to the cleric's austere Christianity" is marked by Oisin's contrasting "the melodious songs of the blackbirds and thrushes with the gloomy bells of St. Patrick" (275). The prospect of the Saint's return leads to the most heartfelt prayer in *The Well of the Saints*: "The Lord protect us from the saints of God!"(III, 133)

Furthermore, whereas Martin submitted meekly, even eagerly, the first time, he is now in a defiant mood, willing to challenge the authority of a Christian saint in order to defend his hallowed imaginative ground. Forced to kneel and be cured a second time, "MARTIN DOUL *with a sudden movement strikes the can from* SAINT'*s hand and sends it rocketing across stage*" (III, 147). The stark simplicity of this action stands in marked contrast to the hurried and overdone physical rough stuff at the close of *The Tinker's Wedding*. Here, the Saint's person is physically respected while the symbol of his spiritual power is definitively rejected. In this last heroic stand, and the eloquence it inspires in him, Martin most completely incarnates the spirit of Oisin:

Go on now, holy father, for if you're a fine saint itself, it's more sense is in a blind man, and more power maybe than you're thinking at all. . . . [If it's] a right some of you have to be fasting and praying and talking holy talk the like of yourself, I'm thinking it's a good right ourselves have to be sitting blind, hearing a soft wind turning round the little leaves of the spring and feeling the sun, and we not tormenting our souls with the sight of the grey days, and the holy men, and the dirty feet is trampling the world. (III, 149)

Despite its claim to be a revival, there was very little the Irish Literary Renaissance could look to in the native tradition by way of precedent and example in the area of drama. Douglas Hyde argued in his *A Literary History of Ireland* of 1899 that "the Irish never developed a drama. The nearest approach to such a thing is in [the] Ossianic poems" (511). Declan Kiberd has demonstrated in detail "Synge's debts to the work of Douglas Hyde . . . , in particular, his scholarly use of *A Literary History of Ireland*" (*Synge and the Irish Language* 149). So Hyde's argument with respect to a native Irish drama would have had a particular impact on Synge:

The dialogue between St. Patrick and Ossian . . . is quite dramatic in its form. Even the reciters of the present day appear to feel this, and I have heard the censorious, self-satisfied tone of Patrick, and the querulous vindictive whine of the half-starved old man, reproduced with considerable humour by a reciter. . . . The conception of bringing the spirit of Paganism and of Christianity together in the persons of the last great poet and warrior of the one, and the first great saint of the other, was truly dramatic in its conception, and the spirit and humour . . . in the pieces which have come down to us are a strong presumption that under happier circumstances something great would have developed from it. (511)

Five years after Hyde's *Literary History* was published, something "great" and "truly dramatic in its conception" emerged with the staging of Synge's elaborately Ossianic *The Well of the Saints* at the new Abbey Theatre.

Synge's apotheosis as a playwright came with *The Playboy of the Western World*, immediately in terms of the first-week riots it engendered and generally as the most complex and achieved of his dramas. In a letter to *The Irish Times* written four days after the famous opening night, Synge made a rare public pronouncement on his work: "There are, it may be hinted, several sides to 'The Playboy' " (Saddlemyer 286). The truth of its creator's statement has been borne out by the apparent inexhaustibility of the play when it comes to interpretation. The principles of ironic qualification and contradiction that Synge has built into the fabric of *The Playboy* ensure that no one line of interpretation can claim to be exhaustive, since any train of imagery or symbolic reference that a critic may start to trace is bound not to complete itself or else be disrupted and brought into conflict by another. One example of this in *The Playboy* is its treatment of the theme of Christianity and paganism.

The lines at first, as we acclimatize ourselves to the Mayo shebeen and its inhabitants on this particular night, seem clearly drawn. The one consistent spokesman for Catholic beliefs as promulgated by the local priest, Father Reilly, is Shawn Keogh, Pegeen's fiancé. What constitutes the traditional comic obstacle to an imminent marriage between the pair, opening up a delaying gap into which a more appropriate suitor will step, is never explicitly indicated. Whatever it may be (an earlier draft suggested they were first cousins), the obstacle requires "Father Reilly's dispensation from the bishops or the Court of Rome" (IV, 59). Synge did not bother to specify since he was evidently more concerned to establish the literalism with which the question of the satisfactoriness or unsatisfactoriness of the match is proposed. He and the play suggest other and more convincing grounds for choice: the spineless, endlessly whining Shawn Keogh is no match for the lively, spirited Pegeen Mike. She counters his references to Father Reilly and the pope with a lament for the passing of pugnacious men who would knock "the eye from a peeler" or would prove "a great warrant to tell stories" (IV, 59). When she asks him to stay the night as her protector, Shawn's cringing refusal, couched in response to what he imagines Father Reilly would say, carries within it Synge's Protestant critique of the oppressive system of hierarchical authority, proceeding from the local priest via the bishops to the Court of Rome, to which the individual Catholic conscience is subject and which has, if Shawn is anything to go by, an emasculating effect. But the contrast is even more than between the servile Christianity of the present and a more authentic pagan past, which would yield flesh-and-blood heroes willing to stand up and defend themselves. The ground is being prepared for the arrival of Christy Mahon, the locals' acclaim for his father-slaying and the rapid development of his romance with Pegeen.

This opening exchange between Pegeen and Shawn is amplified with the entrance of her father, Michael James, and his drinking companions. They enlarge on the scorn directed at Shawn for his fear of incurring the priest's disapproval by elaborating a scapegoating game and threatening to make him stay:

MICHAEL: [*catching him by the coattail*] You'd be going, it is?

SHAWN: [*screaming*] Leave me go, Michael James, leave me go, you old Pagan, leave me go or I'll get the curse of the priests on you, and of the scarlet-coated bishops of the courts of Rome. [*With a sudden movement he pulls himself out of his coat and disappears out of the door.*]

MICHAEL: [*holding up coat*] Well there's the coat of a Christian man. (IV, 65)

On its verbal and physical surface, this scene clearly represents the conflict of Christianity (Shawn Keogh and, by extension, the Catholic priests, bishops, and pope) versus paganism (Pegeen, her "old Pagan" father and his cronies). But Synge had no sooner demarcated the lines of conflict than he began, character-istically, to complicate them. The meanspiritedness of their attack on the hapless Shawn and the disparity in strength of numbers draw a timely rebuke from Pegeen: "What right have you to be making game of a poor fellow for minding the priest?" (IV, 65)

But the play's more consistent and developed approach to Christianity is to affirm at a more archetypal level what its characters verbally asperse or disparge. When Shawn has earlier reported that he passed by "a kind of fellow above in the furzy ditch, groaning wicked like a maddening dog" (IV, 61), Pegeen's reply draws on the parable of the Good Samaritan, as more than one critic has pointed out: "And you never went near to see was he hurted or what ailed him at all?" (IV, 61) This use of the biblical archetype as implicit model for behavior does not contradict the disparagement of Christianity if we regard the first as a Protestant affirmation of the Bible against the legalism, literalism, and hierar-chical decision making of the Roman Catholic Church. But at another level it sets up a disturbing tension between the play's fluctuating affirmation and denial of Christianity.

The most widespread use of biblical archetypes noted by critics has been the suggestive parallels between Christy son of Mahon ("a name pronounced as if almost of one syllable, Maan" [Johnston 34]) and Christ son of Man (MacLean). Howard D. Pearce's important essay "Synge's Playboy as Mock-Christ" ex-amines the process by which the unlikely, impoverished figure taken in by the Mayo people gradually discloses a messianic identity that offers a "kind of salvation" to various of the play's characters (90). This is truest where the women are concerned: three "stranger girls" who have heard the legend of the father-slayer travel to meet him and bring a series of gifts that "effectively parody the gifts of the Magi" (Pearce 91). The Widow Quin may be redeemed if she can persuade Christy to marry her and save her from the worst fate Synge can imagine, loneliness and isolation in the face of an approaching death. Pegeen is offered an escape from the materialistic bargain with the unsatisfactory Shawn Keogh into the romantic fulfilment of a life with Christy. But Synge's play also shows Christy's impact on the community as a whole; his storytelling fires up the rich imaginations of these literally impoverished people, whose existence is not only on the edge of the Western world but on the margins of survival itself. Christy's apotheosis occurs at the climax of the races, when they carry him on their shoulders in a scene reminiscent of Christ's Palm Sunday acclamation. There is an equally precipitate fall, whereby the crowd, feeling he has betrayed their belief, turn on him and come within inches of putting him to death—by rope and by fire. But Christy rises up in the last of the play's numerous death-and-resurrection scenes patented by old Mahon and proclaims the new life they have made possible for him, as he gives his final blessing: "Ten thousand blessings upon all that's here, for you've turned me a likely gaffer in the end of all, the way I'll go romancing through a romping lifetime from this hour to the dawning of the judgement day" (IV, 173). This speech also indicates the way Synge uses biblical references to extend the play's sense of time and place from the local to the universal ("from this hour to the dawning of the judgement day"). But even in a relatively straight reading of the Christ/Christy parallel, it is impossible to suppress completely the disturbing ironic disruptions that refuse to confirm and complete the parallel. Mary C. King best described Synge's method of deploying the Bible by remarking how the "dramatic strategy" draws "its symbolic strength from the Bible and at the same time stands the sacred text on its head" (80). It does so through Synge's characteristic use of irony, parody, and inversion, reflecting a modernist tendency to refer selectively to biblical motifs without endorsing a one-on-one identification of meaning or implying an entire value system (cf. Beckett's use of biblical references in *Waiting for Godot*).

In *The Playboy*, what prevents a thoroughly Christian interpretation are the pagan elements that persistently obtrude at every level—most notoriously, the father-slaying for which Christy is applauded, not condemned, *and* the vision of endless women, "a drift of chosen females, standing in their shifts itself maybe" (IV, 167), at which the opening night audience broke up in disorder. Anyone who knows Irish literature will find this speech echoing the incident in the Ulster saga whereby the warrior Cuchulain, still in the throes of a battle-rage, was finally calmed (and abashed) by the sight of thirty naked virgins sent from Emain Macha. Declan Kiberd drew on this incident as part of a detailed comparison, first suggested by Michael J. Sidnell, between Christy Mahon the champion of the Western world and Cuchulain the Red Branch hero of the Ulster court (*Synge and the Irish Language* 118). Like Cuchulain, Christy, too, according to Kiberd, "is filled with the battle-rage of triumph after the sports and his frantic speech recalls the parade of chosen virgins at Emain Macha" (118–19).

Other mythic avatars for Christy's pagan heroism have been put forth. Kiberd, in a separate essay, "The Frenzy of Christy," has suggested a parallel with mad

Sweeney, whose poem pivots around a similar pagan/Christian contrast to those of Oisin and St. Patrick. Toni O'Brien Johnson has looked outside the Irish tradition to *Sir Gawain and the Green Knight*, identifying Christy with the "green man" or fertility figure (66). The point, surely is that no single figure from the legends can be unequivocally identified with Christy. In this play, Synge's procedure differs from the unmistakable centrality of the Oisin/St. Patrick myth to *The Well of the Saints*. If Martin Doul draws strength from the identification, here the process is reversed and Christy subsumes his great number of heroic predecessors, drawing on their mythic energies but reshaping them in his own name and image. The technique is best exemplified by one of Synge's poems, "Queens":

> Seven dog-days we let pass
> Naming Queens in Glenmacnass,
> All the rare and royal names
> Wormy sheepskin yet retains,
> Etain, Helen, Maeve, and Fand,
> Golden Deirdre's tender hand, . . .
> Yet these are rotten—I ask their pardon—
> And we've the sun on rock and garden,
> These are rotten, so you're the Queen
> Of all are living, or have been. (I, 34)

The area in which *The Playboy of the Western World* most richly mixes its Christian and pagan elements is in the love talk between Christy and Pegeen. In her presence, he declares himself "a good Christian" (IV, 149) and appears to demonstrate it by the fervor of his praying, which has the petitioning force of a litany (like the naming in "Queens") and is irradiated by liturgical imagery: "Isn't there the light of seven heavens in your heart alone, the way you'll be an angel's lamp to me from this out" (IV, 149). But a subtle process of subversion is underway whereby the traditional imagery of worship shifts, in the manner of courtly love, from the divine to the human, and the love object is invested with the sacramental charisma of prayer. When Martin Doul considered the role of the Saint and acknowledged considerable affinities with the man of God in their mutual quest for a spiritual reality, he finally drew back from the comparison on the grounds that "if bell-ringing is a fine life, . . . it's better I am wedded with the beautiful dark woman of Ballinatone" (III, 87). Similarly, the true paradise Christy seeks, for all the symbolic energy it draws from the Christian Heaven, is the one that is shared—and created—between a man and a woman. In Christy's and Synge's most audacious inversion, the lovers' otherworld renders the Christian equivalent a place of isolation and confinement, more Hell than Heaven. Christy thus talks of "squeezing kisses on your puckered lips till I'd feel a kind of pity for the Lord God is all ages sitting lonesome in his golden chair" (IV, 147). Synge expressed almost identical sentiments in his poem "Dread":

Beside a chapel I'd a room looked down,
Where all the women from the farms and town,
On Holy-days, and Sunday used to pass
To marriages, and Christenings and to Mass.

Then I sat lonely watching score and score,
Till I turned jealous of the Lord next door . . .
Now by this window, where there's none can see,
The Lord God's jealous of yourself and me. (I, 40)

The three periods mark not only a dramatic pause before the poem's triumphant reversal of situation and mood but also the two-year gap before he had met Molly Allgood and added the last two lines (Greene and Stephens 204).

Synge sensed his own approaching death and wrote several epitaphs marred by excessive self-pity and literary self-consciousness. His question "Will you go to my funeral?" provoked a response from his fiancée that he turned into one of his finest poems, drawing as in his plays on the speech of others as a means of freeing up his own powers of self-expression. The poem "A Question" serves as fitting epitaph. Synge, as Yeats remarked, "was not sure of any world to come" (328). Yet his end was marked with a Church of Ireland funeral acknowledging the Protestant dimension of his life. But the conflict between those beliefs and the pagan passion he sought to express is finely caught in the living speech of the woman he loved:

I asked if I got sick and died, would you
With my black funeral go walking too,
If you'd stand close to hear them talk or pray
While I'm let down in that steep bank of clay.

And, No, you said, for if you saw a crew
Of living idiots, pressing round that new
Oak coffin—they alive, I dead beneath
That board—you'd rave and rend them with your teeth. (I, 64)

References

Benjamin, Walter. "The Storyteller." *Illuminations*. Translated by Harry Zohn. Edited by Hannah Arendt. New York: Schocken, 1969. pp. 83–109.

Bourgeois, Maurice. *John Millington Synge and the Irish Theatre*. London: Constable, 1913.

Clark, David R. "Synge's 'Perpetual Last Day': Remarks on *Riders to the Sea*." *A Centenary Tribute to John Millington Synge, 1871–1909: Sunshine and the Moon's Delight*. Edited by S. B. Bushrui. New York: Barnes & Noble, 1972. pp. 41–51.

Corkery, Daniel. *Synge and Anglo-Irish Literature: A Study*. Dublin and Cork: University Press; London: Longmans, Green, 1931.

Donoghue, Denis. "Synge: *Riders to the Sea*: A Study." *University Review* 1 (1955):

52–58. Reprinted in *John Millington Synge: Riders to the Sea*. Edited by David R. Clark. The Merrill Literary Casebook Series. Columbus: Charles E. Merrill, 1970. pp. 46–53.

Fay, William G., and Catherine Carswell. *The Fays of the Abbey Theatre: An Autobiographical Record*. New York: Harcourt, Brace; London: Rich and Cowan, 1935.

Greene, David H., and Edward M. Stephens. *J. M. Synge, 1871–1909*. New York: Macmillan, 1959.

Grene, Nicholas. *Synge: A Critical Study of the Plays*. Totowa, N.J.: Rowman and Littlefield, 1975.

————, ed. *The Well of the Saints by J. M. Synge*. Irish Dramatic Texts. Washington, D.C.: Catholic University of America Press; Gerrards Cross, Bucks: Colin Smythe, 1982.

Henn, T. R. "*Riders to the Sea*: A Note." *A Centenary Tribute to John Millington Synge, 1871–1909: Sunshine and the Moon's Delight*. Edited by S. B. Bushrui. New York: Barnes & Noble, 1972. pp. 33–39.

Hillgarth, J. N., ed. *Christianity and Paganism, 350–750: The Conversion of Western Europe*. Philadelphia: University of Pennsylvania Press, 1969.

Hyde, Douglas. *A Literary History of Ireland*. London: Unwin, 1899.

Johnson, Toni O'Brien. *Synge: The Medieval and the Grotesque*. Irish Literary Studies 11. Gerrards Cross, Bucks: Colin Smythe; Totowa, N.J.: Barnes & Noble, 1982.

Johnston, Denis. *John Millington Synge*. Columbia Essays on Modern Writers 12. New York and London: Columbia University Press, 1965.

Kiberd, Declan. "The Frenzy of Christy: Synge and *Buile Shuibhne*." *Éire-Ireland* 14, no. 2 (1979):68–79.

————. *Synge and the Irish Language*. Totowa, N.J.: Rowman and Littlefield; London: Macmillan, 1979.

King, Mary C. *The Drama of J. M. Synge*. Irish Studies. Syracuse: Syracuse University Press, 1985.

Krause, David. "The 'Rageous Ossean': Patron-Hero of Synge and O'Casey." *Modern Drama*, 4, no. 3 (1961):268–91.

MacCana, Prionsias. *Celtic Mythology*. London: Newnes, 1983.

MacLean, Hugh H. "The Hero as Playboy." *The University of Kansas City Review* 21 (1954):9–19.

Mercier, Vivian. "*The Tinker's Wedding*." *A Centenary Tribute to John Millington Synge, 1871–1909: Sunshine and the Moon's Delight*. New York: Barnes & Noble, 1972. pp. 75–89.

————. "Victorian Evangelicalism and the Anglo-Irish Literary Revival." *Literature and the Changing Ireland*. Edited by Peter Connolly. Irish Literary Studies 9. Totowa, N.J.: Barnes & Noble, 1982. pp. 59–101.

Meyer, Kuno, ed. and trans. *The Voyage of Bran Son of Febal*. 2 vols. London: David Nutt, 1895.

Pearce, Harold D. "Synge's Playboy as Mock-Christ." *Modern Drama* 8, no. 3 (1965):303–10. Reprinted in *The Playboy of the Western World: A Collection of Critical Essays*. Edited by Thomas R. Whitaker. Twentieth Century Interpretations. Englewood Cliffs, N.J.: Prentice-Hall, 1969, pp. 88–97.

Roche, Anthony. "The Two Worlds of Synge's *The Well of the Saints*." *Genre* 12 (1979): 439–50.

Saddlemyer, Ann, ed. *The Collected Letters of John Millington Synge, I: 1871–1907*. Oxford: Clarendon, 1983.

Sidnell, M. J. "Synge's Playboy and the Champion of Ulster." *Dalhousie Review* 45 (1965):51–59.

Skelton, Robin. *J. M. Synge*. The Irish Writers Series. Lewisburg, Pa.: Bucknell University Press, 1972.

———. *The Writings of J. M. Synge*. Indianapolis and New York: Bobbs-Merrill, 1971.

Stephens, Edward. *My Uncle John: Edward Stephens's Life of J. M. Synge*. Edited by Andrew Carpenter. London: Oxford University Press, 1974.

Synge Manuscripts, MS 4378, 4382, Trinity College, Dublin.

Thornton, Weldon. *J. M. Synge and the Western Mind*. Irish Literary Studies 4. New York: Barnes & Noble, 1979.

Yeats, William Butler. *Mythologies*. New York: Macmillan, 1959.

J. M. Synge and Irish Mythology

During the lifetime of J. M. Synge (1871–1909), Irish mythology went from being an obscure interest of a few antiquarians, scholars, and poets to being part of the common heritage of Ireland and indeed of the English-speaking world. Many people contributed to this development, but the irreplacable roles were played by W. B. Yeats and Lady Gregory: Yeats through his creative works based on the old stories, *The Wanderings of Osin, On Baile's Strand, Deirdre,* and others, and through his repeated insistence that Ireland had a mythological heritage equal to any other; Lady Gregory through her prose retellings of the old stories in *Cuchulain of Muirthemne* (1902) and *Gods and Fighting Men* (1903), which gave the common reader a version of the myths one could read and enjoy. Hand in hand with this reclaiming of the Irish literary heritage went the creation of a contemporary Irish literature in English, particularly an Irish national drama. Against the skepticism of those like George Moore who unforgettably if unforgivably said that Ireland needed a theater about as much as a mule needed a holiday, Yeats and Lady Gregory created living and important theater in Ireland. In keeping with the literary interests of Yeats and Lady Gregory, the plays initially performed by what was to become the Abbey Theatre were to a large extent recreations of the old Irish mythology: AE's (George Russell's) *Deirdre,* Yeats's *Deirdre* and *On Baile's Strand,* and most strangely, *Diarmuid and Grania* coauthored by Yeats and George Moore.

Synge was in the middle of all of this activity, intimately involved with Lady Gregory and Yeats in the running of the Abbey. He also knew the Irish saga material much more intimately and directly than any of the other writers of the

Revival, since he spoke Irish well and had studied the language at Trinity College and the literature with the noted scholar de Jubainville in Paris. But Synge avoided the mythological subjects favored by Yeats and AE. None of Synge's plays performed in his lifetime were on mythological subjects. Instead, with the exception of *Deirdre of the Sorrows,* left unfinished at Synge's death, his plays are set in the present and set in the rural areas of Ireland, Wicklow, the West, and the Aran Islands. The characters are predominantly peasants who speak in a version of Anglo-Irish dialect that makes no attempt to make them sound more genteel. It has been argued (correctly, I think) that it was Synge's peasant drama that turned the Irish dramatic movement away from mythological subjects toward the peasant drama that for a time became its signature.

This raises the central question in any consideration of Synge and Irish mythology: Why did he avoid it as subject matter for his plays for so long? Why did he finally change his mind? It is clear that his earlier, pre-*Deirdre* choice of subject matter was deliberate. When his close friend Stephen MacKenna urged him to write a play on the old mythological characters, Synge responded with a passage that has become famous: "I do not believe in the possibility of a purely fantastic unmodern ideal breezy spring-dayish Cuchulainoid National Theatre. We had the 'Shadowy Waters' [Yeats's play] on the stage last week, and it was the most *distressing* failure the mind can imagine" (quoted in Ó Tuama 2). He went on to make it clear why he felt this way: "No drama can grow out of anything other than the fundamental realities of life which are never fantastsic, are neither modern nor unmodern and, as I see them, rarely spring-dayish, or breezy or Cuchulainoid." So even if Synge—not wishing to attack his fellow dramatists and theater directors—never made such sentiments public, we can interpret his own plays as a deliberate response to the Cuchulainoid theater of AE, Yeats, and others. They were interested in "spring-dayish" cleaned-up and idealized images from the past; he was interested in "the fundamental realities of life," to be found in contemporary Ireland. This attitude was made unforgettably explicit in his poem "The Passing of the Shee," subtitled "After looking at one of AE's pictures":

> Adieu, sweet Angus, Maeve and Fand,
> Ye plumed yet skinny Shee
> That poets played with hand in hand
> To learn their ecstasy
>
> We'll search in Red Dan Sally's ditch,
> And drink in Tubber fair,
> Or poach with Red Dan Philly's bitch
> The badger and the hare. (I, 38)

The subtitle could easily have been "after seeing one of Yeats's plays" instead of one of AE's pictures, and the poem's attitude gives us a clear understanding of Synge's choice of subject matter. Synge as a playwright is going to search in Red Dan Sally's ditch and poach the badger and the hare, not play hand in hand with the "plumed yet skinny Shee." It therefore comes as a shock to turn to Synge's last play and find that he has abandoned his world of poachers and tinkers to turn to the world of Maeve and Fand.

What led him to change his mind and write *Deirdre of the Sorrows*, a play of the kind he had earlier avoided? Had he simply abandoned his earlier objections and joined the "Cuchulainoids"? Or is his final play somehow consistent with his earlier work and with his earlier objections to his fellow dramatists' work on subjects such as the Deirdre story? This is an important question, for how one answers it determines not only how one sees *Deirdre of the Sorrows* but also how one sees the rest of Synge's career. In what follows, I first summarize the various answers to this question that have been proposed in Synge criticism. But then, since none of the answers tells the whole story, I conclude by advancing a perspective that reconciles what I take to be the best work on this question in a larger perspective. For the question is not only how does *Deirdre* fit in with Synge's other work but also why did Synge turn to mythology when he did? It is obvious that there is a turn here to be explained, even if—as many critics have argued—it isn't the complete inconsistency Synge's remarks about Cuchulainoid theater would indicate.

One line of argument has been simply that Synge's *Deirdre* is an inconsistency that isn't very successful. Yeats, whose writings about Synge have been so powerful in shaping our perceptions of his life and work, seems to have felt this way. His comments on *Deirdre*, though few, separate it from his other works: "It was only at the last in his unfinished *Deirdre of the Sorrows* that his mood changed" (*Essays and Introductions* 309). Here he anticipates a line of criticism on *Deirdre* (to which I've contributed elsewhere) that sees *Deirdre* as, above all, Synge's attempt to come to terms with his own impending death. Yeats doesn't seem to have thought very highly of the play, for his diary of 1909, made prominent by its inclusion in his *Autobiographies*, shows his anxiety before the first performances: "*Deirdre of the Sorrows* (first performaces). I was anxious about this play and on Thursday both Lady Gregory and I felt the strain of our doubts and fears. Would it seem mere disjointed monotony? Would the second act be intelligible?" (*Autobiographies* 523) The distinguished Synge critic and editor Robin Skelton is only one of the critics who share Yeats's view of *Deirdre* as both a new and a less than totally successful departure: "*Deirdre of the Sorrows* is in many ways, therefore, an entirely new departure for Synge" (139). But "unfortunately the play remains narrative rather than drama for much of its length" (139). The new departure for Skelton is primarily in the more explicitly poetic nature of the language, close to the language of the translations Synge was experimenting with in these same years. Yet Synge has also been criticized for using essentially the same Anglo-Irish dialect in *Deirdre* that he had developed in the peasant drama: Sean Ó Tuama argued that "the language is completely inadequate tonally to create a milieu in which kings and princes can operate" (12–13). So there seems to be little agreement on what Synge was trying to do

with the language of the mythological characters in *Deirdre* but there is agreement
that he wasn't successful.

Generally, critics have seconded this judgment, if only—as Henry Kissinger
might say—by voting with their feet. *Deirdre* has not been considered one of
Synge's best plays, *Riders to the Sea* and *The Playboy of the Western World*
customarily being assigned that role, and less has been written on *Deirdre* than
on these other plays. So the question of what Synge was up to in *Deirdre* is
linked to the issue of evaluation: for *Deirdre* to find an honored place in Synge's
canon, it seems necessary for critics to see it as consistent with the rest of the
canon, which means to explain how and why Synge is using the mythology he
had earlier avoided.

One approach to this issue has been simply to argue that *Deirdre* does not
represent as radical a shift as Yeats and Skelton assumed, and the criticism of
Donna Gerstenberger, Hugh Kenner, and Alan Price exemplifies this approach.
According to Gerstenberger, "Synge did not abandon his ideas about the proper
nature of and material for drama in his last play, despite an apparent contradiction
between his theory and practice in the creation of *Deirdre of the Sorrows*" (97).
So the contrast is only apparent: the center of Synge's dramatic practice, according to Gerstenberger, is to bring out the human dimensions of every character, and this is what Synge does with his mythological characters as well, "by
choosing to emphasize all that was most human in them instead of all that was
most traditional" (97). Synge had expressed some anxiety during the writing of
Deirdre on precisely this point. In a letter to John Quinn, Synge wrote that
"these people, when one comes to deal with them, seem very remote" (quoted
in Saddlemyer 93). Gerstenberger's central point about the mythological elements
in *Deirdre* is that Synge—unlike AE or Yeats—wanted to overcome that re-
moteness and did so by going against the tradition he was borrowing from. So
the mythological setting and origins of *Deirdre* in Gerstenberger's view simply
presented Synge with a challenge that he successfully met. Deirdre as a character
may have a different origin from Christy Mahon or Nora Burke, but Synge's
dramatic art succeeded in bringing them to the same place, to life on the stage.

Hugh Kenner's brief analysis of Synge's plays in *A Colder Eye* makes much
the same point. All of Synge's plays tell essentially the same story: "Synge, it
may be, handled but the one story six times, a story of setting out and then
dying, in which those who set forth have chosen better than those who choose
to stay" (120). *Deirdre* is particularly close to *The Shadow of the Glen*, the
story of two lovers who deny social convention, except that *Deirdre* takes the
story to its conclusion. So for Kenner as for Gerstenberger, the sources of *Deirdre*
are less important than what Synge made of them, and what he makes of the
Deirdre story brings it into close correspondence with his other, nonmythological
plays.

Alan Price made virtually the same point: *Deirdre* for Price "does not mark
a change in him as a dramatist; it is not a new departure but a development"
(192). There are thematic links between *Deirdre* and other Synge plays, partic-

ularly *Riders to the Sea* and *The Shadow of the Glen*, and the way the saga characters are portrayed, "mainly in terms of peasant life," links *Deirdre* to his other plays in the way Gerstenberger and Kenner argued. But Price also praised Synge's rendition of the myth as avoiding "the shortcomings of the contemporary versions of the legend which treated Deirdre rather like Tennyson treated King Arthur" (192). So Synge's choice of a mythological subject "does not revoke the attitude antagonistic to the romanticizing of Celtic myth, expressed in his lines 'The Passing of the Shee' " (192). This is an important point: *Deirdre* needs to be read *against* the other contemporary versions of the Deirdre myth as well as alongside Synge's other plays.

Thus Synge has not abandoned his earlier criticism of the other versions of the saga stories, but the existence of *Deirdre* ensures that we understand that earlier criticism to be of the other contemporary versions of the stories, not of the stories themselves. What he was criticizing them for was their tendency to romanticize the original myths. Part of what enabled him to do that, as Declan Kiberd has shown, was his superior knowledge of the original sources. Kiberd's excellent study *Synge and the Irish Language* is the most authoritative treatment of Synge's knowledge of Irish and of the Irish sources for Synge's treatment of Deirdre. He showed beyond any doubt Synge's grasp of the original sources that AE, Yeats, and Lady Gregory knew only through translations:

The fundamental differences between Synge's play and the other works may be explained by the fact that, unlike Yeats and Russell, Synge did not rely on nineteenth-century English translations. Instead, he went back to the original texts of the legend in the Irish language. There had been many Gaelic versions of the tale, from the stark and primitive text in the *Book of Leinster* down to the sentimental and romantic version published by Douglas Hyde in Synge's own lifetime. Synge understood the development of the legend and the characteristic qualities of each of the major versions. (178)

Already while on Aran in 1901 Synge had translated one version of the story, that transcribed by Aindrias MacCuirton in 1740, and this remained his major source for the play. But he knew other versions as well. His 1905 review of A. H. Leahy's *Heroic Romances of Ireland* criticizes Leahy's "deplorable misrepresentation" of the twelfth-century *Book of Leinster* version (II, 371–73), and Synge had studied this version with de Jubainville in Paris. Earlier, in 1902, he had reviewed Geoffrey Keating's *Foras Feasa Ar Éirinn* (II, 360–63), which included another version of the legend. Kiberd's discussion (176–95) traces the influence of these various versions on Synge's own *Deirdre*.

Kiberd's painstaking scholarship enables a deeper understanding of the nature of Synge's play. Deirdre is more like a peasant from one of Synge's other plays than like Tennyson's Arthur at least partially because the original Deirdre was too. Dissenting from Ó Tuama's judgment that the peasant diction fails Synge in *Deirdre*, Kiberd argued that it captures the earthy flavor of the original extremely well:

Many critics of the play have argued that its blunt peasant idiom is inappropriate on the lips of noble personages; but this robust idiom is an integral part of the barbarbic tale in the *Book of Leinster*. . . . Alone among the Abbey dramatists, Synge succeeded in recapturing the vivid and robust idiom of the *Book of Leinster*(181).

So the continuity in Synge's work between the peasant drama and the one mythological play reveals Synge's deeper apprehension of both the mythology and the Irish peasantry: they don't need to be presented as differently as Synge's critics assume. Kiberd has a good discussion of the close connection between the ancient legends and the peasant culture Synge's earlier work had been set in. Relevant in this context is Kiberd's discussion of the parallelism between the exploits of Christy Mahon in *The Playboy* and the exploits of Cuchulain (109–21). Christy is a mock-Cuchulain, and the parallels Kiberd found are largely ironic. But this shows that even before writing *Deirdre*, Synge's work had exploited the connection between ancient and peasant Ireland, revealing a radically different and more authentic conception of ancient Ireland. *Deirdre* merely made that reinterpretation explicit. Thus Synge's journeys in the West of Ireland that led to his earlier plays and his work with the ancient literature that led to *Deirdre* are complementary—not antithetical—as each enabled him to get a better handle on the other.

This is also the argument made in Weldon Thornton's *J. M. Synge and the Western Mind*. Thornton's argument is that the criticism has always overstated Synge's lack of interest in religious issues and that much of his interest in the culture of the West of Ireland and the Aran Islands lay in its archaic, largely pre-Christian and pagan viewpoint and values, one congruent with the world of the sagas. This certainly places Synge in a larger intellectual current of his time, for Synge was a contemporary of Frazer, and it makes a deeper sense of the persistently and deliberately anticlerical themes of plays such as *The Well of the Saints* and *The Tinker's Wedding*. In this context, writing a play about Deirdre that makes her seem much like a peasant from Synge's earlier plays is not a dramatic flaw or incongruity because the culture of those peasants descended directly from Deirdre's and because Synge's interest in those peasants stemmed directly from what they held in common with her. Thus, in Thornton's presentation as well as in Kiberd's, Synge's turn to the saga materials in his final play is nothing more than a return to the most basic sources of his art. This is confirmed not only by his earlier translation of the Deirdre story and his scholarly work in Gaelic literature expertly traced by Kiberd but also by the existence of fragmentary 1902 drafts of two plays on mythological subjects, "A Vernal Play" (III, 189–93) and "Luasnad, Capa, and Laine" (III, 194–205).

So the work of these critics and scholars certainly goes a long way to remove any appearance of inconsistency or even of a new departure in Synge's shift in subject matter from contemporary Ireland to the mythological story of *Deirdre of the Sorrows*. In fact, my only objection to the criticism just surveyed is that the critics have done too good a job in linking *Deirdre* to the rest of Synge's canon. For it remains true, despite all of Synge's interest in the old stories, that he stayed away from them until his final play. Despite his private concern that the other writers of the Literary Revival were distorting the old stories, he seemed content to let them go on doing it. So the question remains, why turn back explicitly to the old stories at that particular point? Inasmuch as criticism has tried to answer that question, it has done so by reference to the themes of the play. Clearly, even painfully, the story of Deirdre is one with personal resonance for Synge, dying young while he wrote the play just as Deirdre died young in his play. But I don't think that is the whole story. If *The Playboy of the Western World* can be seen, as Kiberd has shown, as a contemporary version of the Cuchulain myth, Synge could have retold Deirdre's story in modern dress in the same way. This is a central strategy of modernist literature, and Kiberd's reading of the *The Playboy* makes it a precursor of such works as *Ulysses*. So the question still remains as to why Synge chose in his last play to treat explicitly the saga and mythological material that he had earlier approached so much more indirectly.

I think the anwer lies in the juxtaposition of two things, the turbulent reception of his earlier plays, particularly *The Playboy*, and the use being made in nationalist circles of Irish myth. The "Cyclops" chapter of Joyce's *Ulysses* offers one useful reference point. The Cyclops of the chapter is called the "Citizen," and the Citizen displays a characteristic and relevant set of responses and opinions. He is a Gaelic Leaguer who thinks that everyone should speak Irish, although his command of it seems less than absolute. He thinks that everything English—not just the language—is an abomination, and that salvation for the Irish consists in returning in all ways to Irish tradition and custom. He therefore has a particularly virulent hatred of foreigners of any description; the presence of Leopold Bloom, a Jew who has the audacity to declare himself Irish, causes a particularly hostile response by the Citizen.

If the Citizen is something of a caricature, his opinions nonetheless bear a close resemblance to those that led Arthur Griffith, Padraic Pearse, and other nationalists to attack Synge's plays with such fury. A crucial part of nationalist rhetoric was that England was entirely evil; Ireland correspondingly was entirely good, except where and when it had been corrupted by English influence. The locus of corruption within Ireland was that part of the country oriented toward England, and Synge, a Protestant educated at Trinity College, had close associations with some of the most suspect institutions in the country. Conversely, the locus of virtue, geographically, was the West, particularly the Gaeltacht, that part of the country least sullied by English influence; temporally, the locus of virtue was the past, before the seven centuries of English domination.

Nationalist rhetoric had therefore already linked the Gaelic past and the Gaelic countryside but in a different way from the link delineated in Synge's work: that which was all Irish (or all too Irish, as Joyce might emend) was spotless in virtue and an important resource in the struggle against the English. So the Gaelic League injunction to go west and learn Gaelic was one with the injunction to go back to Irish mythology and learn about Cuchulain: both were ways to deanglicize Ireland. Joyce made the connection perfectly explicit in the mock-heroic depiction of the Citizen as if he were Cuchulain or Finn MacCool. But Padraic Pearse had already lived the connection, with his cult of Cuchulain, his denigration of English in favor of Gaelic, and his violent revolutionary position, a combination that led inexorably to the Easter Rebellion. If Pearse seems like an extreme case, even Yeats and AE comparably tended to locate virtue in the Irish countryside and in the Irish past. Yeats saw the connection I am drawing here between that idealization and revolutionary violence. His reflections late in life in "The Man and the Echo" on the connection between "that play" of his, *Cathleen Ni Houlihan*, and the Easter Rebellion were not wholly melodramatic. Cuchulanoid theater was serious business in Ireland, or to put it another way, the Easter Rebellion was perhaps the most effective piece of Cuchulanoid theater ever staged.

Synge had died several years before, but the riots over his work already showed where that line of nationalism was heading, and this explains his earlier avoidance of mythological subjects. Synge just as clearly as Joyce saw the connection between the cult of Irish mythology and the intolerance of the *Playboy* rioters. He had wanted to play no role in this attempted "deanglicization" of Ireland, which he felt was neither practical nor desirable. Given his disdain for the Gaelic League, so memorably expressed in his unfinished sketch "Deaf Mutes for Ireland" (III, 218–19), he wanted to have nothing to do with the cleaned-up, "spring-dayish" images of the Irish past being passed off—so successfully—as the real thing. But my sense is that the riots over *The Playboy* showed him that he could ignore the misappropriation of the Irish past no longer. If audiences were to break up in disorder at the word *shift* and consider the mention of such an article of clothing on the stage as un-Irish, obviously they had no idea what their old stories were like. If a Pearse could denounce Synge yet celebrate a Cuchulain whose exploits make Christy Mahon look like the parish priest, the time had come to show the Irish some of the truth about their own mythology. It wasn't just a repository of heroic images urging young men to die heroically; there were other values and moods obtaining there.

This is the context in which Synge's turn to Irish mythological subjects in his last play should be seen. In *Deirdre of the Sorrows*, he inaugurated what was to become an important current in modern Irish literature, the conscious de-mythologizing of Irish mythology. The "Cyclops" chapter of *Ulysses* and Flann O'Brien's *At Swim-Two-Birds* are more extended, more self-conscious, and more comic efforts in the same direction. These later works are closer to *The Playboy* in tone than to *Deirdre*, but they should all be seen as antidotes to Cuchulainoid attitudes toward the Irish past. The struggle over what is to be made of the Irish past continues today, but the balanced and informed work with Irish mythology done by contemporary writers such as Thomas Kinsella and Seamus Heaney owes at least as much to the demythologizers as to the mythologizers Synge was reacting against. In this context, Synge's work with Irish mythology has proven to be influential indeed.

References

Gerstenberger, Donna. *John Millington Synge*. Twayne's English Authors Series 12. New York: Twayne, 1964.

Kenner, Hugh. *A Colder Eve: The Modern Irish Writers*. New York: Knopf, 1983.

Kiberd, Declan. *Synge and the Irish Language*. Totowa, N.J.: Rowman and Littlefield; London:Macmillan, 1979.

Ó Tuama, Seán. "Synge and the Idea of a National Literature." *J. M. Synge: Centenary Papers, 1971*. Edited by Maurice Harmon. Dublin: Dolmen, 1972, pp. 1–17.

Price, Alan. *Synge and Anglo-Irish Drama*. London: Methuen, 1961.

Saddlemyer, Ann. "Deirdre of the Sorrows: Literature First . . . Drama Afterwards." *J. M. Synge: Centenary Papers 1971*. Edited by Maurice Harmon. Dublin: Dolmen, 1972, pp. 88–107.

Skelton, Robin. *The Writings of J. M. Synge*. Indianapolis and New York: Bobbs-Merrill, 1971.

Thornton, Weldon. *J. M. Synge and the Western Mind*. Irish Literary Studies 4. New York: Barnes & Noble, 1979.

Yeats, W. B. *Autobiographies*. London: Macmillan, 1955.

———. *Essays and Introductions*. London: Macmillan, 1961.

Additional Sources

Dasenbrock, Reed Way. "Synge's Irish Renaissance Petrarchism." *Modern Philology* 83, No. 1 (1985): 33–44.

Art as Collaboration: Literary Influences on J. M. Synge

The study of literary influences on Synge began in bitter controversy. As early as 1903, Arthur Griffith, the Irish nationalist, insisted that the plot of *The Shadow of the Glen* was borrowed wholesale from Petronius. Synge was, Griffith said, a plagiarist who libeled Irish womanhood with a stolen plot and wrote with the "Decadent Cynicism" of the Parisian Latin Quarter. Synge responded that he had actually heard his plot from an Irish storyteller, but even with his first produced play the controversies about literary influences in his work had begun (Greene and Stephens 153 and 181). They continue to the present. Was Synge an "original" artist or an imitator? How much did he owe to Ibsen? Shakespeare? Molière? Was he more than superficially an "Irish" playwright?

Synge's enemies among the nationalists instinctively sensed something foreign, un-Irish, in his work. Whatever their misjudgments on other matters, they were right to feel that his drama participated in a broader literary culture than provincial Ireland's. Synge envisioned himself as a European artist, one who recognized that all art is a collaboration and understood the idea of collaboration in complex ways. The Dublin audiences of his own time assumed that his artistic mode was expressive realism. They assumed his plays were meant as true-to-life images of Irish life, those colored by their author's personal attitudes. From that misunderstanding arose much of the controversy in Synge's lifetime.

Yet the difficulties around Synge's plays involve more than just this misunderstanding. His drama rejects the mentality of *petit bourgeois* nationalism just as it rejects that of the Ascendancy Ireland of his own upbringing. Instead, it seeks marginalized positions. One margin we easily recognize is the Gaelic-speaking or Gaelic-remembering peasantry living physically around the edges of "civilized" Ireland. Another is the sensibility of that European avant-garde considered "Decadent" in Synge's day and to be called "modernist" later on. Like other modernist works, Synge's plays seek resonances by inviting audiences to sense, often ironically, that what is presented is only indicative of what is suggested. There is a modernist emphasis on dislocations—physical, historical, personal—and a modernist sense of alienation. These qualities are present in texts that seem clear examples of intertextuality with their mosaics of citations in which every text absorbs and transforms others (Kristeva 146).

Like Yeats, Pound, and Eliot, Synge employed a creative method related to the comparativist methods of nineteenth-century literary and anthropological scholarship. He studied philology and cultural anthropology at the Sorbonne, and the method he learned there "took." Thus he came to believe that Irish beliefs and ways of seeing things were living survivals of patterns that most of Europe had lost long before. To be truly an *Irish* artist required involvement in these cultural survivals. To be truly an Irish *artist* required a creative position in contemporary—as well as past—European contexts. To assert, as Synge did, "all art is a collaboration" (IV, 53) was to give allegiance to a demanding intellectual and creative position.

Perhaps the clearest way to examine these collaborative processes in Synge—the roles of influences in his mind and art—is to move in roughly chronological fashion. Synge's life before he became a playwright deserves careful attention. The plays on which his reputation rests were produced in less than a decade, but the creative sensibility in which they were produced had been developing for years.

He grew up in a deeply religious family. Thus we can assume that the images, cadences, and narrative patterns of the Authorized Version of the Bible, the *Book of Common Prayer*, and *Hymns Ancient and Modern* helped form his early consciousness. Many of his poems are in the meters of the hymnal; "Danny" can be sung to any tune in "common measure" with fairly outrageous results. Although Synge lost his faith in his youth, he spent half of his life in a household in which The Word mattered far more than the mere words of literature.

Synge was reticent about his early reading, but he admitted that "English literature I read with much care, although I was painfully conscious of my uncertain judgement and formed my opinions reluctantly for fear a blunder might lower me in my own estimation" (Greene and Stephens 26). He added that he did not permit himself to like a book that was not famous, although there were some famous books—Tennyson's poems among them—he disliked.

Wordsworth's poems he did care for. Wordsworth was a great favorite among Evangelical families, and Synge said he preferred Wordsworth to any other English poet (Price 219). His autobiography has some striking accounts of communion with nature in his youth—and of nature teaching by fear. Weldon Thornton has argued that Synge's basic mode of perception was Wordsworthian, that

Synge shared the sense that the mystery behind all things is too great for reason alone to be considered the definitive interpreter of truth (*J. M. Synge and the Western Mind* 40). Wordsworth was certainly an important influence in his early poetry. The "Ballad of a Pauper" is Wordsworthian in its dialogue of classes, "Prelude" in its setting. For "In a New Diary," the speaker positions himself oddly like Wordsworth's Lucy (Stallworthy 147–48). The direct influence of Wordsworth declined as Synge matured, but his prefaces assert a Wordsworthian desire to recuperate the language of ordinary people, and the Deirdre of his last play begins with a Wordsworthian simplicity derived from living close to nature.

The influence of Wordsworth is demonstrable, but to show the same for some other classics of English literature is not so easy. Synge read widely, though: Chaucer, Shakespeare, Jonson, Herrick, the Elizabethan and Jacobean dramatists, Dryden and others. Occasional echoes from Shakespeare, for example, can be found in his plays, but Synge said he had trouble remembering the plots. Among Shakespeare's contemporaries, he admired Thomas Nashe, Francis Beaumont, Robert Greene, George Peele, and John Marston (Bourgeois 51). He certainly admired Ben Jonson's "living speech"—a minority opinion in his time—and there are parallels between Jonson's *Bartholomew Fair* and *The Playboy* and *The Tinker's Wedding*, especially between Jonson's Ursla and Synge's Molly (Duncan 214–15).

At Trinity College, Synge earned prizes in Hebrew and Irish to complement his "gentleman's pass" degree. We know that he worked hard at his Irish, and it is plausible that his study of Hebrew encouraged his fondness for verbal parallelisms. But it is not really exaggeration to state that in fundamental ways he was self-educated and that much of the education he would actually use as an artist came after he could put B.A. behind his name. During the Trinity years, Synge was also studying music with enthusiasm. He became a capable violinist, enjoyed playing in orchestras (another form of artistic collaboration), and later used the violin to invite himself into peasant Ireland as he would also use it to imagine an alternative self in *Étude Morbide*. Beyond the violin, he studied counterpoint and theory, and some concepts from those studies may have transferred to his dramatic practice (Johnson 23).

It was to study music that Synge left Ireland for Germany in 1893, returning there again the next year. Maurice Bourgeois, the first careful student of literary influences on Synge, was convinced that the visits to Germany affected his dramatic practice. He reminded us that Synge could have seen or read some of the popular Viennese farces or plays by German naturalists such as Arno Holz and Johannes Schlaf. But their grim realism is a long way from that of Synge, and the only thing the peasant theater of Ludwig Anzengruber seems to have in common with Synge is the use of a contrived dialect, although one wonders if Synge's German was good enough to appreciate this. On the other hand, Synge may have learned something from the construction of Gerhardt Hauptmann's earlier plays (Bourgeois 13). If Synge did see or read naturalist drama in Germany, these plays may have joined in his mind with Ibsen's, which he also read in German, as examples of the kind of realism he would later attack in the prefaces to his own plays.

Nevertheless, Synge's years in Paris were surely of far greater importance. These were years of serious education, formally and informally, in what was then the Western world's intellectual and artistic capital. Synge's French was good enough for him to seem bilingual; he studied at the Sorbonne and read extensively on his own in a milieu radically different from that of provincial Dublin. His reading was that of an intelligent young man of "advanced" tastes. In 1897, for example, he recorded that he had read Thomas à Kempis, Huysmans, Keats, Wagner, de Musset, Pater, Wilde, Wordsworth, Chaucer, Blake, Swedenborg, and various texts on the occult (Saddlemyer, "Synge and the Doors of Perception" 103).

That seems a characteristically Decadent reading list, especially when supplemented by Flaubert, Maupassant, and Anatole France (Bourgeois 27 and 55–57). Synge was certainly aware of the French Decadent movement and seems to have responded to it with a mixture of fascination and repulsion. Jon Stallworthy demonstrated Synge's debts to Baudelaire and Verlaine (154). On the other hand, Synge later was anxious to distance himself from Baudelaire's morbidity and the urban culture that sustained it (IV, 3), and he was harshly critical of Huysmans, although he read Mallarmé with pleasure. Certainly, by the latter part of his time in Paris, Synge was ready to place himself against the decadence at times, rejecting Zola, Ibsen, Mallarmé, and Huysmans for failing to convey the fullness of life and praising Burns, Villon, and Herrick for using "the whole of their personal life as their material" (Saddlemyer, "A Share" 212).

To us, Maurice Maeterlinck may seem as much a Decadent as any of those Synge rejected, but he saw in his work "a virile—almost transcendental common sense of the greatest interest and importance" (Saddlemyer, "A Share" 212). Katharine Worth has argued that much of modern Irish drama derives from Maeterlinck and that Maeterlinck's sense of solitariness carried over to Synge. A Maeterlinckian anxiety becomes an active force in *The Shadow of the Glen*. *Riders to the Sea*, like *L'Intruse*, is a simply structured play about waiting for death. *The Well of the Saints* has tonal and situational parallels with *Les Aveugles* (127–28). Surely, Synge's work is earthier, less static, more human than Maeterlinck's, but the sense of influence is there, nevertheless.

Synge also had a lively interest in the French drama of the past. Yeats insisted that he meant to write a critical study of Racine, although the evidence for influence from French heroic drama seems slight. On the other hand, Synge's papers included scene analyses of Racine's *Phèdre* and Molière's *L'Avare*. Bourgeois was sure he saw many of Molière's plays at the Comédie Française (53–54). *Les Fourberies de Scapin* seems a likely influence on *The Well of the Saints*, and indeed Synge directed Lady Gregory's translation of *Scapin* at the Abbey in 1908 (Greene and Stephens 284). But Toni O'Brien Johnson may well be right that the greatest influence from Molière came not from his plays but from the image of the comic master presented by Louis Petit de Julleville, one of Synge's lecturers at the Sorbonne. De Julleville, defending Molière against charges of plagiarism, insisted that comic material is a common heritage in drama, and his approach to Molière as a remaker of the comic inheritance may help to account for Synge's insistence on art as collaboration (45–46).

It is also fruitful to look even further in French literature—to the Renaissance and the Middle Ages. Synge had strong interests in Villon, Rabelais, the poets of the era of the Pleaide, and medieval poetry in general. He translated Villon, Ronsard, Marot, Colin Musset; the spirits of Villon and Rabelais seem very much present in his stage work.

In 1895 Synge attended de Julleville's lectures on French medieval literature and read several of his histories of French drama then and later. With de Julleville, Synge came to see Villon as a Romantic figure, his art an expression of his full and varied life, his life itself an image of the life of the artist as outcast. Likewise, Synge came to see Rabelais as master of "grotesque realism," an art that is positive and festive in its glorification of the body and degrading only "in the sense that it brings down to earth all that is high, spiritual, ideal, and abstract" (Johnson 19). Thus a Villonesque sense of artistic and personal self-identification joined to a Rabelaisian sense of ecstasy arising from the physical, the earthly, and the grotesque (Johnson 24–26 and 47–48).

French was not the only literature Synge studied in Paris. He left Dublin with only a limited knowledge of Irish, but his enthusiasm increased in Paris. As late as 1898, on the first visit to Aran, Synge was frustrated that his Irish was no better, but by then he had already begun to study Celtic literature and philology with de Jubainville. As de Julleville helped to make his image of the French masters, so de Jubainville had a strong influence on his understanding of the Irish tradition.

De Jubainville's method was essentially comparative, and the first lectures Synge heard him give were on parallels between Celtic and Homeric cultures (Kiberd 32). It is characteristic of Synge's absorption in this historicist and comparativist method that his first published article, "A Story from Inishmaan," glosses a tale he heard on Aran with comments on its analogues in European folklore. Declan Kiberd argued that Synge's great contribution to the study of Irish folklore was his emphasis on the comparative method, derived directly from de Jubainville (32). The method would serve him well later when he came to imagine Maurya as an old Irish woman invested with the spirit of the Greek tragedies or Christy as a Dionysiac eruption in the alienated little world of Mayo.

Synge's study of the Irish langue and its literature extended well beyond lectures on the myths and sagas. As early as 1892, he had read the Munster poets of the seventeenth century, and Kiberd stressed the influence of Geoffrey Keating, the priest-poet of the same era. Synge reviewed an edition of Keating's poems in 1900 and in 1902 reviewed David Comyn's edition of Keating's *Foras Feasa ar Éirinn (History of Ireland)*. Synge saw in Keating's fantastic, credulous, yet oddly sophisticated *History* "the shrewd observation, and naïve reasoning

that are common to the learned men of his age and the peasants of our own''
(II, 358). Kiberd concluded that Keating exerted a strong influence because
Synge could see in his work ''the whole cast of mind of the western countryman''
allied to a ''fusion of scholarship and creative imagination'' (57). Thus Synge
could model himself on a figure such as Keating who had ''managed to Euro-
peanise Irish writing without making it any less Gaelic'' (59).

During the Paris years, Synge's interest in Celtic folklore also led him to two
writers who based their work on Breton materials: Pierre Loti and Anatole Le
Braz. Apparently, Synge encountered Loti's work first, and there was a time
when he admitted that Loti had a great influence on him. Bourgeois asserted
that Synge thought of him as the greatest living writer of prose and said that he
wished to do for the peasantry of Ireland what Loti had done for the Breton
fisherfolk (56). Loti's three novels of Breton fishing life, *Mon Frère Yves,
Pêcheur d'Islande*, and *Matelot*, have similarities to *Riders to the Sea* in their
themes of the struggle between men and the sea and the anxiety of kinfolk left
behind. Synge may also have responded to Loti's recurring theme of a restless
search for wisdom and spiritual goals. Loti's influence was greatest, though, in
the inception of *The Aran Islands*. Synge acknowledged at one point that his
book drew its general plan from Loti, whose *Pêcheur d'Islande* he had read just
before his first visit to the island (Greene and Stephens 58). Nevertheless, Synge
outgrew Loti's exotic primitivism as his knowledge of Aran life increased. He
suppressed the admission of debt for *The Aran Islands* and became generally
dismissive of Loti's importance (II, 48, 395).

The influence of Anatole Le Braz was probably more important. Synge heard
him lecture on Brittany in 1897, read several of his books on Breton life and
folklore, and they became friends (Skelton 25). Le Braz's *Au Pays des Pardons*
seems to have been especially influential, but Synge took notes on *La Légende
de la Morte en Basse Bretagne* while on Aran in 1899, and he reviewed Le
Braz's work in a Dublin newspaper the same year. Kiberd suggested that Le
Braz's theories of Celtic drama may have helped Synge position himself as a
playwright (101–2), and Nicholas Grene surmised that Le Braz's Breton enthu-
siasms may have helped to reawaken Synge's old interest in Ireland's Celtic
culture (*Synge: A Critical Study* 21). Synge would have recognized in Le Braz
a substantial folklorist who collected tales in the field—as Synge would do—
and had chosen—as Synge would choose—to publish them in translation. In
sum, one could argue that a combination of things—reading Loti and Le Braz,
attending de Jubainville's lectures—did a good deal more to send Synge toward
Aran than the famous meeting with Yeats at the Hotel Corneille.

Yeats's sense that the Synge he had met in Paris was a man who had not yet
found himself is a half-truth. The Parisian Synge cast himself in the role of
serious student, his mode essentially reactive. Baudelaire, Verlaine, Anatole
France, and even Maeterlinck offered a means by which he could create himself
as an aesthete and urban *sensitif*. On the other hand, the Synge who found
himself on the Aran Islands found an identity that was in many ways modernist.

His fascinations with Villon, Rabelais, and Keating served approximately the same purposes as Pound's with the troubadours or Eliot's with Dante. This mixture of aestheticism, scholarship, and alienation was hardly rare in its time, but it did mean that when Synge became an Irish playwright he would become one different from most of his predecessors or contemporaries.

As Yeats and others have reminded us, Synge spent much effort in the Paris years on his creative work—and on being, in effect, a failed artist. Nothing he wrote in Paris seems of much importance in itself, although this early work does show how much he needed models and influences. *Vita Vecchia*, the collection of autobiographical poems linked by prose commentaries, is extremely imitative, even in the revision of 1907. Begun, apparently, in 1895, after Cherrie Matheson refused to marry him, it adapts its general form from Dante's *Vita Nuova* (probably from Rossetti's translation). The poems, Synge himself admitted, "were written from all the influences of the so-called decadent and symbolist schools" (Stallworthy 154). Another autobiographical work, "Under Ether" (1897), derives from De Quincey, perhaps W. E. Henley, perhaps Maupassant. Yet a third, *Étude Morbide* (1899), participates in the rhetorics of autobiographical sincerity, Thomas à Kempis, damned Byronic heroes, and Decadent introspection.

In short, Yeats and the others who have seen Synge's trips to Aran between 1898 and 1901 as crucial in his artistic development are right. Yet we should remember that the Synge who first went to the islands took his Parisian sensibility with him—literally, in his luggage. Among the books accompanying him in 1898 were *Madame Bovary*, *Auscassin et Nicolette*, Rossetti's poems, and works by Loti and Swedenborg (Greene and Stephens 90). The visit that year may have helped Synge imagine himself as a picaresque hero or living out the life he admired in George Borrow and Lafcadio Hearn (Bourgeois 13), but he was a highly sensitized and passive wanderer who read Maeterlinck's *Pelléas et Mélisande* by the turf fire in a cottage where the wash was drying.

The book Synge wrote about his experiences, *The Aran Islands,* was not published until 1907, but it was completed in 1901 and clearly reflects his personal and creative maturation,"[M]y first serious piece of work," Synge called it (II, 47). It suggests Loti's influence in its themes of the mysterious isolation of the islands, the simplicity of island life, the physical desolation, and the power of the past. But it takes a tough view of its subject, tough enough that Lady Gregory wished it dreamier and less specific (Greene and Stephens 127). One could say that it reacts against the attitudes toward subject found in Loti or Yeats's *Celtic Twilight*. For the attitude of the narrator toward the tales he is told, the model seems more Le Braz than Loti or Yeats.

The Aran Islands should also be read in the tradition of spiritual autobiography with Borrow, perhaps, as a distant model. Mary C. King noted how it reflects Synge's own sense of alienation, in this going well beyond Loti (199). At one level, the book is an intense account of creating the illusion of a nonalienated self, a fiction one can live by and create by. It is the culmination of the autobiographical works that had occupied Synge in the Paris years. Like *Vita Vecchia* and the others, it is an exploitation of the writer's sensibility. But the narrator's growing sense of control of himself is here a central theme, that exemplified by his growing command of the Irish language and a parallel sense of identity with the Aran people. Thus by the end of the book the narrator has found a position in relation to his overt subject and to his own subjectivity. He has created a self ready to become the artist known as J. M. Synge.

Synge began to write plays in earnest around 1900. It is striking how quickly he developed as a playwright; by the end of 1902, *Riders to the Sea, The Shadow of the Glen,* and *The Tinker's Wedding* were all under way. Yet his development as a playwright was very much a process of working reactively and imitatively, of absorbing models and freeing himself from them.

The imitative qualities—and the continuing sense of submerged autobiography—are very much in evidence in Synge's first completed play, *When the Moon Has Set*, first written in 1900–1901. Yeats remembered it later as "morbid" and "conventional." Its protagonist, Colm, is obviously a spokesman for Synge's views just as Sister Eileen, the nursing nun who gives up the habit for Colm, combines attributes from three women Synge had loved and failed to win (Greene and Stephens 121). These autobiographical elements are presented in a distinctly Ibsenesque form: middle-class setting, plain language, a hero restless in the provinces, a heroine prepared to break with convention (Worth 138).

When the Moon Has Set is, in fact, Synge's one play demonstrably modeled on Ibsen, although Jan Setterquist has argued that Ibsen's influence pervades all of his plays: *The Shadow of the Glen* resembles *A Doll's House, The Playboy* resembles *Peer Gynt*, and so on. But this argument seems exaggerated and neglects Synge's hostility to Ibsen's "joyless and pallid words" (IV, 53). As Weldon Thornton noted, Setterquist found parallels that "can be accounted for more readily as ideas whose time had come than through the influence of Ibsen on Synge" ("J. M. Synge" 360).

As Synge continued to work at becoming a playwright, he continued to work from received models. In March 1902, for example, he tried his hand at two verse plays, both set in ancient Ireland. *A Vernal Play* imitates the early Yeats and is, for Synge, oddly Arcadian. *Luasnad, Capa, and Laine* is closer in tone and themes to his mature work, but it, too, is a dramatic failure. Its plot, derived from Geoffrey Keating, is too big for its constricted space, and its language— often highly reminiscent of Edgar's speeches in *King Lear*—is constricted by the blank-verse form.

By the end ot 1902, Synge had written *Riders to the Sea* and *The Shadow of the Glen* and was working on *The Tinker's Wedding*. At least two of these plays are also fairly derivative in the plots—the reactive quality in Synge's imagination still at work—but in these three Synge has found his stage language, and that was a crucial breakthrough for him.

Much scholarly ink has been shed on just how accurate Synge's "Irish dialect" is, and Declan Kiberd has examined the matter recently in detail to argue, in effect, that the issue of linguistic accuracy is almost beside the point. Irish was, in effect, the substratum of Synge's stage language: English, as it was spoken in Ireland, the immediate source. But Kiberd pointed out that Synge was fond of Goethe's dictum that "Art is art because it is not nature" (214). Thus when Synge wrote in the Preface to *The Playboy* of the value to the artist of living in a country "where the imagination of the people, and the language they use, is rich and living" (IV, 53), he was not only arguing against the language of realist drama but also against a veneer-like use of dialect. Yeats was surely right to note that Synge failed as a dramatist when he did not use dialect "because only through dialect could he escape self-expression, see all that he did from without, allow his intellect to judge the images of his mind as if they had been created by some other mind" (345).

Thus in contrast to all of his previous dramatic work, *Riders to the Sea* offers an immensely rich language and seems a play in which Synge is truly himself. Nevertheless, Robin Skelton has suggested that it was written partially in response to Yeats's *Cathleen ni Houlihan*. Both plays are set in cottages; both begin with questions. The main action in each begins with the examination of clothing. Both are centered on old women who devote much time to catalogues of deaths of men attached to them (43).

Some elements in *Riders* derive directly from Synge's experiences on the Aran Islands and from his correspondence with friends there. It is characteristic of his imaginative process that Maurya's great phrase "No man at all can be living for ever, and we must be satisfied" (III, 27) echoes both a letter from an Aran friend and Dante's *"In la sua voluntade è nostra pace."* The immediate focus of the play is on Aran folk and their beliefs, but with the imagery organized so "as to refer us, not only to the world of Irish history and folklore, but also to the world of archetypal symbolism" (Skelton 43). In that way, then, the play is virtually an enactment of de Jubainville's theories of mythology and folklore. Maurya's Irish identity is enriched by all sorts of classical resonances. The play's riders and their horses evoke Aran life, Poseidon the god of horses and the sea, the tale of Hippolytus, the biblical apocalypse, and Odin's gray horses. Kiberd noted that the tragic ending would be no surprise to a folklorist: "All through the play . . . members of the family have violated folk prohibitions" (167). But the play is also reminiscent of Greek tragedy in its fated action, keening women as chorus, offstage events, and foreboding speech and dramatic irony (Skelton 49). If Synge began with the model of Yeats's little patriotic play in mind, he transcended it entirely.

Written about the same time as *Riders, The Shadow of the Glen* was, as we have seen, the first of Synge's plays to excite public controversy. Synge insisted that his *shanachie* friend Pat Dirane was his immediate source for the plot, but Arthur Griffith was right that it was an analogue to "The Widow of Ephesus," one of the most widespread folktales in Western Europe. Its motif of feigned death is common in French and Italian literature, and de Julleville stressed the frequency of the motif of the faithless wife in medieval French literature (Johnson

163). There are analogues, too, in Chaucer, Boucicault's *The Shaughran,* Crofton Croker's *The Corpse Watchers,* Molière's *Le Malade Imaginaire,* and Voltaire's *Zadig* (Bourgeois 156–57). Defending Synge, Lady Gregory pointed to a parallel in Jeremiah Curtin's edition of Irish tales (198), and Greene and Stephens observed that the story was so current in the West of Ireland in Synge's day that the Folklore Commission recorded four versions (158). As Synge remarked to Edward Stephens, "people are entitled to use these old stories in any way they wish" (Kiberd 169).

Discussions of sources and parallels to the plot have overshadowed discussion of other influences. But surely it is no coincidence that the situation of the Nora of this play resembles that of the Nora of Ibsen's *A Doll's House.* A number of critics have also heard strong literary echoes in the play's language. T. R. Henn, for one, heard the language of *Antony and Cleopatra* as well as Villon in the tramp's lyrical outbursts and elsewhere (27, 33, 324). Declan Kiberd heard echoes from Gaelic poetry in Nora's language (127–33) and noted in detail the extent to which the play's action and tone derive from the verbal customs of the Irish wake, even to the taunting and mockery (171–72).

The third of the plays begun in 1902, *The Tinker's Wedding,* generally draws its plot from a tale Synge heard in County Wicklow, and the "literary" influences in it seem to come largely from the common talk of peasant Ireland. For example, Act One ends with that immensely popular ballad "The Night Before Larry Was Stretched." A song Douglas Hyde collected may be a source for the incident of the priest tied up in the sack (Bourgeois 179), but it seems plausible that Synge's most basic sources were tales he heard and recorded in two of his pieces about Wicklow, "At a Wicklow Fair" and "The Vagrants of Wicklow," even though neither was published until after he had begun work on the play. Hyde may have influenced the play in another way too. Synge had seen his *Casadh an tSúgáin,* the first modern play in Irish, while working on his own play and may have followed to some extent his technique of dramatizing folk story and song (Kiberd 149).

In terms of literary influences, these three plays of 1902 are all essentially based on stories or ways of experiencing life that Synge identified with Irish folklore. Skelton called them "shanachie plays" and stressed how each involves conflict between folk beliefs and conventional Christian attitutdes (56–57). One might also note that the *donnée* in each, while specifically Irish, invites associations with mythic and folkloric resonances of European provenance. As Ann Saddlemyer said, the Synge who "came home" from Paris to commit himself to the Irish theater was a literary sophisticate for whom Ireland was "the most westerly point of Europe" ("A Share" 213).

Thus it is not surprising that Synge prefaced the rollicking farce of *The Tinker's Wedding* with a statement that, in highly compressed form, summarized his artistic position. Like any good aesthete, he asserted that drama "does not teach or prove anything." Yet he found it necessary to argue that drama should be "serious," its seriousness coming not from dealing with "seedy problems" but from the way in which it nourishes the imagination. Humor, he argued, is a "most needful" nourishment, and "it is dangerous to limit or destroy it," lest morbidity result, be it the morbidity of a Baudelaire or of a puritanical Irish town. This is a richly allusive little essay, grounded in Fielding's comparison of the types of literature to dishes on the table, positioned so that Synge can claim social value for his work and yet insist that his farce— like one of Molière's or Jonson's—comes from a comic spirit as natural and perpetual as "the black-berries on the hedges" (IV, 3).

The ambivalence here may reflect Synge's own creative ambivalence after he had completed those first "shanachie" plays. Certainly, his next work, *The Well of the Saints*, seems a new departure, not the least in its interactions with literary influences. The play is not based on an Irish source, and its parablelike nature may result from its specifically literary source. As he did with *Deirdre* of a few years later, Synge turned to a medieval text as the basis for his work, in this case of fifteenth-century French *moralité*.

Arthur Griffith, the great hunter of Synge's foreign sources, was among the first to sense that the *The Well of the Saints* was not Irish. Synge himself was fairly vague on the subject, admitting only that it derived from an old French farce (Bourgeois 187). In 1921, that source was identified as André de la Vigne's *Moralité de l'aveugle et du boiteux*. But by then all sorts of sources, probable and improbable, had been suggested: Georges Clemenceau's *Le Voile du Bonheur*, Maeterlinck's *Les Aveugles*, books on Lourdes by Zola and Huysmans, even a tale by Bulwer Lytton (Bourgeois 186–87).

It is evident that de la Vigne's *Moralité* was a starting point for Synge, even though it would have suggested only about two-thirds of the first act (Roche 446). One of Synge's notebooks preserves comments on it from de Julleville (III, 265–67). The *Moralité* is essentially a dialogue between a cripple and a blind man who have formed a begging partnership. By accident, they are cured in the presence of the corpse of St. Martin. The blind man is delighted, but the cripple curses the saint until he realizes that he can pretend to be crippled still for begging while also getting the use of his limbs. As Nicholas Grene noted in the Introduction to his edition of *The Well of the Saints*, the *Moralité* does not seem very close to Synge's play either in its mode or theme. But both are based on the "ironic perception that the gifts of God are not gifts to everyone," and Synge may have been attracted by the *Moralité*'s robust comedy and parable-like structure (7). It may also be, as Johnson has argued, that de Julleville's approach to the *Moralité* actually influenced Synge more than the play itself (31–36).

Despite the influence of the source, *The Well of the Saints* has the feel of rural Ireland. In *The Aran Islands*, Synge recorded a visit to a holy well and the story of a child brought there to be cured of blindness (II, 56–57), and he was alert to the nuances of folk belief and practice throughout the play. Folklore influences may also include memories of poems collected in Hyde's *Love-Songs of Connacht* (Henn 50). On the other hand, the claim of influence from Maeterlinck's *Les*

Aveugles also seems plausible (Worth 128–29). Moreover, as Vivian Mercier has noted, the play works on the archetype of the Christian fall with the blind couple expelled from visionary blindness to a postlapsarian world of labor and frustration (82). The biblical references could also be extended to include New Testament stories of the curing of blindness or even Oscar Wilde's parody of them in "The Doer of Good" (Henn 50). In other words, *The Well* uses its influences in Synge's characteristic way: the given of the plot is enriched and made ambivalent by the interplay of Irish and international literary and folkloric associations.

It is tempting to read Synge's last comedy, *The Playboy of the Western World*, as something of a parable too. A good many critics have sensed that one way to get a fix on its ambiguities is to stress some parabolic intent. Certainly, the sense that the text is full of references, general and specific, is very strong. Our response to that sense will inevitably encourage us to choose one set of influences as particularly important. But *The Playboy* remains an insistently ambivalent text. Synge claimed its central incident was "suggested by an actual occurrence" (IV, 363), thus implying a kind of realism. Yet he also argued that it was not a modern play with a "a purpose." Some of it was "extravagant comedy," but much more was "perfectly serious when looked at in a certain light" (IV, 364).

Thus the search for direct influences on *The Playboy* may show more about the reader than the text. On the other hand, it is useful to note how wide the range of plausible references is, even if we focus only on Christy Mahon. Like Keats's Adam, for example, his dream becomes reality, and Christy becomes a self-created mythmaker (Price 175). In that, his tale has something to do with Synge's own image of himself. Yet Christy lives in a highly ironic world, as many critics have noted. They stress the Widow Quin's importance, how the play parodies in Christy Synge's own attraction to the outrageous, and how the play's language can be seen as direct satire on the blather of Irish Romanticism (Grene, *Synge: A Critical Study* 133–35). Like Don Quixote, Christy is a fantasist and an outsider, a fool—but less a fool than the conventional realists around him—and very good at convincing them to share his fantasy (Skelton 117–18). It is also tempting to put Christy in broadly mythic contexts. In the third act, like Christ in Passion Week, he moves from triumphant entry through suffering to atonement with his father (Skelton 120). Or Christy could be seen as a kind of Odysseus or a mock-Oedipus. Or we could move from the classics to nine-teenth-century classical scholarship to see in his tale a localized reenactment of Nietzsche's Apollonian and Dionysiac principles (Martin 62).

If we move to more specific matters, the range of literary reference—and perhaps influence—seems as great. Henn noted that the slanging match at the end of the first act seems to come from Restoration comedy as the macabre discussion of skulls recalls *Hamlet*, Webster, and Villon (345). Johnson thought the Widow Quin was a distinctly Rabelaisian figure (27), and we should re-member Synge's own observation that "the romantic note and a Rabelaisian note are working to a climax through a great part of the play" (IV, xxv). Johnson and Kiberd have also stressed the parallels to Irish medieval texts. The plot contains some elements reminiscent of the Ulster tale of Bricriu's feast (Johnson 54–62). Christy as wooer and man of violence parallels the tales of Cuchulain as told in the medieval sources in Lady Gregory's *Cuchulain of Muirthemne* (Kiberd 115–21).

One could also argue that the play reflects Synge's Decadent consciousness. The lonely hero finally rejects the "civilization" symbolized by Michael James's pub and Father Reilly's church, but he does that more in the spirit of Huck Finn than Des Esseintes. Even so, he attains insight through suffering to become, like Melmoth, Childe Harold, Rimbaud, and Wilde an outcast for whom experience is invaluable because it means a tale to tell. His rejection of society specifically involves getting clear of women, women as objects of Romantic nympholepsy or women as schemers and harridans. The mythmaker/vagrant creates his own reality through visionary experience. It is no matter if the world sees his myth as "gallous story" or "dirty deed." It's the narcissistic self-fulfillment that counts.

In sum, *The Playboy* is not "explained" by its influences and literary parallels any more than Joyce's *Ulysses* or Yeats's Cuchulain plays. It is, instead, a myth about myths. Skelton put it well by calling it "a play which has precisely the same kind of richness as the shanachie material, a play fitfully illuminated by archetypal echoes and allusions, which, nevertheless, retains coherence, not upon the mythic, but upon the narrative level" (123).

Even before the controversy over *The Playboy* erupted, Synge seemed to feel the need for a new direction in his work. As he wrote to Molly Allgood: "My next play must be quite different from the P.Boy. I want to do something quiet and stately and restrained and I want you to act in it" (Synge 250). The "next play," Synge's last, would be *Deirdre of the Sorrows*. Work on it began in the context of reading Stevenson, Meredith, Scott, Tolstoy, the *Mabinogion*, and Arthurian tales and perhaps of revising *When the Moon Has Set*, with which *Deirdre* has some things in common. But a particularly important activity at this time was preparing a volume of poems for publication (Saddlemyer, "Deirdre of the Sorrows" 89).

In a sense, the work on his poetry was necessary preparation for *Deirdre* as Synge sought to find a stage language appropriate to his subject. Some of the items eventually published in *Poems and Translations* went back to the early phase of Synge's career, but some of the translations—the Petrarch sonnets among them—were prepared while he worked on *Deirdre*. The thematic relevance is self-evident. Johnson provided a detailed discussion of Synge's work as a translator and its effect on the play (97–114). One might add that Synge's dependence on models was not limited to his translations. "Queens," for example, is an "Irished" version of Villon's "Ballade des dames du temps jadis," and Villon seems steadily a presiding spirit in the poems. But Synge worked also from popular Irish balladry, Wordsworth, Herrick, and Ronsard. Ben Jonson is another presiding spirit, most evidently in the preface. There modern poetry is dismissed as "usually a flower of evil or good" so as to assert—in the spirits of Jonson and *Deirdre*—that "it is the timber of poetry that wears most surely, and there is no timber that has not strong roots among the clay and worms" (I, xxxvi).

At one level, it is very easy to define the literary influences on *Deirdre of the Sorrows*. Here, for the only time in his career, Synge dramatized a well-known tale, a story that goes back in the Irish tradition to the eighth or ninth century. A version of it appears in the twelfth-century *Book of Leinster*, an austere account of elopement, entrapment, and suicide that Synge knew and admired (II, 371–72). Nevertheless, it would oversimplify to state that he simply based his play on that version of the tale. As Kiberd explained in a painstaking analysis of sources, Synge's *Deirdre* is influenced by several versions of the Deirdre tale. The emphasis on her as the central character may derive from later medieval versions, de Jubainville's lectures, and Lady Gregory. Geoffrey Keating's version may help account for some of Synge's imagery. Synge's presentation of motives for the play's action probably derives from Andrew MacCuirtín's *Oide Chloinne Uisnigh*, an eighteenth-century rendering of the tale that Synge translated into English while on Aran in the fall of 1901 (179–90). Ann Saddlemyer found no evidence that Synge used his own translation as the basis for his dramatization, and that may be literally the case (IV, 393). Nevertheless, Kiberd made a strong argument for the general influence of MacCuirtín.

When Synge began work on *Deirdre*, he was taking up matter already well established in modern Anglo-Irish literature, and there were at least two plays available on the theme. AE's (George Russell's) *Deirdre* (1901) stressed the sense of fate and prophetic doom in the tale, though with a heroine who seems as passive as her lover is energetic. Yeats's *Deirdre* (1906) is more lyrical evocation of mood than motivated action. Both plays were almost self-consciously poetic; Synge was wise not to attempt a verse drama. Instead, as Robin Skelton observed, he modified his usual prose to give "musically cadenced sentences in which the balance of clause and phrase is given harmony by the consistent use of the highly mannered locutions of Irish speech" (137).

Synge's *Deirdre* seems in conscious reaction against the plays of AE and Yeats. It has a forceful heroine who initiates much of the action, unlike AE's. Yet his play also has a broader scope than Yeats's concentration on Deirdre herself offers. For all of this, the stronger influences are likely Synge's knowledge of the Gaelic sources and his own instinctive sense of how to handle folklore. Perhaps, as Johnson suggested, his version owes something to AE for its plot structure, but it owes more to Lady Gregory's *Cuchulain of Muirthemne* for its focus on the grave and the knife as dominant symbols (90–91). At least in its tonality, Synge's *Deirdre* also has debts to his European interests. Villiers de l'Isle-Adam's *Axël* had colored Synge's first play, *When the Moon Has Set*; it comes back to color this one as well. In the rough outline of the plot and the control of symbolic motifs, one may sense Wagner's *Tristan und Isolde*. In rhythm and atmosphere, Maeterlinck's *Pelléas et Mélisande* seems also an in-fluence.

So, in a sense, with the unfinished *Deirdre*, Synge ended his career as he had begun it. Its subject reflects his interests in Celtic legend from his studies with de Jubainville in Paris. The theme of death-demanding passion reiterates the autobiographical motif of frustration in *Vita Vecchia* and beyond. The central character—however much she is a sublimation of women from Cherrie Matheson to Molly Allgood—is viewed with high Romantic intensity and more than a bit of Villonesque and modernist irony. In its repertory of influences—ancient Irish tales, philological scholarship, Anglo-Irish literature, Wagner, Maeterlinck, Villon—*Deirdre* is a logical completion as well as a circling back.

Synge was, in sum, a profoundly *influenced* artist. The Romantic cult of originality meant little to him. His self-positioning as a European and an Irish artist meant, perhaps, that he seemed an original and thus controversial figure in the Ireland of his time. His work had modernist tendencies of several kinds, notably in its double vision of ancient inheritances and present occasions, and Ireland had not seen a playwright like that. Yeats sensed in the man he knew an unusual mixture of passivity, toughness, and curiosity. The Synge we now read seems most "Synge" when those qualities are in evidence in works that are also complexly engaged with other texts. Some of the poems, perhaps even some of the plays, seem merely imitative, but in most of Synge's work there is a complicated involvement with other literary contexts. To state that is not to deny his integrity. Nor is it a way of suggesting that his work can be conveniently explained simply by tracing obvious influences and parallels. Instead, it is meant to assert that in his self-construction as an artist, he understood himself most thoroughly when he was constructing texts responsive to other texts, overtly responsive. When Synge called all art a collaboration, he meant exactly what he said.

References

Bourgeois, Maurice. *John Millington Synge and the Irish Theatre*. London: Constable, 1913.

Duncan, Douglas. "Synge and Jonson (with a parenthesis on Ronsard)." *A Centenary Tribute to John Millington Synge, 1871–1909: Sunshine and The Moon's Delight*. Edited by S. B. Bushrui. New York: Barnes & Noble, 1972. pp. 205–18.

Greene, David H., and Edward M. Stephens. *J. M. Synge, 1871–1909*. New York: Macmillan, 1959.

Gregory, Lady. *Our Irish Theatre: A Chapter of Autobiography*. New York and London: G. P. Putnam's, 1913.

Grene, Nicholas. *Synge: A Critical Study of the Plays*. Totowa, N.J.: Rowman and Littlefield; London: Macmillan, 1975.

————, ed. *The Well of the Saints by J. M. Synge*. Irish Dramatic Texts. Washington,

D.C.: Catholic University of American Press; Gerrards Cross, Bucks: Colin Smythe, 1982.

Henn, T. R., ed. *The Plays and Poems of J. M. Synge*. London: Methuen, 1963.

Johnson, Toni O'Brien. *Synge: The Medieval and the Grotesque*. Irish Literary Studies 11. Gerrards Cross, Bucks: Colin Smythe; Totowa, N.J.: Barnes & Noble, 1982.

Kiberd, Declan. *Synge and the Irish Language*. Totowa, N.J.: Rowman and Littlefield; London: Macmillan, 1979.

Kristeva, Julia. *Semiotike*. Paris: Seuil, 1969.

Martin, Augustine. "Christy Mahon and the Apotheosis of Loneliness." *A Centenary Tribute to John Millington Synge, 1871–1909: Sunshine and the Moon's Delight*. Edited by S. B. Bushrui. New York: Barnes & Noble, 1972. pp. 61–73.

Mercier, Vivian. *"The Tinker's Wedding." A Centenary Tribute to John Millington Synge, 1871–1909: Sunshine and the Moon's Delight*. Edited by S. B. Bushrui. New York: Barnes & Noble, 1972. pp. 75–89.

Price, Alan. *Synge and Anglo-Irish Drama*. London: Methuen, 1961.

Roche, Anthony. "The Two Worlds of Synge's *The Well of the Saints*." *Genre* 12 (1979): 439–50. Reprinted in *The Genres of the Irish Literary Revival*. Edited by Ronald Schleifer. Norman, Okla.: Pilgrim; Dublin: Wolfhound, 1980. pp. 27–38.

Saddlemyer, Ann, ed. *The Collected Letters of John Millington Synge, I: 1871–1907*. Oxford: Clarendon, 1983.

———. "Deirdre of the Sorrows: Literature First . . . Drama Afterwards." *J. M. Synge: Centenary Papers 1971*. Edited by Maurice Harmon. Dublin: Dolmen, 1972. pp. 88–107.

———. " 'A Share in the Dignity of the World': J. M. Synge's Aesthetic Theory." *The World of W. B. Yeats*. Edited by Robin Skelton and Ann Saddlemyer. Seattle: University of Washington Press, 1965. pp. 207–19.

———. "Synge and the Doors of Perception." *Place, Personality, and the Irish Writer*. Edited by Andrew Carpenter. Irish Literary Studies 1. New York: Barnes & Noble, 1977. pp. 97–120.

Setterquist, Jan. *Ibsen and the Beginnings of Anglo-Irish Drama: I. John Millington Synge*. Uppsala Irish Studies. Uppsala, Swed.: Lundequistka, 1951.

Skelton, Robin. *The Writings of J. M. Synge*. Indianapolis and New York: Bobbs-Merrill, 1971.

Stallworthy, Jon. "The Poetry of Synge and Yeats." *J. M. Synge: Centenary Papers, 1971*. Edited by Maurice Harmon. Dublin: Dolmen. pp. 145–66.

Thornton, Weldon. "J. M. Synge." *Anglo-Irish Literature: A Review of Research*. Edited by Richard J. Finneran. New York: The Modern Language Association of America, 1976. pp. 315–65.

———. *J. M. Synge and the Western Mind*. Irish Literary Studies 4. New York: Barnes & Noble, 1979.

Worth, Katharine. *The Irish Drama of Europe from Yeats to Beckett*. Atlantic Highlands, N.J.: Humanities Press, 1978.

Yeats, William Butler. *Autobiographies*. London: Macmillan, 1955.

Additional Source

King, Mary C. *The Drama of J. M. Synge*. Irish Studies. Syracuse: Syracuse University Press, 1985.

Synge and the Irish Literary Renaissance

At the end of James Joyce's *A Portrait of the Artist as a Young Man*, Stephen Dedalus, budding Irish poet, proclaims his intention "to forge in the smithy of my soul the uncreated conscience of my race" (253). By "conscience" Stephen means, among other things, "consciousness," and it is typical of the writers of his generation that Stephen regards the Irish racial or national consciousness as something that must be developed through literature; most writers, however, imagined that their poems, novels, and plays were a means of resuscitating Ireland's national cultural identity rather than creating it *ab ovo*. Supposedly written in Stephen's diary on April 26, 1902, the passage also implies that the ongoing Irish Literary Renaissance or Revival—an identifiable phenomenon at least since 1894, when William Patrick Ryan wrote a book on the subject—had not succeeded in creating or even resurrecting the "conscience" of the Irish race. That task would remain for Stephen and his own creator, both of whom believed that forging the Irish national consciousness was a task best performed somewhere on the continent, out of reach of Irish lawsuits, censorship, and other threats to artistic integrity.

The flights from Ireland of Joyce and Stephen, and their rejection of the Irish Renaissance, reverse the pattern of John Millington Synge's career. In his early and mid-twenties Synge had traveled and studied extensively on the continent, first studying music and then immersing himself in the works of Goethe, Lessing, Ibsen, Huysmans, and other European writers, but by 1902 he had turned his attention to his native land, making several trips to the Aran Islands in search of authentic Irish cultural roots and determining that he would make his own contributions to the Irish conscience within (if not always in full agreement with) the established national literary and dramatic movement. It seems ironic that Synge, a product of the Anglo-Irish Ascendancy class, would play a major role in the revival of interest in native Irish culture while the Catholic-educated Joyce felt so alienated from the literary movement that he had Stephen write in his diary about his fear of the Gaelic-speaking Irish peasantry. The fact is, however, that the Irish Literary Renaissance was dominated by Anglo-Irish writers like William Butler Yeats, Lady Augusta Gregory, and Synge. Joyce was less an Irishman than a Dubliner, and his disdain for rural life may have led him to feel a greater affinity with nineteenth-century Continental writers than with the primitive and archaic Celtic literature that drew its power from an identification with natural forces; conversely, Synge, an accomplished amateur naturalist, was attracted to the concept of an Irish cultural identity defined in terms of imagination and natural spontaneity rather than religion and social class. This somewhat romantic version of Irish nationality served as a foundation for many of the productions of the Literary Revival.

Frank O'Connor (194) has noted that "the [literary] tradition that Yeats, Synge and Lady Gregory had picked up from Petrie, Ferguson and Standish O'Grady, was largely a Protestant one"; yet he has also observed that the major writers of the literary movement were "people who had spent a considerable part of their youth in the country, whereas its opponents were mainly . . . townsmen." In the Preface to *The Playboy of the Western World*, Synge wrote of his fascination with the Irish peasantry's "popular imagination that is fiery and magnificent, and tender," citing qualities that Joyce rarely found in Ireland. Years later, in "The Municipal Gallery Revisited," Yeats was to write movingly of the faith in the common life of the countryside that underlay his own writings as well as those of Synge and Lady Gregory:

> John Synge, I and Augusta Gregory, thought
> All that we did, all that we said or sang
> Must come from contact with the soil, from that
> Contact everything Antaeus-like grew strong.

Like Tolstoy and other Slavophile writers of nineteenth-century Russia, the advocates of the Irish Renaissance stressed the importance of basing a modern cultural identity upon contact with the soil. There are, however, two crucial differences between the literary situations in Ireland and in Russia: Russia was not ruled by another country, nor was the Russian language in serious danger of disappearing. In Ireland, on the other hand, the nation's political subservience to England and the consequent loss of the Irish language as a major factor in Irish life meant, for many people, that a national literary renaissance could take place only in the medium of a foreign tongue.

The Irish Literary Renaissance, which attempted this compromise between the native tradition and the imported language, was one of three distinct, although in some ways parallel, movements that challenged the English political and cultural domination of late nineteenth- and early twentieth-century Ireland. The other movements were those of Irish political nationalism, which took as its goal land reform, "home rule," or even complete independence from Great Britain; and the revival and promotion of Irish Gaelic culture, especially through the Gaelic League's attempt to return the Irish language to a position of prominence and influence within Irish life. Synge had contact, at various times, both with Irish nationalism and with the Gaelic League, but the relationship was rarely a happy one. In Paris he was for several months a member of Maud Gonne's nationalistic organization L'Association Irlandaise, but in April 1897 he resigned, citing as his reason the "revolutionary and semi-military" nature of the organization (Saddlemyer I, 47). Later, he supported the goal of Irish economic self-sufficiency but objected to the idea that the Abbey Theatre should produce didactic, nationalistic dramas. As to the Gaelic League, Synge was enthusiastic about preserving the Gaeltacht (Gaelic-speaking) areas of the West, but he "declared himself opposed to the reimposition of the language on the rest of the country" (Kiberd, *Synge* 216). Synge's ambivalent attitudes toward political and linguistic forms of nationalism are similar to those of Yeats and other writers closely associated with the Irish Literary Renaissance, for whom Irish political independence and the promotion of the Irish language were less important for their own sakes than as part of the attempt to forge a distinctly Irish cultural identity that incorporated both the Celtic and the Anglo-Irish populations.

Opinions vary as to when the Irish Literary Revival began, but most literary historians would agree that the phase of Irish literature during which writers were most conscious of the Literary Renaissance as a significant factor in Irish cultural life started around 1890 and came to a conclusion shortly after the establishment of the Irish Free State in 1922. As the terms revival and renaissance imply, the writers believed they were resurrecting a national literature that had once been extensive and important. Critics often call attention to the 1878 publication of Standish O'Grady's *History of Ireland: Heroic Period*, with its redactions and adaptations of Irish myths, as a seminal event in the years leading up to the Literary Renaissance, for O'Grady's book reminded the Irish that they were the inheritors of a significant body of literature whose forms and values owed nothing to those of the English literary tradition. George Russell (AE), who articulated a central belief of the Irish Renaissance when he said that "A nation exists primarily because of its own imagination of itself," described his response to O'Grady's stories as that of a man "who suddenly feels ancient memories rushing at him, and knows he was born in a royal house" (Kain and O'Brien 26). The patriotic pride engendered in many Irishmen by O'Grady's books was reinforced over the next few decades by other English versions of Gaelic stories and poems. One of the most popular and influential of those versions was Lady Gregory's *Cuchulain of Muirthemne*, whose Preface, written by W. B. Yeats, includes the claim that "If we will but tell these stories to our children the Land will begin again to be a Holy Land, as it was before men gave their hearts to Greece and Rome and Judea'' (16). Rarely was the Literary Revival's claim for the merits of pagan Ireland made more explicitly, but similar assumptions about the revitalizing power of myth underlay much of the literature of the time.

Cuchulain of Muirthemne (1902) and its companion volume, *Gods and Fighting Men* (1904), were important not only because they presented readers with English versions of Irish myths, but because Lady Gregory's prose style, which she called the "Kiltartan dialect," showed that an Irish dialect of English could be a sensitive and flexible medium for literary expression. Even earlier uses of Irish dialect may be found in Douglas Hyde's *Beside the Fire* (1890) and *Love Songs of Connacht* (1893). As Richard Fallis observes, Hyde's demonstration of the literary possibilities of Irish English constituted "a process of preservation and innovation," both a reminder of the richness of the Gaelic literary tradition and a means of helping some aspects of that tradition survive in the English-speaking world (63–64). This combination of traditional and individual elements helped to make the Literary Renaissance a particularly vital phase of Irish literature, but it also led to conflicts with traditionalists who objected to the more experimental productions of the movement or to language and themes that they regarded as inaccurate portrayals of Irish life.

Since he was one of the authors most often attacked for these reasons, it is interesting to note that in "An Epic of Ulster," his review of *Cuchulain of Muirthemne*, Synge dealt with the issue of linguistic authenticity in literary works. After noting Hyde's pioneering use of an authentic Irish dialect and crediting Hyde with influencing Yeats's style and that of other recent Irish writers, Synge observed that some of Lady Gregory's passages contain echoes of Old Testament or Oriental style. Far from objecting to the book on the grounds that its speech is not always legitimate peasant dialect, however, he argued that "This union of notes, fugitive as it is, forms perhaps the most interesting feature of the language of the book", and that "in her intercourse with the peasants of the west Lady Gregory has learned to use [an Elizabethan] vocabulary in a new way, while she carries with her plaintive Gaelic constructions that make her language, in a true sense, a language of Ireland" (II, 368). As the subject of Synge's language is dealt with elsewhere in this book, I will not go into it in detail here, but it is worth noting that Hyde's style, and Lady Gregory's, appealed to Synge in part because they seemed to capture the ancient spirit of the country while allowing the individual writer the freedom to develop an individual mode of expression and that Synge's own dramatic dialogues involve a similar combination of genuine peasant speech and some other effects that, if not always linguistically accurate, are faithful to the very intense and concrete nature of rural Irish speech.[1]

Aside from the use of dialect by Hyde and Lady Gregory, the most significant influence of Synge's style was probably the Irish language itself, which he first studied at Trinity College, beginning in 1888. The Professor of Irish was a Protestant clergyman, James Goodman, whom Synge later accused of ignorance, or at least indifference, toward "the old literature of Ireland [and] the fine folk-tales and folk-poetry of Munster and Connacht" (Greene and Stephens 38). At Trinity, a bastion of pro-British sentiment, the course in Irish was taught in the Divinity School, and the motivation for offering the course was religious rather than literary: training in Irish was deemed useful to Protestant clergymen who might be assigned to Gaelic-speaking areas of the country. The reading material for the course, an Irish version of the Gospel of St. John, was uninspiring, but Synge took a prize in Irish and went on to read, in the original Irish, both *The Children of Lir* and *Diarmuid and Grainne*. In 1898, Synge studied Old Irish at the College de France under the direction of the distinguished scholar Henri d'Arbois de Jubainville and met Richard Irvine Best, whose translation of de Jubainville's *Le Cycle mythologique irlandais et la mythologie celtique* Synge later reviewed. Shortly after completing his course of study with de Jubainville, Synge set out on his first trip to the Aran Islands.

The trip to Aran has become part of the folklore of histories of the Irish Literary Renaissance. William Butler Yeats several times told the story of how he had met Synge in Paris in 1896 (originally Yeats's arithmetic would have made it 1899) and had told him to "go to the Aran Islands and find a life that had never been expressed in literature, instead of a life where all had been expressed" (*Autobiography* 230). Declan Kiberd (*Synge* 36–37) has argued persuasively that the influence of Best and de Jubainville was a more significant factor than Yeats's advice in Synge's decision to make his historic journey, but Yeats nonetheless came to regard Synge as in some sense his creation and defended his plays against hostile critics. After Synge's death, Yeats idealized him as "that enquiring man John Synge. . . . That dying chose the living world for text" ("In Memory of Major Robert Gregory"), and in his Nobel Prize acceptance speech, Yeats said that Synge and Lady Gregory should have been standing on either side of him as he accepted the award from the King of Sweden (*Autobiography* 387). Yeats's proprietary interest in Synge was of considerable value in promoting Synge's career and preserving his place within the pantheon of the Literary Revival, so that the literal truth of Yeats's story is in one sense less important than the crucial combination of Yeats's influence and the Aran trip in bringing Synge to a prominent position within the literary movement.

A consideration of Synge's relationship to Yeats is inseparable from an understanding of his place in the Irish Renaissance, for Yeats was far more than an important poet within the literary movement: he was also its chief organizer and propagandist and the first internationally known writer to place his reputation squarely behind the movement. In many ways, the Irish Literary Renaissance was an extension of Yeats, an organ for the achievement of his goal of creating a national (but not nationalistic) literature for Ireland. Synge, however, was far from being a mere follower or imitator of Yeats, as we might gather from a 1904 letter to Stephen MacKenna in which Synge declares,

I do not believe in the possibility of "a purely fantastic, unmodern, ideal, spring-dayish, Cuchulainoid National Theatre," because no drama—that is to hold its public—can grow out of anything but the fundamental realities of life which are neither modern or unmodern, and, as I see them, are rarely fantastic or spring-dayish. (Saddlemyer I, 74)

Synge's emphasis on "the fundamental realities of life" sets him apart from Yeats, who was usually more concerned with rising above those realities. The difference may be seen in their treatments of the Deirdre legend: Yeats's *Deirdre* (1907) is concentrated, ritualistic, highly symbolic, whereas Synge's *Deirdre of the Sorrows* (1910) is almost a domestic tragedy by comparison. Likewise, the blank verse of *Deirdre*, with its elevated diction, contrasts with the prose style of *Deirdre of the Sorrows*, which closely resembles that of Synge's peasant dramas. The same rejection of what Synge regarded as "fantastic or spring-dayish" tendencies in the literary movement's uses of Irish mythology may be seen in his poem "The Passing of the Shee," whose subtitle—"*After looking at one of A.E.'s pictures*"—singles out the most otherworldly Irish Revival figure as the inspiration for its more profane vision of saying adieu to the fairies while

> We'll search in Red Dan Sally's ditch,
> And drink in Tubber fair,
> Or poach with Red Dan Philly's bitch
> The badger and the hare. (I. 38)

Similarly, the description of Kate Cassidy's wake in *The Playboy of the Western World* includes Michael James Flaherty's boast that "you'd never seen the match of it for flows of drink, the way when we sunk her bones at noonday in her narrow grave, there were five men, aye, and six men, stretched out retching speechless on the holy stones" (IV, 151). This scene is a long way removed from the delicate lyricism of "The Wanderings of Oisin" or the sentimental idealism of *Cathleen Ni Houlihan*, whose author was to invoke the name of this popular play when he rebuked the crowd that protested Synge's far greater play.

The *Playboy*, in fact, contains several elements that distinguish it from more conventional Abbey Theatre fare and from the "Cuchulainoid" aspect of the literary movement generally. Chief among these elements is the parody of Irish mythic heroism embodied in the portrayal of Christy Mahon, a timid young man who becomes a champion athlete, successful ladies' man, and great braggart "by the power of a lie." Several critics, of whom M. J. Sidnell was the earliest and Declan Kiberd (*Synge* 109–21) the most thorough and persuasive, have called attention to Synge's use of mythic elements in this play, although Kiberd wisely warns against seeking extensive one-to-one correspondences between the play and mythic narratives such as those included in Lady Gregory's *Cuchulain of Muirthemne*. More subversive of the professed aims of the Literary Renaissance, perhaps, is the play's constant insistence that greatness is always found elsewhere—in another county, perhaps, or in a heroic past like the one that Pegeen invokes in the first act, asking:

Where now will you meet the like of Daneen Sullivan knocked the eye from a peeler, or Marcus Quin, God rest him, got six months for maiming ewes, and he a great warrant to tell stories of holy Ireland till he'd have the old women shedding down tears about their feet. Where will you find the like of them, I'm saying? (IV, 59).

The irony here cuts both ways, satirizing both the present, in which we constantly imagine that there are no more great men (although we might create one, if he tells the right story), and the supposedly heroic past itself, a time when a prison term for molesting animals gives a man the status of a hero.

Ironically, Synge's parodic versions of Irish mythic tales are often close in spirit to the original stories, since medieval Irish literature contains more than its share of ludicrous and grotesque elements.[2] In *The Irish Comic Tradition*, Vivian Mercier has written of the pervasiveness in Irish and Anglo-Irish literature of the very elements—satire, parody, the macabre and the grotesque, and the like—that characterize Synge's plays and some of his poems; and in *Synge: The Medieval and the Grotesque*, Toni O'Brien Johnson has demonstrated that Synge frequently used medieval sources in a manner consistent with the spirit of the originals. Synge was, in fact, capable of adopting the persona of a medieval Irish satirist, for example in his poem ''The Curse,'' which plays on the belief in the magical power of the satirist to cause his victims severe physical pain (cf. Robinson, 103, 110, 114–15).

Although he recognizes the satiric element in Synge's work, Mercier argues that Synge ''stands almost entirely outside the Gaelic literary tradition'' because, ''unlike the class-conscious Gaelic poets and satirists, Synge sympathizes with the underdog and the outcast, be he tramp or tinker, parricide or blind beggar'' (239). Indeed, one of the sharpest distinctions between Synge and Yeats might be seen in their different satiric perspectives: both satirize the money-grubbing tendencies of the Irish bourgeoisie—Synge in the persons of Dan Burke and Michael Dara, Yeats in the person of William Murphy and others who, in ''September 1913,'' believe that ''men were born to pray and save''—but Synge's critique of the middle class comes from the perspective of the outcast, whereas Yeats imagined that he was defending the ideals of a vanishing aristocracy.

The distinction here may be related to the difference between Synge's and Yeats's attitude toward the Irish past.[3] For Yeats, the past represented a coherent, organic state like the one Ruskin associated with the Middle Ages. Alex Zwerdling says, accurately, that Yeats found Irish heroic literature appealing, in part, because it ''presented a picture of a hierarchical society ruled by kings, a world whose simplicity of organization emphasized both the sharp distinction between noble, freeman, and slave and the unity created by their mutual interdependence'' (50). The association of the Irish myths with a vision of organic unity is implied also in Yeats's recurrent concern with the heroic figure of Cuchulain, for Cuchulain ''combined the roles of warrior, aristocrat, political leader, and visionary'' in a manner that is impossible in the modern world (Zwerdling 24–25).

To the extent that the recovery of a coherent community is associated with the desire to resurrect the sense of national cultural identity, this emphasis on the stability and coherence of the past, and on the importance of a model of community based on the heroic tales, is one of the most salient features of the Irish Renaissance. It is not, however, an important aspect of Synge's work: the only model of a coherent community to be found in the plays is the one in *Riders to the Sea*, a contemporary (although highly archaic) society in which people are bound together through their common struggle against the destructive forces of Nature.[4] Elsewhere—for example, in *The Well of the Saints* and *The Playboy of the Western World*—Synge satirized communities as places dominated by pettiness, conformity, and hypocrisy. To Hugh Kenner's perceptive comment that in Synge's plays "those who set forth have chosen better than those who choose to stay" (120), we might add G. J. Watson's observation that "the tramp-figure or social reject is [Synge's] version of the isolated artist type, the more so as Synge always endows him (the Tramp and Nora, Martin Doul, Christy) with the artist's imagination and heightened eloquence" (84). This sympathy for the outcast and alienation from all communities, so characteristic of Synge, would later become an important factor in Yeats's poems (the Crazy Jane poems are particularly good examples), as Yeats's disillusionment with the course of events in Ireland led him to a position not far removed from the one Synge had occupied years before.

Synge's preference for outcasts and dissenters, which is evident from the beginning of his career, is related not only to his alienation from some aspects of the literary movement but also to the movement's increasing alienation from the public. The twin attacks on *The Playboy of the Western World*—by nationalists and by religious zealots—were undoubtedly spurred, in part, by suspicions about the "Irishness" of an Irish Literary Revival dominated by Anglo-Irish Ascendancy writers, and the split deepened when Yeats called in the Royal Irish Constabulary, an arm of the British government, to quell the disturbances. Synge believed that he was making a good argument for the legitimacy of his art when he wrote, in the Preface to the *Playboy*, that the play included "one or two words only, that [he had] not heard among the country people of Ireland" and that much of his material for *The Shadow of the Glen* had come from listening to servant girls through "a chink in the floor of the old Wicklow house where [he] was staying" (IV, 53); the first comment was dismissed as obviously untrue and the second as an admission that he was an Ascendancy interloper whose works could be nothing more than a caricature of the real Ireland. Nor did the controversy end with Synge's death, for more than two decades later, in 1931, Daniel Corkery's *Synge and Anglo-Irish Literature* praised Synge for his attempt to portray the Irish peasantry but often faulted the works for what Corkery believed were inaccuracies of portrayal.

Corkery's book is often regarded as the production of an ethnic chauvinist; yet it must be admitted that conflict between the Irish Literary Revivalists and the community whose cultural identity they set out to resurrect and reshape was inevitable. The example of Charles Stewart Parnell, another Ascendancy class champion of the Catholic peasantry who had been rejected by many of his countrymen, became for Joyce and Yeats the prototype of the martyred culture hero, and Robin Skelton has argued persuasively that the nationalists who objected to the *Playboy* did so in part because Christy's career—adulation followed by betrayal and scapegoating—"bore sufficiently close a resemblance to that of Parnell to make them uncomfortable" (21). It might well be added that the public was more likely to see itself portrayed by the small-minded communities of the *Playboy* or *The Well of the Saints* than by the drifters and beggars who are supposed to gain our sympathy.

The conflict between individual and community that is central to Synge seems at times almost a paradigm of the tension between the literary movement and its public. Christy Mahon, it might be argued, resembles Synge himself as much as he does Parnell, so that the action of the play accurately predicts the public hostility that in engendered. Later, in his poem "On Those that Hated 'The Playboy of the Western World', 1907," Yeats depicted Synge as "great Juan" stared at and reviled by the "eunuchs" of Dublin, and elsewhere Yeats campaigned to install Synge within the ranks of the great Irish heroes. Synge's view of heroism was considerably more ironic than Yeats's, and the plays often constitute a critique of the cult of the hero: the *Playboy* and, in a different way, *The Well of the Saints* examine the extent to which illusions are necessary to produce a semblance of heroism. Nonetheless, as Seamus Deane has argued, "Synge is not writing out the failure of heroism. He is registering its failure in regard to society or, conversely, society's failure in regard to it" (53).

Finally, it may be remarked that the plays continually reflect the dominant concerns of the movement for Irish cultural revival. The fact that the only people who actually die in the plays are members of two endangered species—Aran Islanders, in *Riders to the Sea*, and Irish mythic heroes, in *Deirdre of the Sorrows*—is typical of the concern that traditional Irish life, in many ways so superior to the urban life surrounding the Abbey Theatre, is slipping away, never to be recovered; the revolt against authority figures—a significant factor in every play except *Riders to the Sea*, and a minor factor even there, through Maurya's recognition of the limitations of priestly knowledge—has a good deal to do with the demand for Irish cultural self determination; and the struggle of the lonely artist-figure against his or her imaginative inferiors suggests the parochialism against which Synge and the other Literary Revivalists believed they were doomed to struggle. If Synge objected to the "Cuchulainoid" aspects of the literary movement, he never doubted the importance and validity of its main goal: to develop in the English language an Irish literature whose range and subtlety are comparable to those of the best English writers of the time and to do so by relying on subjects that are grounded in Irish life and legend but are universal in their handling of the fundamental problems of life. As the first authentic genius of the Irish theater, Synge was one of the few writers who were most responsible for the success of the Irish Literary Renaissance and the development of a modern Irish literature that is both rooted in Celtic tradition and relevant to the cultural needs of twentieth-century Ireland.

Notes

1. One other point of special interest in the review is Synge's invocation of the popular parallel between Gaelic and classical Greek literature: "The epic of Cuchulain began to take shape in pagan Ireland probably in the same way as the Homeric stories grew up in ancient Greece" (II, 368). Analogies between the ancient Irish and Greek literatures were so common during the Irish Literary Renaissance that Synge felt no need to justify offhand remarks such as the references to Cuchulain as "l'Achille de l'Irlande" and to Lugh as "Celtic Hermes . . . " (II, 353, 365). In Joyce's *Ulysses*, Buck Mulligan claimed to quote Yeats on the subject of *Cuchulain of Muirthemne*: "The most beautiful book that has come out of our country in my time. One thinks of Homer" (178). The first sentence paraphrases Yeats's opening sentence from his preface to Lady Gregory's book; the second sentence is Joyce's invention, but its suggestion that medieval Irish literature may logically be compared to the Greek epics is characteristic of the claims that were made for the Irish tradition by Anglo-Irish writers of the Literary Revival.

2. Similarly, Una Ellis-Fermor, in *The Irish Dramatic Movement* (164), observes that "Synge, who thinks less than any of his predecessors about Nationalism or the Gaelic League or the past civilizations of Ireland, is one of the few followers of the movement who, through affinity of spirit, seem to carry on unbroken the tradition of ancient Irish nature poetry. In that poetry a distinctive quality is the sense of intimacy between man and nature about him."

3. I am dealing here specifically with the differences between Synge's and Yeats's attitudes toward the Celtic past, as represented by Irish mythology, but it should also be noted that Synge's dramatic works totally ignore the Anglo-Irish Ascendancy class to which he and Yeats both belonged, whereas Yeats portrayed this class as a coherent intellectual and cultural aristocracy. On Yeats's treatment of the Ascendancy see Deane, pp. 28–37, and Kiberd, "The Perils of Nostalgia," pp. 17–19.

4. Although it is more intense in Synge's other plays, the conflict between individual and community is also a factor in *Riders to the Sea*. See W. A. Armstrong's argument that "Maurya is never at one with her community. At the beginning of the play, she is at odds with it. In the final phase, she is above it, thinking and feeling on a higher and more articulate plane of sympathy, understanding, and imagination than any of those around her" (121). Synge's emphasis on "less enlightened communities" in his other plays, Armstrong contends, is meant "to sharpen the conflict between his dissenters and their social environment" (127).

References

Armstrong, W. A. "Synge's Communities and Dissenters." *Drama and Society*. Edited by James Redmond. Cambridge: Cambridge University Press, 1979. pp. 117–28.

Corkery, Daniel. *Synge and Anglo-Irish Literature: A Study*. Dublin and Cork: Cork University Press; London: Longmans, Greens, 1931. Reprint. New York: Russell & Russell, 1965.

Deane, Seamus. *Celtic Revivals: Essays in Modern Irish Literature, 1880–1980*. London and Boston: Faber and Faber, 1985. Reprint. Winston-Salem: Wake Forest University Press, 1987.

Ellis-Fermor, Una. *The Irish Dramatic Movement*. London: Metheun, 1939; Reprint. London: Methuen, 1967.

Fallis, Richard. *The Irish Renaissance*. Syracuse: Syracuse University Press, 1977.

Greene, David H., and Edward M. Stephens. *J. M. Synge, 1871–1909*. 1959. Reprint. New York: Collier, 1961.

Gregory, Lady. *Cuchulain of Muirthemne: The Story of the Men of the Red Branch of Ulster*. Preface by W. B. Yeats. 1902. Reprint. Gerrards Cross, Bucks: Colin Smythe, 1973.

Johnson, Toni O'Brien. *Synge: The Medieval and the Grotesque*. Irish Literary Studies 11. Gerrards Cross, Bucks: Colin Smythe; Totowa, N.J.: Barnes & Noble, 1982.

Joyce, James. *A Portrait of the Artist as a Young Man: Text, Criticism, and Notes*. Edited by Chester G. Anderson. New York: Viking, 1968.

Joyce, James. *Ulysses*. Edited by Hans Walter Gabler. New York: Random House, 1986.

Kain, Richard M., and James H. O'Brien. *George Russell (A.E.)*. The Irish Writers Series. Lewisburg, Pa.: Bucknell University Press, 1976.

Kenner, Hugh. *A Colder Eye: The Modern Irish Writers*. New York: Knopf, 1983.

Kiberd, Declan. "The Perils of Nostalgia: A Critique of the Revival." *Literature and the Changing Ireland*. Edited by Peter Connolly. Irish Literary Studies 9. Gerrards Cross, Bucks: Colin Smythe; Totowa, N.J.: Barnes & Noble, 1982.

———. *Synge and the Irish Language*. Totowa, N.J.: Rowman and Littlefield, 1979.

Mercier, Vivian. *The Irish Comic Tradition*. Oxford: Clarendon, 1962.

O'Connor, Frank. *A Short History of Irish Literature: A Backward Look*. New York: Capricorn, 1968.

Robinson, Fred Norris. "Satirists and Enchanters in Early Irish Literature." *Studies in the History of Religions*. Edited by David Gordon Lyon and George Foot Moore. New York: Macmillan, 1912.

Ryan, William Patrick. *The Irish Literary Revival: Its History, Pioneers and Possibilities*. London, 1894. Reprint. New York: Lemma, 1970.

Saddlemyer, Ann, ed. *The Collected Letters of John Millington Synge*. 2 vols. Oxford: Clarendon, 1983–1984.

Sidnell, M. J. "Synge's Playboy and the Champion of Ulster."*Dalhousie Review* 45 (1965): 51–59.

Skelton, Robin. "The Politics of J. M. Synge." *Massachusetts Review*, 18, no. 1 (1977): 7–22.

Watson, G. J. *Irish Identity and the Literary Revival: Synge, Yeats, Joyce, O'Casey*. New York: Barnes and Noble; London: Croom Helm, 1979.

Yeats, W. B. *The Autobiography of William Butler Yeats*. New York: Macmillan, 1965.

———. *The Variorum Edition of the Poems of W. B. Yeats*. Edited by Peter Allt and Russell K. Alspach. New York: Macmillan, 1965.

Zwerdling, Alex. *Yeats and the Heroic Ideal*. New York: New York University Press, 1965.

Synge's Language of Women

In her essay "Synge and the Nature of Woman," Ann Saddlemyer expressed what many have felt about the power and importance of his depiction of women characters. His "women are not only more clearly defined than most of the men but also treated with a sympathetic complexity which frequently determines plot, mood and theme" (58).[1] The power of his women may come in part from deeply Irish sources, like the strong women who inhabit Irish myths, or the survivors and lively beauties Synge found living primitive Irish life-styles in the Aran Islands, Kerry, and the Wicklow hills.[2] He said of the islands, "it seemed that there was a possible link between the wild mythology that is accepted on the islands and the strange beauty of the women" (II, 54). Woman, the artist, and nature are strongly connected by Synge in his early autobiographical writings. His own psychology and the primitive, natural aspects of life that he probed offered Synge alternatives to traditional male ways of doing things in patriarchal, rational, Western male civilization.

Synge's complex female characters often fail to behave as traditional genres might dictate. Weldon Thornton noted how numerous scholars have stumbled over classical definitions of tragedy in their attempts to explain the outcome of *Riders to the Sea*. Errol Durbach suggested that there is a complex dramatic tension in which Maurya becomes her own antagonist and her tragedy unfolds, atypically, without a crisis (365). In an essay that contributes to feminist analysis of gender, Ellen Spangler developed a definition of "feminine tragedy" to account for *Deirdre of the Sorrows:* "Feminine tragedy involves not struggle and then the horror of sudden discovery, as does masculine tragedy, but the horror of a perpetual knowledge, whose presence means that the self can never be entirely deluded into active struggle. This is the kind of tragedy with which Synge was most deeply sympathetic'' (98).

Robin Wilkinson brought structuralist analysis to the study of character in *The Shadow of the Glen* and *Deirdre*. By assigning characters, regardless of sex, to positions along a masculine/feminine axis, he called our attention to complexities such as "virile" women (Nora Burke and Deirdre), "feminine" men (Dan Burke and Michael Dara of *The Shadow*), and variability of gender type, especially in couples that achieve a balance in their relationship, like Deirdre and her lover Naisi or Nora and the tramp with whom she exits the drama (91–93).[3] By opening up a concept of gender, Wilkinson's work offers a good direction for future feminist analysis of Synge, which should move beyond the rather basic analytical principle of selecting out characters of the female sex.

Synge's sympathetic depiction of female characters has led a number of critics to the theme of woman as victim of social and geographical entrapment. Synge took pains to divorce his dramatic intentions from the tradition of the problem play and, more specifically from the work of Henrik Ibsen, describing his own work as much more the product of the imagination (IV, 3). Still, both Joan Templeton (97) and Durbach (363) made comparisons to Ibsen's women. Templeton considered the Romantic demand for freedom of the individual self "over the norms of a restrictive society" the "major theme" of Synge (92) and located it in female heroes like Maurya, Pegeen, Deirdre, Nora Burke, and Mary Byrne of *The Tinker's Wedding*. In the consistent theme of woman as victim of a societal double standard, she hastily found an allegory for a "redemptive future" of Ireland itself (97).[4] F.A.E. Whelan and Keith N. Hull, like Templeton, detect a repeated theme of women's dissatisfaction with their frequently isolated lives; in seeking escape, they become the "movers and shakers of the dramatic action" (36).

Women posed interesting problems of interpretation in biographical studies of Synge. Andrew Carpenter offered the most deliberate treatment of Synge's relationships with women, deriving much from his autobiographical writing and making initial connections to his drama.[5] A summary of Synge's interactions with the women in his life will prepare a discussion of the language of women in his dramas.

The most criticized woman in Synge's life is his mother, Kathleen M. Synge, whose home he shared for most of his life and whom he survived by only five months. Since she was widowed when he was a year old and never remarried, one might expect that she was singularly influential on her youngest child. Her Calvinistic, Evangelical Church of Ireland religious convictions are usually seen as a negative influence on the impressionable child as well as the man. His autobiography records nightmares over his mother's depictions of hell, although he found her "judicious" in other matters: "the well-meant but extraordinary cruelty of introducing the idea of Hell into the imagination of a nervous child has probably caused more misery than many customs that the same people send missionaries to eradicate'' (II, 4–5). Synge's Darwinian conversion (II, 10–11) marked the onset of a deliberate atheism and a silence on the subject of religion between mother and son. Jeanne Flood, operating from Freudian theory and frequently analyzing statements on women and sexuality in the autobiography, suggested that Mrs. Synge's teachings on hell encouraged a dual flight from sexuality and religion. The pattern was reinforced when Cherrie Matheson, a young woman of considerable imaginative as well as emotional importance to Synge, rejected his proposals of marriage, presumably because of his atheism (Flood 176–77, 182).

Mrs. Synge may have contributed some lasting habits of the mind to her son—a value for truth in ideas and attention to small details (Thornton 18, 23). Seamus Deane has detected a ''salvational vocabulary'' derived from the religious training she provided (51). But the language and mind frame provided by Kathleen Synge belong more to a language of the father (or God the Father) than of the mother (or the ''feminine language'' sought particularly in contemporary French feminist theory). Mary C. King suggested that Synge needed to work free of the fundamentalist demand for an unalterable word of God, which was inadequate to the artist's need to work more imaginatively and individualistically with words as signs and symbols (2–3, 9). For Synge, as for James Joyce, the combination of woman and religion was perceived as destructive, and it was in their mothers that they first saw the combination and resisted it; Joyce, however, retained the theme of mother and religion more deliberately in his works, particularly in *A Portrait of the Artist as a Young Man*. Synge's greatest mother figure, Maurya of *Riders to the Sea*, has her own pagan, supernatural admixture to Catholic religion and is not particularly impressed by priestly authority, especially where the workings of nature (particularly the sea) are involved (III, 21). Kathleen Synge's encouragement of her son's studies of natural history, and her positive attitude about his walking out into the country with Florence Ross and Molly Allgood (II, 8; Saddlemyer, *Letters to Molly* 79) should not be overlooked. As I argue later, Synge found an alternative, more ancient mother and language in nature than he did in his own mother.

That Synge had a profound respect for the basic, nurturant practice of motherhood is abundantly evident in his prose works and in his final commendation of his recently deceased mother to Molly Allgood, his fiancée in his final years. He noted of a newly married woman in Kerry, ''she had her full share of the passion for children which is powerful in all women who are permanently and profoundly attractive'' (II, 257). His message to Molly has an undertone of self-serving demand that Molly take on an aspect of his mother, but his appreciation also puts his own artistic endeavors in perspective:

There is nothing in the world better or nobler than a single-hearted wife and mother. I wish you had known her better, I hope you'll be as good to me as she was—I think you will. . . . It makes me rage when I think of the people who go on as if art and literature and writing were the first thing in the world. There is nothing so great and sacred as what is most simple in life. (Saddlemyer, *Letters to Molly* 299)

The dominance of Synge's mother in his upbringing brings to the attention of some scholars his lack of a father. Flood made Synge's missing father the object of a literary quest. Hence her arguments serve as a counter to studies that emphasize the positive influences of the mother and indeed other women in Synge's life and identity as an artist. Flood found the ultimate, theoretically necessary father figure in Pat Dirane, the storyteller Synge met on the Aran Islands and whom he replaced as a storytelling, reborn son (187–96). Despite the closeness of the argument, it is encumbered by the male bias of Freudian theory and the male-centered versions of the vegetation myths characteristic of Sir James Frazer's *The Golden Bough*. Flood's analysis embraces the patriarchal tradition of male public performance and the norm of patrilineal cultural inheritance. This model functions in only two of Synge's plays—*Playboy* and the very early play, *When the Moon Has Set*.

Synge's attraction to Cherrie Matheson [Houghton], a religious, Ascendancy, middle-class young woman, remains poorly documented and understood. The long letters he wrote her from Paris have been lost. Her own memoir gives no hint of sexual attraction on her part, although she described his strong build and delicate health with sensitivity. Her account ("John Synge as I Knew Him") recalls Synge's enthusiastic sharing of his aesthetic interests in Wordsworth and the French painter Corot and reports their sitting in the half-wild garden of Castle Kevin, as well as more conventional visits to Dublin art galleries and concerts. Synge seems to have been unable to attain the openness of communication on a variety of more personal and primitive subjects that he had achieved as a child with his cousin Florence Ross and would later manage in more casual exchanges with "preconventional" rural Irish women, with the artistic women he met abroad, and with his fiancée, Molly Allgood. Carpenter and Flood have detected Matheson figures in Synge's autobiographical writings, his early sketches, and *When the Moon Has Set* (a work he continued to rewrite into his final years). *Étude Morbide* records the interrupted attempt of the central male character, like Synge a violinist, to perform in front of his mistress (II, 28; cited by Flood 184). Synge recalled with greater equanimity the ridicule he occasionally received from Aran women, when their men were not around, for his unmarried state (II, 138). Dread of female ridicule remains in early drafts of *Playboy* (IV, 82 n. 2). The progressive insanity of the mistress in *Étude Morbide* may be her punishment for inflicting male suffering. More directly relevant to the Matheson affair is the two-generation plot of *When the Moon Has Set*. In the elder generation, Mary Costello (now a mad, wandering old woman who has visions of her unborn children) had refused to marry her lover because of his atheism. This lover is the uncle of young Colm, a persona of Synge and another atheist. Colm follows the advice of his just deceased uncle to exercise "the male power" and "subdue" his own beloved, a nun who has been ordered back to the church. Carpenter joined W. B. Yeats in finding it a very bad play (98). The middle-class Irish woman, the Ibsenian situation, and the direct challenge of masculinity to religion did not bring into play Synge's full imaginative potential and his sensitivity to gender.

Beginning in childhood, and particularly during the years when he visited Germany, Italy, and Paris, Synge cultivated a number of relationships with talented women, most of them associated with art, as painters, critics, writers, or musicians. His cousin Florence Ross, the girl described in his autobiography as one of his first loves, collaborated in the keeping of a nature diary and later became an artist and writer; she lived with the Synges for some time following her mother's death in 1891. In the autobiography, there are extraordinary passages about the child-couple's sharing of nature and their discussions of sexuality in the forthright manner of folklore (II, 6–7). Synge seemed to be evaluating masculinity when he noted that he found himself telling her "with more virile authority that I since possess, that she was to be my wife" (II, 8). He is also interested in the "curious" effect of male competition for her; not only was he superseded for a time, but he behaved differently, no longer touching her but kissing her notes and even the chairs she sat on, after the intrusion from a wider society (II, 9). Even toward the end of his life, Synge frequently mentioned Ross's visits, his concern for her endeavors, and the merits of her pursuits to Molly (Saddlemyer, *Letters to Molly* 149, 172, 217). An older cousin from England, Mary Synge, was a musician whom he helped with concert arrangements in Dublin. It was she who encouraged his musical studies, helping set him up in Germany.

Synge's personal reticence with men was not characteristic of his exchanges with sympathetic, intelligent women (Greene and Stephens 49). He told them his dreams and emotional struggles. Like the central character of *Vita Vecchia*, he was helped to self-awareness by them. Synge exchanged long, personal letters with Valeska von Eicken, one of four sisters he lodged with in Germany (Greene and Stephens 38–39, 45–46). He returned to the family for a visit at the end of his life. Synge debated religion, politics, and philosophy with English art historian Hope Rea, another woman who continued to visit with him. Synge confided his heartbreak over Matheson to Thérèse Beydon, an art teacher, feminist, and anarchist who exchanged language lessons with Synge in Paris (Greene and Stephens 49; Saddlemyer, "Synge and the Nature of Woman" 71); he was briefly in love with the etcher Margaret Hardon and cultivated a friendship with an art student, Marie Antoinette Zdanowska (Carpenter 93–97; Saddlemyer, "Synge and the Nature of Woman" 71–72).

Molly Allgood's artistry came in the form of acting, although Synge's letters to her suggest his confidence that the young woman, fifteen years his junior, had a variety of talents that could be cultivated. Their love began while Synge was coaching the Abbey Theatre players in his *The Shadow of the Glen*. *Playboy* and, more so, *Deirdre of the Sorrows* were written with her as the model actress for the young female lead parts. As Carpenter and Thornton have remarked,

Synge's letters to Molly are capable of petulance, pettiness, self-centered jealously, and physical complaints. He sometimes takes on the role of educator, steering her reading to a list of writers that included Shakespeare, Milton, and Meredith. He said he hoped to be able to rely on her as a critic (Saddlemyer, *Letters to Molly* 46, 223) and proposed that she become a playwright as well as a performer (40, 180). He could accept her criticisms of his verses (124) and gave her credit for the poem "A Question," which Yeats particularly admired (283). The poem develops a woman's fierce, primitive response to her lover's death. In its second stanza, she answers the question, "would you / With my black funeral go walking too":

> And, No, you said, for if you saw a crew
> Of living idiots, pressing round that new
> Oak coffin—they alive, I dead beneath
> That board,—you'd rave and rend them with your teeth. (I, 64)

As the poem predicts, Allgood did not attend her fiancé's funeral, but she showed perfectly consistent strength by assisting with the assembly of the unfinished play *Deirdre of the Sorrows*, directing it, and playing the part designed for her when it opened. Synge idealized their relationship at its best—their wanderings in the wild hills of Wicklow—in letters, poems, and *Deirdre*, contributing to a language of woman in nature, to which we will return at the end of this chapter. In Molly, Synge may have found a combination of natural sexual attraction and the type of the artist-woman who had helped him recover from the Matheson affair. Although she was a Roman Catholic, Synge called Molly "heathen" (Saddlemyer, *Letters to Molly* 236), an appropriate companion to an atheist enamored of the primitive. She was released somewhat from middle-class social mores by her lower origins and, more so, by the widened perspective that came from work and travel with the theater. Synge was not always comfortable with her commonplace amusements apart from him, but he compared their genius for wandering: "I, and some other people of *genius* I have known, in my youth nearly always got a wild impulse to wander off and tramp the world in the spring and autumn, the time the birds migrate, so as you're a genius too it's right and proper that you should have the impluse" (Saddlemyer, *Letters to Molly* 98). That they never married is indicative of Synge's psychology; he used his mother, his health, and his writing as reasons for postponements. He served his imagination better than his real living and assigned his marriage to his favored imaginative category.

A problem with many critical studies that deal with a succession of strong, complex, or victimized women in Synge is that they have little theoretical grounding, tend to select a few supportive speeches, and offer an inordinate proportion of plot summary. In discussing Synge's woman characters in this chapter, I focus on their capacity for speech. This relates to the feminist issue of silence imposed on women as authors, members of society, and in literary representation.[6] I argue that Synge, unlike many male authors, delights in women's talk and makes powerful speakers, storytellers, advisers, and even prophetesses of his female heroes. I do not mean to suggest that he is alone among Irish writers or dramatists in offering speaking women. Shaw and Ibsen set recent precedents for outspoken women in drama, although their female speakers were modern and bourgeois, whereas Synge's female characters suggested a more fundamental women's speech.

Synge listened to a great deal of female telling on the Aran Islands and other rural parts of Ireland. He seems to have had a rare potential for summoning forth female confidences, whether from a pair of little girls (II, 52–53) or a teenager in a state of "tumult," who disclosed to him a "sense of prehistoric disillusion" (II, 114). His friend John Masefield noted Synge's special demeanor with women: "his grave courtesy was only gay when he was talking to women. His talk to women had a lightness and charm. It was sympathetic; never self-assertive, as the hard brilliant Irish intellect often is" (Saddlemyer, "Synge and the Nature of Woman" 71). This might suggest that, with women, Synge abandoned the norms of male discourse and found things that other male interviewers could not.

It may be an aspect of Synge's training and interest in folklore that even details of a female-dominated domestic environment spoke to him. This was particularly true in Inishmaan, characterized by Synge as the most primitive of the Aran Islands, where his command of local Gaelic and English language was commendable but incomplete. Synge spent many of the frequent intervals of adverse weather in the female domestic realm of the kitchen, and he found "beauty and distinction" there. "The red dresses of the women who cluster round the fire on their stools give a glow of almost Eastern richness, and the walls have been toned by the turf-smoke to a soft brown that blends with the grey earth-colour of the floor" (II, 58). The walls and the rafters hold the masculine items of fishing tackle and nets (II, 58). It was a description he would reuse for the set of *Riders to the Sea*. Synge attributed "personal character" to this simple inventory. "The curaghs and spinningwheels, the tiny wooden barrels that are still much used in the place of earthenware, the home-made cradles, churns, and baskets, are all full of individuality and . . . they seem to exist as a natural link between the people and the world that is about them" (II, 59). The making and attempted delivery of a cake to Bartley function as a form of female communication in the drama. Durbach has noted how the spinning-wheel operated by the daughter Cathleen communicates: "The whirring of the wheel and its sudden silence generate an ominous sense of tension"; Durbach thought that this prepares for another female domestic rite, the identification of the sisters' drowned brother from the stitches made in his stocking (366–67). The stitches in stockings, like the designs in quilts or the disarray of a kitchen, are seen in feminist analysis as female symbolic systems.[7] Women's crafts also communicate in *Deirdre of the Sorrows*, and the play opens with the prophetess-nurse Lavarcham sewing at a tapestry that is officially Deirdre's work. Lavarcham uses the skill shown in the stitches to win the approval of Conchubor, who inspects the work closely. Yet Deirdre has subverted the task of learning suitable ladies' activities for Conchubor's court at Emain to her own expressive ends. She has told the story of her desire for Naisi and her love of nature in her subject matter: "Three young men, and they chasing in a green gap of a wood" (IV, 191). Deirdre has also expressed her rejection of Emain by failing to display any of the fine housewares Conchubor has brought her. Clearly, Synge is sensitive to women's symbolic systems and their nonverbal powers of communication through domestic arrangements.

Synge's descriptions of women's dress offer another way of examining his attitude toward them. His use of verbs attributes to the dressers an active, practical response to circumstances: "The women wear red petticoats and jackets of the island wool stained with madder, to which they usually add a plaid shawl twisted round their chests and tied at the back. When it rains they throw another petticoat over their heads with the waistband round their faces" (II, 59). Deirdre is an active dresser in Synge's play, donning the apparel of a queen only when she has the purpose of taking on a new role with Naisi and not at the bidding of Conchubor. Another of Synge's descriptions of a young Aran woman has been compared to the famous bird-girl of James Joyce's *A Portrait of the Artist as a Young Man* (Mercer; Solomon):

The water for washing is also coming short, and as I walk round the edges of the sea, I often come on a girl with her petticoats tucked up round her, standing in a pool left by the tide and washing her flannels among the sea-anemones and crabs. Their red bodices and white tapering legs make them as beautiful as tropical sea-birds, as they stand in a frame of seaweeds against the brink of the Atlantic. Michael, however, is a little uneasy when they are in sight, and I cannot pause to watch them. (II, 76)

Synge's young Aran companion will not gaze, although Synge is so inclined. There is a clear difference in attitude—Synge as a member of Western culture perhaps inheriting the aesthetics of the gaze (an act shared by Stephen Dedalus in Joyce's passage), the Aran young man perhaps respecting her vulnerability, perhaps being prudish.[8] Synge strained to offer this view a conventional "frame." Its seaweed substance is unconventional, but predictable for Synge, who tended to surround woman with nature, as we shall see in further examples. Like Joyce, he made a bird analogy. His bird-girl is of an exotic, "tropical" strain, a comparison encouraged by the Aran love of red garments for women. Synge was not so elaborate or fetishistic in developing the analogy over specific parts of the girl's body. Neither did he suggest a religious response in worshipful behavior, language, or comparison to the Virgin, as did Joyce in his consistent portrayal of Stephen Dedalus as perceiver.[9] Synge presented her as one of a recurrent type and took interest in the real conditions of her washing; she engaged actively in a task, rather than suffering his gaze or making seductive movements of her limbs. Solomon has found her "antiseptic and sterile . . . one-dimensional, unresponsive, unalive'' in comparison to Joyce's rendition and that of another bird-girl in George Moore's *Hail and Farewell* (273). I would suggest that, without speaking, she conveys a way of life and an integrity of action although certainly through the filter and form of Synge's aesthetics. The peasant woman who offers Davin a drink and an overnight accommodation in Joyce's *A Portrait* is also suggestive of Synge. She is ''without guile'' and engages Davin ''in talk a long while'' (183). Unlike Davin or Synge in Aran, Stephen has little interest in her ''talk'' and abstracts her for his artistic project of forging ''the uncreated conscience of my race'' (253).

Most women Synge encountered or set into drama were speakers and notable ones at that. Speech may serve as the most available form of action for women with relatively few possibilities in life. Synge's younger women may admit to having sharp tongues and are apt to make stark, revealing admissions; some achieve changes in situation. The men who are attracted to them value their speech.

Nora Burke of *The Shadow of the Glen* expresses directly the frustrations of her childless, mist-locked existence. Speaking of her husband, she openly admits, ''he was always cold, every day since I knew him—and every night, stranger'' (III, 35). Her speech has the power of eliciting change in the form of the Tramp's invitation to join him in the glen. As noted by Whelan and Hull, who have focused more than most critics on women's speech, the Tramp considers Nora's talk ''an indication of her worth'' (39). In *The Well of the Saints*, the blind Martin Doul never tires of hearing the speech of the young Molly Byrne (Whelan and Hull 43). Conchubor thinks that he likes the ''Light and airy'' Deirdre as a counterpart to the ''weight and terror'' of his ''store of knowledge,'' but Deirdre tries to deprive him of these illusions, noting her own lonesome days and bad nights (IV, 193). She is determined and direct, though quiet, in pronouncing ''I will not be your mate in Emain'' (IV, 193).

In *The Playboy of the Western World*, Christy Mahon is in ''rapture'' with the prospect of hearing Pegeen Mike's ''words'' as one of the daily experiences of working at the shebeen (IV, 113). Pegeen admits to being ''the fright of seven townlands for my biting tongue'' (IV, 151), and this capacity surfaces in her dealings with both Christy and the Widow Quin. But her frank revelations predominate over sharp remarks. These include an assessment of the available men in her area: ''you'll meet none but Red Linahan, has a squint in his eye, and Patcheen is lame in his heel, or the mad Mulrannies were driven from California and they lost in their wits'' (IV, 59). She regrets the loss of more violent types who have stories to tell of confrontations with the peelers. No wonder she goes after the outlaw Christy as an improvement in her condition or that the village girls and the Widow Quin have comparable aspirations. Pegeen has been credited with building Christy to heroic stature through her talk. We are told in stage directions near the end of Act I that Christy was ''*expanding with delight at the first confidential talk he has ever had with a woman*'' (IV, 81), an effect not unlike Synge's positive experiences with artistic women. In

the wake of Virginia's Woolf's *A Room of One's Own* (35), we may find that
some of Pegeen's talk with Christy fulfills the traditional female role of male
magnification.[10] Such are the compliments for his small feet and noble brow and
the expressions of interest in his violent deed. When Pegeen compares him to
wandering tellers of tales "like Owen Roe O'Sullivan or the poets of the Dingle
Bay" (IV, 81), she is appreciating more the romantic possibilities of artist and
wanderer. The latter is an extrasocietal role she has aspired to herself and more
conducive to a mutual love talk. She has thought of "sailing the seas" herself
(IV, 151). She associates "great rages" with being a poet (IV, 81), although
she feels incapable of them herself. Near the end of the drama, Pegeen gives a
candid reason for joining the violent public uproar against Christy: "there's a
great gap between a gallous story and a dirty deed" (IV, 169). The division is
intelligent and the preference of story over violence, hardly despicable. Ironically, she goes on to demonstrate that she, too, is capable of grotesque violence,
placing the noose around Christy's neck and burning him with a sod. But from
the opening stage directions, she has been described as a "wild-looking" girl,
and her raised broom evoked his first version of his murderous tale. Synge had
observed violence in both sexes in rural Ireland and was faithful to that reality
in *Playboy*. Pegeen is left in a spirit of self-reproach, a victim of her misjudgment
and of Christy's newfound authority. Frank as ever is the admission "Oh my
grief, I've lost him surely. I've lost the only playboy of the western world"
(IV, 173). For all of Christy's grand talk, Pegeen has the last words of the
drama, and we are still left with the problem of knowing her vision of a
"Playboy."

A number of Synge's female heroes, particularly the older ones, have stature
as fashioners of tales, often told to serve ulterior motives that are as complicated
as their situations in life. In *Playboy*, the Widow Quin tries to woo Christy with
tales of her murderous deed and her desirable cottage. She is sufficient realist
to see that Pegeen is Christy's only goal in love and shifts her attention to
obtaining goods and rights as a bribe for her help. In Christy's service, she
works just as hard to fashion lies that will throw his enraged father off his track
and explanations that will destroy the father's credibility with the community.
Mary Byrne of *The Tinker's Wedding* uses speech to preserve her own tenuous
familial position in the marginal existence of the tinkers. With her talk, she
serves as a mediator with foreign elements like the priest, who finds himself
talking about his own problems to an old heathen (IV, 17). In an attempt to
soothe her loneliness, she promises Sarah Casey a story about great queens and
the spring if only she will stay behind with her at night (IV, 23). Mary also uses
her talk to try to persuade Michael and particularly Sarah of the superiority of
their way of life and is particularly expansive on its natural delights. At the start
of Act Two, Sarah and Michael try to leave quietly in the morning, knowing
that, if they awake Mary, she will use her talk as a tactic to delay their arrival
at the chapel, where the priest is waiting to marry them. At the end of the play,
it is Mary's talk to the priest that secures his promise not to report the three of

them to the authorities for binding and gagging him (IV, 47). Earlier, the priest has been *"half terrified at the language"* he has heard Mary using with Sarah (IV, 33). Although he does not summon the authorities, the priest calls upon God for the divine language of a curse on the tinkers. Like this priest, the saint of *The Well of the Saints* has no love of female language. He offers a prayer against "words of women and smiths" by St. Patrick (III, 91) and instructs Mary Doul that raising the voice is "a bad thing in a woman"(III, 101). Synge's sympathies surely do not lie with the figures of religious authority and their attempts for verbal dominance over women in his plays.

In her use of language, Lavarcham, the nurse-satirist of *Deirdre of the Sorrows*, serves as medial figure between Deirdre and Conchubor, a position comparable to Mary Byrne's intermediacy between Sarah Casey and the priest in *The Tinker's Wedding*. Lavarcham outspokenly tells Conchubor that he is going against nature in his pursuit of the wild young girl, while allying herself in age with him:

she's little call to mind an old woman when she has the birds to school her, and the pools in the rivers where she goes bathing in the sun. I'll tell you if you seen her that time, with her white skin, and her red lips, and the blue water and the ferns about her, you'd know maybe, and you greedy itself, it wasn't for your like she was born at all. (IV, 187, 189)

Like the lovers, Lavarcham senses betrayal when Naisi and Deirdre return to Conchubor's court, and she tries to stay the action until Fergus' help can arrive— characteristically, by telling stories. Her efforts to discourage Conchubor's interest in the returned Deirdre (which include lies about her looks) are met with the censoring words, "It's too much talk you have"(IV, 243). Lavarcham offers him a threatening view of nature overrunning Emain, should he proceed with his deadly plans. An eternal nurturer, she leads the mute Conchubor away to rest at the tragic end of the drama. She is given the final, barren words of the play.

The same, ultimate pronouncement is also reserved for Maurya, the wise old woman of *Riders to the Sea*. Maurya has more difficulty over words than Synge's other major female heroes, but they are critical in relation to her. Maurya's daughters consider it essential that she break the "dark word" and speak her blessing to her last son, Bartley, as he leaves for a treacherous passage to the mainland. It is part of the tragedy of *Riders to the Sea* that her words stick in her throat. The failure is ironic, since the daughters have also complained about the abundance and repetition of her speech in mourning her lost son Michael.

As a final perspective on Synge's language of women, I should like to suggest that Synge partook of the tradition that associates nature romantically, psychologically, and even scientifically with the female. It is an assignment that has both troubled feminists and stimulated them creatively.[11] Other typologies of nature and Synge have been offered. Wilkinson assigned the "exterior" world, with its potentials of danger and adventure, movement and madness, to a "virile" category (192–93). Nature is to a great extent synonymous with his "exterior." Wilkinson's typology is understandable, given his typical use of "interior" domesticity as a contrasting "feminine" value, but it does not take full advantage of Synge's feminine depiction of nature in his early writing.

The association of woman and nature is essential to Synge, from the time of his early recollections. As noted earlier, Synge had his first serious love of a girl in a period of close, mutual experience of nature. Later, when the relationship had become distanced by male competition, Synge engaged in a complicated blending of wooing a real girl and exploring the feminine in nature. With the relentless invasiveness of the late nineteenth-century naturalist, he collected eggs, blew them out, mounted them as specimens, and displayed them to his cousin— a process that he said gave him rare pleasure in every stage (II, 6).[12] He reported his "amorous fellowship" with birds (II, 7) and the "passionate and receptive mood like that of early [man]" that walks in the Dublin mountains inspired (10). In one revelation he reported, "I saw in one hour that both nature and woman seemed an always intangible glory" (II, 10).

In his early work, Synge treated nature itself as female. A poem of the 1890s presents nature as a female God to "court" and mate with:

> The wealth of sun, moon, sea, cloud-vesture drains,
> The loneliness of heather breathes delight,
> I court steep steamlets, withered woods, and lanes. (I, 6)

In place of Christian religion, he vowed he "with Earth's young majesty would yearning mate" (I, 6). Landscape could seem a voluptuous womb for his poet persona's creativity while still reminiscent of his death in *Vita Vecchia*. The triple goddess, who sometimes appears as an earth-goddess, has the same birth-to-death range in her incarnations as maiden, mother and hag:

[An] earth breath came up across the bogs, carrying essences of heath, and obscure plants and the ferment of the soil. . . . In a little while the same moon will rise and there will be wonderful perfumes and darkness and silver and gold lights in the pathways of Wicklow, and I will be [lying] under the clay. . . . I am [haunted] by the briefness of my world. It brings me at times a passionate thirst for the fulfilment of every passive or active capacity of my person. (II, 20–21).

A passage more suggestive of an affirmative return to the ancient mother is recorded as "A Dream":

> And still sad songs intoning touched in me
> A quivering of passions pale with ecstasy.
> Toward banking violets in dreaming rest,
> A woman from the shadow passed to sight

And I beheld drowse on her drooping breast
A babe that breathed with bliss of bland delight. (II, 22–23)

In that same work, Synge's poet-persona had defined *art* as the "soul in harmony with some mood of the earth" and vowed that "unless we are able to produce some myth more beautiful than nature" it is "better to be silent" (35). By his own definition, the feminine, the maternal, as found in nature, is the foundation of his art. Contemporary French feminist theory concerns itself with a return to a pre-Oedipal, ancient mother as a source of language and even literary form and investigates a basic "semiotics" of desire, to use the vocabulary of Julia Kristeva. This is fitting to Synge's early immersion in nature. Far from insisting on a male line of creativity, as suggested earlier in Flood, Synge entertained feminine models of creativity. He speculated in *Étude Morbide* that "the finer organism of women seems to be able to preserve the intensity and delicacy of perception necessary for an artist . . . in a way that is rare with men" (II, 25). A romantic but pessimistic statement from *Vita Vecchia* places woman and artist in a common mortal condition in nature: "Nature is cruel to living things. Rubies and crystals that do not feel are beautiful for ever, but flowers and women and artists fulfil [*sic*] their swift task of propagation and pass in a day" (II, 23). Synge sensed early the relentlessness of time as an aspect of nature and wrote with increasing frequency of its violent, unpredictable aspects and their human counterparts, particularly after the Aran experiences. Whereas nature fosters isolation and loneliness, as it does in the early parts of *The Shadow of the Glen*, it is antithetical to the survival of men and women of all sorts and must be countered with human relationship. Nora Burke begins in peril, partially from nature; Patch Darcy has perished in madness. Nature is kinder to young characters in love, Deirdre and Naisi, or Nora and the Tramp, than to old ones in loneliness, like Mary Byrne of *The Tinker's Wedding* or Conchubor, who finds in it images of his own ageing: "the dry leaves are blowing back and forward at the gate of Emain . . . furze breaking and the daws sitting two and two on ash-trees by the Duns of Emain" (IV, 193). For the imaginative old couple of *The Well of the Saints*, however, it still offers an attractive alternative to the corrupt community that tries to normalize them.

Nature very regularly provides the language of male courtship in Synge; hence it has another strong linguistic connection to the female. Synge used nature language himself in wooing Molly Allgood, as we see in his poems of the period and in letters recollecting their wanderings in the glens, appropriately signed "Your old tramp." The poem "Is It a Month" recalls an evening spent with her in Glen Dubh, where nature and Synge's beloved merge: "And stars grew wilder, growing wise, In the splendour of your eyes!" (I, 50) Nature also takes on characteristics of the lovers as a favorite image, the "moon sank tired through the ledge / Of the wet and windy hedge" (I, 52). Typically, the men who use this language in his plays are marginals who work outside the structures of political and religious power—the tramps, tinkers, hunters, and poachers who live in the "exterior" and love nature as they experience it there. As outsiders to power, they have something in common with the women they woo, and it is not too surprising that this language can be both appreciated and appropriated by these women. When her piously proper fiancé Shawn Keogh accuses her of picking up "a dirty tramp up from the highways of the world," Pegeen summarizes the contrasts in their romance imagery: "it's sooner on a bullock's liver you'd put a poor girl thinking than on the lily or the rose" (IV, 155). The materialistic, establishment man, Shawn, thinks of farm holdings; Christy, of nature.

Christy's delight in "walking down where you'd see the ducks and geese stretched sleeping on the highway" stands in stark contrast to the snoring, cursing father who waits at home, a man who would hurl clods at the stars (IV, 85) and complains of his son's interest in little birds (IV, 123). The elder Mahon's proposal that Christy marry the Widow Casey for his own material gain is a violation of nature as severe as Conchubor's insistence on a young bride. Although she qualifies as an ancient mother (she nursed Christy in infancy), this "hag" is in discord with nature; she is feared even by the birds.

Christy's love speeches have been observed to grow with his enhanced sense of self (Spacks 84–86). One example that echoes Synge's own lines to Molly Allgood will suffice here: "it's then yourself and me should be pacing Neifin in the dews of night, the times sweet smells do be rising, and you'd see a little shiny new moon maybe sinking on the hills" (IV, 147). Pegeen reciprocates, extending his vision of love in an outlaw, natural setting. She imagines a future of love in nature with Christy as a poacher and offering the service of her language to counter authority: "If I was your wife, I'd be along with you those nights, Christy Mahon, the way you'd see I was a great hand at coaxing bailiffs, or coining funny nicknames for the stars of night. . . . Yourself and me would shelter easy in a narrow bush" (IV, 149). Pegeen worries, realistically, that she is indulging only in talk, an insight shared by Nora in her response to the Tramp's vision of love-in-nature in *The Shadow of the Glen*.

The Tramp is perhaps the most eloquent advocate of a loving life in the glens, acknowledging the bad weather but looking forward to the good, offering his abilities to put food in Nora's mouth, and extolling fine songs and the crying of herons as replacements for the civilized talk of getting old that has so troubled Nora (III, 57). Deirdre finds her first images of Naisi in nature. She seeks a mate with skin like snow and "lips like blood spilt on it "(IV, 191). She uses natural analogies in persuading Naisi to fulfill their love, despite the prophecy of early death: "I'm a long while in the woods with my own self, and I'm in little dread of death, and it earned with richness would make the sun red with envy and he going up the heavens, and the moon pale and lonesome and she wasting away" (IV, 211). Naisi woos her in the same natural idiom. They are appropriately wed by natural, not institutional, authority, when Ainnle proclaims, "By the sun and moon and the whole earth, I wed Deirdre to Naisi," and offers the blessing, "May the air bless you, and water and the wind, the sea, and all the hours of the sun and moon"(IV, 215).

The tragic ending of *Deirdre* is a departure from nature and from love, an insertion into patriarchy. Similarly, Christy Mahon's much celebrated departure at the end of *Playboy* is a patriarchal act. Although he and his father plan a return to the roads, theirs will not be the loving venture in nature Pegeen and Christy had anticipated. It is an exercise in dominion. Christy lists the old man's culinary duties as his "heathen slave" and, significantly, denies him speech: "Not a word out of you" (IV, 173). That Christy should turn master and censor in the final moments of the play is a failure that corresponds to Pegeen's inability to separate herself from village judgments and her fear of the authority of the peelers, whom both she and the villagers think will accuse them of murder. Both *Deirdre* and *Playboy* set an ideal, nurturing, natural world against the authoritarian realms of kings or priests or peelers. A tragedy for both sexes is the destruction of the natural language of love in cultural situations involving power. Nature provides a resource for feminine creation and a foundation metaphor for male-female relationship that is informing, nurturing, and promoting of affirmative language in both partners. In *Playboy* and *Deirdre* we see its amorous potential and the counter principles of patriarchal society that challenge and subvert it.

Notes

1. For comments on psychological complexity in Pegeen Mike of *Playboy of the Western World* and Deirdre of *Deirdre of the Sorrows*, see Thornton (138, 146–48). Female changeability is a positive psychological characteristic in Thornton's reading. Synge called his fiancée Molly Allgood "changeling" in his letters.

2. Thomas Kinsella in his "Introduction" to *The Táin* remarked of the women of the Ulster Cycle that the action continually turns on their "strong and diverse personalities." Deirdre is high on his list. "It may be as goddess-figures, ultimately that these women have their power; it is certainly they, under all the violence who remain most real in the memory" (xiv–xv). Saddlemyer identified the Widow Casey of *Playboy* as a parody of the hag-goddess of sovereignty (Saddlemyer, "Synge and the Nature of Woman" 56).

3. Wilkinson's scheme, like the anima/animus construct of Carl Jung, is more positive about virile women than feminine men. The variable gender typing or "oscillation" in couples is suggestive of androgyny.

4. Seamus Deane in *Celtic Revivals* had more difficulty with Synge's heroic themes as related to a politics of Ireland, finding real oppressors like landlords left out of the scheme of his dramas (57–59). Synge's *The Aran Islands* encourages a critical attitude toward evictions, however. See his descriptions of an eviction that features two women, the woman of the house, to whom "the outrage to the hearth is the supreme catastrophe" (II, 89), and the bailiff's mother, who takes on with a "fury of . . . speech" against her own son, the villain of the piece (II, 92).

5. Saddlemyer provided a convenient listing of Synge's female friendships in "Synge

and the Nature of Woman'' and useful annotations to the women relevant to Synge's letters to Molly Allgood. More may be garnered from Robin Skelton's introduction to Volume I of the *Collected Works*, and his book *The Writings of J. M. Synge* and from Thornton (36–41). Basic information, including sections of drafts of lost and unpublished letters, is available in the Greene and Stephens biography. Stephens's unpublished, fuller account of his uncle, housed in the National Library of Ireland, has been read by many scholars in an effort to understand better Synge's relationships with women.

6. On the silencing of women as authors see Woolf (*A Room of One's Own*) and Olsen (*Silences*). Ardener discussed women as a muted social group.

7. See Kolodny's pioneer article ''A Map for Rereading'' in this area. She discussed women characters' reading of the symbols detected in a distressed farm wife's kitchen in Susan Glaspell's story ''A Jury of Her Peers.'' Like the people of Aran, these women also have their own system of justice. Aran sweaters have been marketed for years with the information that each woman knitter has her own distinct stitches to identify drowned men.

8. Templeton considered lovely girls of her type ''entrapped'' by Michael's attitude. In another incident, ''Michael never gave a look at the half-naked girls on Galway Beach, but was 'intense' in his interest in a horse'' (92). Solomon found Michael ''pious'' (273). This is not clearly established in *The Aran Islands*. Elsewhere, Synge found that the islanders' ''direct sexual instincts are not weak . . . but they are so subordinated to the instinct of the family that they rarely lead to irregularity'' (II, 144).

9. See Joyce's *A Portrait* (171).

10. ''Women have served all these centuries as looking-glasses possessing the magic and delicious power of reflecting the figure of man at twice its natural size,'' stated Woolf (35). As if to fulfill the figure, Christy is caught with a looking-glass at the start of Act II.

11. See Griffin, *passim*.

12. See Griffin on John James Audubon (13–14).

References

Carpenter, Andrew. ''Synge and Women.'' *Études Irlandaises* 4 (1979): 89–106.

Deane, Seamus. *Celtic Revivals: Essays in Modern Irish Literature, 1880–1980*. London and Boston: Faber and Faber, 1985.

Durbach, Errol. ''Synge's Tragic Vision of the Old Mother and the Sea.'' *Modern Drama* 14, no. 4 (1972): 363–72.

Flood, Jeanne. ''Synge's Ecstatic Dance and the Myth of the Undying Father.'' *American Imago* 33 (1976): 174–96.

Greene, David H., and Edward M. Stephens. *J. M. Synge, 1871–1909*. New York: Macmillan, 1959.

Griffin, Susan. *Woman and Nature: The Roaring Inside Her*. New York: Harper & Row, 1980.

H., H. C. [Cherrie Matheson Houghton]. ''John Synge as I Knew Him.'' *J. M. Synge: Interviews and Recollections*. Edited by E. H. Mikhail. New York: Barnes & Noble; London: Macmillan, 1977. pp. 3–7.

Joyce, James. *A Portrait of the Artist as a Young Man*. New York: Viking, 1964.

King, Mary C. *The Drama of J. M. Synge*. Irish Studies. Syracuse: Syracuse University Press, 1985.

Kinsella, Thomas. "Introduction." *The Táin*. Translated by Thomas Kinsella. London: Oxford University Press, 1970.

Kolodny, Annette. "A Map for Rereading: Or, Gender and the Interpretation of Literary Texts." *New Literary History* 2 (1980): 451–67.

Mercer, Caroline G. "Stephen Dedalus's Vision and Synge's Peasant Girls." *Notes and Queries* 7, no. 12 (1960);473–74.

Olsen, Tillie. *Silences*. New York: Delacorte, 1978.

Saddlemyer, Ann. *Letters to Molly: John Millington Synge to Maire O'Neill, 1906–1909*. Cambridge: Belknap of Harvard University Press, 1971.

———. "Synge and the Nature of Woman." *Woman in Irish Legend, Life, and Literature*. Edited by S. F. Gallagher. Irish Literary Studies 14. Gerrards Cross, Bucks: Colin Smythe; Totowa, N.J.: Barnes & Noble, 1983. pp. 58–73.

Skelton, Robin. *The Writings of J. M. Synge*. Indianapolis: Bobbs-Merrill, 1971.

Solomon, Albert J. "The Bird Girls of Ireland." *Colby Library Quarterly* 10, no. 5 (1974): 269–74.

Spacks, Patricia Meyer. "The Making of the Playboy." *The Playboy of the Western World: A Collection of Critical Essays*. Edited by Thomas R. Whitaker. Twentieth Century Interpretations. Englewood Cliffs, N.J.: Prentice-Hall, 1969, pp. 75–87.

Spangler, Ellen S. "Synge's *Deirdre of the Sorrows* as Feminine Tragedy." *Éire-Ireland* 12, no. 4 (1977): 97–108.

Templeton, Joan. "Synge's Redeemed Ireland: Woman as Rebel." *Caliban* 17 (1980): 91–97.

Thornton, Weldon. *J. M. Synge and the Western Mind*. Irish Literary Studies 4. New York: Barnes & Noble, 1979.

Whelan, F.A.E., and Keith N. Hull. " 'There's Talking for a Cute Woman'! Synge's Heroines." *Éire-Ireland* 15, no. 3 (1980); 36–46.

Wilkinson, Robin. "The Shadow of Deirdre: A Structuralist Approach to Two Plays by John Millington Synge." *Cahiers du Centre d'Etudes Irlandaises* 4 (1979): 87–100.

Woolf, Virginia. *A Room of One's Own*. New York: Harcourt Brace World, 1957.

Additional Sources

Saddlemyer, Ann. "Art, Nature, and 'The Prepared Personality': A Reading of *The Aran Islands* and Related Writings." *A Centenary Tribute to John Millington Synge, 1871–1909: Sunshine and the Moon's Delight*. Edited by S. B. Bushrui. New York: Barnes & Noble, 1972. pp. 107–20.

Synge's Use of Language

In *Ascendancy and Tradition in Anglo-Irish Literary History from 1789 to 1939*, W. J. McCormack set forth the two perspectives within which this study of Synge's use of language is located. McCormack reminded us that "the emergence of Anglo-Irish literature lies close to the heart of European romanticism. The Anglo-Irish Renaissance is central to modernist literature in the English language" (*Ascendancy and Tradition* 1). The works of Yeats, Joyce, and Beckett have been studied with attention to the interplay of Romanticism and modernism. It is probably not an exaggeration to claim that John Millington Synge is more often perceived as one of the last Romantics, while his contribution to modernist literature remains largely unassessed, not least because of the strenuous efforts of W. B. Yeats to rewrite Synge *as* a Romantic and to insert him into the Yeatsian historiography of Protestant Ascendancy, with its related myth of Celticism. This historiography required for its viability "the complementary notion that Ireland had no middle class" (McCormack, *Ascendancy and Tradition* 9). The nation, therefore, had to be remade in the image of an indomitable Irishry, a rural-based community of noble and beggarman. Synge, or so Yeats would persuade us, combined key features of both roles. A member of an Ascendancy family that had once owned estates in Wicklow and Galway, he not only gave voice to the voiceless poor when he wrote his peasant plays, but he was, himself, the very type of peasant-aristocrat, the Celtic incarnation of Arnold's scholar gypsy. "It was, as I believe," wrote Yeats in "J. M. Synge and the Ireland of his Time," "to seek that old Ireland which took its mould from the duellists and scholars of the eighteenth century and from generations older still, that Synge returned again and again to Aran, to Kerry, and to the wild Blaskets'' (*Essays and Introductions* 324). Thus do we find Yeats assimilating Synge into a version of eighteenth-century primitivism that is symptomatic of his own modernist anxieties about his class and time.

Taking its cue from Yeats's projection of him as a Romantic writer of peasant plays, much of the critical debate about Synge's use of language has focused on the question of its vernacular authenticity.[1] Such debates can, however, distract attention from a more significant dimension of his work, his preoccupation with the nature of language itself. It is within the context of European philology and its relationships with the Celtic Revival that Synge's interest in the Gaelic tongue and in the related peasant vernacular must be located. Only then is it possible to assess the significance of that heightened awareness of language *as* language in his plays, which, together with their self-conscious theatricality, caused Katharine Worth to declare him to be ''in a way one of the most modern of the moderns'' (139).

No consideration of Synge's use of language responsive to this insight can afford to ignore the genesis of his interest in the word. The interest may be traced to the pathological insistence on a literal interpretation of the Divine Word, which characterized the Synge household. This literalism was mediated to the young Synge largely through his mother, who took on herself the role of the absent, because dead, father. In terms of the history of Protestant Ascendancy in Ireland, I have argued elsewhere that, as the privilege of earthly authority faded, sectarian insistence on privileged access to the authority of the Divine Word became for Synge's class a substitute for political power (*The Drama of J. M. Synge* 1–14). Under the influence of Victorian middle-class values and ideologies, and Synge's class was predominantly bourgeois and Victorian, not aristocratic or Augustan, spoken and written English were becoming emasculated. Sexual puritanism, especially, asserted its repressive powers, making the frank expression of emotion traumatic. The process, and its origins and legacy, may be seen at work in Synge's first, highly autobiographical play, *When the Moon Has Set*.[2] This early text also bears witness to his turning toward ''peasant'' language and characters in an attempt to confront and resolve the tensions inherent in his Ascendancy experience. The emasculation of language in the Ascendancy sequence of *When the Moon Has Set*, together with fear of and fascination with miscegenation and *mésalliance*, are not without relevance for an assessment of the tensions and antinomies inherent in Synge's relationships with the people of Aran, for his interest in Celtic studies and in the spoken Gaelic of the Aran people, and for his use of a highly self-conscious, metalinguistic version of the peasant speech of Catholic Ireland in his plays. As Synge's nephew Edward Stephens suggested, and as W. J. McCormack has argued, in their very recourse to peasant language and peasant characters, these plays are ''symbolic products of the Anglo-Irish ascendancy at the crux of its historical development'' (McCormack, *Sheridan LeFanu* 265).[3]

If we examine Synge's autobiographical prose writings, upon which he draws for much of the language and action of *When the Moon Has Set,* it is not difficult to trace therein characteristics that are recognizably those of a late Romantic preoccupation with language as the creative expression of the individual psyche. The narrators in these works, the *Autobiography,* the *Vita Vecchia,* and the *Étude Morbide,* as well as the unpublished novel, are all artists. All are engaged, generally unsuccessfully, in the struggle to give voice to artistic identity through the medium of aesthetic utterance. In this respect, they all foreshadow the artist *par excellence* in Synge's drama, the poetry-talking Christy Mahon in *The Playboy of the Western World.* For Synge, as for Yeats, this effort to establish an identify is part of an often desperate search for persistence of the personality, a personality constantly threatened, as in the *Vita Vecchia* and the *Étude Morbide,* by fear of and longing for dissolution. Unity of Being is located in an idealized past and is guaranteed and simultaneously threatened by the quasi eternality of the work of art. Synge's *Autobiography,* a protomodernist text that Yeats had by him as he wrote his own versions of his autobiographies, is a portrait of the young man as a failed artist, searching for forms of expression that elude him in the very process of their formulation. The narrator strives for "the expression of a personality [which] will reveal evolution from before history to beyond the science of our epoque" (II, 8). The sense of personality or, more precisely, the striving for its expression in language, is, however, presented as constantly under threat. It is threatened by recourse to words, just as Christy Mahon's verbally constructed persona in *The Playboy* and Martin and Mary Doul's poetic vision of each other as "the finest man and the finest woman, of the seven counties of the east" (III, 73) in *The Well of the Saints* are threatened by the authoritarian word of the father.

In Synge's *Autobiography* the quest for identity is jeopardized by the fallibility of the word as the vehicle of chronologically articulated memory: "If I could know the dates of my nurses I could trace the whole course of my opening memory, but they are lost" (II, 3–4); by the fear of hell and of the mother, surrogate bearer of the Father's Word, and by abortive efforts at poetic utterance: "I remember walking into the drawing room and telling the company that I had 'invented' a poem. I was proud of the achievement and wanted to read it aloud, but got very nervous in the middle and had to give it up" (II, 5). So, too, in the *Vita Vecchia,* the narrator dreamed of playing on the violin for his beloved and endured the nightmare of breaking down when "a crowd of people" (II, 16) rushed into the room. He then played for her in reality and was frustrated when "a number of children ran into the room and began to make fun of my performance. I was playing from memory. I began to lose notes, and in the end I broke down utterly" (II, 16). The theme is repeated in the *Étude Morbide,* when the narrator and his beloved, the Chouska, debate the nature of art (love). He responds to her suggestion that "art is but expression" (II, 35) by declaring that "music is the finest art, for it alone can express directly what is not utterable, but I am not fitted to be a composer. . . . There is little poetry that I can read here, *except the songs of the peasants* and some of Wordsworth and Dante'' (II, 35, my emphasis). The narrator's desire in the autobiographical prose for gen-erational, sexual continuity is darkly shadowed by the spectre of ill-health, by deep psychic guilt, and by fear of a polluted inheritance: ''I said, I am unhealthy, and if I marry I will have unhealthy children . . . so I will never marry'' (II, 9). These preoccupations linking expression and identity with generation and sex-uality, and both with dread of hereditary pollution, are central to *When the Moon Has Set*. They also make their presence felt in the Oedipal themes in *The Playboy of the Western World,* where Christy becomes capable of speaking poetry-talk, of using the word creatively, only through and because of the slaying of his father; in *Deirdre of the Sorrows,* where Conchubar reverses the Oedipal cycle by slaying his nephew so that he may possess that nephew's bride, Deirdre; and in the appearance of the *tyrannos* as the not-dead spouse in the person of the word-hating Daniel Burke in *The Shadow of the Glen.* Together with the me-taformal and metalinguistic features of his work, such preoccupations place Synge firmly within the mainstream of Anglo-Irish and, therefore, of European, modernism. In *When the Moon Has Set,* theme and technique anticipate by some forty years Yeats's exposition, in his most modernist play, *Purgatory,* of the inauthentic tradition of Ascendancy to which he appealed for legitimation of his aesthetic of history and of art.

In his *Autobiography.* in his notebooks, and in *When the Moon Has Set,* close and profoundly symptomatic affinities may be traced between the wrestling of the creative artist with the problematic of language and self-expression and Synge's struggle with the impact of Darwin and Darwinism on the received tradition of Ascendancy history and religion, bound up as it was with a literal interpretation of the Bible, the Book of the Word. If class for the Ascendancy was a matter of divinely ordained distinction and privileged separation, the Darwinian theory of evolution insisted on common ancestry and relationships as the source of biological generation and continuity. This view of life as con-tinuity through reciprocity and change was reinforced and historicized for Synge when he added to his acquaintance with Darwin his reading of the works of Hegel and Marx.[4] His study of Darwin necessitated a dramatic revision and eventual rejection of the parental attitude toward language. Forcing him to aban-don the literal interpretation of the Divine Word, it entailed an epistemological questioning of the nature and status of language itself. If language, like ancestry, evolved, the Word was not a divinely underwritten literal expression of Ultimate Truth, or a ''mere copy of the world'' (II, 35). With the realization that words change, that they, too, have a history, Synge embarked on a journey beyond the literal that led him after his Aran experiences, toward an appreciation that language was essentially *symbolic* and that this symbolic power made possible a *transformation* of the past. Through the creative power of the word, history, instead of being fixed and accusing, could become the locus of action directed toward a creative making of the self.

If his reading of Darwin, Hegel, and Marx was important for Synge's development of a historical imagination, his studies of the European Romantic movement in philology, his familiarity with the works of Zeuss, Meyer, de Jubainville,
Herder, Renan, and Nietzsche, can scarcely be overestimated either.[5] In its
approach to language, the Romantic movement's philosophical orientation was
both nationalist and historical. The movement came, also, to the defense of the
expression of individual consciousness as the highest aim of language. It incorporated into its epistemology the concept of the word as symbolic and polyse-
mantic. The very theory of self-expression, however, became prey to idealistic
a priori-ism, which was not without affinities with belief in the ineffable Divine
Word, presupposing as it did that the expressible "exists first in one form and
then switches to another form" (Volosinov 84). The consequence of this belief
is that the expressed or languaged form is almost inevitably perceived as less
perfect, more polluted, than the a priori content it expresses. The hopeless
ambition and fate of the artist, as the *Étude Morbide* suggests, thus becomes
that of an endlessly recessive striving for perfect utterance, perfect either because
the aesthetically inspired word alone can "tell it like it is," or because my words,
as an artist, "tell it like it is for me" (Silverman and Torode 42). As David
Silverman and Brian Torode pointed out,

the first path proposes a transcendental discourse and engenders a silence of absolute
truth; the second path proposes a relativized discourse and engenders the silence of
solipsism. Following either path we would not be able to converse, to construct the world
together and thus to make history. (42)

This dilemma is confronted, but not resolved, in *When the Moon Has Set*, where
the desire of the central character, Columb, to make a new history for himself
and his class issues in solipsistic escape from the "diseased" world of habit
(38). These contradictions are dramatized and transcended in *The Well of the
Saints*, a play characterized by the density of its references to language as
language and by its preoccupation with the relationships between language and
reality.

In *When the Moon Has Set*, written before Synge completed his major prose
work *The Aran Islands* and therefore "before he discovered the method of art
to be virtually the nature of language itself," the hero, Columb, like Aleel in
Yeats's *The Countess Cathleen*, is a writer-musician with a mission (Mc-
Cormack, *Ascendancy and Tradition* 392). This mission combines aesthetic
proselytizing with political aspirations. The play gives to the European Romantic
agony, anatomized by Columb and typified by his cellist friend O'Neill, a local
Irish Ascendancy habitation in the decaying Big House, the dead uncle, and his
insane peasant-aristocrat bride. At the same time it anticipates Synge's later use
of peasant themes, characters, and dialect and his deployment, in his later plays,
of metalinguistic and metadramatic strategies. It is the only play in which we
can observe the dramatist tentatively exploiting the tensions between the polite,

"educated," and sexually repressed language of the Ascendancy and the more concrete, explicit, and frank "peasant" dialect of the servants—servants who, it must be stressed, are related by sexual (mis)alliance and symbolic association with their masters and mistresses. The setting of the play, the library of the decaying, death-ridden Big House with its collection of books, predicates the self-conscious textuality of the work, just as Pegeen Mike's writing out of her spoken order-list for her wedding with Shawn Keogh in *The Playboy of the Western World* announces the self-referential theatricality of that drama and ironically foreshadows Pegeen's treacherous insistence on "a great gap between a gallous story and a dirty deed" (IV, 169) when she betrays her playboy to the villagers. The play's attention, in *When the Moon Has Set*, to its own status as text is further reinforced when Sister Eileen reads from an aesthetic manuscript written by her artist-musician cousin Columb comparing life with music. In this Nietzschean disquisition, life is projected as part of a cosmic symphony. The aesthetic debate continues as the manuscript is explicated in a series of faltering efforts to bring about and give expression to changing relationships between the protagonists. But as in Kafka's *The Castle*, the two protagonists, K and Joseph K, are driven by their desire "to grasp the whole truth in an abstraction" and are thus directed "towards a fruitless search for the essence of language, as if there were some position outside language from which to attack the truth," so, too, Columb and Sister Eileen trace "what seems to be a circle around the limits of language" from which they cannot break through into meaningful relationships with each other or with life (Silverman and Torode 77). Their attempts at intercourse are simultaneously forms of linguistic evasion and repression of explicit sexuality. The emphasis is not so much on the drawing together of the couple as man and woman, as with Christy and Pegeen when they reciprocate each other's poetry-talk in *The Playboy*. It is, rather, on the power of music, in particular of symphonic form, to give aesthetic shape to the Ideal Life and thus to facilitate evasion of the processes of history. Unlanguaged Ultimate Form is prioritized and valorized over verbal and bodily intercourse, over the materiality of language. The aesthetic act is postulated, as in Yeats's "Sailing to Byzantium," as a means of going out of nature from the generational imperative of Darwinian evolution and the horrible concretions of history, time, and context-bound, relativized identity. The hero's final panegyric, with its dubious praise of release from the flesh-bound *logos*, leads to the act of escape itself. Using a formula that is repeated almost *verbatim* by Ainnle in Synge's last play, *Deirdre of the Sorrows*, when he pronounces Naisi and Deirdre man and wife in the green world of Alban's woods; Columb calls on Sister Eileen, dressed in the symbolic green robe of their uncle's "peasant-aristocrat" bride, Mary Costello, to go with him to a world of unadulterated arboreal beauty:

COLUMB: The world of habit is diseased. . . . We will go out among the trees. . . . In the Name of the Summer, and The Sun, and the Whole World, I wed you as my wife. (38)

There is no trace here of the compassionately ironic skepticism about the viability of the desiderated life in the a-social green world that we find in *Deirdre of the Sorrows* nor any of the controlling, self-reflective awareness of the nature and limits of "fine talk" that repeatedly subverts, in Synge's later comedies, the impulse toward solipsistic introversion or transcendental Romanticism.

If Columb's last speech were an assertion of escapist aesthetics unchallenged by the rest of the text, we might perhaps dismiss *When the Moon Has Set* as a failed Romantic drama and be inclined to accept that in the poetry-talk of the later plays we have the peasant equivalent of "an assertion, an imposition of romance on reality" (Innes 74). We might thus be tempted to subscribe to the critical tradition that sees the fine language of Synge's plays as part of a process through which "the transformation of the real world, the joining together of reality and joy, takes place only *within* the work of art, which by that very transformation becomes alienated from the 'reality' on which it is based" (Innes 75). Not only, however, does his first play bear witness to the closeness of Synge to late European Romanticism, but it is also an experimental drama that pushes beyond that movement, to explore with characteristic modernist anxiety what Frederic Jameson has called "the vain attempt of subjectivity to evolve a human world completely out of itself" (148). That exploration is carried out in *When the Moon Has Set* through a search for language, form, and technique that attend to the problematic relationships between word and "reality." The play provides a key to the role and function of the "peasant" characters and use of "peasant" language in Synge's later work, alerting us to the degree to which these features and this use of language are "a mask for tensions in his Protestant upbringing" as well as a means for resolving some of these tensions (Mc-Cormack, *Sheridan LeFanu* 6).

In *When the Moon Has Set,* Columb, the putative Ascendancy heir of a recently deceased uncle, attempts to win over to his politico-aesthetic philosophy, and his marriage bed, a woman who is his first cousin. He thus appears to avoid the threat of miscegenation that was the downfall of his uncle's romance, but because of the blood relationship, he flirts with the equally traumatic risk of a depraved gregariousness. Not only is Sister Eileen a celibate nun, however, and a Roman Catholic, she is also related by symbolic association to the peasant girl, Bride, and, through her donning of the green dress at the end, to the mad peasant bride of the deceased uncle. An alliance with his cousin, like that of the dead uncle with Mary Costello, who is also Bride Kavanagh's aunt, is fraught, therefore, with historical traumas that are reflected in the inability of Columb to speak of sexual attraction except by recourse to aesthetic masks and a vicarious identification with the peasant characters that borders at times on the allegorical. The nightmares and desires to which the "polite" register of the main characters cannot give voice erupt as suppressed subtexts in the play, as history is translated into aesthetics. Whereas, however, the main action is powerfully directed at a surface level toward a stylized, linguistically effete escape into the artifice of eternity, the attempt to cope with life as language, and with text as a form of history capable of transformation by human action, is present in the metatextual devices of the aesthetic manuscripts and the various letters. These letters—from Columb's uncle, from his musician friend and *alter ego* O'Neill, and from Columb ostensibly to O'Neill but effectively to Sister Eileen—are all texts within the text. All are failed attempts also to use the emasculated register of polite middle-class English to explore and express dimensions of sexual attraction. All of them, too, urge the protagonists neither to repeat nor to deny enigmatic sins and guilt of the past. These sins and guilt relate to the failure of the uncle and his Catholic servant to consummate their nuptial union and to the failure of the artist to find a form of expression that, going through and beyond "the Christian synthesis" where "each separate faculty has been dying of atrophy," will create instead "new discords resolving in what are to us inconceivable harmonies" (32).

In *When the Moon Has Set,* it is only through the displaced mediation of the aesthetic manuscript and the letters, *and the masklike, ventriloquistic mediation of the peasant characters and their language,* that Synge/Columb finds it possible to express the sexual-relational themes of the main plot. It is, finally, Bride Kavanagh's "peasant" commitment to vigorous languge, to expressive life, and to sexuality—she is pregnant by Pat Murphy before marriage—that is the operative stimulus and occasion for the repressed hero's sexual overtures to his cousin toward the end of the play:

COLUMB:Did you notice anything?

SISTER EILEEN:What do you mean?

COLUMB:The girl is enceinte.

SISTER EILEEN:Oh, Columb.

COLUMB:[*going to the window*] She is nobler than you are.
     [*speaking very slowly*] I am not a woman. I cannot judge of your feelings. Yet I
     know, you have a passionate instinct for children. (36)

These issues take us far beyond immediate stylistic questions of vernacular authenticity, local color, or escapist poetry-talk in the language of Synge's better-known plays. By contrast with the prurient *politesse* of the anglophone middle class, to speak Gaelic in Ireland, or to speak the peasant dialect so strongly influenced by the Gaelic vernacular "was to make explicit aspects of human biology which English was tending to disguise" (McCormack, *Ascendancy and Tradition* 267). Of equal significance is the fact that "within the United Kingdom, where its political role was anomalous and its economy divergent, Ireland experienced an intense cultural trauma through the medium of linguistic change" (McCormack, *Ascendancy and Tradition* 267). Part of that trauma, for the Protestant bourgeoisie, was their perception of the emergence of an English-speaking Catholic Irish middle class, a class that was to demonstrate all too clearly by its shocked response to the use of the word *shift* in *The Playboy of the Western*

World just how effectively it could act as a mirror and a lamp to its Protestant counterpart. Peering in that mirror, by the light of that lamp, Protestant Ascendancy saw its own bourgeois reflection and found itself related to its Catholic cousins by bonds more powerful than blood: by the *commercium hominis* of the cash nexus. Yeats, for one, did not like what he saw. His "Celtic Twilight," therefore,

> sought a "dream of the noble and the beggarman" and thus sought both to acknowledge the immiseration of the nineteenth century and to leapfrog back across the Famine to an era of Whiggish hegemony. In more specifically linguistic terms, he sought a cultural synthesis under the guise of "a written speech." (McCormack, *Ascendancy and Tradition* 268)

For Synge, as his first play testifies, a related synthesis was not without its attractions. However, his sojourns on the Aran Islands; his genuine empathy with the Aran people; his awareness of history, sharpened by his socialist sympathies; and his acutely perceptive insight into the contemporaneity and revolutionary potential of the folk tradition of the Aran people all enabled him to engage in an act of imaginative synthesis no less effective than, but very different from, that postulated by Yeats for himself or, indeed, for John Millington Synge.

When Synge visited the Aran Islands at the turn of the century, Irish Gaelic was still the main vernacular. The people's use of language, like the economy of their islands, was, however, very obviously in the state of revolutionary change, with increasing pressure and interference from the colonizing English tongue. Most of the islanders were eager, for economic reasons, to speak English, envying their visitor his anglophone fluency that they associated with access to the currency and coinage they needed to keep pace with the commodification of their subsistence way of life.[6] Without doubt, Synge was impressed by the vitality and exuberance of the islanders' Gaelic as well as of their idiomatic English, whose syntax and phraseology derived much from direct calquing from Gaelic. Without doubt, too, he was tempted to regard this use of language as a manifestation of that exoticism, that blessed exclusion from history and its attendant industrializing rationalism, which Arnoldian Celticism offered to the Saxon as antidote to the philistinism attendant upon progress and power. Synge, however, was alerted by his formal philological studies and his study of Hegel, Marx, and Darwin to the need to historicize myth and to the dangers attendant upon failure to do so. Listening to the islanders' folktales and stories, and sharing their daily lives, he came to appreciate that the folk tradition, like the word, was a living, changing form of social *activity,* not a repository of past culture frozen in "artistic" isolation from the modern world. The islanders' stories and poems, like their language, reflected their past, but these stories and poems were undergoing a continual transformation as the people deployed their myths and traditions to mediate between past, present, and future and to help them make their history. The strategies of mediation and articulation in Synge's plays are rooted in a sense of the negotiations that language, literature, and tradition must enter into in their engagement with the outer world and its ineluctable objectivity. It is this historicizing imagination that informs the awareness of language as language remarked upon by Katharine Worth. It manifests itself in his plays not just in the peasant dialect but in the references to fine talk, stories, games, rites and rituals, myth, legend, and role playing. Synge learned from his acquaintance with the people of Aran how art, like language, can be a means of access to history and a mode of action within it. In this respect, his vision is essentially dramatistic, if *dramatism* means a perspective on language and art that regards them "primarily as modes of action" rather than as "means of conveying information" (Burke xxii).

The ways in which language becomes a form of symbolic action and the word itself can be considered a kind of act are explored in *The Well of the Saints,* where the dependence of the protagonists, Martin and Mary Doul, on linguistic mediation for their knowledge of self, other, and world is foregrounded by their blindness. The couple's lack of sight makes them doubly dependent for their sense of identity on language: a blind person, like a word, is, in Tony Tanner's phrase, "almost literally a presence and an absence combined" (302). In *The Well of the Saints,* Synge called upon the conventions and practices of language to reveal the part they play in making the relationship between what Nietzsche called "the designations and the things" (Bell 506). The well of the title reputedly contains water that, when combined with the Latin formula uttered by the Saint, confers a particular way of seeing—and behaving—on Martin and Mary, a way that is diametrically at odds with their previous, also linguistically mediated, vision of themselves as "the finest man, and the finest woman, of the seven counties of the east" (III, 73). But if consciousness can harbor only in the image or the word, is it, then, solipsistic? For the German philosopher the answer appears to be yes, "for between two utterly different spheres, as between subject and object, there is no causality"; all that can be offered is "at the utmost an *aesthetical* relation" (Bell 507). The objective world is thus handed over to a subjective language-as-art, and art itself becomes fabulation.

In the opening scene of *The Well of the Saints,* the protagonists appear to be hopelessly trapped in such a circularity of linguistic constructs. Freedom from dependence on the words of the villagers for confirmation of their good looks seems to materialize with the advent of the Holy Father. Ironically, however, the longed-for escape from dependence on language into unmediated knowledge or their a priori perfection is turned by the words of the ascetic priest into a declaration that they are "wrinkled and poor, a thing rich men would hardly look at at all" (III, 89). They are exhorted to practice self-renunciation in this diseased world in return for occasional glimpses of "the splendour of the Spirit of God, you'll see an odd time shining out through the big hills" (III, 101). Unlike Columb in *When the Moon Has Set,* however, Martin and Mary Doul hold fast, through their trials and tribulations, to the hope of achieving in this world the satisfaction of their desires. As the curtain rises on the once-more-blind couple in Act Three, the rush lights that they are again producing remind us that they are *makers* of light who earn thereby their few halfpence on the road. The couple are not game-playing pastoral characters indulging the aesthetic illusion of being able to convert life into style. Such strategies are no longer open to Martin and Mary because they have experienced their failure. They can no longer delude themselves into thinking that the words of people or of priest can confer on them eternal beauty or lasting identity as the perfect man and woman. But recognition of the reality of their involvement in process and change is to become for them neither pathetic fallacy nor resigned determinism. The couple learn to move away from "the tendency of the middle classes to understand our relationship to external objects (and consequently our *knowledge* of those objects) in static and contemplative fashion . . . as though our primary relationship to the things of the outside world were not one of making or use, but rather that of a motionless gaze" (Jameson 185). Language becomes for them instead the vehicle of a new form of action that leads beyond mere passivity as victims in a failed stylistic game. Rejecting the Saint's way of seeing, they choose, rather, a form of transfigured realism that revels in "things growing up, and budding from the earth" (III, 131). Their new awareness issues in a superbly triumphant transformative act when Martin defiantly knocks over the Saint's can of water and they opt instead for "seeing lakes and broadening rivers, and hills are waiting for the spade and plough" (III, 41). In place of the aesthetics of reflection and contemplation, of a "static relationship to the objects of knowledge [which] is itself but a reflection of the life experience of the middle classes in the economic and social realm," Martin and Mary opt for an embracing of the word "as a form of action, as a social force" (Jameson 185).

In *The Well of the Saints,* language becomes for the protagonists a medium through which they learn to articulate the production of consciousness with practical activity. *The Playboy of the Western World* takes the metalinguistic qualities developed in that play to a level of linguistic and dramatic intensity in which the very exuberance of the style calls attention to its histrionic nature. If we accept as a working definition of *metalinguistic*, "language the use of which calls attention, with a degree of explicitness, to the linguistic status of utterances" and by analogy define *metadramatic* as "drama, including dramatic language, which with a degree of explicitness draws attention to the 'play' status of events, episodes or elements within a play," in this work we find a concentration of both.[7] As Pegeen Mike, in the opening lines, speaks *and writes* an order for

Six yards of stuff for to make a yellow gown. A pair of lace boots with lengthy heels on them and brassy eyes. A hat is suited for a wedding-day. A fine tooth comb. To be sent with three barrels of porter in Jimmy Farrell's creel cart on the evening of the coming Fair. (IV, 57)

language and action momentarily coincide, only to be projected rapidly into a relationship of dramatic tension when she scornfully informs Shawn Keogh of the doubts surrounding the very marriage for which she is making preparations. Her reasons for questioning Shawn's certainty about their wedding are closely related to his lack of histrionic or playboy qualities. She listens to her suitor's drab characterization of himself as a man with "little will to be walking off to wakes or weddings in the darkness of the night" (IV, 59) and to his supine subjection of his desires to the word of a whole constellation of holy fathers. Shawn is timidly and fearfully "waiting these days on Father Reilly's dispensation from the bishops or the Court of Rome" (IV, 59) to absolve him from the risk of a depraved gregariousness should he marry his cousin Pegeen. Scornfully, she mocks him by comparing the squint, lame, and mad antiheroes left in the village with past heroes and storytellers who would "have the old women shedding down tears about their feet" (IV, 59). Shawn Keogh is the type of repressed silent man represented by the failed artists of the prose works and epitomized in *The Shadow of the Glen* by Michael Dara, "a quiet man, God help you" (III, 59). Shawn's references to language, like those of both Michael Dara and his older alter ego Daniel Burke, are frequently negative: "don't let on I was speaking of him. Don't tell your father and the men is coming. . . . Will you whisht, I'm saying" (IV, 61). Ironically, his introversion, fear of self-expression, and exaggerated deference to authority are matched, indeed almost surpassed, by the initial appearance and speech, or lack of it, when Christy Mahon makes his entry. This early identity between Shawn and Christy, focusing as it does upon their mutual reluctance to use words, defy authority, or lay claim to heroic deeds, is crucial to the play's exploration of the tensions and relationship between language and action. It is by experiencing these tensions and accepting and acting upon their implications that Christy eventually *becomes* a playboy when he is challenged with being a mere sayer of words, not a doer of deeds.

When the Widow Quin appears, Christy seems to her to be merely a "curiosity man," "a little smiling fellow," "sitting so simple with your cup and cake, and you fitter to be saying your catechism than slaying your da" (IV, 87). His contributions to the heated exchange between Pegeen and the Widow over which of them should lay claim to him display, in the opening sequences, little of the poetry-talk for which the play, as well as the playboy, are renowned:

CHRISTY:[*shyly*] God save you kindly.

CHRISTY:[*doubtfully*] It should, maybe.

CHRISTY:[*innocently*] Did you kill your father? (IV, 87, *passim*).

Far from being an equal of "the great powers and potentates of France and Spain" (IV, 79), with "as much talk and streeleen, I'm thinking, as Owen Roe O'Sullivan or the poets of Dingle Bay" (IV, 81), the Christy of Act One is more like a changeling child in danger of being "stolen off and kidnabbed while himself's abroad" (IV, 89). He is, to use Kenneth Burke's words, the victim of an ongoing exploratory process of "lifting, smelling, tasting, tapping, holding in different lights, subjecting to different pressures, dividing, matching, contrasting, etc." (504). The object of this is not just to help establish his own identity but to make it possible for him to perceive himself in others and for others to perceive themselves both in and apart from him. In this process the self-referential use of language and the attendant self-conscious role playing are part of Synge's innovative creation of a dramaturgy of the word. The strategy invites comparison with that of Brecht in, for example, *Man Equals Man*:

> Herr Bertolt Brecht maintains man equals man
> —A view that has been around since time began.
> But then Herr Brecht points out how far one can
> Manoeuvre and manipulate that man. (Brecht 100)

Christy is cast in *The Playboy* not in the simple role of hero but in that of potential hero *and* potential antihero. He takes part in a series of plays within the play, in each of which he is called upon to formulate and then try out his status in relation to those who have encouraged him in a process and practice of verbal creativity. By the end of Act One he has rehearsed his role as murderer/hero in a heavily prompted dramatic *mimesis* of the murder of his da. In Acts Two and Three he is placed in a situation in which he must measure the assertions made and the role assumed against that version of his past character and deeds that materializes in the person of his father. Before he does so, however, he engages in a series of poetic exchanges with Pegeen Mike. Such exchanges give him the courage and the flair that enable him to dress himself in Shawn Keogh's wedding jacket and transform the empty "coat of a Christian man" IV, 65) into the very incarnation of a swaggeringly confident suitor:

CHRISTY:From this out I'll have no want of company when all sorts is bringing me their food and clothing [*he swaggers to the door, tightening his belt*], the way they'd set their eyes upon a gallant orphan cleft his father with one blow to the breeches belt. (IV, 119)

When Christy's father appears, however, we are reminded that the playboy's progressively constructed identity remains as yet at the level of poetry-talk unarticulated with history or "reality." The downfall of the poet and his poetry seems at first complete, his heroism nothing but a Romantic assertion. Going out in Shawn's coat to seek Pegeen, Christy comes face to face with the nightmare of his past, "the walking spirit of my murdered da," "that ghost of hell" (IV, 119), from which, it seems, he cannot as yet fully waken into his dream of heroic action. Shawn-like and inarticulate once more, he scuttles away to hide behind the door.

With the materialization of old Mahon, we are offered yet another metalinguistic reconstruction of Christy's persona, reminding us that the hero's past, like his dream of future freedom and integrity, is mediated by language. The formula of question and answer used in Acts One and Two to elicit from Christy an account and a dramatization of the murder of his father recurs as the Widow questions old Mahon. This time, the character constructed by the dialogue emerges not as a hero but as "an ugly young streeler with a murderous gob on him," "a lier on walls, a talker of folly, a man you'd see stretched the half of the day in the brown ferns with his belly to the sun," a shirker of work who'd be "making mugs at his own self in the bit of a glass we had hung on the wall" (IV, 119–23, *passim*). There can be little doubt that aspects of Christy's persona are reflected in his father's description of him, but in a play in which references to role playing and to the ambivalent status of language are pervasive, we as audience are scarcely willing to take this characterization of our many-faceted hero/antihero as literally true. The Widow Quin reminds us, in any case, of the dangers of doing so when she calls attention explicitly to the linguistic status of old Mahon's account of Christy's character and actions:

WIDOW QUIN:[*clasping her hands*] Well, I never till this day *heard tell* of a man the like of that. (IV, 123, my emphasis)

Her words also suggest that singularity and identity are social constructs that cannot be either exhaustive or definitive. If Christy is "the looney of Mahon's" (IV, 123)—as well as the playboy of the Western world—perhaps he became so because that is a part that old Mahon called on him to play, or perhaps, like Lear's fool, he sometimes wears motley by consent. The parallel, again, might be with Brecht's Gayly Gay, the Western playboy sent East:

GALY GAY:All over Ireland the Galy Gays are famous for banging the nail home in any situation.

URIAH:[*to Polly*] Before the sun has set seven times this man must be another man.

POLLY:Can it really be done, Uriah? Changing one man into another?

URIAH:Yes, one man is like the other. Man equals man. (Brecht 37)

By the end of the play's second act, then, the quest for the hero has by no means succeeded in identifying him as such or in confirming, either, his antiheroic status any more than the "lies" of the villagers or the miracle-working *fiat* of the Holy Father can of themselves authoritatively determine whether or not Martin and Mary Doul are fine-looking people. Is Christy's "dream," then, the victim of the relativity of language, the product and prisoner of an ultimately solipsistic Romantic imagination? The final act of *The Playboy of the Western World* brings the play's metadrama, and its metalinguistic exploration of the word-deed relationship, to a climax that, like Martin's action of defiance in *The Well of the Saints* when he spills the water from the can, transcends the theme of role playing as game, uniting but not identifying image with action and thus offering to resolve the solipsistic dilemma created and confronted by the self-regarding modernist text.

In Act Three of *The Playboy* the most intense of the love scenes between Pegeen and Christy precedes her rejection of him for those very qualities that make this one of the most complex explorations of the nature of poetry-talk in Synge's plays. In this last love scene, which Synge in his diagrammatic draft labeled poetical, the incidence of metalanguage is highly concentrated. It is this language, too, that has led many critics to detect in the play a stylistic exuberance approaching self-parody. The scene has been variously interpreted either as a direct satire on Irish Romanticism or as an ironic qualification of the Romantic vision of the play itself. What is at work here, however, is something far more central to Synge's preoccupations and far more significant for his contribution to a critical modernism. The critical perspective, the sense of both the irony and the achievement of the work of art in its relation to "reality," is present within the vision and words of the characters themselves. Christy and Pegeen refer repeatedly to the linguistic nature of their poetic declarations of love. They are aware of the precarious, at times hyperbolical, and yet creatively transfiguring relationship between word and referent. They are conscious also, however transiently, of poetry as making and of the limitations of purely contemplative reflections on, and of, each other. Christy's existential "pity for the Lord God is all ages sitting lonesome in his golden chair" (IV, 147) is inspired by his acceptance of the waking, if passing, love of time-bound life as finer than the static solitude of eternity's gaze.

As they participate consciously in the play of words, Christy's poetry-talk inspires in Pegeen "*real tenderness*" (IV, 149) and awakens rapture in himself. The context- and time-bound, conditional nature of their dream is, however, acknowledged by the repetitive, stylized, formal placing of the "if" participle at the beginning of their antiphonal exchanges: "If the mitred bishops . . . " "If I was your wife . . . " "If I wasn't a good Christian . . . " "If that's the truth . . . " (IV, 149, *passim*). They neither ignore nor undervalue the element of gaming, of playing with language, in their imaginative projection of their love, nor do they gloss over the presence within the vision of the possibility of "taking your death in the hailstones or the fogs of dawn" (IV, 149). The world they imagine is transfigured by their poetry-talk, but it is not a discrete, insulated paradise or an isolated green world. It is, rather, a transfiguration and embracing of the everyday world of "jack straw . . . roofing" and "stony pebble" (IV, 149). In the name of this transfigured realism—the phrase in Synge's—Pegeen *renounces* the illusory quest for an exotic world beyond the seas and her desires of marrying "a Jew-man with ten kegs of gold" in favor of the world of the shebeen, with "the like of you drawing nearer like the stars of God" (IV, 151). Her final tragedy is that she realizes, too late, that it is fidelity to this sense of reality articulated with vision that Christy asks of her in the end. This is what she refuses to concede when he triumphantly relates gallous story to heroic deed and thus she loses her "only playboy" (IV, 173).

The village people have encouraged Christy Mahon, throughout *The Playboy*, to assume the identity of a hero who lays claim to having slain his father. He badly misjudges, however, the nature of the social sanctions that will be brought to bear upon him by the villagers and Pegeen when he dares to realize his role. The danger of his becoming merely their perpetual sport, just as the villagers in *The Well of the Saints* force the newly sighted Martin and Mary Doul to engage in a cruel game of blindman's buff, is made dramatically explicit by their final attempts to dress him up not as playboy hero on this occasion but in a woman's petticoat and shawl, as if in fulfilment of his father's emasculating account of how he once dispatched him to "the females' nurse" (IV, 123). When Pegeen herself leads the villagers toward their victim in the end and they snare him in their noose, Christy's agonized question "And what is it you'll *say* to me and I after *doing* it this time in the face of all?" (IV, 169, my emphasis) brings fully and finally into the open the word/deed, play/reality tensions that permeate this drama. Unlike Kafka, however, in whose writings the "red of sensuous human practice" remains absent from the language-reality dialogue, Synge once more forges a practical link between transcendent reality and mundane appearance (Silverman and Torode 89). When their playboy's suffering is at its most intense and Pegeen Mike burns his leg with a sod of turf—a shocking enactment of mundane cruelty—it is revealed to his tormentors that the very element of play that they encouraged and now deny has won through into action. As the anarchic old Proteus leans forward to free Christy from bondage he also frees himself. Old Mahon, the father-figure all of them fear, is both dead and not dead: he acts out the slaying of his dominating role as *tyrannos* when he releases his son, thus ushering "all that has outlived its day into the realm of shadows" (Zis 224). Christy's and old Mahon's mutual rehabilitation of each other is a social act. It is a product of a process wherein the people use the word and the story to appropriate the myths and traditions of the past into a form of imaginative activity. This vision, this use of language and art as a making of reality, Synge learnt from the people of Aran, as his prepared imagination attended to their transforming practice.

Synge's interest in the nature of language led him to recognize the role of the word as mediating *process*. Although he shared with the late Romantics a distaste for the petty-bourgeois "nullity of the rich" (II, 103) he did not subscribe, as Yeats would suggest, to the atavistic belief in the possibility of an aesthetically contrived escape therefrom to a hypothetical past state of heroic/peasant innocence or an Arnoldian Celtic enclave. In this context, it is, perhaps, illuminating to compare his comic, even laughing, acceptance of process and change and the necessity of death with Yeats's dangerously embittered protest, in 1938, against the disappearance of the Ascendancy. Yeats is referring to his play *Pugatory*, the conclusion of which, when the father slays the son but fails to lay to rest the ghost of a polluted past, offers a neat contrast to *The Playboy*:

In some few cases a house has been destroyed by a mesalliance. I have founded my play on this exceptional case, partly because of my interest in certain problems of eugenics, partly because it enables me to depict more vividly than otherwise would be possible the tragedy of the house.

In Germany there is special legislation to enable old families to go on living where their fathers lived. (Torchiana 357–58)

Ascendancy, Synge once noted, with a finely tuned sense of the bearing of etymology on the history, fate, and ideology of classes, involves a belief in astrology.[8] For Synge, once he had freed himself from the literalism of the authoritarian Word, the act of creation through language opened up the possibilities of transforming the paralyzing antinomies of his class and time into the grounds for human action. His sophisticated attention to the processes of the origination of all ideologies in our use of language was the product of a modern and modernist sensibility committed to exploring the relationships between word and deed, between text and world. His plays celebrate the claims of art to be part of the making of the world rather than a substitute for the business of living. Yeats's and Joyce's relationships to the philosophical, political, and aesthetic contexts from which they wrote and to which they contributed have long been acknowledged. O'Casey's Marxism, Shaw's socialism, and Beckett's existentialist sympathies have all been recognized as relevant to the assessment of their contribution to twentieth-century literature. Synge's awareness of and responses to the turbulent spirit of his age have largely been ignored. Above all, Yeats's authoritative and authoritarian statements have helped to keep the emphasis on the "primitive" at the expense of the "civilized" sources of his themes, his technique, and his style. In certain respects, not the least their use of dialect, his plays are peasant plays. They are peasant plays in the sense in which Goethe's *Faust* might be said to be a folk drama or the comic epics of Rabelais popular narratives. They draw strength, as does his use of language, from the historicity of the folk tradition and continue the mental and poetic activity of the people. Synge's mature vision, like that of James Joyce, seeks dynamic psychic wholeness rather than static Unity of Being. Casting a warm, laughter-loving but ironic eye on life, on death, like Joyce he refuses, while celebrating the creative power of language, to grant any ultimate privilege to the aesthetic word.

Notes

1. The question of the authenticity of Synge's use of dialect is comprehensively discussed by Kiberd in *Synge and the Irish Language*. pp. 196–215.

2. All references to *When the Moon Has Set* in this chapter are to the original two-act version of the play, published in *Long Room*, edited by Mary C. King. The version of *When the Moon Has Set* in the *Collected Works* is a conflation of several of the manuscript versions of the play.

3. Stephens's reading of Synge's plays has been published in part in David H. Greene

and Edward M. Stephens's *J. M. Synge, 1871–1909* and in *My Uncle John: Edward Stephens's Life of J. M. Synge,* edited by Andrew Carpenter.

    4. Synge recorded his reading of Marx in his 1896 diary. Substantial notes he made on and from *Das Kapital* are contained in the Trinity College Manuscript Collection, TCD MS 4379. His readings of Darwin, Herbert Spencer, William Morris, Nietzsche, Spinoza, Comte, and Hegel are also recorded there.

    5. For Synge's study of philology, see Kiberd, pp. 26–37.

    6. For further consideration of Synge's visits to Aran, see King, "Synge and 'The Aran Islands.' "

    7. These features of the text are more fully discussed in King, *The Drama of J. M. Synge,* Chapter 7.

    8. Comment in notes on Trench's *On the Study of Words,* Trinity College Manuscript Collection, TCD MS 4373.

References

Bell, Clive, ed. *The Philosophy of Nietzsche.* New York: Mentor, 1965.

Brecht, Bertolt. *Man Equals Man* and *The Elephant Calf. Collected Plays,* volume 2. Part 1. London: Methuen, 1977.

Burke, Kenneth. *A Grammar of Motives.* New York: Prentice-Hall, 1945.

Carpenter, Andrew, ed. *My Uncle John: Edward Stephens's Life of J. M. Synge.* Oxford: Oxford University Press, 1974.

Greene, David H., and Edward M. Stephens. *J. M. Synge, 1871–1909.* New York: Macmillan, 1959.

Innes, C. L. "Naked Truth, Fine Clothes, and Fine Phrases in Synge's *Playboy of the Western World.*" *Myth and Reality in Irish Literature.* Edited by Joseph Ronsley. Waterloo, Ont.: Wilfred Laurier University Press, 1977. pp. 63–75.

Jameson, Frederic. *Marxism and Form: Twentieth-Century Dialectical Theories of Literature.* Princeton, N.J.: Princeton University Press, 1971.

Kiberd, Declan. *Synge and the Irish Lanugage.* Totowa, N.J.: Rowman and Littlefield; London: Macmillan, 1979.

King, Mary C. *The Drama of J. M. Synge.* Irish Studies. Syracuse: Syracuse University Press, 1985.

————. "Synge and 'The Aran Islands': A Linguistic Apprenticeship." *Irish Studies* 1 (1980):61–72.

————, ed. Introduction, "J. M. Synge's *When the Moon Has Set.*" *Long Room* [Trinity College, Dublin] 24–25 (1982):9–40.

McCormack, W. J. *Ascendancy and Tradition in Anglo-Irish Literary History from 1789 to 1939.* Oxford: Clarendon, 1985.

————. *Sheridan LeFanu and Victorian Ireland.* Oxford: Clarendon, 1980.

Silverman, David, and Brian Torode. *The Material Word: Some Theories of Language and Its Limits.* London, Boston, and Henley: Routledge and Kegan Paul, 1980.

Stephens, Edward. *My Uncle John: Edward Stephens's Life of J. M. Synge.* Edited by Andrew Carpenter. London: Oxford University Press, 1974.

Tanner, Tony. *Adultery in the Novel: Contract and Transgression.* Baltimore and London: The Johns Hopkins University Press, 1979.

Torchiana, Donald. *Yeats and Georgian Ireland.* Evanston, Ill.: Northwestern University Press, 1966.

Volosinov, V. W. *Marxism and the Philosophy of Language*. Translated by Ladislaw Matejka and I. R. Titunik. New York and London: Seminar, 1973.

Worth, Katharine. *The Irish Drama of Europe from Yeats to Beckett*. Atlantic Highlands, N.J.: Humanities Press; London: Athlone, 1978.

Yeats, William Butler. *Essays and Introductions*. London and Basingstoke: Macmillan, 1961.

Zis, Avner. *Foundations of Marxist Aesthetics*. Translated by Katharine Judelson. Moscow: Progress, 1977.

Toward an Assessment

Although of little literary worth, the *Autobiography* (II, 3–15) is a good starting place for a discussion of Synge's contribution because it sketches several early influences on later work and because it provides some material for psychological sleuthing.

The piece describes Synge's early difficulties with and attraction to females. In one of his first memories, he is trapped in a woman's bathing box, complete with occupant, during a storm. Also, his mother taught him about hell and horrified him for a while, until the concept of the Holy Ghost (significantly, for the future writer, the religious symbol of verbal expression) temporarily rescued him. In addition, Synge seems to have been shattered when the cousin (Florence Ross) with whom he frankly discussed sex using folktales as illustrations jilted him, seemingly without a second thought or the least remorse.

The *Autobiography* also records Synge's discovery of Darwin: this caused thoughts of "Incest and parricide" (II, 11), both conspicuously present in *Playboy*, and led two or three years later to his abdicating formal Protestantism. The essay records Synge's gazing at street Arabs, foreshadowing a habit of observation that increased as Synge grew older. The pages show his isolation, a trait of the sympathetic characters in his plays; until he was twenty-three, he had never met a person who agreed with his ideas. The *Autobiography* details Synge's love of nature and his desire to describe the *thisness* (to borrow a term from Gerard Manley Hopkins and Duns Scotus) of natural phenomena, the latter resulting in one semimystical experience that terrified him.

But the *Autobiography* is not wholly reliable concerning Synge's views on religion. It may be true that he did replace formal theology with a "temperate Nationalism" (II, 13), but he certainly did not ever relinquish completely the kingdom of God.

Vita Vecchia, a series of fourteen poems linked by a prose narrative, is dated and proceeds more from early Decadent influences on Synge than from any type of death wish. Stemming from Cherrie Matheson's rejection of Synge's marriage proposal, the prose-poem delineates the narrator's hypersensitivity and his attachment to a melancholy, ethereal woman; this is the type of love that is felt by the boy-narrator of Joyce's "Araby," but Synge, writing in his midtwenties, lacked Joyce's irony. The work also features a Wordsworthian escape to the country to avoid the city's ills and several silly statements: "a man who has passed thirty is not able to experience" (II, 23). In addition, some of the poetry is very poor: "Cold, joyless I will live, though clean" (II, 19). The *Vita Vecchia* does contain two often-quoted sentences: "The world is an orchestra where every living thing plays one entry and then gives his place to another. We must be careful to play all the notes" (II, 24).

In the *Étude Morbide,* Cherrie Matheson is seen in two women who are really two aspects of one woman, the stolid, oaklike Chouska and the delicate, shadowy, nervous Celliniani, who goes insane during the narrator's poor concert performance, is dragged to a madhouse, and then dies. The tougher-minded Chouska refuses marriage with the narrator, fearing that such a union would spoil the unique qualities of their relationship. Both girls wear a green dress, as does Sister Eileen in *When the Moon Has Set.*

Two short prose pieces, also from Synge's midtwenties, are noteworthy: "On a Train to Paris" and "Under Ether." The former describes sleeping dancing girls whom Synge somewhat priggishly concluded, amidst a welter of other patronizing conjectures, are better off asleep than parading their scantily clad bodies before men. "Under Ether," on the other hand, effectively reproduces Synge's experiences while undergoing surgery for swollen glands late in 1897: his hallucinations, his fear of revealing secrets under the anesthetic, and his eventual sense of rapture. Plausible, too, is Synge's depiction of the reluctance of medical personnel to share his quips before the operation but their relieved smiles when the job is finished. De Quincey need not be invoked as possibly influencing the work; Synge's material came from his own ordeal.

Of much greater significance is *The Aran Islands,* which is important apart from its obvious usefulness as a prime source of material for interpreting the plays. The book documents Synge's increasing knowledge of Gaelic through four (actually, five) visits to Aran, and it records both his alienation from and his fascinated identification with the people of the three islands. Synge both understood and liked the people of Aran, two issues that are frequently debated by critics although they are not totally relevant to an evaluation of the book's literary merit. There was no communication gap between Synge and the islanders, just as there was hardly any such gap between generations during the 1960s in America: each side knew what the other thought and usually disagreed with the opposition. Also, *The Aran Islands* limns what was for Synge a purification rite, a rite of passage, and an experience that he had to undertake before he could write the six produced plays.

Synge defined the Aran Islands with impressive physical acuity. The islands are thirty miles from Galway "up the centre of the bay, (II, 47) although Synge could not have foreseen the creaky aircraft that today transports visitors to these limestone formations. Synge stated accurately that the islands are "not far" (II, 47) from "the corner of Connemara on the north" (II, 47): today the wise pilgrim boards a boat at Spiddal, a "corner" of Connemara, for a shorter but still tumultuous journey to Aranmor, the largest of the islands. Synge captured the physical danger of travel by curagh between the islands over an open sea, reporting that his craft was confronted with breech waves that threatened to turn over the canvas rowboat. Conversely, he also depicted the dreadful sameness that characterizes the three islands on consecutive rainy days and nights, when even the constantly changing patterns of the breaking ocean offer no relief.

But Synge's finest perceptions are reserved for the islanders themselves. He located the glint of malice that contrasts with their virtues, such as hospitality: the islanders have little compassion for a person or animal in pain, unless there is danger of death, often laughing at boys and girls with throbbing toothaches and, as a practice, tying donkeys' heads to the beasts' ankles so that they cannot run away. Veiled, leering sexual references are often voiced by young and old men alike, and the women and young girls frequently jeered at Synge because he was not married.

But the book does capture the essence of the islanders' existence. They feared loss of American support from their emigrated family members. They suffered deeply from the evictors, and Synge became one with the people when soldiers arrived to desecrate the islanders' hearths and when a distraught woman denounced her son, the informer. Arguments among the islanders lasted through the night, and the people still spoke in wonder about a knife fight that occurred sixty years before Synge's arrival. Also, the islanders treated Synge well even though he was not a part of them, and their warmth is seen in the sups of whiskey that they slipped into his room and in the gregariousness of Michael's semiliterate letters.

The worst parts of *The Aran Islands* are those that retell the fairy lore, with Synge admitting that sometimes the lengthy tales fade into gibberish; the reader is glad that Synge resisted the example of Hyde, Lady Gregory, and Yeats, who viewed their subjects too frequently as mainly a source of folklore collecting. Specific sections of *The Aran Islands*, many vivid and meaningful in several ways, are discussed throughout the *Companion*.

The rest of Synge's prose in Alan Price's edition (II) deserves more attention than all but a few critics have given it—again, for its intrinsic value and not merely for its utility as source material. "A Landlord's Garden in County Wicklow" (II, 230–33) encapsulates Synge's regret over the dying of the Anglo-Irish landlord class, a subject that he rarely broached but one that deeply involved

Yeats. Synge's description of a circus in Dingle in *In West Kerry* (II, 241–44) captures the carnival atmosphere of the scene, in which all things are leveled, the tawdry exhibition contrasting with the wild beauty of the Dingle peninsula itself: "One wonders in these places why anyone is left in Dublin, or London, or Paris, when it would be better, one would think, to live in a tent or hut with this magnificent sea and sky" (II, 246). Fascinating, too, is Synge's description of his stay on the Great Blasket Island, where his host ordered his sleepy daughter to serve the two men whiskey at 6 A.M.

Noteworthy, in addition, are Synge's description of the Puck Fair, held in Kerry in August; his meticulous account of kelp making (used for iodine), which shows the industry of the rural Irish of Connemara; and his recording of the ineffective means taken to alleviate conditions in the Congested Districts, for example, replacing thatch roofs with metal ones.

Synge's criticism, too, reveals occasional insights into French and medieval Irish works. But it is useful mainly in tracing influences on his own writing.

Synge's unproduced *When the Moon Has Set* differs considerably from his later plays in both its one-act form and in the two-act version that was rejected by Lady Gregory and Yeats in 1901. It is not a peasant play, taking place, rather, in the library of an old country estate. But although it deals with the problems of a Decadent aristocrat, Colm Sweeny, it does contain some elements found in subsequent works, for example, the themes of aging and loneliness and the thought that free individual expression is a remedy for suffocating conformity. Yet the play is poor, and its conclusion—even with final lines suggestive of the later *Deirdre* and with Sister Eileen in green, vernal dress—fails to convince.

Synge's spokesman for the uninhibited life, Colm, is a reed crushed by a mountainous assignment, more a Lockwood than a Lövburg. He is a weakling, needing to have his feet warmed and becoming lost and requiring the services of a madwoman, Mary Costello, to redirect him. His gesture of locking the door to debate the future of the timorous Eileen is the kind of act that one expects from a Torvald Helmer, not from Synge's liberated intellectual.

Sister Eileen is equally implausible, a Corinna without earthiness, and her decision to abandon her calling for Colm is unrealistic, more a matter of head than heart. The symbolism surrounding Eileen is also trite and obvious. Her green dress is "*cut low at the neck*" (III, 175), and she leaves her veil, the emblem of her sisterhood and, in Synge's view, the symbol of the obtuseness of organized religion, in the room of Colm's dead uncle when she decides to yield to Colm's wishes.

Some suggestion of the later power of Synge's writing is seen briefly in Mary Costello, although one could never guess that the Widow Quin or Mary Byrne could issue from such an origin.

Vastly different in quality and subject matter is *The Shadow of the Glen*, which shares a surprising number of common elements with *Riders, Well, Playboy*, and *Deirdre*. In *The Tinker's Wedding*, the parallels are evident, with Dan Burke transmogrified into the priest, the incarnation of the authoritative Word, and with external nature, somewhat less convincingly, being contrasted to the Establishment.

Riders ends in a caoine, and *Shadow* centers upon a wake, albeit a mere similacrum of one for a physically still alive but emotionally dead Dan Burke. Both works, too, portray nature as implacable, with the destructiveness of the sea paralleling the equally destructive rainy, misty, and consummately lonely glen: Nora's death of spirit is no less real than the losses of fishermen to the ocean. In each of the plays, also, an attempt to assuage the ravages caused by a desolate environment takes the form of cake baking, an attempt at communion that, in each work, falls far short of its mark.

The ending of *Shadow* resembles to some extent the conclusion of *Well*. Both couples start off to address an uncertain fate, faced with difficult terrain and roaring waters, as they wander like Adam and Eve from their prelapsarian home, perhaps dropping a few natural tears along the way. However, the dangers are more immediate in Synge's often crabbed *Well*. Also, in both plays Synge presents women who take to the road, and although neither Mary nor Nora leaves alone, their portrayals are a welcome balance to the male-oriented stereotypes embodied (later) in Charlie Chaplin's Little Tramp and in the American cowboy, who rides off into the sunset, eschewing possible romantic entanglements.

In comparing *Shadow* to *Playboy* too much can be made of similarities between Nora and Pegeen. Nora is older than Pegeen, both chronologically and experiencially, a Widow Quin more than a lissome lass, although she may be "much younger" (III, 31) than the Father Time figure Dan. A more profitable exercise might be to focus on Synge's similar portraits of Dan and old Mahon: both men are totemic, falsely (or truly) dead, half mad, isolated but quirkishly filial, and, as one would say today, drug dependent, keeping their illusions going through alcohol. Also, they both embody a great deal of Christocentric symbolism.

Two other similarities between the two plays deserve mention. Newspaper commentary of 1903 said little about the fact that Nora is indeed "alone" with the Tramp, perhaps feeling that Dan, though dead, might qualify as the type of chaperone that was later found to be missing when Pegeen and Christy spent the night together. Also, neither Patch nor Christy, two picaros, receives much attention as they lie in their respective ditches, a poignant commentary by Synge on Irish courage and hospitality.

In both *Shadow* and *Deirdre,* a wild night in external nature foreshadows a volatile relationship between the sexes. In addition, both plays show Synge's obsession with aging, with the characterization of the ruined Peggy Cavanagh anticipating Lavarcham. Most important is Nora's refusal to seek the safety, though squalid, of the Union, a decision that foreshadows Deirdre's preference of the grave to Conchubar's castle.

Shadow is important for many reasons: its political and social implications, its wild bursts of poetry, the consistent characterization of Nora, the elusive picture of the Tramp, whose early stage portrayals included a hint of the sinister at the start as he held a lighted match to his haggard face, and its splendid suggestiveness of the vastness and indifference of nature.

The effectiveness of *Riders* rests in part upon the play's deft and highly suggestive exploration of several opposites: Christianity and paganism, classic tragedy and modern capitalistic necessities, Maurya as the Universal Mother and Maurya as an emotionally exhausted old woman, and details anchored in the real that plausibly augur the symbolic. Above all, the inner working of *Riders* is true metadrama, with what is not said being as significant as what is uttered.

The play contains so many pre-Christian references that it might be convincingly argued that *Riders* is shaded in the direction of the pagan, with the work reflecting Synge's amazement at his discovery in Aran that superstition assumed an importance in the day-to-day practical lives of the islanders that was definitely equal to their Christian beliefs.

Thus the prayers that Maurya says in the dark night are probably not Christian but seem to be almost trancelike and incantatory, trailing off at their end into a kind of inspired babble. The Holy Water drawn from the spring well is associated with Samhain, more than with All Saints' Day or Halloween. Maurya's gesture of placing the cup mouth-down as part of her funeral ritual for Bartley has little to do with Christian hope for a resurrection, and the well-dressed Michael of Maurya's vision resembles more closely someone who has been seized by the fairies than a saved Christian who has been assumed into a heavenly afterlife. Nor do Maurya's daughters question their mother's vision, no matter how bizarre or "unchristian" it may be. Michael has probably been keened by the "black hags," the sea birds (III, 17), in his tenebrous journey towards Donegal.

The spokesman for Christianity in *Riders* is the "young" priest, who is as ineffective as Pastor Manders in Ibsen's *Ghosts,* although not quite the caricature that Ibsen's negligent villain is. The priest is portrayed as a harried administrator more than a traditional clergyman, hopping from island to island, scuttling up and down Ireland's western coast gathering details of the discovery of Michael's body by poteen peddlars, abdicating responsibility, and, probably because of his inexperience and stressed existence, enunciating bland and senseless adjurations to desperate islanders to trust in God.

The priest, who has learned young to connive, suggests that the girls wait until Maurya takes one of her walks to the beach (to search for the fulfillment of her "vision" of Michael's body being returned from the sea) before they examine the stocking and shirt. He tells them not to mention the bundle to Maurya if its contents do not identify Michael since such a sight might drive her to another emotional display.

Maurya and her daughters seem to place more confidence in their pagan rituals than in the assurances of the clergy. Nora's report of the priest's assertion that Maurya will not be left "destitute" since she says prayers through the night (ironically, prayers of probably maculate Christianity) is met by the curtly realistic query of Cathleen: "Is the sea bad by the white rocks Nora?" (III, 5)

Maurya's response to the priest's assurances is equally abrupt: "It's little the like of him knows of the sea" (III, 21). The priest's invocation of Almighty God at the start of the play parallels Maurya's use of the expression at its conclusion, and the playgoer or reader must question the willingness of the Divinity to intervene and must wonder whether the Western Maurya's definition of God resembles at all the concept of the Lord endemic to Dubliners in 1904.

The vastness of *Riders,* its Aeschylean, apocalyptic archetypes, examined carefully by many critics, is founded in concrete, vivid details, some of which, for example, realistically portray Bartley's mission and its end. Bartley is in part a victim of economic forces. The Galway Fair promises to be lucrative, but it will be over before Bartley can get to it if he waits for the arrival of the next ship in two weeks. Indeed, he has only a half hour to reach the pier, and his precipitousness perhaps occasions (on a literal level) his demise. Again, Maurya is thinking in commodities when she avers that Cathleen will be unable to secure a fair price for the willful pig with black feet if Bartley is absent. Also, the circumstance of Bartley's death, probably by drowning, is plausible since very few Aran Islanders in Synge's day could swim; Bartley would have been doomed even were he alive after he had been knocked over into the surf by the gray pony.

Synge's cogent details lend realism as well to the portrait of Maurya, who is too often seen as a combination of evil goddess and Pietà figure. Maurya, besides symbolizing suffering humanity, is also merely a very old woman who no longer has the strength to place order upon her household, who confuses past with present, who has given in to the strange fancy of recovering Michael's body on the beach (possibly at the same spot as his point of departure), and who must be goaded by Cathleen into even the most minimal actions, such as going to the spring well to intercept Bartley with the bread. Yet some critics have found in Maurya a sensitivity that sets her above the other islanders, regarding her as the first female outsider of Synge's six produced plays.

Synge's details, grounded as always in the actual, are used to develop his motif of interchangeability, in which individuality takes third place to the decaying and renewing process of nature and time. The same rope that was to lower Michael into a deep grave is used as a halter by Bartley and afterwards will assist in his funeral. Maurya uses Michael's walking stick, and Bartley appropriates his shirt. The new boards, originally meant to build Michael's coffin, will now serve the corpse of Bartley, and the coffinmakers, in the concluding antithesis of the Christian Communion ceremony, will devour what the resilient (and deceptive) Cathleen calls a "new cake" (III, 25) as they work.

Of much less importance is *The Tinker's Wedding,* which contradicts several points that Synge adumbrates in his Preface to the play. It is difficult to locate good-hearted humor in the work, easy to detect a hint of malice in its anticlericalism. Also, there are a good deal of gratuitous unpleasantness in all of the characters and several points of confusion in regard to their motivations. Marriage is treated cynically, almost bitterly, a tone that is only partially alleviated by

Synge's themes of external nature versus interior "authority" and of common parlance, supposedly purified by the wonders of the physical universe, versus the doctrinaire *fiat lux*.

It is indeed possible that in *Wedding* Synge's anticlericalism got out of hand, for the violent treatment of the priest at the conclusion is reinforced by a current of anticlericalism and antireligious sentiment that runs from beginning to end of the play. Mary slyly suggests that the sins of the country people, sexual by implication, must be especially hard to listen to in the spring. She considers the priest's Latin prayers (at least at the start of the play) a "great game" (IV, 21). Later she intends to "cool" her "gullet at the blessed well" (IV, 31). Sarah's threat to inform on the priest to the bishop is placed in the context of the Via Crucis: "if I walked to the city of Dublin with blood and blisters on my naked feet" (IV, 33). The three empty bottles parody the Trinity, the allusion being signaled by Sarah's "Glory to the saints of joy!" (IV, 41) Also, the disrespectful use of the priest at the end by the tinkers suggests a parody of several sacraments. A ring is placed on his finger by Sarah in a parody of matrimony; Michael feels his mouth (Holy Communion) and pats him on the back (Confirmation); an especially striking parody of penance is Mary's gesture of placing her mouth next to the sacking—evoking the image of the confessional screen—to whisper in his ear; and the priest himself is a living parody of Holy Orders. Throughout the play the tinkers show constant disrespect for the priest's office by touching and tapping him and by the very tone of their conversation, Michael at one point yoking Sarah and the priest as "the two of you" (IV, 17) when commanding them to be silent.

The priest has some redeeming traits, but mostly those that Synge saw as differentiating him from the stereotypical Irish clergyman of the day: his sharing a pint with and his human revelations to peasants, his willingness to negotiate and to compromise with underlings, and his partially justifiable wrath when the bargain is broken (and when the alcohol has worn off).

Yet, in general, the portrait of the priest would not have won Synge many new friends among Dublin Irish Catholics had it been produced at the Abbey before his death. Besides being rapacious and simoniac, the priest is the victim of several veiled sexual innuendos. They refer to both his supposed effeminate nature as a priest, in opposition to the "strong lads" (IV, 43) that Sarah has known, and to his voyeurism and fantasizing about sex with female parishoners. Also, he thinks nothing of gorging himself during Lent with laying pullets that the tinkers might continue to smuggle to him; he advises Michael and Sarah to steal the rest of the money that he demands to wed them; and he lives in constant terror of a complaint being made to his bishop, no matter how unjustified such a complaint would be or how tainted its source.

The other characters in *Wedding* are equally unpalatable and are not even drawn with the consistency of the clergyman's characterization. Mary's portrait is an apprentice attempt at creating a Wife of Bath—though it does excel the earlier effort at earthiness, Mary Costello—but although she expresses Synge's theme of life's transitory nature set against the Movements of May, Mary is no Dame Alice. Sarah has little to recommend her. She is a total flirt, although usually unwashed, and a violent woman who is willing to use any weapon available, a hammer, the back of her hand, or an empty bottle. The portrait of Sarah might deserve more artistic respect did not the impetus for the play stem from her menstrual period and were she not compared with Synge's later, brilliant creation, Pegeen Mike, who combines violence with poetry. Michael is flat: timorous and uxorious at the start and then a bully and a coward, in turn, at the conclusion.

In many ways *The Tinker's Wedding* is a poorly constructed work, containing major contradictions and confusion. It is unclear whether Michael and Sarah have had children or, if they have, what has happened to them. Prayer is treated disdainfully at the beginning of the play; yet the priest's ending malediction fills the tinkers with dread—although they perhaps fear more the return of the peelers than his curse. The complacency with which the tinkers contemplate the actual murder of the priest violates whatever comic tone and verisimilitude might have been established in the play.

In addition, *Wedding* seems to be as much concerned with the evils of marriage as with the joys of the nomadic life, and one cannot help but see in this negativism Synge's rejection by Cherrie Matheson and his other obsessions, such as his detestation of aging. Yet despite all of Mary's arguments against matrimony, her derision seems ultimately to be as implausible as Sarah's wish to be married, apparently a perennial desire, although there is some realism in Sarah's wanting to avoid being called a whore when she enters a village.

Wedding does have some artistic merit, such as its occasionally effective lyricism and its attempts at symbolism: the ring will not fit Sarah's plump finger. Yet in the final analysis, *Wedding* is the type of play one discusses in the classroom mainly because it blends so well with the themes and characters in the rest of Synge's canon.

The Well of the Saints, too, has much in common with other works of Synge, although this is not always emphasized by critics: a dreary patch of rural area relieved only temporarily by Cavalier or carpe diem poetry meant to seduce, a jostled holyman, and an oft-stated aversion to bodily decay, at one point in this work voiced by the otherwise imperceptive Molly Byrne, who also briefly utters her fear of the loss of love. In addition, in both *Well* and *Playboy,* the rebels are driven from communities partially because of villagers' fears: in *Playboy,* fear of peelers and magistrates; in *Well,* fear of God, as the heretofore tolerant Saint implies that the Almighty might indeed refuse to forgive Martin and Mary, the impenitent blind beggars, who may become Jonahs.

The play must be seen, however, as essentially a contrast between the Establishment and the two outsiders; yet the antithesis that Synge presented between the two worlds is as complex and paradoxical as Kafka's in "The Hunger Artist" and as Huxley's in *Brave New World,* a work that, Huxley later lamented, delineates two types of insanity but offers no third choice of reason. Synge's ruthless presentation of the deficiencies of Martin and Mary, on the one hand, and of the Saint, Molly, and Timmy the smith (Synge's Hephaestus), on the other hand; his refusal to glorify either side; and his insistence upon the cruel, Rabelaisian element in both partially account for the play's being viewed as a direct precursor of Beckett and Black Comedy.

The Establishment figures, with the exception of the almost unrelievedly vicious Molly, deftly balance for some time civility with nastiness, even though at the conclusion their blindness of mind prevails. The Saint possesses a naive goodness as he voices his belief that young girls like Molly Byrne are disingenuous and pure of mind, even though in his role of a symbolic St. Patrick he does warn against the wiles of women and smiths. He does try to treat Martin and Mary with charity, excusing Martin's sacrilegious behavior on the basis of his blindness; also, he offers the plausible suggestion that Martin use his newly regained vision to look upon the joys of the world. Undercutting the Saint's effectiveness, though, is his bland assumption that the hurried marriage of Timmy and Molly will be more fulfilling than the union of the two beggars who are now stumbling along to a probable death by drowning.

Timmy is the epitome of the conventional life, an embodiment, in modern parlance, of the work ethic. He is genuinely sorry that the villagers have deceived the Douls for years (*Doul* in Irish means "blind," so Martin and Mary are not "Mr. and Mrs. Doul"); he fears that harm will come because of their regained sight; and he does show considerable perceptiveness when he castigates Martin for his "talk of fine looks" (III, 111). Yet he cruelly strips Martin of his coat (note the hagiological analogy with St. Martin of Tours who *gave* half of his cloak to a beggar) on a cold day because of his complaints about being overworked, and he helps to drive the beggars out of the village after he has reduced their dreams to a mere desire to avoid labor through choosing "wilful blindness" (III, 143).

Nor are Martin and Mary quite so heroic as Yeats suggested, that is, "transformed" by a "dream" (III, 67). Yet they do grow during the play: they begin under the complete delusion of their mutual comeliness but end with their acceptance of the chaff of life: in a very important phrase, "a bit of comfort" (III, 131). It is this "bit of comfort," long white hair for Mary and a distinguished beard for Martin, that adds artistic control to the play's conclusion. The beggars do not choose total illusion over total truth. They have been almost completely divested of their false self-images throughout the play, and they undoubtedly feel that the little that is left to them does not bear overly close scrutiny or an unsparing light. The Douls's compromise, then, suggests that Synge himself did not abdicate his customary insistence upon truth in both life and art. Whether Martin and Mary are likeable or not is beside the point, as is the issue of whether they are factotum spokespersons for Synge himself.

Synge's greatest work, *Playboy*, must be read on many levels, all of which, intertwining and interfusing, both amplify the play's high suggestiveness and at the same time help to account for the hostility directed against it by Dubliners in 1907 and by Gaelic-Americans in 1911–1912.

One level of meaning is psychosexual. Some critics focus so somberly on the play's theme of father killing as essential to the growth and fulfillment of the young (rarely stopping to question whether this process is always necessary) that they miss entirely the hilarious phallic connotation of Christy's means of executing his Da, his raising of the long-handled loy against his archetypal sire. Also, the loy, in turn, carries the ironic suggestion of the French *loi* or law, as opposed to the scythe, the former representative of the new mandate of free-flowing sexuality, sublimated by Christy and Pegeen through their pantheistic love ecstasies; the latter, indicative of the death of emotion. In addition, the play has much to do with breasts. The Widow Casey suckled Christy during his first six weeks. The implication of Nelly, who has brought Christy a pullet, is obvious: "Feel the fat of that breast, Mister" (IV, 99).

The sexual theme is seen, too, in Synge's view of Western women, which was not intended to please nationalists. Pegeen reveals a fear of rape by the tinkers or the harvest men, an attack that Irishmen did not like to admit as a possibility in their pastoral Mayo. Jimmy speculates that Christy's crime may have been rape. The Limerick girls are scarcely models of feminine decorum, but they are fit companions for old Mahon as they help him through a three-week drinking spree. The sweethearts that Widow Quin promises to find for Christy "at each waning moon" (IV, 165) are surpassed only in his fantasy of eager womanly flesh, a "drift [a bovine term] of chosen females, standing in their shifts itself maybe, from this place to the Eastern World" (IV, 167), to whom he prefers Pegeen, with or without *shift* not being made clear.

Additionally, the play comments mordantly on social issues, with a good deal of time being spent excoriating Irish cowardice, fear of the peelers being most prominent. Pegeen recalls her fear of the law early in the play in her apprehension that should the man who is groaning in a ditch die, the pub frequenters will have to answer to the peelers or to the Justice of the Peace. Later, Pegeen's conventional trepidation, seen in her refusal to follow her dream, however flawed, of a lifetime romancing with the playboy, is revealed through her burning his leg in the third act. Certainly, her barbaric gesture comes partially from her frustration and public embarrassment, but it also stems from her fear of peelers. In turning hated informer, the once poetic, Deirdre-like playgirl of the Western world becomes again the bargirl smelling of poteen, who consigns herself to a lifetime of conformity. Finally, Shawn avers at one point that he would turn in Christy to the authorities except for his fear that Christy might escape from Kilmainham Gaol and do him harm.

The psychological, sexual, and social themes in *Playboy* are commingled with religious imagery that is so pervasive that it has not been entirely parsed by previous critics, most of whom admit that despite the injunctions of Lady Gregory and others, the *Playboy* does contain some gratuitous blasphemies and a good deal of anticlericalism. For example, the reason that Shawn needs a dispensation is not stated clearly (though it may have something to do with his second-cousin relationship with Pegeen) and represents for Synge merely one more emblem of addiction to authority. Jimmy Farrell's dog hangs for three hours while the peelers—read Roman soldiers—swear that it has life in it. Pegeen plays the part of Veronica as she wipes Christy's face with a shawl—veil—at noon, the same hour at which Kate Cassidy's bones are sunk, sans resurrection. Christy's envisioned lovemaking with Pegeen, it should be emphasized, is certainly opposed to Catholic practice. In Synge's day, Catholics abstained from all joys on Good Friday, the most solemn holy day of the year, but Christy sees Pegeen and himself "astray in Erris when Good Friday's by, drinking a sup from a well, and making mighty kisses with our wetted mouths" (IV, 149). Through his religious satire, Synge is both striking the bourgeoisie on the pate and, in his positive antedote to theological entrapment, building his tabernacle, his shrine, of nature for the two lovers. Synge's conscious intent in much of his religious symbolism is seen in his having Christy use his full name in Act One when introducing himself to the pub denizens: Christopher Mahon (IV, 77). St. Christopher, the Christ-bearer, is the patron saint of travelers.

Thus one can detect many reasons why the Irish (including Lady Gregory) hated *Playboy*. It proved enbarrassing to Dubliners who were not far removed socially from their cousins in the West, who had still not achieved the affluence of their Eastern relatives. It attacked the myth of the virginal west of Ireland, confounding, in American terms, John Wayne's deeds at the Alamo with Ozzy Osbourne's. It was seen, as Joyce's *A Portrait of the Artist* was to be seen, as encouraging emigration, It was said to play into the hands of the English, who for centuries had judged the Irish barbaric. The *Playboy,* besides refuting the myth of Irish fighting courage, questions the ideal of hospitality, venerated, for example, in Joyce's "The Dead": in Mayo madmen are stoned and driven into the sea, where they drown. The play was performed so as to inflame passionate hostility: Old Mahon's bandaged head was emphasized in the production, as were the physical filth and small stature of Willie Fay as the playboy (in Chicago, where crowds outside of a theater called for the hanging of the author of the "Cowboy" of the Western world, who had been dead for two and a half years, newspapers lamented the fact that the Abbey players appeared on the stage in bare feet). Above all, the opening-night crowd of January 26, 1907, had been led to believe by advance notices that what they were about to see performed was a faithful portrait of life in the rural West. Therefore, given the political, religious, and social conditions of Synge's Dublin, his masterpiece could not possibly have been granted a fair hearing in the Ireland of 1907.

Deirdre is perhaps the best-organized of Synge's plays, despite the fact that the work was unfinished when Synge died. The plot line is cogent, depending upon Synge's consistent characterization of Deirdre; her motivation, contrary to critical theory that has often tended to obfuscate the point of the play, is clearly delineated from beginning to end. The play is not about death, as Yeats implied in his Preface to the work, but rather is about the unalterable affront of the aging process, with its accompaning loss of joy and excitement. Deirdre's actions reflect, then, not so much Synge's obsession with his own death, his "death wish," some critics would maintain, but rather his dread of the effects of growing old, with the loosening of teeth, a recurrent dontological image in his plays. One might fault Deirdre's and Synge's viewpoint, especially if one subscribes to *Modern Maturity;* yet one must grant Deirdre and Synge their données. Also, although the type of obsession that *Deirdre* presents might be more plausible in the thirty-six-year-old Synge than in his twenty- to twenty-seven-year-old heroine, Deirdre's intimations of old age are clearly presented from the start, and her actions do stem from her loathing of bodily decay. Deirdre may not be likeable, but she unerringly carries out her goals, refusing to find wisdom in bodily decrepitude.

Deirdre's only lapse in her single-minded quest to preserve her youth and beauty and, in passing, to nurture the eternal flame of Naisi's love for her and joy in her day-to-day existence during the seven-year stay in Scotland occurs when she sends him off with a hard word to die beside his brothers. Yet this climactic scene (IV, 255, 257) is realistic given the fact that Deirdre is now confronted with actual death as opposed to the thanatopic fantasies that infused the hours before the lovers' decision to depart Alban. Her subsequent suicide, which makes up for her cruelty to Naisi and solidifies her promise to join him in death, however, is just as much an embodiment of her wish to be "rid of grey hairs and the loosening of the teeth" (IV, 267). The home to which the old king (the Dan Burke of the sagas) had offered to lead his prospective queen had resembled a pre-Viking burial place more than a palace: "with red gold upon the walls, and ceilings that are set with bronze" (IV, 259).

Other flaws in *Deirdre* include the introduction of the Elizabethan fool-figure Owen, although assuredly, Synge, had he lived, would have more stringently woven his character into the fabric of the play. Another problem is found in the dialect, especially as it is attributed to Conchubor; he is the only consecrated noble in the play; yet often his language smacks too much of a peasant Kiltartan, with Synge trying to minimize the problem by having him at one point speak "*very stiffly*" (IV, 189) while bantering with Lavarcham. Additionally, the term *blue stew* (IV, 185) seems less than proper to describe the rage of the king of Ulster. Also, one may well wonder what the two lovers did for seven years in the woods. We may assume that they practiced effective birth control, and Deirdre tells us explicitly that she kept their tent meticulously clean, but there is little else of a concrete nature to go on.

Despite its flaws, *Deirdre* deserves more attention than has been paid to it by critics and by producers of plays, and part of its power stems from its occasionally magnificent poetry. Some of this high poetic utterance includes the effective elevation of the characters of Deirdre and Naisi through their identification with the vicissitudes of nature, a process that resembles Shakespeare's paralleling of the fates of Antony and Cleopatra with the rise and fall of the Nile; Deirdre's moving evocation of a nostalgic Ireland seen through the mists of exile in Alban; the play's portrayal of the minutiae and, through this detail, the expansiveness of external nature: "the smell of June in the tops of the grasses" (IV, 231); Deirdre's justly reknowned farewell speeches to the Woods of Cuan and to Alban; and Synge's startling description of the destruction of Emain Macha.

Thus as many critics have said should be done, although few have done so, *Deirdre of the Sorrows* must be examined as a rewarding work in its own right, as having faults and virtues, and with the autobiographical elements used sparsely to define the play's worth.

Most of Synge's poetry is poor, with whatever importance it might possess coming mainly from the fact that it was written by a significant playwright. Although Synge's prose translations from the poetry of Villon and Petrarch included in *Poems* (I) do at times capture the spirit of their originals, the rest of the offerings in Skelton's edition of the first volume of Synge's works contains only a handful of poems that bear scrutiny. "Queens" rests upon a counter-pointing of opposites, which is typical of Synge in his poetry. Here the slightly naughty but still regal queens, whose "finger once did stir men" (I, 34), have been eaten by "fleas and vermin" (I, 34). While the queens are "rotten," Synge and his beloved have the "sun on rock and garden" (I, 34), external nature, again, typically, being contrasted with the artificiality of hierarchy. "The Passing of the Shee," Synge's antedote to the Celtic twilight as it is exemplified by George Russell (AE), is important for its obvious historicity, as Synge would rather poach and drink at the fair than study AE's portrait of heroic, prehistoric figures whom previous poets "played with hand in hand" (I, 38). Yet although the sexual innuendo may be humorous considering Russell's staunch demeanor, the reader wonders what meaning attaches to the line "Ye plumed yet skinny Shee" (I, 38). Additionally, "The Curse" is a partially effective adaptation of ancient Celtic nastiness to contemporary events.

"Danny," Synge's most highly regarded poem, is possessed of a crude force-fulness and does expose the seamier side of the Mayo peasantry, exemplified here by twenty-nine men who mutilate the sexually astute but now defenseless Danny, stomp him to death, and then take his sparse possessions—apparently the last being the worst violation of all. Yet the allusions to dying widows seem gratuitous, as does the accusation that Danny attacked the parish priest. On the other hand, "The Mergency Man" has a tight narrative structure and some vivid details. He drowns on a "night of rains you'd swamp a star in" (I, 58) and is "found in the ebb tide stuck in a net" (I, 58). Finally, in "A Question," Synge's "question" to his beloved Molly, whether she would go to his funeral since only chattering fools would be there, avoids self-pity and bathos by rooting itself in the brutal, "you'd rave and rend them with your teeth" (I, 64).

A postscript: In any chapter dealing with a beginning assessment of Synge, mention should be made of the numerous sources available for analyzing the criticism, both in newspapers and in journals and books, spent on Synge's works.

There are three full-length secondary bibliographies devoted to Synge: by Paul M. Levitt (1974), by E. H. Mikhail (1975), and by Edward A. Kopper, Jr. (1979). Levitt's book, which is in the main accurate, is complete through 1969, with some items of 1970 and 1971 added. E. H. Mikhail's work is exhaustive, listing about twenty-five hundred items, and is especially helpful with out-of-the-way items, such as reviews of productions of Synge's plays found in popular magazines, and unpublished works. Kopper's book is the only one of the three to be annotated. It summarizes books and articles on Synge from 1900 to 1976, with a few items from 1977. The work includes foreign-language items and several items not found through the usual methods of searching indices: many items were located by sifting through books by and about central figures such as Steinbeck, Wolfe, Faulkner, and Dreiser, and these findings offer a few workpoints for future investigations of Synge's influence on other major writers.

Indispensable are two critical reviews of Synge criticism by Weldon Thornton. His first essay, published in *Anglo-Irish Literature: A Review of Research* (1976), analyzes critical commentary on Synge from the beginnings; his second essay, which appears in *Recent Research on Anglo-Irish Writers* (1983), evaluates research on Synge from 1976. A third analysis of Synge criticism also is forth-coming from the Modern Language Association of America. This essay by Edward A. Kopper, Jr., which will appear in *Anglo-Irish Literature: A Guide to Research,* analyzes writings about Synge from 1900, as did Thornton's 1976 chapter; it has the advantage of citing books and articles through 1987 and of viewing the whole of Synge criticism from a new perspective.

Although there is no book-length primary bibliography of Synge's writings, Volumes III and IV of the *Collected Works,* edited by Ann Saddlemyer, provide a wealth of data concerning matters such as variant readings and detailed de-scriptions of previous editions. Her two volumes are certainly adequate for even the most dedicated Syngean. Other important sources of information about pri-mary Synge materials are *The Synge Manuscripts in the Library of Trinity Col-lege, Dublin,* compiled by Nicholas Grene and published by Trinity College; *John Millington Synge, 1871–1909: A Catalogue of an Exhibition Held at Trinity College Library, Dublin, on the Occasion of the Fiftieth Anniversary of His Death,* compiled by Ian MacPhail and M. Pollard; and Ann Saddlemyer's '' 'Infinite Riches in a Little Room'—the Manuscripts of John Millington Synge.'' In contrast to Volumes III and IV, the first two volumes of the *Collected Works: Poems,* edited by Robin Skelton; and *Prose,* edited by Alan Price, are simply not reliable, with a good deal of material being omitted, in Price's case, apparently for lack of space.

Synge's works have been translated into several languages and performed in various parts of the world, usually with disastrous results. Several essays are devoted to analyses of these adaptations: the Aran World (Ghassan Maleh); Breton (Per Denez); Chinese (Irene Eber); Czech (O. F. Babler); France (Gérard Leblanc); Germany (Paul Foley Casey, Johannes Kleinstück); Italy (Carlo Bi-gazzi, Esther Menascè); and Japan (Shotaro Oshima).

Unfortunately, distortions abound. The Arabs see *Riders* in terms of their own massive calamities. The Chinese view Synge's peasants in the light of their farmer-rebels of the 1920s and 1930s , although they demur at Synge's political passivity. The French have virtually ignored Synge, translating "Playboy" as "Buffoon." German productions have given Synge's tinker couple children and made Sarah Casey pregnant again; East Germans see Christy's raising of the loy against his father as a means of striking out against the capitalist Establishment, represented, somewhat illogically, by old Mahon, with the son at last willing to divest himself of the "playboy" (American connotation) image.

Several commentators have dealt specifically with Synge's dialect and with the technicalities of his prose cadences. A representative list of these critics includes P. L. Henry, Seamus Deane, Lorna Reynolds, Brigitte Tielert, Uwe Stork, Klaus Naseband, and Roger McHugh and Maurice Harmon.

Helpful in "translating" the dialogue of Synge's characters are the two-page glossary in Volume IV of the *Collected Works;* T. R. Henn's lengthy glossary in his edition of *The Plays and Poems of J. M. Synge;* and "A Synge Glossary," by Alan Bliss, which explicates 282 head-words.

Finally, an important source of data about Synge's attitudes and his works is the *Collected Letters,* edited in two volumes by Ann Saddlemyer (1983, 1984), which supersedes all previous editions of Synge's correspondence. For example, these letters offer insight into Synge's social and political views. Synge's letter to Maud Gonne of April 6, 1897, through which he resigns from the Association Irlandaise, documents his reluctance to "get mixed up with a revolutionary and semi-military movement" (Saddlemyer, ed., *Collected Letters* I: 47); yet it also contains the prophetic statement of the twenty-five year old Synge: "I wish to work in my own way for the cause of Ireland . . . " (Saddlemyer, ed., *Collected Letters* I: 47). Synge's letter to Stephen MacKenna of July 13, 1905, written shortly after his return from his trip with Jack Yeats through the Congested Districts, excoriates the greedy, grubbing side of some Western Irelanders who prey upon their countrymen. These include the "groggy-patriot-publican-general shop-man who is married to the priest's half sister and is second cousin once-removed of the dispensary doctor . . . " (Saddlemyer, ed., *Collected Letters* I: 116). Synge's insistence upon a mordantly realistic assessment of Irish society, stemming in part from his aversion to the Catholic middle class (but his respect for the peasantry), extends to his reluctance to whitewash Irish mythology. He felt that his colleagues in the theater movement were doing this in their dramatic treatments of Cuchulain, Deirdre, and other saga figures. As Synge wrote to MacKenna on January 28, 1904, he did "not believe in the possibility of 'a purely fantastic, unmodern, ideal, spring-dayish, Cuchulainoid National Theatre', because no drama—that is to hold its public—can grow out of anything but the fundamental realities of life which are neither modern or un-modern . . . " (Saddlemyer, ed., *Collected Letters* I: 74).

Also, Synge's often complicated relationships with other principals of the Irish Revival may be partially elucidated through his letters. After his meetings with

Joyce in Paris early in 1903, Synge confided to Lady Gregory his opinion that the younger Joyce, though possessed of a very "keen" intellect (Saddlemyer, ed., *Collected Letters* I: 68), would probably not amount to more than a good essayist, and even this, only if he could straighten himself out and manage to hold himself together. Additionally, Synge resisted George Moore's pleas to have him write a happy ending for *Playboy,* though Synge appreciated Moore's public praise of *The Well of the Saints.* Also, the correspondence reveals Synge's frequent differences with Lady Gregory and, especially, with Yeats over theatre business. Synge charged that his plays were not being performed as often as theirs, and he suspected that his codirectors' reticence about bringing *Playboy* across the ocean for a contemplated American tour came from their fear of possible Gaelic-American protests.

The letters are important, of course, for the significant insight they provide into Synge's methods of composition: his perpetual insistence upon authenticity and the proper organization of his works and wording of the characters' speeches and his never-ending wrestling with his compositions. And Synge's comments about the reception of *Playboy* show a toughness in his nature that helps palliate Yeats's depiction of him as an Adonais-Shelley destroyed by middle class hostility. In his correspondence, Synge writes of his opposition to Yeats's holding his famous debate over *Playboy* (February 4, 1907) since the theatre would be filled with "low ruffians" (Saddlemyer, ed., *Collected Letters* I: 289) who wouldn't give Yeats a hearing. Also, Synge was assiduous in having his friends collect several copies of press clippings describing the *Playboy* row, during what he called the Playboy Week. And Synge apparently kept meticulous count of the number of peelers needed to quell each disturbance.

Lastly, much of the *Collected Letters* is taken up with Synge's tumultuous relationship with Molly. Synge constantly complains to her of his poor health and of her neglecting him. He invariably appears as the wary jealous older man, though he jauntily signs himself Your Old Tramp (not Dan Burke) in his letters to her. He lectures Molly on the dangers of associating with medical students and of the evils of cigarettes. He is constantly apprehensive that their relationship will be found out before he is ready to reveal the facts. He patronizingly insists that Molly read Dickens and Shakespeare. Yet often the letters suggest a sense of deeply shared harmony between the two. Not entirely facetious is his suggestion that she write the male dialogue for a scenario that he would devise, while he writes the women's lines. And frequently the extent of Synge's passion is revealed through passages in the letters that are as fervent in their pictured assimilation of Molly with external nature as parts of *Deirdre* which border on the pantheistic.

References

Babler, O. F. "John Millington Synge in Czech Translations." *Notes and Queries* 191 (1946):123–24.

Bigazzi, Carlo. " 'Riders to the Sea': Problemi di traduzione." *English Miscellany* 26–27 (1977–1978):361–72.

Bliss, Alan. "A Synge Glossary." *A Centenary Tribute to John Millington Synge, 1871–1909: Sunshine and the Moon's Delight*. Edited by S. B. Bushrui. New York: Barnes & Noble, 1972. pp. 297–316.

Casey, Paul Foley. "German Productions of the Drama of J. M. Synge." *Maske und Kothurn* 27, nos. 2–3 (1981):163–75.

Deane, Seamus. "Synge's Poetic Use of Language." *Mosaic* 5, no. 1 (1971):27–37.

Denez, Per. "On the Breton Translations of Synge's Plays." *Cahiers du Centre d'Etudes Irlandaises* 2 (1977):87–88.

Eber, Irene. "Chinese Views of Anglo-Irish Writers and Their Works in the 1920's." *Modern Chinese Literature and Its Social Context*. Edited by Göran Malmqvist. Nobel Symposium 32. Stockholm, 1977. pp. 46–75.

Henn, T. R., ed. *The Plays and Poems of J. M. Synge*. London: Methuen, 1963.

Henry, P. L. "The Playboy of the Western World." *Philologica Pragensia* ns. 8 (1965):189–204.

Kleinstück, Johannes. "Synge in Germany." *A Centenary Tribute to John Millington Synge, 1871–1909: Sunshine and the Moon's Delight*. Edited by S. B. Bushrui. New York: Barnes & Noble, 1972. pp. 271–77.

Kopper, Edward A., Jr. *John Millington Synge: A Reference Guide*. A Reference Publication in Literature. Boston: G. K. Hall, 1979.

Leblanc, Gérard. "Synge in France." *A Centenary Tribute to John Millington Synge, 1871–1909: Sunshine and the Moon's Delight*. Edited by S. B. Bushrui. New York: Barnes & Noble, 1972. pp. 265–70.

Levitt, Paul M. *J. M. Synge: A Bibliography of Published Criticism*. New York: Barnes & Noble, 1974.

MacPhail, Ian, and M. Pollard, comps. *John Millington Synge, 1871–1909: A Catalogue of an Exhibition Held at Trinity College Library, Dublin, on the Occasion of the Fiftieth Anniversary of His Death*. Dublin: Dolmen Press for the Friends of the Library of Trinity College, Dublin, 1959.

Maleh, Ghassan. "Synge in the Arab World." *A Centenary Tribute to John Millington Synge, 1871–1909: Sunshine and the Moon's Delight*. Edited by S. B. Bushrui. New York: Barnes & Noble, 1972. pp. 245–52.

McHugh, Roger, and Maurice Harmon. *A Short History of Anglo-Irish Literature: From Its Origins to the Present Day*. Totowa, N.J.: Barnes & Noble, 1982.

Menascè, Esther. "Une traduzione di James Joyce: La cavalcata al mare, di J. M. Synge." *Acme* 33, nos. 1–2 (1980):23–44.

Mikhail, E., H. *J. M. Synge: A Bibliography of Criticism*. Totowa, N.J.: Rowman and Littlefield, 1975.

Naseband, Klaus. *John Millington Synges dramatische Poesie*. Frankfurt am Main: Peter Lang, 1981.

Oshima, Shotaro. "Synge in Japan." *A Centenary Tribute to John Millington Synge, 1971–1909: Sunshine and the Moon's Delight*. Edited by S. B. Bushrui. New York: Barnes & Noble, 1972. pp. 253–63.

Reynolds, Lorna. "The Rhythms of Synge's Dramatic Prose." *Yeats Studies* 2 (1972):52–65.

Saddlemyer, Ann, ed. *The Collected Letters of John Millington Synge*. 2 vols. Oxford: Clarendon, 1983–84.

————. " 'Infinite Riches in a Little Room'—the Manuscripts of John Millington
     Synge." *Long Room* 1, no. 3 (1971):23–31.
Stork, Uwe. *Der sprachliche Rhythmus in den Bühnenstücken John Millington Synges.*
     Salzburg Studies in English Literature. Salzburg: Institut für Anglistik und Amer-
     ikanistik, Universität Salzburg, 1980.
Weldon, Thornton. "J. M. Synge." *Anglo-Irish Literature: A Review of Research.* Edited
     by Richard J. Finneran. New York: The Modern Language Association of Amer-
     ica, 1976. pp. 315–65.
————. "J. M. Synge." *Recent Research on Anglo-Irish Writers: A Supplement to Anglo-
     Irish Literature: A Review of Research.* Edited by Richard J. Finneran. The Modern
     Language Association of America Reviews of Research. New York: The Modern
     Language Association of America, 1983. pp. 154–80.
Tielert, Brigitte. "Rezeption von Synge und Situationsmodell." *Semiotische Versuche
     zu Literarischen Strukturen.* Edited by Walter A. Koch. Studien zu Philologie
     und Semiotik 2. Hildesheim and New York: Olms, 1979. pp. 1–142.
Trinity College, Dublin [Nicholas Grene]. *The Synge Manuscripts in the Library of Trinity
     College, Dublin.* Dublin: Dolmen and Trinity College Library, 1971.

Select Bibliography

Akin, Warren, IV. " 'I Just Riz the Loy': The Oedipal Dimensions of *The Playboy of the Western World.*" *South Atlantic Bulletin* 45, no. 4 (1980):55–65.

Armstrong, W. A. "Synge's Communities and Dissenters." *Drama and Society*. Edited by James Redmond. Cambridge: Cambridge University Press, 1979. pp. 117–28.

Ayling, Ronald. "Synge's First Love: Some South African Aspects." *English Studies in Africa* 6 (1963):173–85

Babler, O. F. "John Millington Synge in Czech Translations." *Notes and Queries* 191 (1946):123–24.

Bariou, Michel. "Margaret Flaherty: The Awakening and Failure of Love in *The Playboy of the Western World.*" *Cahiers du Centre d'Etudes Irlandaises* 2 (1977):43–54.

Barnett, Pat. "The Nature of Synge's Dialogue." *English Literature in Transition (1880–1920)* 10, no. 3 (1967):119–29.

Bauman, Richard. "John Millington Synge and Irish Folklore." *Southern Folklore Quarterly* 27, no. 4 (1963):267–79.

Beckerman, Bernard. *Dynamics of Drama: Theory and Method of Analysis*. New York: Knopf, 1970.

Beckson, Karl. "Arthur Symons on John Millington Synge: A Previously Unpublished Memoir." *Éire-Ireland* 21, no. 4 (1986):77–80.

Benson, Eugene. "Demythologising Cathleen ni Houlihan: Synge and His Sources." *Irish Writers and the Theatre*. Edited by Masaru Sekine. Irish Literary Studies 23; IASAIL-Japan Series 2. Gerrards Cross, Bucks: Colin Smythe, 1986; Totowa, N.J.: Barnes & Noble, 1987. pp. 1–16.

———. *J. M. Synge*. Grove Press Modern Dramatists. 1982. Reprint. New York: Grove Press, 1983.

Berlin, Normand. *The Secret Cause: A Discussion of Tragedy*. Amherst: University of Massachusetts Press, 1981.

Bessai, Diane E. "Little Hound in Mayo: Synge's Playboy and the Comic Tradition in Irish Literature." *Dalhousie Review* 48, no. 3 (1968):372–83.

Bickley, Francis. *J. M. Synge and the Irish Dramatic Movement*. London: Constable; Boston and New York: Houghton Mifflin, 1912.

Bigazzi, Carlo. " 'Riders to the Sea': Problemi di traduzione." *English Miscellany* 26–27 (1977–1978):361–72.

Bigley, Bruce M. *"The Playboy of the Western World* as Antidrama." *Modern Drama* 20, no. 2 (1977):157–67.

Botheroyd, Paul F. " 'Athenry That Was, Galway That Is, Aran That Will Be': Recent Works on Aran." *Etudes Irlandaises* 5 (1980):105–12.

———. "J. M. Synge's *The Aran Islands, Riders to the Sea,* and Territoriality: The Beginnings of a Cultural Analysis." *Studies on Synge*. Edited by Dapo Adelugba. Ibadan, Nig.: Ibadan University Press, 1977. pp. 75–86.

———. "The Years of the Travellers: Tinkers, Tramps, and Travellers in Early Twentieth-Century Irish Drama and Society." *Studies in Anglo-Irish Literature*. Edited by Heinz Kosok. Wuppertaler Schriftenreihe Literatur. Bonn: Bouvier, 1982. pp. 167–75.

Boulaire, François. "Quelques ancêtres de John Millington Synge." *Cahiers du Centre d'Etudes Irlandaises* 2 (1977):19–23.

Bourgeois, Maurice. *John Millington Synge and the Irish Theatre*. London: Constable, 1913.

Bushrui, S. B., ed. *A Centenary Tribute to John Millington Synge, 1871–1909: Sunshine and the Moon's Delight*. New York: Barnes & Noble, 1972.

Carpenter, Andrew. "Synge and Women." *Etudes Irlandaises* 4 (1979):89–106.

———. "Two Passages from Synge's Notebooks." *Hermathena* 120 (1976):35–38.

Carpenter, Charles A. *Modern Drama Scholarship and Criticism, 1966–1980: An International Bibliography*. Toronto: University of Toronto Press, 1986.

Casey, Daniel J. "An Aran Requiem: Setting in 'Riders to the Sea.' " *Antigonish Review* 9 (1972):89–100.

Casey, Paul Foley. "German Productions of the Drama of J. M. Synge." *Maske und Kothurn* 27, nos. 2–3 (1981):163–75.

Clark, David R., ed. *John Millington Synge: Riders to the Sea*. The Merrill Literary Casebook Series. Columbus: Charles E. Merrill, 1970.

Clements, William M. "Pious and Impious Peasants: Popular Religion in the Comedies of Lady Gregory and John M. Synge." *Colby Library Quarterly* 14 (1978):42–48.

Collins, Michael J. "Christy's Binary Vision in *The Playboy of the Western World*." *Canadian Journal of Irish Studies* 7, no. 2 (1981):76–82.

Collins, R. L. "The Distinction of *Riders to the Sea*." *The University of Kansas City Review* 13 (1947):278–84.

Colum, Mary. *Life and the Dream*. Garden City, N.Y.: Doubleday, 1947.

Combs, William W. "J. M. Synge's *Riders to the Sea:* A Reading and Some Generalizations." *Papers of the Michigan Academy of Science, Arts, and Letters* 50 (1965):599–607.

Conacher, D. J. "Some Profane Variations on a Tragic Theme." *Phoenix: The Journal of the Classical Association of Canada* 23 (1969):26–38.

Corkery, Daniel. *Synge and Anglo-Irish Literature: A Study*. Dublin and Cork: Cork University Press; London: Longmans, Green, 1931. Reprint. New York: Russell & Russell, 1965.

Coxhead, Elizabeth. *J. M. Synge and Lady Gregory*. Writers and Their Work 149. London: Longmans, Green, 1962.

Cronin, Anthony. *Heritage Now: Irish Literature in the English Language*. Dingle, Ire.: Brandon, 1982.

Cusack, Cyril. "A Player's Reflections on *Playboy*." *Modern Drama* 4, no. 3 (1961):300–305.

Dalsimer, Adele M. "Players in the Western World: The Abbey Theatre's American Tours." *Éire-Ireland* 16, no. 4 (1981):75–93.

Daniels, William L. "AE and Synge in the Congested Districts." *Éire-Ireland* 2, no. 4 (1976):14–26.

———. " 'A Local Human Intensity': The Unities of Synge's *In Wicklow*." *Éire-Ireland* 15, no. 2 (1980):91–104.

———. "Synge's *In West Kerry*: 'Brilliant Liveliness.' " *Éire-Ireland* 17, no. 1 (1982):74–90.

Dasenbrock, Reed Way. "Synge's Irish Renaissance Petrarchism." *Modern Philology* 83, no. 1 (1985):33–44.

Davie, Donald A. "The Poetic Diction of John M. Synge." *The Dublin Magazine* ns. 27, no. 1 (1952):32–38.

Deane, Seamus. *Celtic Revivals: Essays in Modern Irish Literature, 1880–1980* London and Boston: Faber and Faber, 1985. Reprint. Winston-Salem: Wake Forest University Press, 1987.

Denez, Per. "On the Breton Translations of Synge's Plays." *Cahiers du Centre d'Etudes Irlandaises* 2 (1977):87–88.

Ditsky, John. *The Onstage Christ: Studies in the Persistence of a Theme*. Barnes & Noble Critical Studies. Totowa, N.J.: Barnes & Noble, 1980.

Donoghue, Denis. "Flowers and Timber: A Note on Synge's Poems." *Threshold* 1, no. 3 (1957):40–47.

———. "Synge: *Riders to the Sea*: A Study." *University Review* 1 (1955):52–58.

———. " 'Too Immoral for Dublin': Synge's 'The Tinker's Wedding.' " *Irish Writing* 30 (1955):56–62.

———. *We Irish: Essays on Irish Literature and Society*. New York: Knopf, 1986.

Durbach, Errol. "Synge's Tragic Vision of the Old Mother and the Sea." *Modern Drama* 14, no. 4 (1972):363–72.

Eber, Irene. "Chinese Views of Anglo-Irish Writers and Their Works in the 1920's. *Modern Chinese Literature and Its Social Context*. Edited by Göran Malmqvist. Nobel Symposium 32. Stockholm, 1977. pp. 46–75.

Eckley, Grace. "Truth at the Bottom of a Well: Synge's *The Well of the Saints*." *Modern Drama* 16, no. 2 (1973):193–98.

Ellis-Fermor, Una. *The Irish Dramatic Movement*. London: Methuen, 1939.

Ellmann, Richard. *James Joyce*. New York and London: Oxford University Press, 1959.

Ervine, St. John. "Some Impressions of My Elders: Bernard Shaw and J. M. Synge." *The North American Review* 211, no. 5 (1920):669–81.

Estill, Adelaide Duncan. *The Sources of Synge*. A Dissertation in English. Philadelphia: University of Pennsylvania Press, 1939.

Everson, Ida G. "Young Lennox Robinson and the Abbey Theatre's First American Tour
    (1911–1912)." *Modern Drama* 9, no. 1 (1966):74–89.
Fackler, Herbert V. "J. M. Synge's *Deirdre of the Sorrows:* Beauty Only." *Modern
    Drama* 11, no. 4 (1969):404—409. Revised and reprinted as "J. M. Synge's
    Deirdre of the Sorrows (1909)." *That Tragic Queen: The Deirdre Legend in
    Anglo-Irish Literature.* Salzburg: University of Salzburg, 1978.
Fallis, Richard. *The Irish Renaissance.* Syracuse: Syracuse University Press, 1977.
Farris, Jon R. "The Nature of the Tragic Experience in *Deirdre of the Sorrows.*" *Modern
    Drama* 14, no. 2 (1971):243–51.
Faulk, C. S. "John Millington Synge and the Rebirth of Comedy." *Southern Humanities
    Review* 8, no. 4 (1974):431–48.
Fay, Gerard. *The Abbey Theatre: Cradle of Genius.* New York: Macmillan, 1958.
Fay, William G., and Catherine Carswell. *The Fays of the Abbey Theatre: An Autobio-
    graphical Record.* New York: Harcourt, Brace; London: Rich and Cowan, 1935.
Fehlmann, Guy. "J. M. Synge, dramaturge irlandais *ou* dramaturge de l'Irlande?" *Gae-
    liana* 3 (1981):71–85.
Feito, Francisco E. "Synge y Lorca: De *Riders to the Sea* a *Bodas de sangre.*" *Garcia
    Lorca Review* 9, no. 2 (1981):144–52.
Flood, Jeanne. "The Pre-Aran Writing of J. M. Synge." *Éire-Ireland* 5, no. 3 (1970):63–
    80.
————. "Synge's Ecstatic Dance and the Myth of the Undying Father." *American Imago*
    33, no. 2 (1976):174–96.
————. "Thematic Variation in Synge's Early Peasant Plays." *Éire-Ireland* 7, no. 3
    (1972):72–81.
Foster, John Wilson. "*The Aran Islands* Revisited." *University of Toronto Quarterly*
    51, no. 3 (1982):248–63.
Foster, Leslie, D. "Heroic Strivings in *The Playboy of the Western World.*" *Éire-Ireland*
    8, no. 1 (1973):85–94.
————. "Maurya's Tragic Error and Limited Transcendence in *Riders to the Sea.*" *Éire-
    Ireland* 16, no. 3 (1981):98–117.
Frechet, René. "Le Thème de la parole dans le théâtre de J. M. Synge." *Etudes Anglaises*
    21, no. 3 (1968):243–56. Reprinted as "The Theme of Speech in the Plays of
    J. M. Synge." *Studies on Synge.* Edited by Dapo Adelugba. Ibadan, Nig.: Ibadan
    University Press, 1977. pp. 34–51.
Free, William J. "Structural Dynamics in *Riders to the Sea.*" *Colby Library Quarterly*
    11, no. 3 (1975):162–68.
French, Frances-Jane. *The Abbey Theatre Series of Plays: A Bibliography.* Dublin: Dol-
    men; Chester Springs, Pa.: Dufour Editions, 1970.
Gallagher, Brian. "About Us, for Us, near Us: The Irish and Harlem Renaissances."
    Éire-Ireland 16, no. 4 (1981):14–26.
Garratt, Robert F. *Modern Irish Poetry: Tradition and Continuity from Yeats to Heaney.*
    Berkeley, Los Angeles, and London: University of California Press, 1986.
Gaskell, Ronald. "The Realism of J. M. Synge." *Critical Quarterly* 5, no. 3 (1963):242–
    48.
Gerstenberer, Donna. "Bonnie and Clyde and Christy Mahon: Playboys All." *Modern
    Drama* 14, no. 2 (1971):227–31.
————. *John Millington Synge.* Twayne's English Authors Series 12. New York:
    Twayne, 1964.

Glandon, Virginia E. *Arthur Griffith and the Advanced-Nationalist Press Ireland, 1900–1922*. American University Studies Series 9. New York; Berne; Frankfurt am Main: Pater Lang, 1985.

Gmelch, George [and Ann Saddlemyer], ed. *In Wicklow West Kerry and Connemara by J. M. Synge*. Dublin: O'Brien; Totowa, N.J.: Rowman and Littlefield, 1980.

Gogarty, Oliver St. J. *As I Was Going Down Sackville Street: A Phantasy in Fact*. London: Rich and Cowan; New York: Reynal and Hitchcock, 1937.

Greene, David H. "The *Playboy* and Irish Nationalism." *Journal of English and Germanic Philology* 46, no. 2 (1947):199–204.

———. "The Shadow of the Glen and the Widow of Ephesus." *Publications of the Modern Language Association of America* 62, no. 1 (1947):233–38.

———. "Synge in the West of Ireland." *Mosaic* 5, no. 1 (1971):1–8.

———. "Synge's Unfinished Deirdre." *Publications of the Modern Language Association of America* 63, no. 4 (1948):1314–21.

———. "*The Tinker's Wedding*, A Revaluation." *Publications of the Modern Language Association of America* 62, no. 3 (1947):824–27.

Greene, David H., and Edward M. Stephens. *J. M. Synge, 1871–1909*. New York: Macmillan, 1959. Reprint. New York: Collier, 1961.

Gregory, Lady. *Our Irish Theatre: A Chapter of Autobiography*. New York and London: G. P. Putnam's, 1913.

Grene, Nicholas. *Synge: A Critical Study of the Plays*. Totowa, N.J.: Rowman and Littlefield; London, Macmillan, 1975.

———. "Synge's Creative Development in *The Aran Islands*." *Long Room* (1974):30–36.

———. ed. *The Well of the Saints by J. M. Synge*. Irish Dramatic Texts. Washington, D.C.: Catholic University of America Press; Gerrards Cross, Bucks: Colin Smythe, 1982.

[Griffith, Arthur]. "All Ireland." *United Irishman* [Dublin], 17 October 1903, p. 1.

H., H.C. [Cherrie Matheson Houghton]. "John Synge as I Knew Him." *Irish Statesman* [Dublin], 5 July 1924, pp. 532–34.

Harmon, Maurice, ed. *J. M. Synge: Centenary Papers 1971*. Dublin: Dolmen, 1972.

Hart, William. "Synge's Ideas on Life and Art: Design and Theory in *The Playboy of the Western World*." *Yeats Studies* 2 (1972):35–51.

Heilman, Robert Bechtold. *The Ways of the World: Comedy and Society*. Seattle and London: University of Washington Press, 1978.

Henn, T. R. *The Harvest of Tragedy*. New York: Barnes & Noble, 1966.

———. "John Millington Synge: a Reconsideration." *Hermathena* 112 (1971):5–21.

———, ed. *The Plays and Poems of J. M. Synge*. London: Methuen, 1963.

Henry, P. L. "The Playboy of the Western World." *Philologica Pragensia* ns. 8 (1965):189–204.

Hirsch, Edward. "The Gallous Story and the Dirty Deed: The Two *Playboys*." *Modern Drama* 26, no. 1 (1983):85–102.

Hogan, Robert. *'Since O'Casey' and Other Essays on Irish Drama*. Irish Literary Studies 15. Gerrards Cross, Bucks: Colin Smythe; Totowa, N.J.: Barnes & Noble, 1983.

Hogan, Robert, and James Kilroy. *The Abbey Theatre: The Years of Synge, 1905–1909*. The Modern Irish Drama: A Documentary History 3. Dublin: Dolmen; Atlantic Highlands, N.J.: Humanities Press, 1978.

Holloway, Joseph. *Joseph Holloway's Abbey Theatre: a Selection from His Unpublished*

    Journal "Impressions of a Dublin Playgoer." Edited by Robert Hogan and Michael J. O'Neill. Carbondale and Edwardsville: Southern Illinois University Press; London and Amsterdam: Feffer & Simons, 1967.

Howarth, Herbert. *The Irish Writers, 1880–1940: Literature under Parnell's Star.* New York: Hill and Wang, 1959.

Howe, P. P. *J. M. Synge: A Critical Study.* London: Martin Secker, 1912.

Hull, Keith N. "Nature's Storms and Stormy Natures in Synge's *Aran Islands.*" *Éire-Ireland* 7, no. 3 (1972):63–71.

Innes, C. L. "Naked Truth, Fine Clothes, and Fine Phrases in Synge's *Playboy of the Western World.*" *Myth and Reality in Irish Literature.* Edited by Joseph Ronsley. Waterloo, Ont.: Wilfrid Laurier University Press, 1977. pp. 63–75.

Jeffares, A. Norman. *Anglo-Irish Literature.* History of Literature Series. New York: Schocken, 1982.

Jochum, K.P.S. "Maud Gonne on Synge." *Éire-Ireland* 6, no. 4 (1971):65–70.

————. *W. B. Yeats: A Classified Bibliography of Criticism: Including Additions to Allan Wade's Bibliography of the Writings of W. B. Yeats and a Section on the Irish Literary and Dramatic Revival.* Urbana, Ill.; Chicago; and London: University of Illinois Press, 1978.

Johnson, Kenneth E. "J. M. Synge's *When the Moon Has Set.*" *Canadian Journal of Irish Studies* 9, no. 2 (1983):35–42.

Johnson, Toni O'Brien. *Synge: The Medieval and the Grotesque.* Irish Literary Studies 11. Gerrards Cross, Bucks: Colin Smythe; Totowa, N.J.: Barnes & Noble, 1982.

————. "*The Well of the Saints* and *Waiting for Godot:* Stylistic Variations on a Tradition." *The Irish Writer and the City.* Edited by Maurice Harmon. Irish Literary Studies 18. Gerrards Cross, Bucks: Colin Smythe; Totowa, N.J.: Barnes & Noble, 1984. pp. 90–102.

Johnston, Denis. *John Millington Synge.* Columbia Essays on Modern Writers 12. New York and London: Columbia University Press, 1965.

Kain, Richard M. "The Image of Synge: New Light and Deeper Shadows." *Sewanee Review* 84, no. 1 (1976):174–85.

————. "A Scrapbook of the '*Playboy*' Riots." *The Emory University Quarterly* 22, no. 1 (1966):5–17.

Kelsall, Malcolm. "The *Playboy* before the Riots." *Theatre Research* 1 (1975):29–37.

————. "Synge in Aran." *Irish University Review* 5 (1975):254–70.

————, ed. *The Playboy of the Western World.* The New Mermaids. London: Ernest Benn, 1975.

Kenner, Hugh. *A Colder Eye: The Modern Irish Writers.* New York: Knopf, 1983.

Kiberd, Declan. "The Frenzy of Christy: Synge and *Buile Shuibhne.*" *Éire-Ireland* 14, no. 2 (1979):68–79.

————. "The Perils of Nostalgia: A Critique of the Revival." *Literature and the Changing Ireland.* Edited by Peter Connolly. Irish Literary Studies 9. Gerrards Cross, Bucks: Colin Smythe; Totowa, N.J.: Barnes & Noble, 1982. pp. 1–24.

————. *Synge and the Irish Language.* Totowa, N.J.: Rowman and Littlefield; London: Macmillan, 1979.

————. "Synge's *Prós* and Verse in *Vita Vecchia.*" *Éire-Ireland* 15, no. 3 (1980):75–85.

Kilroy, James F. "The Playboy as Poet." *Publications of the Modern Language Association of America* 83, no. 2 (1968):439–42.

————. *The 'Playboy' Riots*. The Irish Theatre Series 4. Dublin: Dolmen, 1971.

Kilroy, Thomas. "Synge the Dramatist." *Mosaic* 5, no. 1 (1971):9–16.

King, Mary C. *The Drama of J. M. Synge*. Irish Studies. Syracuse: Syracuse University Press, 1985.

————. "Synge and 'The Aran Islands': A Linguistic Apprenticeship." *Irish Studies* 1 (1980):61–72

————, ed. Introduction, "J. M. Synge's *When the Moon Has Set.*" *Long Room* [Trinity College, Dublin] 24–25 (1982):9–40.

Knowlson, James. "Beckett and John Millington Synge." *Gambit* 7, no. 28 (1976):65–81. Reprint. James Knowlson and John Pilling. *Frescoes of the Skull: The Later Prose and Drama of Samuel Beckett*. New York: Grove Press, 1980.

Kopper, Edward A., Jr. *John Millington Synge: A Reference Guide*. A Reference Publication in Literature. Boston: G. K. Hall, 1979.

Krause, David. "The 'Rageous Ossean': Patron-Hero of Synge and O'Casey." *Modern Drama* 4, no. 3 (1961):268–91. Revised and reprinted as *The Profane Book of Irish Comedy*. Ithaca, N.Y., and London: Cornell University Press, 1982.

Laigle, Deirdre M. "The Liberation of Christy Mahon." *Cahiers du Centre d'Etudes Irlandaises* 2 (1977):55–62.

Leblanc, Gérard. "Ironic Reversal as Theme and Technique in Synge's Shorter Comedies." *Aspects of the Irish Theatre*. Cahiers Irlandais I. Edited by Patrick Rafroidi, Raymonde Popot, and William Parker. Paris: University of Lille, 1972. pp. 51–63.

————. "The Three Deaths of the Father in *The Playboy of the Western World.*" *Cahiers du Centre d'Etudes Irlandaises* 2 (1977):33–42.

Leech, Clifford. "John Synge and the Drama of His Time." *Modern Drama* 16, nos. 3–4 (1973):223–37.

Levitt, Paul M. *J. M. Synge: A Bibliography of Published Criticism*. New York: Barnes & Noble, 1974.

————. "The Structural Craftsmanship of J. M. Synge's *Riders to the Sea.*" *Éire-Ireland* 4, no. 1 (1969):53–61. Revised and reprinted as "The Whole Analysis: *Riders to the Sea.*" *A Structural Approach to the Analysis of Drama*. The Hague and Paris: Mouton, 1971. pp. 84–116.

————. "The Two-Act Structure of *The Playboy of the Western World.*" *Colby Library Quarterly* 11, no. 4 (1975):230–34.

Lydon, J. F. "John Millington Synge: The Man and His Background." *Mosaic* 5, no. 1 (1971):17–25.

MacKenna, Stephen. *Journal and Letters of Stephen MacKenna*. Edited by E. R. Dodds. London: Constable; Toronto: Macmillian, 1936.

————. "Stephen MacKenna on Synge: A Lost Memoir." Edited by Nicholas Grene and Ann Saddlemyer. *Irish University Review* 12 (1982):141–51.

MacLean, Hugh H. "The Hero as Playboy." *The University of Kansas City Review* 21 (1954):9–19.

MacNeice, Louis. *The Poetry of W. B. Yeats*. Oxford University Paperback. New York: Oxford University Press, 1969.

MacPhail, Ian, and M. Pollard, comps. *John Millington Synge, 1871–1909: A Catalogue of an Exhibition Held at Trinity College Library, Dublin on the Occasion of the Fiftieth Anniversary of His Death*. Dublin: Dolmen Press for the Friends of the Library of Trinity College, Dublin, 1959.

Masefield, John. *John M. Synge: A Few Personal Recollections with Biographical Notes.* New York: Macmillian, 1915.

Maxwell, D.E.S. *A Critical History of Modern Irish Drama, 1891–1980.* Cambridge: Cambridge University Press, 1984.

McHugh, Roger. "Literary Treatment of the Deirdre Legend." *Threshold* 1 (1957):36–49.

————. "Theater: The Synge Centenary." *Art in America* 60 (1972):90–93.

McHugh, Roger, and Maurice Harmon. *A Short History of Anglo-Irish Literature: From its Origins to the Present Day.* Totowa, N.J.: Barnes & Noble, 1982.

McMahon, Seán. "Clay and Worms." *Éire-Ireland* 5, no. 4 (1970):116–34.

————. " 'Leave Troubling the Lord God': A Note on Synge and Religion." *Éire-Ireland* 11, no. 1 (1976):132–41.

————. "The Road to Glenmalure." *Éire-Ireland* 7, no. 1 (1972):142–51.

Menascè, Esther. "Une traduzione di James Joyce: La cavalcata al mare; di J. M. Synge." *Acme* 33, nos. 1–2 (1980):23–44.

Messenger, John C. *Inis Beag: Isle of Ireland.* Case Studies in Cultural Anthropology. New York: Holt, Rinehart and Winston, 1969. Reprint. Prospect Heights, Ill.: Waveland, 1983.

Metwally, Abdalla A. "Synge's When the Moon Has Set." *Studies in Modern Drama* [Beirut Arab University] 1 (1971):38–59.

Mikhail, E. H. *J. M. Synge: A Bibliography of Criticism.* Totowa, N. J.: Rowman and Littlefield, 1975.

————. ed. *J. M. Synge: Interviews and Recollections.* Foreword by Robin Skelton. New York: Barnes & Noble; London: Macmillan, 1977.

Moore, George. *Hail and Farewell: A Trilogy, III: Vale.* New York: D. Appleton, 1914.

Morrissey, Thomas J. "The Good Shepherd and the Anti-Christ in Synge's *The Shadow of the Glen.*" *Irish Renaissance Annual* 1 (1980):157–67.

————. "Synge's Doorways: Portals and Portents." *Éire-Ireland* 17, no. 3 (1982):40–51.

Mortimer, Mark. "Stagecraft in *The Playboy.*" *Cahiers du Centre d'Etudes Irlandaises* 2 (1977):25–31.

————. "Synge and France." *Cahiers Irlandais* 2–3 (1974):183–190.

————. "Yeats and Synge: An Inappropriate Myth." *Studies* 66 (1977):292–98.

Murphy, Brenda. "Stoicism, Asceticism, and Ecstasy: Synge's *Deirdre of the Sorrows.*" *Modern Drama* 17, no. 2 (1974):155–63.

Murphy, Daniel J. "The Reception of Synge's *Playboy* in Ireland and America: 1907–1912." *Bulletin of the New York Public Library* 64, no. 10 (1960):515–33.

Naseband, Klaus. *John Millington Synges dramatische Poesie.* Frankfurt am Main: Peter Lang, 1981.

Nash, Vincent. "*The Well of the Saints*: Language in a Landscape." *Literatur in Wissenschaft und Unterricht* 5, no. 4 (1972):267–76.

Neff, D. S. "Synge's Hecuba." *Éire-Ireland* 19, no. 1 (1984):74–86.

Nethercot, Arthur H. "The *Playboy* of the *Western World.*" *Éire-Ireland* 13, no. 2 (1978):114–20.

Nic Shiubhlaigh, Maire (Mary Walker). *The Splendid Years: Recollections of Maire Nic Shiubhlaigh as Told to Edward Kenny.* Dublin: James Duffy, 1955.

Nonoyama, Minako. "La funcion de los simbolos en *Pellés et Mélisande* de Maeterlinck,

Bodas de sangre de Lorca y *Riders to the Sea* de Synge." *Revista de Estudios Hispánicos* 9, no. 1 (1975):81–98.

O'Casey, Sean. *Drums under the Window*. New York: Macmillan, 1955.

———. "John Millington Synge (1946)." *Blasts and Benedictions: Articles and Stories by Sean O'Casey*. Edited by Ronald Ayling. London: Macmillan; New York: St. Martin's, 1967. pp. 35–41.

O'Connor, Frank. "Synge." *The Irish Theatre*. Edited by Lennox Robinson, London: Macmillan, 1939. pp. 29–52.

O'Connor, Ulick. *All the Olympians: A Biographical Portrait of the Irish Literary Renaissance*. New York: Atheneum, 1984.

Orel, Harold. "Synge's Concept of the Tramp." *Éire-Ireland* 7, no. 2 (1972):55–61.

———. "Synge's Last Play: 'And a Story Will Be Told For Ever.' " *Modern Drama* 4 no. 3 (1961):306–13.

Orr, Robert H. "The Surprise Ending: One Aspect of J. M. Synge's Dramatic Technique." *English Literature in Transition* 15, no. 2 (1972):105–15.

Ó Síocháin, P. A. *Aran: Islands of Legend*. New York: Devin-Adair, 1962.

Parker, Randolph. "Gaming in the Gap: Language and Liminality in *Playboy of the Western World*." *Theatre Journal* 37, no. 1 (1985):65–85.

Partridge, A. C. *Language and Society in Anglo-Irish Literature*. Dublin: Gill and Macmillan; Totowa, N.J.: Barnes & Noble, 1984.

Peacock, Ronald. *The Poet in the Theatre*. London: Routledge and Kegan Paul; New York: Harcourt, Brace, 1946.

Pearce, Howard D. "Synge's Playboy as Mock-Christ." *Modern Drama* 8 no. 3 (1965):303–10.

Pierce, James C. "Synge's Widow Quin: Touchstone to the *Playboy*'s Irony." *Éire-Ireland* 16, no. 2 (1981):122–33.

Pittock, Malcolm. *"Riders to the Sea."* *English Studies* 49, no. 5 (1968):445–49.

Podhoretz, Norman. "Synge's *Playboy*: Morality and the Hero." *Essays in Criticism* 3 (1953):337–44.

Poger, Sidney. "Brecht's *Senora Carrar's Rifles (Die Gewehre Der Frau Carrar)* and Synge's *Riders to the Sea*." *Canadian Journal of Irish Studies* 10, no. 2 (1984):37–43.

Popkin, Henry, ed. *John Millington Synge, The Playboy of the Western World and Riders to the Sea*. The Avon Theatre Library. New York: Avon Books, 1967.

Price, Alan. *Synge and Anglo-Irish Drama*. London: Methuen, 1961.

Pyle, Hilary. *"Many Ferries*: Jack B. Yeats and J. M. Synge." *Éire-Ireland* 18, no. 2 (1983):17–35.

Rajan, Balachandra. "Yeats, Synge, and the Tragic Understanding." *Yeats Studies* 2 (1972):66–79.

Reid, Alec. "Comedy in Synge and Beckett." *Yeats Studies* 2 (1972):80–90.

Reynolds, Lorna. "The Rhythms of Synge's Dramatic Prose." *Yeats Studies* 2 (1972):52–65.

Richard, Lionel. "De Synge à Brecht." *Obliques* 20–21 (1979):39–45.

Robinson, Lennox. *Ireland's Abbey Theatre: a History, 1899–1951*. London: Sidgwick and Jackson, 1951.

Robinson, Paul N. "The Peasant Play as Allegory: J. M. Synge's *The Shadow of the Glen*." *CEA Critic* 36, no. 4 (1974):36–38.

Roche, Anthony. "The Two Worlds of Synge's *The Well of the Saints*." *Genre* 12

(1979):439–50. Reprinted as *The Genres of the Irish Literary Revival*. Edited by Ronald Schleifer. Norman, Okla.: Pilgrim; Dublin: Wolfhound, 1980. pp. 27–38.

[Rodgers, W. R., ed.]. "J. M. Synge." *Irish Literary Portraits . . . W. R. Rodgers's Broadcast Conversations with Those Who Knew Him*. London: British Broadcasting Corporation, 1972.

Rollins, Ronald G. "Huckleberry Finn and Christy Mahon: *The Playboy of the Western World*." *Mark Twain Journal* 13, no. 2 (1966):16–19.

————. "O'Casey and Synge: The Irish Hero as Playboy and Gunman." *Arizona Quarterly* 22, no. 3 (1966):217–22.

Saddlemyer, Ann. "In Search of the Unknown Synge." *Irish Writers and Society at Large*. Edited by Masaru Sekine. Irish Literary Studies 22. Gerrards Cross, Bucks: Colin Smythe; Totowa, N.J.: Barnes & Noble, 1985. pp. 181–98.

————. " 'Infinite Riches in a Little Room'—the Manuscripts of John Millington Synge." *Long Room* 1, no. 3 (1971):23–31.

————. "J. M. Synge on the Irish Dramatic Movement: An Unpublished Article." *Modern Drama* 24, no. 3 (1981):276–81.

————. *J. M. Synge and Modern Comedy*. Dublin: Dolmen, 1967.

————. "Synge and the Doors of Perception." *Place, Personality, and the Irish Writer*. Edited by Andrew Carpenter. Irish Literary Studies 1. New York: Barnes & Noble, 1977. pp. 97–120.

————. "Synge and the Nature of Woman." *Woman in Irish Legend, Life, and Literature*. Edited by S. F. Gallagher. Irish Literary Studies 14. Gerrards Cross, Bucks: Colin Smythe; Totowa, N.J.: Barnes & Noble, 1983. pp. 58–73.

————. "Synge and Some Companions, with a Note Concerning a Walk through Connemara with Jack Yeats." *Yeats Studies* 2 (1972):18–34.

Saddlemyer, Ann, ed. *Theatre Business: The Correspondence of the First Abbey Theatre Directors: William Butler Yeats, Lady Gregory, and J. M. Synge*. Gerrards Cross, Bucks: Colin Smythe; University Park: Pennsylvania State University Press, 1982.

————, ed. *The Collected Letters of John Millington Synge*. 2 vols. Oxford: Clarendon, 1983–1984.

Salmon, Eric. "J. M. Synge's *Playboy*: A Necessary Reassessment." *Modern Drama* 13, no. 2 (1970):111–28.

Sanderlin, R. Reed. "Synge's *Playboy* and the Ironic Hero." *The Southern Quarterly* 6 (1968):289–301.

Sänger, Wolfgang. *John Millington Synges* The Aran Islands: *Material und Mythos*. Neue Studien zur Anglistik und Amerikanistik 6. Frankfort: Lang, 1976.

Setterquist, Jan. *Ibsen and the Beginnings of Anglo-Irish Drama, I: John Millington Synge*. Uppsala Irish Studies 2. Uppsala, Swed.: Lundequistka, 1951.

Sidnell, M. J. "Synge's Playboy and the Champion of Ulster." *Dalhousie Review* 45 (1965):51–59.

Simpson, Alan. "The Unholy Trinity: A Simple Guide to Holy Ireland c. 1880–1980." *Sean O'Casey: Centenary Essays*. Edited by David Krause and Robert Lowery. Irish Literary Studies 7. Gerrards Cross, Bucks: Colin Smythe, 1980; Totowa, N.J.: Barnes & Noble, 1981. pp. 190–211.

Skelton, Robin. *J. M. Synge*. The Irish Writers Series. Lewisburg, Pa.: Bucknell University Press, 1972.

————. *J. M. Synge and His World*. A Studio Book. New York: Viking; London: Thames and Hudson, 1971.

————. "The Politics of J. M. Synge." *Massachusetts Review* 18, no. 1 (1977):7–22.

————. *The Writings of J. M. Synge*. Indianapolis and New York: Bobbs-Merrill, 1971.

————, ed. *J. M. Synge: Some Sonnets from "Laura in Death" after the Italian of Francesco Petrarch*. Dublin: Dolmen, 1971.

————, ed. *Riders to the Sea*. Dolmen Editions 8. London: Oxford University Press, 1969.

Smith, Harry W. "Synge's *Playboy* and the Proximity of Violence." *Quarterly Journal of Speech* 55, no. 4 (1969):381–87.

Smoot, Jean J. *A Comparison of Plays by John Millington Synge and Federico Garcia Lorca: The Poets and Time*. Madrid: Porrúa Turanzas, 1978.

————. "The Living Text in the Drama of John Millington Synge and Federico Garcia Lorca." *Proceedings of the Tenth Congress of the International Comparative Literature Association, New York, 1982*. Vol. 1. Edited by Anna Balakian. New York and London: Garland, 1985. pp. 338–42.

Spacks, Patricia Meyer. "The Making of the Playboy." *Modern Drama* 4, no. 3 (1961):314–23.

Spangler, Ellen B. "Synge's *Deirdre of the Sorrows* as Feminine Tragedy." *Éire-Ireland* 12, no. 4 (1977):97–108.

Stephens, Edward. *My Uncle John: Edward Stephens's Life of J. M. Synge*. Edited by Andrew Carpenter. London: Oxford University Press, 1974.

Stephens, James. "Reminiscences of J. M. Synge." *James, Seumas & Jacques*. Edited by Lloyd Frankenberg. New York: Macmillan, 1964. pp. 54–60.

Stephens, Lilo, ed. *J. M. Synge: My Wallet of Photographs*. Dublin: Dolmen, 1971.

Stilling, Roger. "Synge, Health, and Death." *The Dublin Magazine* 10 (1973):31–42.

Stork, Uwe. *Der sprachliche Rhythmus in den Bühnenstücken John Millington Synges*. Salzburg Studies in English Literature. Salzburg, Institut für Anglistik und Amerikanistik, Universität Salzburg, 1980.

Styan, J. L. *The Elements of Drama*. Cambridge: At the University Press, 1960.

Sullivan, Mary Rose. "Synge, Sophocles, and the Un-making of Myth." *Modern Drama* 12, no. 3 (1969):242–53.

Sultan, Stanley. "The Gospel According to Synge." *Papers on Language and Literature* 4, no. 4 (1968):428–41.

————. *J. M. Synge: The Playboy of the Western World*. Barre, Mass.: Imprint Society, 1970.

Suss, Irving D. "The 'Playboy' Riots." *Irish Writing* 18 (1952):39–42.

Synge, Samuel, Rev. *Letters to My Daughter: Memories of John Millington Synge*. Dublin and Cork: Talbot, 1931.

Taaffe, Maura. "Legend of an Irish Outlaw in Synge's *Playboy of the Western World*." *Papers in Comparative Studies* 2 (1982–83):207–16.

Templeton, Joan. "Synge's Redeemed Ireland: Woman as Rebel." *Caliban* 17 (1980):91–97. Revised and reprinted as "The Bed and the Hearth: Synge's Redeemed Ireland." *Drama, Sex, and Politics*. Edited by James Redmond. Themes in Drama 7. Cambridge: Cambridge Univesity Press, 1985. pp. 151–57.

Thornton, Weldon. "J. M. Synge." *Anglo-Irish Literature: A Review of Research*. Edited by Richard J. Finneran. New York: The Modern Language Association of America, 1976. pp. 315–65.

———. "J. M. Synge." *Recent Research on Anglo-Irish Writers: A Supplement to Anglo-Irish Literature: A Review of Research*. Edited by Richard J. Finneran. The Modern Language Association of America Reviews of Research. New York: The Modern Language Association of America, 1983. pp. 154–80.

———. *J. M. Synge and the Western Mind*. Irish Literary Studies 4. New York: Barnes & Noble, 1979.

Tielert, Brigitte. "Rezeption von Synge und Situationsmodell." *Semiotische versuche zu Literarischen Strukturen*. Edited by Walter A. Koch. Studien zu Philologie und Semiotik 2. Hildesheim, W. Ger., and New York: Olms, 1979. pp. 1–142.

Trinity College, Dublin [Nicholas Grene]. *The Synge Manuscripts in the Library of Trinity College, Dublin*. Dublin: Dolmen and Trinity College Library, 1971.

Truninger, Annelise. *Paddy and the Paycock: A Study of the Stage Irishman from Shakespeare to O'Casey*. Theatrical Physiognomy Series 24. Bern, Switz.: Francke, 1976.

Van Laan, Thomas F. "Form as Agent in Synge's *Riders to the Sea*." *Drama Survey* 3 (1964):352–66.

Vichy, Thérèse. "La mer dans le théâtre de Synge." *Cahiers Victoriens et Edouardiens* 23 (1968):177–88.

Warner, Alan. "Astringent Joy: The Sanity of Synge." *Wascana Review* 6 (1971):5–13.

Waters, Alan. "The Sounds of Aran." *Colby Library Quarterly* 17, no. 1 (1981):46–54.

Waters, Maureen. *The Comic Irishman*. Albany: State University of New York Press, 1984.

Watson, G. J. *Irish Identity and the Literary Revival: Synge, Yeats, Joyce, O'Casey*. New York: Barnes and Noble; London: Croom Helm, 1979.

Whelan, F.A.E., and Keith N. Hull. " 'There's Talking for a Cute Woman' ! Synge's Heroines." *Éire-Ireland* 15, no. 3 (1980):36–46.

Whitaker, Thomas R., ed. *The Playboy of the Western World: A Collection of Critical Essays*. Twentieth-Century Interpretations. Englewood Cliffs, N.J.: Prentice-Hall, 1969.

Wilkinson, Robin. "The Shadow of Deirdre: A Structuralist Approach to Two Plays by John Millington Synge." *Cahiers du Centre d'Etudes Irlandaises* 4 (1979):87–100.

Winkler, Elizabeth Hale. *The Clown in Modern Anglo-Irish Drama*. European University Papers Series 14. Frankfurt: Lang, 1977.

Worth, Katharine. *The Irish Drama of Europe from Yeats to Beckett*. Atlantic Highlands, N.J.: Humanities Press; London: Athlone, 1978.

———. "O'Casey, Synge, and Yeats." *Irish University Review* 10 (1980):103–17.

Wyatt, David. *Prodigal Sons: A Study in Authorship and Authority*. Baltimore and London: The Johns Hopkins University Press, 1980.

Yeats, W. B. *The Bounty of Sweden: A Meditation, and a Lecture Delivered before the Royal Swedish Academy and Certain Notes*. Dublin: Cuala, 1925.

———. *The Death of Synge, and Other Passages from an Old Diary*. Dublin: Cuala, 1928.

———. "Introduction: Mr. Synge and His Plays." *The Well of the Saints by J. M. Synge*. Being Volume Four of Plays for an Irish Theatre. London: A. H. Bullen, 1906.

———. *Synge and the Ireland of His Time by William Butler Yeats with a Note Concerning a Walk through Connemara with Him by Jack Butler Yeats*. Churchtown, Ireland: Cuala, 1911.

Appendix A: Characters, Locales, Motifs

Achill. On the Atlantic, off the west coast of County Mayo (IV, 167).

AE. Poet and theosophist George William Russell, 1867–1939 (I, 38).

Aging. III, 51, 93, 121; IV, 37, 195, 211, 223, 227.

Ainnle. Brother of Naisi and Ardan. Officiates at the marriage of Deirdre to Naisi (IV, 215).

Alban. Scotland, where Deirdre and Naisi spend seven years before their return to Ireland (to die).

The Aran Islands. Three islands about thirty miles into the Atlantic, southwest of Galway city.

Aranmor or Aranmore. The most northern and largest of the three Aran Islands.

Ardan. Brother of Ainnle and Naisi in *Deirdre*.

Arklow. About fifty-five miles south of Dublin, in County Wicklow (IV, 11).

Ballinaclash. Hamlet in south Wicklow about 10 miles northwest of Arklow (IV, 11).

Bangor. In northwest Mayo, about 10 miles northwest of Belmullet (I, 57).

Bartley. Determined son of Maurya in *Riders,* who is knocked into the sea on his way to catch a boat to the Galway Fair.

Bawn, Kitty. A faded beauty spoken of by Mary Doul (III, 129).

The Beauty of Ballinacree. Name given to Sarah Casey by Jaunting Jim (IV, 11). Ballinacree is a small village in County Meath.

Belmullet. Town in the northwest corner of County Mayo (I, 57; II, 327; IV, 97).

Blake, Honor. A village girl in *Playboy.*

Brady, Susan. A village girl in *Playboy.*

Bride. A good-looking girl in *Well;* a young maid in *When the Moon Has Set.*

Brien, Mary. Represents for Nora Burke the aging process (III, 51).

Brittas. About seven miles southwest of Dublin and about forty miles from Aughrim, County Galway (III, 33).

Burial. III, 5, 9; IV, 151, 209.

Burke, Dan. In *Shadow,* the tyrannical, elderly husband of Nora.

Burke, Nora. Wife of Dan Burke in *Shadow*; Synge's exemplum of the loveless Irish marriage.

Byrne, Mary. In *Wedding,* the drunken mother of Michael, who opposes her son's marriage to Sarah Casey for reasons that, apart from Mary's anticlericalism, are not clear.

Byrne, Michael. In *Wedding,* son of Mary Byrne and mate of Sarah Casey.

Byrne, Molly. Beautiful but hard-hearted character in *Well* whose marriage to Timmy the smith helps end the work.

Cahir Iveraghig. Iveragh is in County Kerry. *Cahir* means "height" (III, 115).

Casey, Sarah. In *Wedding,* pretty but coarse, she wants to marry Michael Byrne partially to legitimize their relationship.

Casey, Widow. Two hundred pound grotesque who once suckled Christy; old Mahon wanted his son to marry her for money.

Cashla Bay. On the west coast of County Galway (III, 91).

Cassidy, Kate. Her wake in *Playboy*, attended by Pegeen's father and his intoxicated friends, helps Christy and her to be alone (presumably celibately) for the night.

Cathleen. Pert older daughter of Maurya in *Riders*.

Cavanagh, Peggy. In *Shadow*, the living embodiment of the ravages of time on a woman.

The Celliniani. The narrator's ethereal girlfriend in *Étude Morbide*.

Children, birth, offspring. III, 99, 109; IV, 7, 85, 131.

The Chouska. The narrator's tough-minded girlfriend in *Étude Morbide* who, perhaps with good judgment, refuses to marry him.

Claddagh fishermen. Claddagh, in Galway, is purportedly the oldest fishing settlement in Ireland (II, 151). The famous Claddagh wedding ring consists of two hands holding a heart.

Clash. Near Rathdrum in County Wicklow (III, 71; IV, 49).

Clothing. III, 15, 175; IV, 115, 145.

Conchubor. High King of Ulster but in Synge's version of the Deirdre legend mainly a jealous old man: a December to Deirdre's May.

Coomasaharn. Lake in County Kerry in which the 'mergency man drowns (I, 58).

Costello, Mary. A madwoman in *When the Moon Has Set*, once in love with Colm Sweeny's now dead uncle.

Cruelty. III, 55, 105, 113, 119, 123, 125, 137; IV, 9, 27, 73, 171.

Danny. Roisterer who is beaten to death by twenty-nine Mayo men, mainly because of his sexual misdeeds (I, 56–57).

Dara, Michael. In *Shadow*, Nora's weakling suitor who abandons her after Dan recovers.

Darcy, Patch. Mysterious friend of Nora (probably Platonic) who apparently goes insane, dies, and is eaten by crows.

Death. III, 21, 23, 45, 159; IV, 47, 65, 73, 89, 165, 171, 180, 259, 269.

Deirdre. The heroine of *Deirdre of the Sorrows:* in medieval legend, a tigress; in later translations, a Miss Lonely Heart; in Synge's play, a full creation who far outshines the male characters.

Dingle. Picturesque town in County Kerry mentioned in Synge's works.

Dirane, Pat. Synge's storyteller on Inishmaan. Synge used his actual name possibly because he died after Synge's first visit.

Donegal. County far to the north of the Aran Islands, an unlikely place for Michael's remains to have been washed ashore.

Doul, Martin. Iconoclastic blind beggar in *Well* who is driven from the community at the play's conclusion. Husband of Mary Doul (*Doul* means "blind" in Irish).

Doul, Mary. Wife of Martin in *Well* who is as feisty and salty as her husband.

Dream. III, 67, 119, 129; IV, 229.

Drinking. III, 35, 43, 59; IV, 13, 19, 27, 77, 123.

Eileen, Sister. Implausibly abandons her vocation for Colm Sweeny in *When the Moon Has Set*.

Emain Macha. Home of the Red Branch Knights, destroyed at the end of *Deirdre*. Called by Synge an "Irish Troy" (II, 387).

Farrell, Jimmy. Jovial farmer in *Playboy,* straight man to Philly O'Cullen.

Fergus. One of Conchubor's warriors who foolishly believes in the message of peace that he brings from the High King to Deirdre and Naisi in Scotland.

Flaherty, Margaret. Pegeen Mike, a bargirl who smells of poteen, who becomes the Cleopatra of Mayo through Synge's magnificent love poetry but who loses the only playboy of the Western world at the conclusion because of her inability to accept compromise.

Flaherty, Michael James. Pegeen's drunken father, a stage Irishman with a touch of malice added.

Flaherty, Tim. In *Wedding,* his hens are likely booty for thieving tinkers (IV, 25).

Galway. County in Western Ireland; Galway City is Bartley's destination, which he fails to reach in *Riders*.

Glencree. A river in southwestern County Dublin (I, 47).

Glencullen. Small river in southwestern County Dublin (I, 3).

Glenmalure. The setting of *Shadow,* a glen in County Wicklow that is almost ten miles long. Also, see Sarah's statement in *Wedding* (IV, 11).

Grave of the Four Beautiful Saints. The Church of the Four Beautiful Saints (Teampull an Cheathrair Aluinn), a fifteenth-century church (28 by 12 1/2 feet) on Aranmor. South of the church is a holy well.

Grianan. Really, Greenan, near Rathdrum in County Wicklow. The Douls beg near here in *Well* (III, 75 and 103).

Hearing, senses other than sight. III, 85, 131, 141, 149; IV, 9, 31, 231.

Holymen. III, 5, 83, 101, 149; IV, 43, 59, 87.

Inishere. The smallest and most southern and eastern of the three Aran Islands.

Inishmaan. The middle island of the three Aran Islands, where Synge spent most of his time on his five trips to Aran; also, the setting of *Riders*.

Insanity. III, 37, 161, 173; IV, 137, 143, 145, 235.

Jaunting Jim. Sarah Casey in *Wedding* threatens to run away with Jaunting Jim, another tinker, unless Michael Byrne marries her.

Keel. Near Achill Head on the far west coast of County Mayo. Christy promises to go there and live with the madmen if Pegeen does not turn him in to the peelers (IV, 169).

Keogh, Shawn. Pegeen's cowardly fiancé, to whom she will probably return now that Christy has left.

Kevin's Bed. In *Well*, the bed of the Holy St. Kevin. The wandering friar plans to sleep in St. Kevin's Bed, which is made of stone. St. Kevin was the abbot of Glendalough, a center of learning in the sixth century, in County Wicklow (III, 101).

Kilmainham. Dublin Gaol mentioned in Synge's works.

Kilronan. The main settlement on Aranmor in Synge's day and now.

Kinsella, Mary. Dies under mysterious circumstances in Richmond Asylum in "An Autumn Night in the Hills" (II, 192).

Lambert, Charley. Champion jockey and playboy mentioned in *The Aran Islands* (II, 166–67) who foreshadows Christy Mahon in *Playboy*.

Larry. Unrepentant hero of the anonymous nineteenth-century song "The Night before Larry Was Stretched," sung by the equally anticlerical Mary Byrne in *Wedding* (IV, 17).

Lavarcham. Servant of Conchubor who thinks little of talking back to him and of lying to protect Deirdre.

Linahan, Red. Talking about the "squint in his eye" (IV, 59) provides much of the excitement in the Mayo village which is the setting of *Playboy* (IV, 59).

Loneliness. III, 35, 37, 49, 159; IV, 39, 61, 63, 109.

Lough Nahanagan. A lake in County Wicklow, supposedly inhabited by a monster (III, 35).

Mahon, Christopher. Synge's poacher-poet, who learns that his bent, at the conclusion of *Playboy*, is for satire, not high flights of poetry that are doomed to come down to earth.

Mahon, Old. Christy's dreadful father, who is almost palatable when compared to the male phoneys in Mayo.

Maurice. A fisherman with whom Synge discusses mackerel and other matters while in County Kerry (II, 246, 280).

Maurya. In *Riders,* Synge's great portrait of universal grief and stoic acceptance.

Mayo. The wild coast of County Mayo, in Western Ireland, is the setting of the wild displays of *Playboy*.

McDonough, Martin. "Michael" in *The Aran Islands*. Synge stayed with the Mc-Donough family while on Inishmaan.

McLaughlin, Nelly. A village girl in *Playboy* who brings Christy a pullet, urging him to feel the "fat of that breast" (IV, 99).

Michael. Martin McDonough, Synge's friend on Inishmaan; son (possibly favorite) of Maurya in *Riders;* Mike, *The Aran Islands* (II, 136) source of Michael of *Riders*.

Money. III, 9, 49, 79; IV, 15, 103.

Mor, Rucard. The hero of an Irish folktale that Synge heard on Inishere about a man in search of his horse (II, 172–75).

Mount Jerome. Protestant cemetery in Dublin, which Synge prophetically pictured as his final resting place (I, 47).

Mountjoy. Jail on the outskirts of Dublin to which Synge wishes to consign his enemy in "The Curse" (I, 49).

Mourteen, Old. Martin Coneely, Synge's blind guide on Aranmor.

The Mulrannies. Insane people who were driven from California and now live in Mayo in *Playboy* (IV, 59).

Naisi. In *Deirdre,* would-be rapist turned uxorious mate of the heroine.

Neifin. Mountain in western County Mayo; Christy dreams of escaping there and making love to Pegeen on Neifin (IV, 109 and 147).

Neill, Jemmy. Supplies Mary Byrne with porter in *Wedding.*

Nora. Younger sister of Cathleen in *Riders.*

O'Conor, Lady. In *The Aran Islands,* the faithful wife (II, 61–64).

O'Cullen, Philly. Sly, skeptical farmer in *Playboy* who doubts Christy's story.

Owen. Sent by Conchubor to help trap Naisi and Deirdre; Owen's awkward characterization was left unfinished by Synge at his death.

Patch. One of Maurya's sons. The discovery of his death is described in *Riders* (III, 21).

Patcheen. In *Playboy,* because he is "lame in his heel" (IV, 59), he arouses interest in Mayo's stultified community.

Patrick. An informer to the evictors on Inishmaan who is denounced by his mother (II, 88).

Phelim. Battles an eagle in a folktale in *The Aran Islands* (II, 176–78).

Physical beauty. III, 71, 87; IV, 11, 95, 183, 191.

A Priest. In *Wedding,* his violent treatment by the tinkers kept the play from the Abbey stage until 1971.

Quin, Marcus. A good storyteller in *Playboy* who "got six months for maiming ewes" (IV, 59).

Quin, Widow. Substantial character in *Playboy* who is genuinely attracted to Christy and wants to help him (and herself), even though she knows his story is a hoax.

Rathdrum. About thirty-five miles south of Dublin in County Wicklow (III, 55).

Red Branch House. The most important of the three regal courts of Emain Macha (IV, 247).

Reeks of Cork. As Synge explained (III, 114), mountains in Kerry (bordering on Cork), in *Well* (III, 115).

Reilly, Father. Shawn Keogh lives in terror of him in *Playboy;* the clergyman, who seems to be of a traditional cut, does not appear on stage.

Richmond Asylum. Dublin hospital mentioned several times in Synge's works, for example, in *Shadow* (III, 37).

Roger, Little. An old dancer in *The Aran Islands* who was constrained by Synge's presence (II, 153).

The Saint. In *Well,* Synge's parody of St. Patrick, a friar who is naive although well meaning but ultimately vindictive.

Seven Churches. At Glendalough, St. Kevin's sixth-century monastic center (III, 51).

Sight and blindness. III, 71, 75, 95, 117.

Simon, Mat. A minor character in *Well* who echoes community sentiments.

Slieve Fuadh. Part of the County Armagh mountain range called the Fews; cite of Lavarcham's house (Deirdre's residence) at the start of the play.

Speech. III, 57, 123, 131; IV, 7, 39, 49, 53–54, 81, 151, 173.

Storms and other weather conditions. III, 33, 161; IV, 201.

Sullivan, Daneen. In *Playboy,* he "knocked the eye from a peeler" (IV, 59).

Sweeny, Colm. Willowy protagonist of *When the Moon Has Set* who wins the hand of Sister Eileen through specious arguments.

Tansey, Sara. A village girl in *Playboy.*

Tara Hill. In county Meath, the seat of the High Kings, about twenty miles northwest of Dublin. Tibradden (also, IV, 9) is a mountain in County Dublin, about eight to ten miles from Tara.

Timmy the smith. In *Well,* a good-hearted but mercantilistic blacksmith who is unable to accept either the personality of Martin Doul or his vision. Marries Molly Byrne at the conclusion.

A Tramp. In *Shadow,* the blatherer that Nora leaves with; in his letters to Molly Allgood, Synge's way of signing his name.

Twelve Pins. Twelve hills in County Galway (II, 110).

The Union. The workhouse, dreaded much more than the madhouse by Synge's destitute characters.

Wandering, leave-taking. III, 33, 55, 151; IV, 49, 173.

Wicklow. County and city directly south of Dublin county and city.

Appendix B: Stage Histories

The Shadow of the Glen

October 8, 1903.	Dublin: Molesworth Hall by the Irish National Theatre Society. Cast included: Dan Burke, G. Roberts; Nora Burke, Maire Nic Shiubhlaigh; Michael Dara, P. J. Kelly; A Tramp, W. G. Fay. 3 performances.
March 26, 1904.	London: Royalty Theatre, matinée.
December 28, 1904.	Dublin: Abbey Theatre.
February 7, 1906.	Prague: Inchover Theatre. Translator: Karel Mušek.
August 22, 1907.	Prague: National Theatre.

Note: Paul Foley Casey's "German Productions of the Dramas of J. M. Synge." *Maske and Kothurn* 27, nos. 2–3 (1981):163–75, is meticulous and provides vital information. Other sources of information about the foreign productions are Ghassan Maleh, "Synge in the Arab World"; Shotaro Oshima, "Synge in Japan"; and Gérard Leblanc, "Synge in France." All three are included in S. B. Bushrui, ed. *A Centenary Tribute to John Millington Synge, 1871–1909: Sunshine and the Moon's Delight*. New York: Barnes & Noble, 1972. Useful also is Roger McHugh, "Theater: The Synge Centenary." *Art in America* 60 (1972):90–93. Information about the 1963 Dublin Production of *The Tinker's Wedding* comes from Ann Saddlemyer, *Collected Letters,* II: 128.

1911–1912.	Part of the first American Tour, which began September 23, 1911, and ended at the place of its origin, New Plymouth Theatre on March 4, 1912.
March 11, 1919.	Frankfurt am Main: Schauspielhaus.
October 25, 1928.	London: London Arts Theatre. Produced by W. G. Fay.
November 17, 1934.	New York: Golden Theatre. Cast included: Dan Burke, F. J. McCormick; Nora, Eileen Crowe; Michael, Arthur Shields; A Tramp, Barry Fitzgerald.
1935.	Japan: Staged by the Budo No Kai.
March 6, 1957.	New York: Theater East, with Barry Macollum as Dan Burke.
May 6, 1968.	Dublin: Abbey Theatre.
October, 1971.	Ibadan, Nigeria: Ibadan University's Theatre Arts Department.
July 30, 1973.	Dublin: Peacock Theatre.

Riders to the Sea

February 25, 1904.	Dublin: Molesworth Hall by the Irish National Theatre Society. Cast included: Maurya, Honor Lavelle; Bartley, W. G. Fay; Cathleen, Sara Allgood; Nora, Emma Vernon; Men and Women, Maire Nic Shiubhlaigh, P. J. Kelly, Seamas O'Sullivan; Doreen Gunning, G. Roberts, Maire Ni Gharbhaigh. Three performances.
March 26, 1904.	London: Royalty Theatre, matinée.
June 11, 1907.	London: Great Queen Street Theatre.
June 9, 1909.	London: Royal Court Theatre.
April 17, 1911.	Stratford-upon-Avon.
1911–1912.	Part of First American Tour.
June 17, 1918.	Zurich: Flauen Theatre. Produced by James Joyce and Claude Sykes, with Nora Barnacle playing a small part.
February 19, 1935.	Basel, Switzerland: Stadtheater.
July, 1935.	Tokyo: Jinju Hall. By the players of the Jiyu Butai.

March 6, 1957.	New York: Theatre East, with Elspeth March as Maurya.
1963.	Syrian Arab Television.
April 26, 1971.	Dublin: Abbey Theatre, with Marie Kean as Maurya. Directed by Hugh Hunt.
June 14, 1978.	London: Greenwich Theatre.

The Well of the Saints

February 4–11, 1905.	Dublin: Abbey Theatre, by the Irish National Theatre Society. Cast included: Martin Doul, W. G. Fay; Mary Doul, Emma Vernon; Timmy, George Roberts; Molly Byrne, Sara Allgood; Bride, Maire Nic Shiubhlaigh; Mat Simon, P. Mac Shiubhlaigh; A Wandering Friar, F. J. Fay. Scenery designed by Pamela C. Smith. Molly Allgood played a bit part.
January 12, 1906.	Berlin: Deutsches Theater. Seven or eight performances. Translator: Max Meyerfeld.
May 14, 1908.	Revised version. Costumes and setting designed by Charles Ricketts. Molly Byrne is played by Molly Allgood.
June 8, 1909.	London: Royal Court Theatre.
1911–1912.	Part of the First American Tour.
April 20, 1926	Berlin: Wallner Theatre (today the Schiller). More than seventy performances.
January 32, 1921.	New York: Barbizon Theatre. Martin was played by Augustine Duncan; the Saint, by P. J. Kelly. Five performances.
November 21, 1934.	New York: Golden Theatre. Martin was played by Barry Fitzgerald; Timmy, by P. J. Carolan; the Saint, by F. J. McCormick.
April 7, 1962.	Münster/Westphalia, West Germany: the Kammerspiele. Translator: Christina Pesch. Nine performances.
August 21, 1969.	Beit Meri, Lebanon: Roman Temple. Translator: Unsi El Haj (The Well of Truth).

The Playboy of the Western World

January 26, 1907.	Dublin: Abbey Theatre, by the National Theatre Society Ltd. A week of disturbances and riots. Cast included: Christopher Mahon, W. G. Fay; Old Mahon, A. Power; Michael James Flaherty, Arthur Sinclair; Margaret Flaherty, Maire O'Neill (Molly Allgood); Shawn Keogh, F. J. Fay; Philly O'Cullen, J. A. O'Rourke; Jimmy Farrell, J. M. Kerrigan; Widow Quin, Sara Allgood; Sara Tansey, Brigit O'Dempsey; Susan Brady, Alice O'Sullivan; Honor Blake, Mary Craig; Peasants, U. Wright, and Harry Young.
Spring, 1907.	Performances in Cambridge, Oxford and London.
June 10, 1907.	London: Great Queen Street Theatre.
June 7, 1909.	London: Royal Court Theatre.
April 17, 1911.	Start of Stratford-upon-Avon Festival.
November 27, 1911.	New York: Maxine Elliott Theatre. Part of the First American Tour.
January 18, 1912.	Cast of *Playboy* arrested in Philadelphia for immorality.
November 8, 1912.	Münster/Westphalia, West Germany: Stadttheater.
December 12, 1913.	Paris: Lugné-Poë's Theatre de l'Oeuvre.
Spring, 1918.	London: Royal Court Theatre.
April 16, 1921.	New York: Bramhall Theater. Cast included Glayds Hurlbut as Pegeen and Thomas Mitchell as Christy.
October 12, 1925.	London: Royalty Theatre. Five-week run; play revived by Dennie Eadie and James B. Fagan.
January 2, 1930.	New York: Irish Theatre. Pegeen played by Betty Murry and Christy by Sean Dillon. Twenty-Seven performances.
May 21–22, 1930.	Amherst, Massachusetts: Amherst College. Guest producer: Lennox Robinson.
November 17, 1934.	New York: Golden Theatre. Cast included: Pegeen, Eileen Crowe; Michael James, Barry Fitzgerald; Christy, Arthur

	Shields; Widow Quin, Maureen Delany. Seven performances.
November 20, 1937.	New York: Ambassador Theatre, with Ria Mooney as Pegeen and Arthur Shields as Christy. Nine performances.
January 27, 1939.	London: Mercury Theatre, with Cyril Cusack as Christy.
1941.	Paris. Produced by Marcel Herrand.
October 26, 1946.	New York: Booth Theatre. Ten-week run. First production of Theatre Incorporated. Cast included: Christy, Burgess Meredith; Pegeen, Eithne Dunn; Widow Quin, Mildred Natwick; smaller parts played by Julie Harris and Maureen Stapleton. Directed by Guthrie McClintic.
1954.	Paris: Theatre des Nations. Three performances by Cyril Cusack and the Theatre of Ireland.
1955.	Vienna: Kaleidoskop. Sil-Vara's version of the play.
1955.	Hokuriku and Chugoku districts, Japan: Gekidan Mingei (People's Theatre Art Players).
1958.	London: Westminster Theatre. Musical adaptation entitled *The Heart's a Wonder*.
March 11, 1960.	Cologne: the Kammerspiele. Version of Annemarie and Heinrich Böll.
October 12, 1960.	London: Piccadilly Theatre. Leads: Donal Donnelly and Siobhan McKenna. One hundred forty-one performances.
August 19, 1968.	Dublin: Abbey Theatre.
January 7, 1971.	New York: The Repertory Theater of Lincoln Center. Leads: Martha Henry and David Birney. Closed February 20, 1971.
April, 1971.	Dublin: Abbey Theatre and Lantern Theatre. Director of Abbey production: Colin George of the Sheffield Playhouse.
March 11, 1972.	Ashland, Oregon: Angus Bowman Theatre. Shakespeare Festival Association.
October 14, 1975.	New York: Bert Wheeler Theater. Musical adaptation entitled *Christy*. Forty performances.

August 15, 1978.   Musical adaptation called *Back Country*.
                                    Opened in Boston and closed there
                                    September 24, 1978, after pre-Broadway
                                    tryouts.

February 24, 1983.   New York: The Meat and Potatoes
                                    Company. Twenty performances.

January 30, 1980.   New York: Roundabout Theatre
                                    Company. Leads: Ken Marshall and Kate
                                    Burton. Fifty-five performances.

The Tinker's Wedding

November 11, 1909.   London: Afternoon Theatre at His
                                    Majesty's Theatre. Cast included:
                                    Michael Byrne, Jules Shaw; A Priest,
                                    Edmund Gurney; Mary Byrne, Clare
                                    Greet; Sarah Casey, Mona Limerick.
                                    Directed by Edmund Gurney.

Summer, 1913.   Stratford-upon-Avon: part of Summer
                                    Season of Shakespeare's Plays.

May 12, 1917.   Birmingham: Birmingham Repertory
                                    Theatre. Completes week-long run
                                    despite riot on May 15.

March 6, 1957.   New York: Theater East, with Elspeth
                                    March as Mary Byrne.

September 24, 1963.   Dublin: Pike Theatre, directed by Liam
                                    Miller.

December 4, 1963.   Heidelberg: Zimmertheater. Translator:
                                    Erich Fried. Fourteen performances.

April 26, 1971.   Dublin: Abbey Theatre. First performance
                                    at the Abbey.

October, 1971.   Ibadan, Nigeria: Ibadan University's
                                    Theatre Arts Department.

March, 1974.   Zurich: Theater am Neumarkt.
                                    Translators: Eva Walch and Klaus Tews.

January 19, 1981.   New York: Equity Library Theater. Three
                                    performances.

Deirdre of the Sorrows

January 13, 1910.   Dublin: Abbey Theatre, by the Irish
                                    Players. Cast included: Lavarcham, Sara

	Allgood; Old Woman, Eileen O'Doherty; Owen, J. A. O'Rourke; Conchubor, Arthur Sinclair; Fergus, Sydney J. Morgan; Deirdre, Maire O'Neill (Molly Allgood); Naisi, Fred O'Donovan; Brothers of Naisi: Ainnle and Ardan, J. M. Kerrigan and John Carrick; Two Soldiers, Ambrose Power and Harry Young. Directed by Maire O'Neill.
October, 1959.	New York: Gate. Cast included: Deirdre, Salome Jens; Naisi, Ray Mac Donnell; Conchubor, William Clemens.
1969.	Brittany. Producer: Michel Hermon.
March 30, 1971.	Dublin: Peacock Theatre.

Index

About the Editor and Contributors

ROSEMARIE A. BATTAGLIA, assistant professor of American Thought and Language at Michigan State University, has had her work published in *College Literature,* the *James Joyce Quarterly,* and *Joyce Studies 1985* (University of Delaware).

MICHAEL H. BEGNAL, professor of English and comparative literature at Penn State University, has had numerous books and articles published on James Joyce and other modern writers.

ZACK R. BOWEN is professor of English and chair at the University of Miami and the past president of the James Joyce Society. He is the author of many books and articles on modern literature and is coauthor, with James F. Carens, of *A Companion to Joyce Studies.*

DANIEL J. CASEY, academic dean of Elms College (Chicopee, Massachusetts), has had more than seventy books, articles, and reviews published, as well as fiction and poetry, on Irish themes. He is currently editing *Critical Essays on John Millington Synge* for the Twayne Series.

REED WAY DASENBROCK, associate professor of English at New Mexico State University, is the author of *The Literary Vorticism of Ezra Pound and Wyndham Lewis* and has had work published on Joyce, Yeats, and Synge, as well as other subjects.

RICHARD FALLIS is associate professor of English at Syracuse University. He is the author of *The Irish Renaissance,* a history of modern Anglo-Irish literature, and is editor of the Syracuse University Press's "Irish Studies Series" of books on Irish literature and culture.

LESLIE D. FOSTER is professor of English at Northern Michigan University and has held visiting professorships in Sierra Leone, West Africa, and on the West Bank, near Jerusalem. He has had work published on Synge, Sidney, Shakespeare, and other writers.

MARY C. KING lectures in communications and social sciences at the University of Bradford in the United Kingdom and is the author of *The Drama of J. M. Synge* and the editor of the two-act version of *When the Moon Has Set,* published in a special edition of *Long Room.*

EDWARD A. KOPPER, JR., professor of English at Slippery Rock University, is the author of several books and numerous articles and monographs on James Joyce and other modern writers, and he is the contributor of the Synge section in The Modern Language Association's forthcoming *Anglo-Irish Literature: A Guide to Research.*

PATRICK A. McCARTHY is professor of English and director of graduate studies in English at the University of Miami. He is the author of *The Riddles of Finnegans Wake* and *Olaf Stapledon* and is the editor of *Critical Essays on Samuel Beckett.*

THOMAS J. MORRISSEY is professor of English and chair at the State University of New York College at Plattsburgh. He has had articles published in a number of areas, including Anglo-Irish literature, science fiction, children's literature, and the teaching of writing.

LEONARD ORR teaches Irish literature, the history of criticism, bibliography, and critical methods at the University of Notre Dame. He is the editor of *De-Structing the Novel* and the author of *Semiotic and Structuralist Analyses of Fiction* and many articles.

ANTHONY ROCHE, a native of Dublin, teaches at University College, Dublin, and is the Irish editor of the *Irish Literary Supplement.* He has had essays published on Synge, Joyce, Beckett, and contemporary Irish playwrights.

BONNIE KIME SCOTT is professor of English at the University of Delaware. She is the author of *Joyce and Feminism* and *James Joyce: A "Pollylogue" on Gender* and editor of a forthcoming collection of essays, *New Alliances in Joyce Studies.*